Plant Engineer's Handbook

of

Formulas, Charts

and Tables

Plant Engineer's Handbook

of

Formulas, Charts

and Tables

by

Donald W. Moffat

PRENTICE-HALL, Inc.
Englewood Cliffs, N. J.

Prentice-Hall International, Inc., *London*
Prentice-Hall of Australia, Pty. Ltd., *Sydney*
Prentice-Hall of Canada, Ltd., *Toronto*
Prentice-Hall of India, Private Ltd., *New Delhi*
Prentice-Hall of Japan, Inc., *Tokyo*

Second Printing . . . . . September, 1975

Library of Congress Cataloging in Publication Data

Moffat, Donald W
   Plant engineer's handbook of formulas, charts,
and tables.

   Includes bibliographical references.
   1. Plant engineering—Handbooks, manuals, etc.
I. Title.
TS184.M63   658.2'0021'2   74-1016
ISBN 0-13-680280-X

Printed in the United States of America

About the Author

Donald W. Moffat is a teacher of industrial management and business at San Diego City College, as well as a teacher of upper division and graduate courses in business and economics at LaVerne College.

Before going into full-time teaching, he worked in industry for 26 years, at various levels from construction mechanic to project engineer, industrial teacher, and program management. During that time he presented seven papers to national and international professional conferences, and had over 50 articles published. His previous book, *Charts & Nomographs for Electronics Technicians and Engineers,* simplifies mathematics for industrial technicians and provides many aids for rapid evaluation of frequently used functions.

His formal education includes a B.S. in physics from Hofstra University, graduate studies at Syracuse University and UCLA, and an M.S. in Management Science from United States International University. He is a member of Sigma Pi Sigma, National Physics Honor Society.

A Word from the Author

Decision-making poses no problem when all factors under consideration have numerical values. Even computers make perfect decisions under such conditions. However, real-life decisions inevitably have to be based on less-than-complete information because a point is always reached where a continuation of the information-gathering process would be more costly than the expected benefits of an improved decision. The manager with an edge on his competitors is the one who has been able to obtain the largest amount of pertinent and factual data for a given expenditure on pre-decision research.

This book presents the formulas and tables that practicing plant engineers have had to obtain from a wide variety of sources. The convenience of having the required information collected in one volume will provide that extra amount of results for a given expenditure on research.

Both the content and the organization of this book have resulted from investigations into tasks actually performed by plant engineering departments in industry and government. As for content, the investigations concentrated on two questions: what material should be included? (especially, for what information do plant engineers have to go to sources other than present handbooks?); and, what should not be included? (what parts of present handbooks are felt to be not worth the cost of including them?).

Another test question ruled the organization of each entry. No entry was in final form until there could be a "Yes" to the question, "Are the degrees of detail and explanation just right for providing maximum assistance to a practicing plant engineer?" Every entry was examined to determine the best method of presentation. Consideration was given to how the data will be applied and to what kinds of information plant engineers will require from it. For example, when electrical wiring is specified, one wants only to know what wire will meet the requirements for the equipment he has to power; very seldom would he use wire specifications in a tradeoff analysis. Therefore, tables, rather than graphs of other charts, are used for wiring information. On the other hand, viewing distance for a sign is more likely to be used in a tradeoff analysis over a continuum of conditions and, therefore, data on this topic is presented in a graphical form, making it easier to see the effects of changing a variable. Some topics are presented in more than one manner.

A project of this size leaves the author indebted to individuals and organizations too numerous to mention. Among those whose assistance deserves special mention are: Dover Corporation, which was so generous with information about the entire elevator industry; Hewlett-Packard, which provided the use of a HP 9100B desk computer; Portland Cement Association, which responded so effectively when needed; and The Aluminum Association, whose information was useful in more than one area of the book.

DONALD W. MOFFAT

How to Use This Handbook

In this handbook will be found formulas, tables, graphs, and other quantitative information for immediate use by the reader. It is assumed that the reader has knowledge of the various fields that are a part of plant engineering, and therefore basic tutorial explanations are omitted, resulting in a book of high density which includes that part of plant engineering which can be presented in handbook fashion.

The information has been made as complete as a handbook format allows, and for most tasks it should not be necessary to use other references. For example, suppose a new parking lot is to be laid out—Chapter 9 gives formulas for width requirements of stalls (including a nomogram for fast numerical answers); area requirements per car; minimum aisle width; critical angle; aisle requirements for back-in; length of stall; overhang; intermeshed stalls; area lost at end of a row of angled parking; and ramp requirements. For another example, however, it is not intended that a complete elevator installation be designed from the formulas in this book. Instead, Chapter 8 gives formulas that will help the plant engineer in planning building requirements that will be necessary for an elevator installation. For example, there are formulas for buffer stroke (so the reader will know how much room to provide), buffer reaction (so the reader will know what structural requirements will be needed), minimum rated load (to help determine how much platform area the elevator will have to have), and many others.

All formulas include a list of the symbols used and a demonstration of the formula's use.

Example (from Chapter 4)

A fire-protection sprinkler system uses an air-pressurized water tank. The required pressure is given by

$$P = \frac{30}{A} - 15 + 0.434 \frac{H}{A}$$

where: P = pressure in pounds on the gauge
A = proportion of tank occupied by air
H = height of highest sprinkler above tank bottom
= 0 if tank is located above highest sprinkler

An example is then given: The bottom of a pressure tank is 20 feet lower than the highest sprinkler in the system. What pressure is required if the tank is to be kept 2/3 full of water (1/3 air)?

$$P = \frac{30}{0.333} - 15 + 0.434\frac{20}{0.333}$$
$$= 101 \text{ pounds per square inch}$$

Some entries also include a nomogram for fast numerical answers and for quickly surveying the results of changing one or more of the variables.

Example (from Chapter 9)

In designing a parking lot, the plant engineer is concerned about the interrelationships involving width of stall, angle of stall, and number of stalls possible in a given aisle length. The nomogram presented in Figure 9–2 allows him to examine any number of possibilities simply by rotating a straightedge across the scales. One possible situation would find the plant engineer constrained with a given number of stalls (say 40) to be fit into a given length of aisle (say 800 feet). Now he has a tradeoff to consider: placing the stalls at right angles to the aisle provides the widest stalls but requires the largest amount of aisle space for turning; placing the stalls at a flatter angle to the aisle reduces their widths but allows the aisle to be narrower. To identify the possibilities for a tradeoff analysis, the plant engineer draws a straight line through the given values on the first two scales of Figure 9–2 and then places his pencil point at the spot where that line crosses the middle scale (at 20 in this example). He then rotates a straightedge about that point; every combination of stall width and angle made by the straightedge (last two scales) is a physical possibility that he can consider—such as 20 feet wide at 90 degrees; 17 feet wide at 60 degrees; 14 feet wide at 45 degrees, etc.

List of Tables

Table of Contents

Soil Mechanics and Foundation Design

CHAPTER 1

SOIL MECHANICS

This chapter treats soil mechanics as applied to supporting a structure, but the information presented is applicable to any plant engineering function that interfaces with the ground. Chapter 12 will refer to some of these formulas when evaluating the underbed for a paved area.

Soil Classifications: Comparison of Systems

Table 1–1[1] gives names and size limits for various soil components as defined by five organizations. Further details follow for two of the systems, and Chapter 9 will present details on the AASHO system.

Unified soil classification system

Table 1–2[2] shows successive class breakdowns according to this system. The lower case subdivisions of groups with an asterisk have meaning for airfields and roads only. This system is especially applicable to plant engineering because it includes soils that are high in gravel content.

U. S. Department of Agriculture Soil Classification

This classification defines textural groups composed of particles smaller than 2 millimeters in diameter. Each group name can be prefixed by "gravelly" if it contains 20 percent or more of gravel, but gravel is not included when percentages of the defined textural components are given.

Figure 1–1[3] shows the names applied to various combinations of the basic ingredients: sand, silt, and clay. To use this chart, locate the point at which all three applicable percentages intersect, and read the soil name at that point. At each entry, choose the line that runs to the clockwise side of the applicable percentage.

---

[1] Portland Cement Association, PCA Soil Primer, Skokie, Illinois, p. 10. © Portland Cement Association, 1962.

[2] U.S. Army Corps of Engineers, The Unified Soil Classification System, Military Standard 619, 1960.

[3] U.S. Department of Agriculture, Atlas of American Agriculture, Part III, 1935.

FIGURE 1-1

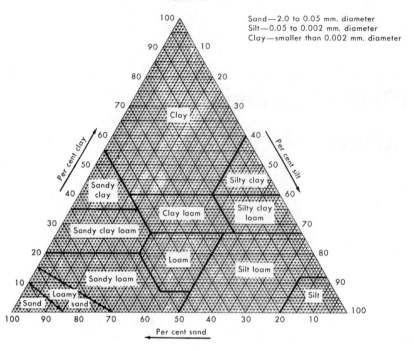

Sand—2.0 to 0.05 mm. diameter
Silt—0.05 to 0.002 mm. diameter
Clay—smaller than 0.002 mm. diameter

TABLE 1-1. Differences in components of soil as defined by five organizations.

American Society for Testing and Materials	Colloids*	Clay	Silt	Fine sand	Coarse sand	Gravel				
American Association of State Highway Officials Soil Classification	Colloids*	Clay	Silt	Fine sand	Coarse sand	Fine gravel	Medium gravel	Coarse gravel	Boulders	
U.S. Department of Agriculture Soil Classification	Clay	Silt	Very fine sand	Fine sand	Medium sand	Coarse sand / Very coarse sand	Fine gravel	Coarse gravel	Cobbles	
Federal Aviation Agency Soil Classification	Clay	Silt	Fine sand	Coarse sand	Gravel					
Unified Soil Classification (Corps of Engineers, Department of the Army, and Bureau of Reclamation)	Fines (silt or clay)	Fine sand	Medium sand	Coarse sand	Fine gravel	Coarse gravel	Cobbles			

Sieve sizes: 270 | 200 | 140 | 60 | 40 | 20 | 10 | 4 | ½" | ¾" | 3"

Particle size, mm.: .001 .002 .003 .004 .006 .008 .01 .02 .03 .04 .06 .08 .1 .2 .3 .4 .6 .8 1.0 2.0 3.0 4.0 6.0 8.0 10 20 30 40 60 80

*Colloids included in clay fraction in test reports.

TABLE 1-2. Unified soil classification system.

Major Divisions			Group Symbols		Typical names
Coarse-grained soils (More than half of material is larger than #200 sieve size)	Gravels (More than half of coarse fraction is larger than #4 sieve)	Clean gravels	GW		Well-graded gravels, gravel-sand mixtures, little or no fines
			GP		Poorly graded gravels, gravel-sand mixtures, little or no fines
		Gravels with fines	GM*	d	Silty gravels, gravel-sand-silt mixtures
				u	
			GC		Clayey gravels, gravel-sand-clay mixtures
	Sands (More than half of coarse fraction is smaller than #4 sieve)	Clean sands	SW		Well-graded sands, gravelly sands, little or no fines
			SP		Poorly graded sands, gravelly sands, little or no fines
		Sands with fines	SM*	d	Silty sands, sand-silt mixtures
				u	
			SC		Clayey sands, sand-clay mixtures
Fine-grained soils (More than half of material is smaller than #200 sieve)	Silts and clays (liquid limit less than 50)		ML		Inorganic silts and very fine sands, rock flour, silty or clayey fine sands, or clayey silts with slight plasticity
			CL		Inorganic clays of low to medium plasticity, gravelly clays, sandy clays, silty clays, lean clays
			OL		Organic silts and organic silty clays of low plasticity
	Silts and clays (liquid limit greater than 50)		MH		Inorganic silts, micaceous or diatomaceous fine sandy or silty soils, elastic silts
			CH		Inorganic clays of high plasticity, fat clays
			OH		Organic clays of medium to high plasticity, organic silts
	Highly organic soils		Pt		Peat and other highly organic silts

Soil types in the lower left hand corner of the figure are further detailed in Table 1–3.[4] This table is especially helpful if the various consultants and contractors do not use identical units or terms.

TABLE 1-3.   Details of sand sizes in three types of soil.

Basic soil class	Subclass	Soil separates				
		Very coarse sand, 2.0-1.0 mm.	Coarse sand, 1.0-0.5 mm.	Medium sand, 0.5-0.25 mm.	Fine sand, 0.25-0.1 mm.	Very fine sand, 0.1-0.05 mm.
Sands	Coarse sand	25% or more		Less than 50%	Less than 50%	Less than 50%
	Sand	25% or more			Less than 50%	Less than 50%
	Fine sand	Less than 25%		—or—	50% or more	Less than 50%
	Very fine sand					50% or more
Loamy sands	Loamy coarse sand	25% or more		Less than 50%	Less than 50%	Less than 50%
	Loamy sand	25% or more			Less than 50%	Less than 50%
	Loamy fine sand	Less than 25%		—or—	50% or more	Less than 50%
	Loamy very fine sand					50% or more
Sandy loams	Coarse sandy loam	25% or more		Less than 50%	Less than 50%	Less than 50%
	Sandy loam	30% or more — Less than 25%		—and—	Less than 30%	Less than 30%
	Fine sandy loam	—or— Between 15 and 30%			30% or more	Less than 30%
	Very fine sandy loam	Less than 15%		—or—	More than 40%*	30% or more

*Half of fine sand and very fine sand must be very fine sand.

---

[4]Ibid.

Example

Because of drainage and other problems, an excavation contractor makes his bid conditional upon the soil's containing less than 50 percent sand under 0.1 millimeter in diameter. An analysis is conducted and the result is:

    5 percent silt
    5 percent clay
    90 percent coarse sand
    no gravel

Enter Figure 1–1 near the top, at 5 percent silt, and follow that line down and to the left until it intersects with the short line coming from 90 percent sand. (A clay content of 5 percent also intersects at that point because the three components add to 100 percent at every point on the chart.) Since the sand has been named coarse sand, refer to the top line of Table 1–3 and note that less than 50 percent of the sand is under 0.1 millimeter. Fifty percent of the 90 percent sand content means less than 45 percent of the soil will be sand smaller than the critical diameter, and the contract condition will be met.

Shrinkage Limit

Formula

$$S = M - \frac{100(V - V_o)}{W_o} (0.0362)$$

where S = shrinkage limit in percent moisture content
            = point at which shrinkage stops as moisture is removed
              6 to 14 for soils which are mostly clay
              14 to 25 for soils which are mostly sand
   M = moisture content of soil subject to shrinkage
            = weight of contained moisture divided by weight of dry soil
   V = volume of soil subject to shrinkage, in $inch^3$
   V_o = volume of dry soil, in $inch^3$
  W_o = weight of dry soil, in pounds

If volume and weight are in cubic centimeters and grams, the equation becomes[5]

$$S = M - \frac{100(V - V_o)}{W_o}$$

Example

What range of moisture contents will have a linear effect on a soil's volume if the following parameters have been determined? A six inch cube of wet soil was carefully formed and baked to complete dryness. Before baking, the soil weighed 15 pounds and after baking, it weighed 12 pounds. Volume decreased from 216 to 215.5 cubic inches.

---

[5]Portland Cement Association, PCA Soil Primer, Skokie, Illinois, p. 15. © Portland Cement Association, 1962.

Moisture content of the wet soil is first determined by dividing the weight of lost water by that of the dry soil:

$$M = \frac{15.0 - 12}{12}$$
$$= 0.25$$
$$= 25 \text{ percent}$$

This value and the weights and volumes given are then used in the equation

$$S = .25 - \frac{100(216 - 215.5)}{(12)}(.0362)$$
$$= .25 - .15$$
$$= .10$$

The soil's volume will be linearly dependent on moisture content over a range of 8 to 100 percent.

Shrinkage Ratio[6]

Formula

$$R = \frac{\dfrac{V - V_o}{V_o}(100)}{M - S}$$

where R = ratio of soil volume for moisture contents of M and S
$\quad\quad M$ = moisture content of soil subject to shrinkage
$\quad\quad S$ = shrinkage limit in percent moisture content
$\quad\quad V$ = volume of soil which has moisture content M
$\quad\quad V_o$ = volume of dry soil

Example

Find shrinkage ratio for conditions used in the preceding example.

$$R = \frac{\dfrac{216.0 - 215.5}{215.5}(100)}{20 - 10}$$
$$= .022$$

Volumetric Shrinkage[7]

Formula

$$C_v = (M_a - S)R$$

where C_v = volumetric shrinkage in percent of dry volume
$\quad\quad M_a$ = moisture content, usually of field sample
$\quad\quad S$ = shrinkage limit
$\quad\quad R$ = shrinkage ratio

---

[6]Ibid.
[7]Ibid.

Example

Soil of the type used in the two preceding examples is found to have 15 percent moisture content on the day a survey is made. What is the maximum shrinkage that must be planned for?

$$C_v = (15 - 10)0.022$$
$$= 0.110 \text{ percent of dry volume}$$

Linear Shrinkage[8]

Formula

$$L = \left[1 - \sqrt[3]{\frac{100}{C_v + 100}} \right] 100$$

where L = linear shrinkage, expressed as a percentage of the same dimension before the soil is dried

C_v = volumetric shrinkage

Table 1–4 is included to give computer-generated solutions for a range of C_v most likely to be encountered.

TABLE 1-4. Linear shrinkage in percent.

C_v	L	C_v	L
.05	.017	.75	.249
.10	.033	.80	.265
.15	.050	.85	.282
.20	.067	.90	.298
.25	.083	.95	.315
.30	.100	1.00	.331
.35	.116	1.50	.495
.40	.133	2.00	.658
.45	.150	2.50	.820
.50	.166	3.00	.980
.55	.183	3.50	1.140
.60	.199	4.00	1.300
.65	.216	4.50	1.457
.70	.232	5.00	1.613

Example

If soil of the type used in the preceding examples is packed into a form 10 feet long, and then dried, how far will the soil draw from the ends of the form?

From the formula:

---

[8]Ibid.

$$L = \left[1 - \sqrt[3]{\frac{100}{0.110 + 100}} \right] 100$$

$$= 0.037 \text{ percent}$$

Using $C_v = 0.10$ in Table 1–4:

$$L = 0.033 \text{ percent}$$

Working with the table value, obtain total shrinkage by multiplying L by 120 inches

$$\text{Shrinkage} = 0.04 \text{ inch}$$

and it can be expected that the soil will draw about half that amount from each end of the form.

Coefficient of Permeability

Formula

$$K = 0.394Q \frac{L}{TAH}$$

where K = coefficient of permeability in inches per second
Q = quantity of water in inch^3
L = thickness of soil in inches
T = time in seconds
A = cross-sectional area of soil in inch^2
H = hydrostatic head in inches

If the basic unit is centimeters instead of inches, the formula is

$$K = Q \frac{L}{TAH}$$

The higher the K value, the more porous a soil is, as shown in Table 1–5. It is not practical to try to reduce water content through tile drains if K is less than 10^{-3} centimeters per second.

Example

A test frame is 20 by 20 centimeters, and tall enough for 5 centimeters of soil plus a 50 centimeter head of water. If water is poured in constantly for 30 seconds to maintain the head of 50 centimeters, and it requires 1.2 litres (1200 cc) to replace the water that seeps out, is drainage by tile practical?

Substituting directly into the metric equation gives

$$K = 1200 \frac{5}{30(400)50}$$

$$= 10^{-2} \text{ centimeters per second}$$

This value of K is an order of magnitude above the threshold; it is practical to drain with tile.

TABLE 1-5.   Correlation between coefficient of permeability and drainage characteristics.

Coefficient of Permeability

Centimeters per Second	Inches per Second	Type of Soil	Drainage
1.0 to 10^{-1}	0.5 to .05	Sand	Easily drained by tile
10^{-1} to 10^{-3}	5×10^{-2} to 5×10^{-4}	Sand	Can be drained by tile
10^{-3} to 10^{-7}	5×10^{-4} to 5×10^{-8}	Silty and Clayey Sand	Difficult to impossible
10^{-7} and less	5×10^{-8} and less	Cohesive Clay	Impervious

Pumping Rate to Reduce Ground Water Level

Formula

(English units):
$$P = \frac{42.5K\,(D_1^2 - D_2^2)}{2.78 + \log \dfrac{(D_1 - D_2)\sqrt{K}}{A}}$$

(metric):
$$P = \frac{58.2K\,(D_1^2 - D_2^2)}{2.477 + \log \dfrac{(D_1 - D_2)\sqrt{K}}{A}}$$

where P = pumping rate in gal/min (litres/min)
K = permeability in inch/sec (cm/sec)
D_1 = distance between normal water level and impermeable level in feet (meters)
D_2 = distance between desired water level and impermeable level in feet (meters)
A = radius of area encompassed by wells, in feet (meters)

Example

Water presently exists from 5 feet below the surface to 22 feet below the surface and must be lowered 5 feet by pumping over a radius of 100 feet. Tests show a soil permeability of 0.394×10^{-2} inch per second. At what rate must water be pumped to hold this new level?

Subtracting 5 feet from 22 feet gives $D_1 = 17$ feet, and 10 from 22 gives $D_2 = 12$ feet. Substituting these and the given values into the first form of the equation gives

$$P = \frac{42.5\,(0.394 \times 10^{-2})\,(17^2 - 12^2)}{2.78 + \log \dfrac{(17 - 12)\sqrt{0.394 \times 10^{-2}}}{100}}$$

$$= 138 \text{ gallons per minute}$$

Number of Wells for Given Pumping Rate

Formula

(English units):
$$N = \frac{P}{41.34\, D_3 D_4 \sqrt{K}}$$

(metric):
$$N = \frac{P}{188 D_3 D_4 \sqrt{K}}$$

where N = number of wells required
P = total pumping rate in gal/min (litres/min)
D_3 = diameter of each well in feet (meters)
D_4 = water level in feet (meters)
K = permeability of soil in inch/sec (cm/sec)

Example

Given 1-foot diameter wells and a water level of 5 feet, how many wells would be required to pump the 138 gallons per minute of the preceding example?

These numbers, and constants from the preceding example, can be substituted directly into the formula

$$N = \frac{138}{188\,(1)\,5\sqrt{0.394 \times 10^{-2}}}$$

$$= 2.34 \qquad \text{(3 wells would be required)}$$

FOUNDATIONS

Of the great number of possible combinations of soil types and foundation types, it is fortunate that those that are mentioned here correspond to those that the plant engineer will use in his projects. Because safety factors are always recommended, this information should satisfy all requirements for estimating the magnitude of a project.

The largest block of information, which is too complex for presenting in summary form, is that of foundations on rock. It is necessary that this topic be dismissed with the statement that safe bearing capacities vary from a low of 6 tons per square foot (6 kilograms per square centimeter) for solid chalk to a high in excess of 100 tons per square foot (100 kilograms per square centimeter) for a solid base of hard rock.

Full Foundation on Sand

Formula

$$B = \frac{N - 3}{5}$$

where B = allowable bearing capacity in tons/ft^2 or kg/cm^2
N = soil type coefficient, given in Table A-1

Example

The soil on which a structure is to be placed without footings is judged to be fairly tight sand. Calculate the allowable rate of bearing.

Sand is represented by the first two rows of Table A–1, and a soil of the description given here would fall about in the middle of the range covered by the second row. An N value of 7 will be a good approximation for planning purposes.

$$B = \frac{7 - 3}{5}$$
$$= 0.8 \text{ tons/ft}^2 \text{ or kg/cm}^2$$

Applying a safety factor of 3 reduces the allowable bearing capacity to 0.27.

Square, Shallow Footings on Sand

Formula

$$B = 0.5 \ DWJ + DF \ (L\text{-}1)$$

where B = allowable bearing capacity in units consistent with those used for D, W, and F

D = density of soil
W = width and length of square footing
J = factor found in Table A–1
F = depth of footing
L = factor found in Table A–1

Example

A soil of 90 pounds per cubic foot and loose consistency is to support 2-foot square footings that are 3 feet deep. How many footings will be required to support a total weight of 32,000 pounds?

Substituting the two factors from Table A–1 ($J = 17$ and $L = 19$) with the given dimensions and soil density gives

$$B = 0.5 \ (90) \ 17 + 90 \ (3) \ (19 - 1)$$
$$= 6390 \text{ pounds per square foot}$$

Applying a safety factor of 3 reduces B to 2130 pounds per square foot. Each footing has a surface of 4 square feet and can therefore carry 8520 pounds. Divide this capacity into the total weight of 32,000 pounds, and the smallest number of footings that will suffice is 4.

Rectangular Footings in Clay

Formula (bottom of footing below ground by less than 2 1/2 times footing width)

$$B = C \left(5 + \frac{F}{W} \right) \left(1 + \frac{W}{5X} \right)$$

Formula (deep footing)

$$B = C \left(7.5 + 1.5 \frac{W}{X} \right)$$

where B = allowable bearing capacity in units consistent with the units of C, F, W, and X

C = cohesion factor of clayey soil, obtained by complex measurements and analysis. For estimating, use 0.1 ton/ft² (0.1 kg/cm²) for thin clays to 1.0 for dense clays

F = depth of footing in consistent units
W = width of footing in consistent units
X = length of footing in consistent units

Example

Rectangular footings 2 feet wide by 3 feet long are to be set 4 feet below the surface in sandy clay soil ($C = 0.4$). What is the allowable bearing capacity?

Depth/width ratio is 4/2, less than 2 1/2; the first equation will be used.

$$B = 0.4\left(5 + \frac{4}{2}\right)\left(1 + \frac{2}{5(3)}\right)$$
$$= 3.17 \text{ tons per square foot}$$

Square and Circular Footings in Clay

Formula (bottom of footing below ground by less than 2 1/2 times footing width)

$$B = 1.2\left(5 + \frac{F}{W}\right)C$$

Formula (deep footing)

$$B = 9C$$

where all variables have the same meaning as for rectangular footings in clay.

Example

A stiff clay with cohesion factor of 1 ton per square foot is to support cubic footings of 2-foot sides. What is the allowable bearing capacity?

Substituting directly into the first equation gives

$$B = 1.2\left(5 + \frac{2}{2}\right)1$$
$$= 7.2 \text{ tons per square foot}$$

General Bearing Equation

Most of the preceding bearing equations are special cases of the general form

$$B = CK + 0.5\,DWJ + DF(L - 1)$$

where J, K, and L are obtained from Table A–1 after either estimating soil consistency or conducting a Standard Penetration Test, and other coefficents have the same meanings as in previous equations.

Example

A medium dense soil of 95 pounds per cubic foot and C of 0.1 is to support footings 3 feet wide at a depth of 5 feet. What is the allowable bearing capacity?

To remain with consistent units, the cohesion factor of 0.1 ton per square foot will be expressed as 200 pounds per square foot. Coefficients J, K, and L are obtained from the "medium dense" line of Table A–1.

$$B = 200(62) + 0.5(95)3(47) + 95(5) \ (46 - 1)$$
$$= 40{,}500 \text{ pounds per square foot}$$

Immediate Settlement Due to Uniform Load of Rectangular Shape

Formula

(English units):	$S = 0.8BWU/E$
(metric):	$S = 2BWU/E$

where S = settlement under corner of load in inches (cm)
$\quad\ B$ = load density in lb/inch (kg/cm^2)
$\quad\ W$ = width of bearing surface in inches (centimeters)
$\quad\ U$ = factor obtained from Table 1–6
$\quad\ E$ = Young's modulus for clay in the compressible layer lb/inch^2 (kg/cm^2)

TABLE 1-6.   Factor U for calculating settlement.

Depth factor*	1	2	3	4	5	6	8	10	15	ultimate
1	.15	.14	.13	.12	.12	.12	.12	.12	.12	.12
2	.30	.29	.28	.27	.26	.26	.27	.27	.27	.27
3	.36	.41	.40	.40	.39	.39	.38	.38	.38	.37
4	.41	.48	.50	.50	.48	.48	.47	.46	.46	.45
5	.44	.53	.56	.56	.55	.55	.54	.53	.53	.52
6	.46	.56	.61	.62	.61	.61	.60	.60	.59	.58
7	.47	.59	.65	.66	.66	.66	.65	.65	.64	.63
8	.48	.61	.67	.70	.70	.70	.70	.69	.68	.67
9	.48	.63	.68	.71	.73	.75	.75	.73	.71	.70
10	.48	.64	.71	.74	.76	.78	.79	.77	.75	.73

*depth factor is equal to depth of the compressible layer divided by W.

Example

Calculate immediate settlement under the corner of a footing that is 50 inches wide by 100 inches long, if the consultant has determined that the compressible layer is 33 feet thick and has a Young's modulus of 20,000 pounds per square inch.

$$\text{Length/width} = 100/50$$
$$= 2$$

and therefore factor U will be found in the second column of Table 1–6.

$$\text{Depth factor} = 33 \ (12)/50 \qquad \text{(converting feet to inches)}$$
$$= 8$$

and factor U from the table is 0.61. Using this factor in the equation gives

$$S = 0.8(100) \ 50 \ (0.61)/20{,}000$$
$$= 0.12 \text{ inch}$$

Ultimate Settlement: One year to tens of years

Formula

$$S_u = T \frac{V_i - V_u}{1 + V_i}$$

where S_u = ultimate settlement in consistent units

$\quad T$ = thickness of compressible layer in consistent units

$\quad V_i$ = initial voids ratio of soil, obtained by test

$\quad V_u$ = ultimate voids ratio of soil

Example

Soil has a voids ratio of 0.95 and tests show that it will ultimately settle to 0.8. Determine the ultimate settlement for a compressible layer 3 feet thick.

$$S_u = 3(12)(0.95 - 0.8)/(1 + 0.95)$$
$$= 2.8 \text{ inches}$$

The factor 12 has been included to convert feet to inches so as to give consistent units.

Bearing Capacity of Pile Driven Into Clay

Formula

$$B = S (9A_p + KA_w)$$

where B = bearing capacity after driving pressures dissipate in about 5 weeks, in pounds (kilograms)

$\quad S$ = soil shear strength in lb/ft^2 (kg/m^2)

$\quad A_p$ = area of pile point in ft^2 (m^2)

$\quad A_w$ = area of pile wall in contact with soil in ft^2 (m^2)

$\quad K$ = dimensionless constant determined by soil analyst, usually between 0.4 and 0.6 for medium soft clay

Example

A soil analyst has determined that a soil is predominantly clay with S of 1000 pounds per square foot, and K is 0.5. What will be the bearing capacity of a pile with 3.5 square feet of point area and 200 square feet of wall in contact with soil?

$$B = 1000(9(3.5) + (0.5)100)$$
$$= 81,500 \text{ pounds}$$

Pile Array Factor: Some or all of the load taken by pile walls

Formula

$$A = 1 - \arctan \left(\frac{d}{s}\right) \frac{R (P - 1) + P (R - 1)}{1.57 \, RP}$$

where A = factor between 0 and 1 which multiplies the load a pile could carry if it were isolated

d = diameter of each pile
s = spacing between centers of piles
arctan is in radians
R = number of rows of piles
P = number of piles in a row

The array factor can be evaluated either by substituting numbers into the equation or by referring to computer-generated solutions for most expected arrangements in Table A–2.

Example

Piles of 1-foot diameter are placed on 6-foot centers in 3 rows of 5 each. Calculations show that, if isolated, they could support 15,000 pounds each. What total load will they support?

In Table A–2 use the fourth group, headed spacing/diameter = 6. The intersection between 3 rows and 5 per row shows that the array factor is 0.85. Total bearing capacity is then

$$P = \text{(array factor) (single-pile capacity) (number of piles)}$$
$$= 0.85 \ (15,000) \ 15$$
$$= 202,500 \text{ pounds}$$

Beam Formulas: (Tables in Appendix)

Forces, deflections, and other quantities resulting from suspending beams can be calculated from formulas presented in Table A–4. Some factors in those formulas, such as I (moment of inertia), depend on the beam's shape and are first calculated from formulas in Table A–3. Other factors, such as E (Young's modulus), are constants that depend only on the type of material; for structural work use the following:

Aluminum $- E = 10 \times 10^3$ kips per square inch
$= 7$ kilogram per square millimeter
Steel $- E = 29 \times 10^3$ kips per square inch
$= 20$ kilogram per square millimeter

Example

The I-beam shown in Figure A–1 is to be suspended but not anchored and will support a single load in the middle, as shown in Figure A–2. Determine the forces, deflections, and other quantities.

The applicable load and support arrangement is found in the first configuration of Table A–4. Moment of inertia for this cross-section is evaluated in the example for Table A–3 ($I = 25.1$ inch^4).

Reaction: $R_1 = R_2 = \dfrac{2000}{2}$

$= 1000$ pounds

Maximum shear forces: $V_1 = \dfrac{P}{2} = 1000$ pounds

$V_2 = \dfrac{P}{2} = -1000$ pounds

Maximum bending moment: $M_{max} = \dfrac{PL}{4}$

$$= \dfrac{2000\ (20)}{4}$$

$$= 10{,}000 \text{ foot pounds}$$

Equation for deflection: $def = \dfrac{Px}{48EI}\ (3L^2 - 4x^2)$

$$= \dfrac{2000\,x}{48\ (10^4)\ 25.1}\ (3\ (20)^2 - 4x)$$

$$= \dfrac{-x^3 + 300x}{1506} \text{ inch}$$

Maximum deflection—deflection in the middle will be:

$$def_{max} = \dfrac{PL^3}{48EI}$$

$$= \dfrac{2000\ (20)^3}{48\ (10^4)\ 25.1}$$

$$= 1.33 \text{ inches}$$

Maximum deflection can also be obtained by substituting $x = \dfrac{L}{2} = 10$ in the equation for deflection.

Concrete, Blocks, and Wood

CHAPTER 2

Formulas and tables for using concrete, blocks, and wood as structural materials are presented in this chapter. The first section, on poured concrete, deals with the product technically known as Portland Cement Concrete: a mixture of portland cement, aggregate, water, and sometimes an admixture. It applies to concrete that is placed and cured at the site; the section after that will cover concrete that is supplied to the user already cured as a block or in another form.

POURED CONCRETE

Compressive Strength

Table 2–1 shows compressive strengths of typical mixtures, at selected ages, for various ratios of water to cement. The ratio is on a weight basis; pounds of water to pounds of cement, where a cubic foot of water weighs 62.3 pounds and a cubic foot of cement weighs 94 pounds. (One litre of water weighs 1 kilogram and 1 litre of cement weighs 1.49 kilograms.)

TABLE 2-1. Compressive strength of non-air-entrained concrete, moist-cured at 70°F (21°C).

Pounds per Square Inch

Water-cement ratio

	0.40	0.45	0.50	0.55	0.60	0.65	0.70
1 day	1000	750	600	450	350	250	200
3 days	2400	2100	1800	1500	1300	1200	1000
7 days	3700	3300	2900	2500	2200	1800	1500
28 days	5600	5200	4700	4200	3800	3300	2900

Kilograms per Square Centimeter

Water-cement ratio

	0.40	0.45	0.50	0.55	0.60	0.65	0.70
1 day	70	53	42	32	25	18	14
3 days	168	147	126	105	91	84	70
7 days	260	232	203	175	154	126	105
28 days	392	364	330	294	266	232	203

Slump Test: Standard method of measuring consistency[1]

After the mold is filled and rodded it is carefully removed and the sample's average height is compared to that of the mold.

Table 2–2 shows slump ranges as indications of workability ranges of concrete mixes for various types of construction.[2]

TABLE 2-2. Typical slump ranges for selected types of construction.

Type of Construction	Maximum Slump In.	Maximum Slump Cm.	Minimum Slump In.	Minimum Slump Cm.
Reinforced foundation walls and footings	3	8	1	3
Unreinforced footings, caissons, and substructure walls	3	8	1	3
Reinforced slabs, beams, and walls	4	10	1	3
Bridge Decks	3	8	2	5
Pavements	2	5	1	3
Building Columns	4	10	1	3
Sidewalks, driveways, and slabs on ground	4	10	2	5
Heavy mass construction	2	5	1	3

Trial Mix

Because batches of cement can absorb differing amounts of water, and because aggregates often contain significant amounts of moisture before mixing, a firm table of proportions for an optimum mix cannot be provided. Instead, a trial mix is prepared several times during construction, and adjustments are made on the basis of slump test results.

Table 2–3[3] shows suggested trial mixture proportions for a goal of 3 to 4 inch (8 to

---

[1]U.S. Department of the Interior, Concrete Manual, Government Printing Office, Seventh Edition, 1966, page 554.
[2]Portland Cement Association, Proportioning Concrete Mixes, Skokie, Illinois. © Portland Cement Association 1969.
[3]Ibid.

TABLE 2-3. Suggested trial mixes for non-air-entrained concrete of medium consistency.

Water-cement ratio, lb. per lb.	Maximum size of aggregate, in.	Air content (entrapped air), per cent	Water, lb. per cu.yd. of concrete	Cement, lb. per cu.yd. of concrete	With fine sand—fineness modulus = 2.50*			With coarse sand—fineness modulus = 2.90*		
					Fine aggregate, per cent of total aggregate	Fine aggregate, lb. per cu.yd. of concrete	Coarse aggregate, lb. per cu.yd. of concrete	Fine aggregate, per cent of total aggregate	Fine aggregate, lb. per cu.yd. of concrete	Coarse aggregate, lb. per cu.yd. of concrete
0.40	⅜	3	385	965	50	1240	1260	54	1350	1150
	½	2.5	365	915	42	1100	1520	47	1220	1400
	¾	2	340	850	35	960	1800	39	1080	1680
	1	1.5	325	815	32	910	1940	36	1020	1830
	1½	1	300	750	29	880	2110	33	1000	1990
0.45	⅜	3	385	855	51	1330	1260	56	1440	1150
	½	2.5	365	810	44	1180	1520	48	1300	1400
	¾	2	340	755	37	1040	1800	41	1160	1680
	1	1.5	325	720	34	990	1940	38	1100	1830
	1½	1	300	665	31	960	2110	35	1080	1990
0.50	⅜	3	385	770	53	1400	1260	57	1510	1150
	½	2.5	365	730	45	1250	1520	49	1370	1400
	¾	2	340	680	38	1100	1800	42	1220	1680
	1	1.5	325	650	35	1050	1940	39	1160	1830
	1½	1	300	600	32	1010	2110	36	1130	1990
0.55	⅜	3	385	700	54	1460	1260	58	1570	1150
	½	2.5	365	665	46	1310	1520	51	1430	1400
	¾	2	340	620	39	1150	1800	43	1270	1680
	1	1.5	325	590	36	1100	1940	40	1210	1830
	1½	1	300	545	33	1060	2110	37	1180	1990
0.60	⅜	3	385	640	55	1510	1260	58	1620	1150
	½	2.5	365	610	47	1350	1520	51	1470	1400
	¾	2	340	565	40	1200	1800	44	1320	1680
	1	1.5	325	540	37	1140	1940	41	1250	1830
	1½	1	300	500	34	1090	2110	38	1210	1990
0.65	⅜	3	385	590	55	1550	1260	59	1660	1150
	½	2.5	365	560	48	1390	1520	52	1510	1400
	¾	2	340	525	41	1230	1800	45	1350	1680
	1	1.5	325	500	38	1180	1940	41	1290	1830
	1½	1	300	460	35	1130	2110	39	1250	1990
0.70	⅜	3	385	550	56	1590	1260	60	1700	1150
	½	2.5	365	520	48	1430	1520	53	1550	1400
	¾	2	340	485	41	1270	1800	45	1390	1680
	1	1.5	325	465	38	1210	1940	42	1320	1830
	1½	1	300	430	35	1150	2110	39	1270	1990

10 centimeter) slump. For a goal of a larger or smaller slump, change quantities in the trial mix according to the following guidelines:

- increase or decrease water by 3 percent to change slump 1 inch
- for less workable concrete, as in pavements, decrease fine aggregate by 3 percent and water by 8 pounds per cubic yard of concrete
- for manufactured fine aggregate, increase fine aggregate by 3 percent and water by 15 pounds per cubic yard of concrete
- with a given amount of water and cement paste, a stiffer mix is obtained by increasing the amount of aggregate

*fineness modulus is defined on pages 44 and 45.

• in general, thin members and heavily reinforced members require more plastic mixtures than large members with little reinforcing.

Abrasion Resistance

Table 2–4 shows comparisons between compressive strength and abrasion resistance, where the depth of wear in concrete of 1000 psi is taken as 100 percent.

TABLE 2-4. Correlation between compressive strength and abrasion resistance.

Compressive Strength, psi	Relative Abrasion Resistance
1000	100%
2000	62%
3000	43%
4000	30%
5000	21%
6000	15%

Curing: Effect on compressive strength

Figure 2–1[4] shows the advantage of moist-curing, and the dramatic degree to which compressive strength tops out with early exposure to air.

FIGURE 2-1

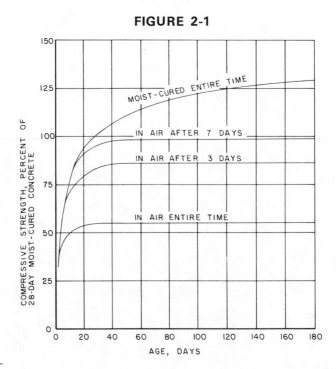

[4]Portland Cement Association, Fundamental Facts About Concrete, Skokie, Illinois © Portland Cement Association 1966.

Rate of Evaporation (Plastic shrinkage cracks can result from tensions set up by fast drying)

Figure 2–2[5] provides an easy way to determine if conditions are present for evaporation to proceed at a rate faster than that at which bleed water rises to the surface. To use this chart, enter at the applicable air temperature, move straight to the applicable relative humidity line, and proceed through the figure with right angle turns.

FIGURE 2-2

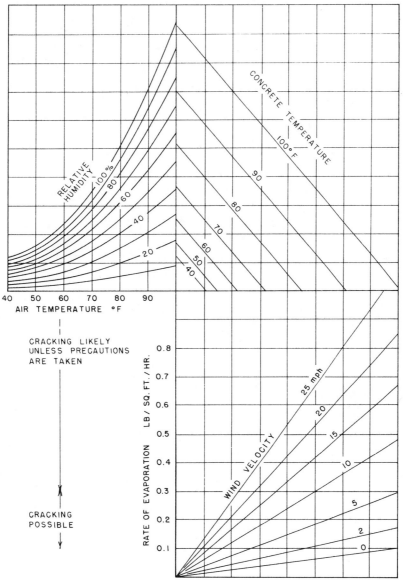

[5]Portland Cement Association, Curing of Concrete, Skokie, Illinois © Portland Cement Association 1966.

Example

The air is 75 degrees at 50 percent relative humidity, and wind is 15 miles per hour. What will be the rate of surface evaporation if the concrete temperature is 80 degrees?

Solution

Locate 75 degrees halfway between 70 and 80 and proceed straight up to the curve of 50 percent humidity. Turn a right angle and proceed horizontally to the curve for 80 degree concrete, then turn another right angle and proceed straight down to the curve for 15 mph wind. At that point make the final right angle and read 0.22 pounds per square foot per hour as the rate of evaporation. Since this rate is in the intermediate band, surface cracking is possible and some measures to retard evaporation are recommended.

Screening: Grading of aggregate mix according to Fineness Modulus

Coarse aggregates pass through screens with openings between 6 inches and 1/4 inch, and fine aggregates pass through screens numbered 4 through 200. Table 2–5[6] shows dimensions of openings and wires. Separating through successively smaller screens provides data from which Fineness Modulus can be calculated.

TABLE 2-5. Dimensions of standard screens for aggregate grading.*

Screen number or size in inches	Average screen opening		Average wire diameter	
	Millimeter	Inch	Millimeter	Inch
200	0.074	0.0029	0.053	0.0021
100	.149	.0059	.110	.0044
50	.297	.0117	.212	.0084
30	.59	.0232	.35	.0140
16	1.19	.0469	.60	.0236
8	2.38	.0937	.92	.0362
4	4.76	.187	1.41	.056
3/8	9.52	.375	2.35	.092
1/2	12.7	.50	2.74	.108
3/4	19.1	.75	3.50	.138
1	25.4	1.00	3.96	.156
1 1/2	38.1	1.50	4.5	.178
2	50.8	2.00	5.2	.202
3	76.2	3.00	6.4	.255

*The dimensions conform to the requirements of ASTM Designation E 11, "Standard Specifications for Sieves for Testing Purposes." (Screen openings given are square openings.)

[6]U.S. Department of the Interior, Concrete Manual, Government Printing Office, Seventh Edition, 1966, p. 518.

Formula

$$M_f = \frac{\text{Summation of \% retained after each screening}}{100}$$

Example

The first two columns of Table 2–6 give the percentages that pass through each screen. Each value in the pass-through column is subtracted from 100 to obtain the percent retained, and the latter values are summed to obtain the last column. Fineness Modulus is then

$$M_f = \frac{283}{100}$$
$$= 2.83$$

TABLE 2-6. Example of Fineness Modulus calculation.

Screen Number	Percent Passed Through	Percent Retained	Cumulative Percent Retained
4	98	2	2
8	85	15	17
16	65	35	52
30	45	55	107
50	21	79	186
100	3	97	283

Aggregates: Usually occupy 60 to 80 percent of concrete volume

Aggregate density, size, and composition are used in concrete according to the classifications of Table 2–7[7]. Weight classifications are intended only for gross groupings, as there are no sharp boundaries between classifications.

Maximum Aggregate Size

The amount of water required decreases as the maximum size of aggregate increases, as shown in Figure 2–3[8]. Therefore, for a given water-cement ratio, the amount of cement required also decreases as aggregate size increases, resulting in lower material costs. However, costs of obtaining and handling rise for very large aggregates, and the rule is that maximum aggregates of 2 or 2 1/2 inches usually result in minimum total costs.

General practice also holds that maximum aggregate size should not exceed:

- One-fifth the dimension of nonreinforced members
- Three-fourths the clear spacing between reinforcing bars or between reinforcing bars and forms
- One-third the depth of nonreinforced slabs on ground.

[7]Portland Cement Association, Aggregates for Concrete, Skokie, Illinois © Portland Cement Association 1968.
[8]Ibid.

TABLE 2-7.   Relation between concrete classification and aggregate.

Concrete Classification	Range of concrete weights*		Range of aggregate weights*		Typical Aggregate Materials
	Pounds per cubic foot	Kilograms per cubic meter	Pounds per cubic foot	Kilograms per cubic meter	
Insulating	15–90	240–1500	6–70	95–1100	Pumice, scoria, perlite, vermiculite, diatomite
Normal-weight	135–160	2200–2600	75–110	1200–1800	Sand, gravel, crushed stone, Air-cooled blast-furnace slag
Lightweight	85–115	1400–1800	30–70	480–1100	Expanded shale, clay, slate, slag
Heavyweight	150–380	2400–6000	110 up	1800	Barites, Limonite, magnetite, Ilmenite, iron, steel

*in pounds per cubic foot

FIGURE 2-3

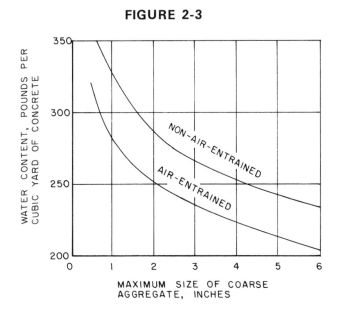

Bulking: Increase in volume when fine aggregate is handled

Figure 2–4[9] shows that bulking can add as much as a third to the volume of a batch of sand, which explains why most mixing instructions are given in terms of weight rather than volume.

FIGURE 2-4.   Increase in fine aggregate volume due to bulking.

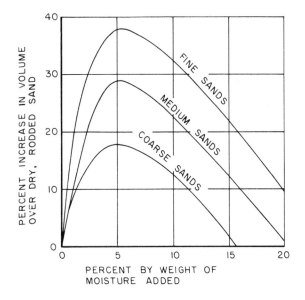

Harmful Substances in Aggregates

A very small percentage of certain organic impurities, such as sugar, may prevent setting of concrete for several days. Other substances and their effects are shown in Table 2–8[10].

TABLE 2-8. Harmful substances in aggregates.

Substance	Effect on Concrete
Organic Impurities	Affect setting and hardening and may cause deterioration
Materials finer than number 200 sieve	Coat aggregate particles, weaken bond, increase water requirement
Coal, lignite, or other lightweight materials	Reduce durability, may cause stains and popouts
Soft particles	Reduced durability, increase water requirements
Friable particles	Affect workability, reduce durability, popouts, may increase water requirement

Air-Entrained Concrete[11]

Figure 2–5 demonstrates the degree to which air-entrainment reduces vulnerability to deterioration from freeze-thaw cycles.

Percentage Entrained Air

A larger percentage air content is required for protection against severe freeze-thaw cycles than for other benefits. Table 2–9 shows recommended air contents for the two types of service, as a function of coarse aggregate size. Expected benefits can be realized if the percentage air content varies by as much as plus or minus 15 or 20 percent from the table values.

TABLE 2-9. Recommended percentages of air content for air-entrained concrete.

Maximum size coarse aggregate		Air content, percent by volume	
Inches	Centimeters	Protection against severe freeze-thaw cycles and de-icers	Air-entrainment benefits other than freeze-thaw
1 1/2, 2, 2 1/2	4, 5, 6	5	3
3/4, 1	2, 2 1/2	6	4
3/8, 1/2	1, 1 1/2	7 1/2	5

---

[10]Ibid.

[11] Portland Cement Association, Air-Entrained Concrete, Skokie, Illinois. © Portland Cement Association 1967.

FIGURE 2-5

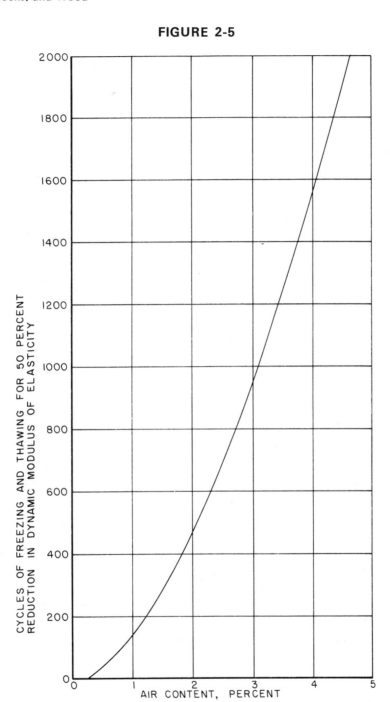

Water-Cement Ratio

Table 2–10 shows the water-cement ratio to use for a given compressive strength of air-entrained concrete.

TABLE 2-10. Compressive strength in psi, air-entrained concrete, moist-cured at 70°F.

	Water-cement ratio						
	0.475	0.500	0.525	0.550	0.575	0.600	0.625
1 day	400	300	250	200	175	150	130
3 days	1450	1300	1200	1100	950	700	650
7 days	2300	2100	1850	1700	1500	1300	1200
28 days	3850	3650	3300	3150	2800	2650	2500

Trial Mix[12]

After percentage air and water-cement ratio are selected, a trial mix can be designed. Table 2–11 gives suggested proportions for a 3 to 4 inch slump; if a different consistency is required, adjust the quantities as follows:

- increase or decrease water by 3 percent to change slump 1 inch
- for manufactured fine aggregate, increase fine aggregate by 3 percent and water by 15 pounds per cubic yard of concrete
- for less workable concrete, as in pavements, decrease fine aggregate by 3 percent and water by 8 pounds per cubic yard.

Example

We will design a trial mix for placing an unreinforced substructure wall of 3100 psi (after 28 days) in a severe freeze-thaw environment, using an aggregate with maximum size of 1 inch. Because of the environment, air-entrained concrete will be selected.

From Table 2–9 we determine that 1 inch aggregate dictates an air content of 6 percent, and Table 2–10 shows that 28–day compressive strength of 3100 pounds per square inch is slightly exceeded in a mixture with a water-cement ratio of 0.55.

Next, near the middle of Table 2–11, we see that a trial mix for 3- to 4-inch slump uses 520 pounds of cement and 285 pounds of water. The consistency should be adjusted for the actual type of construction, from Table 2–2. For unreinforced substructure walls the slump should be 1 to 3 inches, or an average of 2 inches compared to the average of 3 1/2, which the proportions of Table 2–11 will provide.

At a rate of 3 percent per inch, we should reduce the water quantity by 4 1/2 percent, to 272 pounds. Finally, quantities of fine and coarse aggregates can be selected from the last six columns of Table 2–11, depending on the Fineness Modulus of the fine aggregate.

CONCRETE REINFORCING[13]

Reinforcing Bars

Concrete reinforcing bars are designated by a number that is generally equal to the

---

[12] U.S. Department of the Interior, Concrete Manual, Government Printing Office, Seventh Edition, 1966, p. 144.
[13] Concrete Reinforcing Steel Institute, Manual of Standard Practice, Chicago, Illinois © 1970—Concrete Reinforcing Steel Institute.

TABLE 2-11. Suggested trial mixes for air-entrained concrete
of medium consistency.

Water-cement ratio, lb. per lb.	Maximum size of aggregate, in.	Air content, per cent	Water, lb. per cu.yd. of concrete	Cement, lb. per cu.yd. of concrete	With fine sand—fineness modulus = 2.50**			With coarse sand—fineness modulus = 2.90**		
					Fine aggregate, per cent of total aggregate	Fine aggregate, lb. per cu.yd. of concrete	Coarse aggregate, lb. per cu.yd. of concrete	Fine aggregate, per cent of total aggregate	Fine aggregate, lb. per cu.yd. of concrete	Coarse aggregate, lb. per cu.yd. of concrete
0.40	⅜	7.5	340	850	50	1250	1260	54	1360	1150
	½	7.5	325	815	41	1060	1520	46	1180	1400
	¾	6	300	750	35	970	1800	39	1090	1680
	1	6	285	715	32	900	1940	36	1010	1830
	1½	5	265	665	29	870	2110	33	990	1990
0.45	⅜	7.5	340	755	51	1330	1260	56	1440	1150
	½	7.5	325	720	43	1140	1520	47	1260	1400
	¾	6	300	665	37	1040	1800	41	1160	1680
	1	6	285	635	33	970	1940	37	1080	1830
	1½	5	265	590	31	930	2110	35	1050	1990
0.50	⅜	7.5	340	680	53	1400	1260	57	1510	1150
	½	7.5	325	650	44	1200	1520	49	1320	1400
	¾	6	300	600	38	1100	1800	42	1220	1680
	1	6	285	570	34	1020	1940	38	1130	1830
	1½	5	265	530	32	980	2110	36	1100	1990
0.55	⅜	7.5	340	620	54	1450	1260	58	1560	1150
	½	7.5	325	590	45	1250	1520	49	1370	1400
	¾	6	300	545	39	1140	1800	43	1260	1680
	1	6	285	520	35	1060	1940	39	1170	1830
	1½	5	265	480	33	1030	2110	37	1150	1990
0.60	⅜	7.5	340	565	54	1490	1260	58	1600	1150
	½	7.5	325	540	46	1290	1520	50	1410	1400
	¾	6	300	500	40	1180	1800	44	1300	1680
	1	6	285	475	36	1100	1940	40	1210	1830
	1½	5	265	440	33	1060	2110	37	1180	1990
0.65	⅜	7.5	340	525	55	1530	1260	59	1640	1150
	½	7.5	325	500	47	1330	1520	51	1450	1400
	¾	6	300	460	40	1210	1800	44	1330	1680
	1	6	285	440	37	1130	1940	40	1240	1830
	1½	5	265	410	34	1090	2110	38	1210	1990
0.70	⅜	7.5	340	485	55	1560	1260	59	1670	1150
	½	7.5	325	465	47	1360	1520	51	1480	1400
	¾	6	300	430	41	1240	1800	45	1360	1680
	1	6	285	405	37	1160	1940	41	1270	1830
	1½	5	265	380	34	1110	2110	38	1230	1990

number of eighths of an inch of diameter. Table 2–12 shows dimensions and weights for standard bars.

Welded Wire Fabric

Table 2–13 gives dimensions and weights for wires that are generally used for welding at right angles to form fabric. Physical characteristics of some typical wire fabrics are shown in Table 2–14. Table 2–15 presents basic data that can be used for calculating weights of arrangements not shown in Table 2–14.

**fineness modulus is defined on pages 44 and 45.

TABLE 2-12. Characteristics of standard concrete reinforcing bars.

Bar Designation Number	Pounds per foot	Kilograms per centimeter	Diameter		Cross-sectional area		Perimeter	
			Inches	Centimeters	Square Inches	Square Centimeters	Inches	Centimeters
3	0.376	.006	0.375	0.953	0.11	0.713	1.178	2.992
4	0.668	.010	0.500	1.270	0.20	1.270	1.571	3.989
5	1.043	.016	0.625	1.588	0.31	1.979	1.963	4.987
6	1.502	.022	0.750	1.905	0.44	2.850	2.356	5.985
7	2.044	.030	0.875	2.223	0.60	3.879	2.749	6.982
8	2.670	.040	1.000	2.540	0.79	5.067	3.142	7.980
9	3.400	.051	1.128	2.865	1.00	6.447	3.544	9.001
10	4.303	.064	1.270	3.226	1.27	8.173	3.990	10.134
11	5.313	.079	1.410	3.581	1.56	10.074	4.430	11.251
14	7.65	.114	1.693	4.300	2.25	14.523	5.32	13.510
18	13.60	.202	2.257	5.733	4.00	25.812	7.09	18.010

Bar numbers are based on, but not always equal to, the number of eighths of an inch of nominal diameter.

Example

Calculate the weights per 100 square feet of a welded wire fabric that has AS&W
#8 longitudinal wires spaced 4 inches on centers, and AS&W #12 transverse wires
spaced 10 inches on centers.

Solution

Table 2–15 shows that #8 longitudinal wires on 4 inch centers will weigh 22.40
pounds per 100 square feet. In the second half of the same table we see that #12 transverse
wires on 10 inch centers will weigh 3.68 pounds per 100 square feet. Total weight of this
fabric will be the sum, or 26 pounds per 100 square feet when rounded to the nearest
pound.

TABLE 2-13. Characteristics of wire used in welded wire fabric.

Diameter (in.)	AS&W Gauge	Diameter (in.)	Area (sq. in.)	Pounds Per Foot
1/2		.5000	.19635	.6668
	7/0	.4900	.18857	.6404
15/32		.46875	.17257	.5861
	6/0	.4615	.16728	.5681
7/16		.4375	.15033	.5105
	5/0	.4305	.14556	.4943
13/32		.40625	.12962	.4402
	4/0	.3938	.12180	.4136
3/8		.3750	.11045	.3751
	3/0	.3625	.10321	.3505
11/32		.34375	.092806	.3152
	2/0	.3310	.086049	.2922
5/16		.3125	.076699	.2605
	0	.3065	.073782	.2506
	1	.2830	.062902	.2136
9/32		.28125	.062126	.2110
	2	.2625	.054119	.1823
1/4		.2500	.049087	.1667
	3	.2437	.046645	.1584
	4	.2253	.039867	.1354
7/32		.21875	.037583	.1276
	5	.2070	.033654	.1143
	6	.1920	.028953	.09832
3/16		.1875	.027612	.09377
	7	.1770	.024606	.08356
	8	.1620	.020612	.07000
5/32		.15625	.019175	.06512
	9	.1483	.017273	.05866
	10	.1350	.014314	.04861
1/8		.125	.012272	.04168
	11	.1205	.011404	.03873
	12	.1055	.0087147	.02969
3/32		.09375	.0069029	.02344
	13	.0915	.0065755	.02233
	14	.0800	.0050266	.01707
	15	.0720	.0040715	.01383
	16	.0625	.0030680	.01042

ONE-WAY (RECTANGULAR) TYPES

Style designation	Spacing of wires, in.		Size of wires AS & W gauge		Sectional area sq in. per ft		Weight lb per 100 sq ft
	Longit.	Trans.	Longit.	Trans.	Longit.	Trans.	
24-1414 *	2	4	14	14	.030	.015	16
212-04	2	12	0	4	.443	.040	169
212-15	2	12	1	5	.377	.034	144
212-26	2	12	2	6	.325	.029	124
212-37	2	12	3	7	.280	.025	107
212-48	2	12	4	8	.239	.021	91
212-59	2	12	5	9	.202	.017	77
212-610	2	12	6	10	.174	.014	66
212-711	2	12	7	11	.148	.011	56
312-04	3	12	0	4	.295	.040	119
312-15	3	12	1	5	.252	.034	102
312-26	3	12	2	6	.216	.029	87
312-37	3	12	3	7	.187	.025	75
312-48	3	12	4	8	.159	.021	64
312-59	3	12	5	9	.135	.017	54
312-610	3	12	6	10	.116	.014	46
312-711	3	12	7	11	.098	.011	39
312-812	3	12	8	12	.082	.009	32
412-26	4	12	2	6	.162	.029	69
412-37	4	12	3	7	.140	.025	59
412-48	4	12	4	8	.120	.021	51
412-59	4	12	5	9	.101	.017	43
412-610	4	12	6	10	.087	.014	36
412-711	4	12	7	11	.074	.011	31

TWO-WAY (SQUARE) TYPES

Style designation	Spacing of wires, in.		Size of wires AS & W gauge		Sectional area sq in. per ft		Weight lb per 100 sq ft
	Longit.	Trans.	Longit.	Trans.	Longit.	Trans.	
2x2—10/10	2	2	10	10	.086	.086	60
2x2—12/12 *	2	2	12	12	.052	.052	37
2x2—14/14 *	2	2	14	14	.030	.030	21
2x2—16/16 *	2	2	16	16	.018	.018	13
3x3—8/8	3	3	8	8	.082	.082	58
3x3—10/10	3	3	10	10	.057	.057	41
3x3—12/12 *	3	3	12	12	.035	.035	25
3x3—14/14 *	3	3	14	14	.020	.020	14
4x4—4/4	4	4	4	4	.120	.120	85
4x4—6/6	4	4	6	6	.087	.087	62
4x4—8/8	4	4	8	8	.062	.062	44
4x4—10/10	4	4	10	10	.043	.043	31
4x4—12/12 *	4	4	12	12	.026	.026	19
4x4—13/13 *	4	4	13	13	.020	.020	14
4x4—14/14 *	4	4	14	14	.015	.015	11
6x6—0/0	6	6	0	0	.148	.148	107
6x6—1/1	6	6	1	1	.126	.126	91
6x6—2/2	6	6	2	2	.108	.108	78
6x6—3/3	6	6	3	3	.093	.093	68
6x6—4/4	6	6	4	4	.080	.080	58
6x6—5/5	6	6	5	5	.067	.067	50
6x6—6/6	6	6	6	6	.058	.058	42
6x6—7/7	6	6	7	7	.049	.049	36
6x6—8/8	6	6	8	8	.041	.041	30
6x6—9/9	6	6	9	9	.035	.035	25
6x6—10/10	6	6	10	10	.029	.029	21

* Usually furnished only in galvanized wire.

TABLE 2-14. Characteristics of some typical arrangements of welded wire fabric.

TABLE 2-15. Table for estimating weight of welded wire fabric.

For all styles having uniform spacings and gauges of members

Approximate Weights in Pounds per 100 Square Feet—Based on 60″ width c. to c. of outside longitudinal wires.

Steel Wire Gauge Numbers	Weight of Longitudinal Members						
	Spacing						
	2″	3″	4″	6″	8″	10″	12″
0000000	397.05	268.97	204.93	140.89	108.87	89.66	76.85
000000	352.22	238.60	181.79	124.98	96.58	79.53	68.17
00000	306.47	207.61	158.18	108.75	84.03	69.20	59.31
0000	256.43	173.71	132.35	90.99	70.31	57.90	49.63
000	217.31	147.21	112.16	77.11	59.59	49.07	42.06
00	181.16	122.72	93.50	64.28	49.67	40.91	35.06
0	155.37	105.25	80.19	55.13	42.60	35.08	30.07
1	132.43	89.71	68.35	46.99	36.31	29.90	25.63
2	113.96	77.20	58.82	40.44	31.25	25.73	22.06
¼″	103.33	70.00	53.33	36.67	28.33	23.33	20.00
3	98.21	66.53	50.69	34.85	26.93	22.18	19.01
4	83.95	56.87	43.33	29.79	23.02	18.96	16.25
5	70.87	48.01	36.58	25.15	19.43	16.00	13.72
6	60.96	41.29	31.46	21.63	16.71	13.76	11.80
7	51.81	35.10	26.74	18.38	14.21	11.70	10.03
8	43.40	29.40	22.40	15.40	11.90	9.80	8.40
9	36.37	24.64	18.77	12.91	9.97	8.21	7.04
10	30.14	20.42	15.56	10.69	8.26	6.81	5.83
11	24.01	16.27	12.39	8.52	6.58	5.42	4.65
12	18.41	12.47	9.50	6.53	5.05	4.16	3.56
12	13.84	9.38	7.15	4.91	3.80	3.13	2.68
14	10.58	7.17	5.46	3.76	2.90	2.39	2.05
15	8.57	5.81	4.43	3.04	2.35	1.94	1.66
16	6.46	4.38	3.33	2.29	1.77	1.46	1.25

Steel Wire Gauge Numbers	Weight of Transverse Members*							
	Spacing							
	2″	3″	4″	6″	8″	10″	12″	16″
0000	256.43	170.95	128.22	85.48	64.11	51.29	42.74	32.05
000	217.31	144.87	108.66	72.44	54.33	43.46	36.22	27.16
00	181.16	120.78	90.58	60.39	45.29	36.23	30.19	22.65
0	155.37	103.58	77.69	51.79	38.84	31.07	25.90	19.42
1	132.43	88.29	66.22	44.14	33.11	26.49	22.07	16.55
2	113.96	75.97	56.98	37.99	28.49	22.79	18.99	14.24
¼″	103.33	68.89	51.67	34.44	25.83	20.67	17.22	12.92
3	98.21	65.47	49.10	32.74	24.55	19.64	16.37	12.28
4	83.95	55.97	41.97	27.98	20.99	16.79	13.99	10.49
5	70.87	47.24	35.43	23.62	17.72	14.17	11.81	8.86
6	60.96	40.64	30.48	20.32	15.24	12.19	10.16	7.62
7	51.81	34.54	25.90	17.27	12.95	10.36	8.63	6.48
8	43.40	28.93	21.70	14.47	10.85	8.68	7.23	5.43
9	36.37	24.25	18.18	12.12	9.09	7.27	6.06	4.55
10	30.14	20.09	15.07	10.05	7.53	6.03	5.02	3.77
11	24.01	16.01	12.01	8.00	6.00	4.80	4.00	3.00
12	18.41	12.27	9.20	6.14	4.60	3.68	3.07	2.30
13	13.84	9.23	6.92	4.61	3.46	2.77	2.31	1.73
14	10.58	7.06	5.29	3.53	2.65	2.12	1.76	1.32
15	8.57	5.72	4.29	2.86	2.14	1.71	1.43	1.07
16	6.46	4.31	3.23	2.15	1.62	1.29	1.08	.81

NOTE: To determine the weight of any type add the weights of the longitudinal and transverse members, adjust the total to the nearest lb., considering 0.5 lb. or over to be 1 lb., and less than 0.5 lb. to be zero.

*Includes weight of 1″ projection beyond longitudinal selvage wires.

Bar Supports

Table 2–16[14] shows symbols, shapes, and dimensions of standard factory-made bar supports for holding reinforcing material in the proper position while concrete is being placed. Class A in that table refers to Bright Basic material, which has no protection against rusting and which is intended for use in situations where surface blemishes can be tolerated.

TABLE 2-16.   Standard bar supports.

SYMBOL	BAR SUPPORT ILLUSTRATION	TYPE OF SUPPORT	STANDARD SIZES
SB		Slab Bolster	¾, 1, 1½, and 2 inch heights in 5 ft. and 10 ft. lengths
SBR*		Slab Bolster with Runners	Same as SB
BB		Beam Bolster	1, 1½, 2; over 2″ to 5″ heights in increments of ¼″ in lengths of 5 ft.
UBB*		Upper Beam Bolster	Same as BB
BC		Individual Bar Chair	¾, 1, 1½, and 1¾″ heights
JC		Joist Chair	4, 5, and 6 inch widths and ¾, 1, and 1½ inch heights
HC		Individual High Chair	2 to 15 inch heights in increments of ¼ in.
CHC		Continuous High Chair	Same as HC in 5 foot and 10 ft. lengths
UCHC*		Upper Continuous High Chair	Same as CHC
UJC**		Upper Joist Chair	14″ Span. Heights −1″ through +3½″ vary in ¼″ increments

*Available in Class A only except on special order.
**Available in Class A only, with upturned or end bearing legs.

[14]U.S. Department of Commerce, Wire Bar Supports for Reinforced Concrete Construction, Washington, D.C., 1966. Reprinted from Manual of Standard Practice, © 1970—Concrete Reinforcing Steel Institute.

Precast Block Supports

Table 2–17 gives dimensions of standard plain precast block supports for keeping reinforcing material a fixed distance off grade. When vertical bars are to be supported or for any jobs where the block is to be held firmly, blocks are available that are precast with two lengths of #16 wire protruding from the top.

Table 2–18 gives dimensions of standard precast blocks with wires.

The third type of block support is a doweled block, which is always 3 inches high and either 3 or 4 inches square. Such blocks are cast with a 2 1/4 inch deep hole in the middle, large enough for a number 4 bar. The dowel bar that is inserted in the field is usually given a 90-degree bend at the top for supporting reinforcing material.

Reinforcing Bar Bending Dimensions[15]

Recommended inside diameter of a 180-degree hook, shown as D in Figure 2–6, is shown in Table 2–19. When this practice is followed, the other dimensions in the table will be consistent.

TABLE 2-17. Dimensions of standard plain precast concrete block supports.

Length	Width	Height
2 inches	2 inches	3/4 inch
2	2	1
2	2	1 1/2
2	2	2
3	3	2
3	3	3
3	3	4
4	4	3
4	4	4
6	6	3

TABLE 2-18. Dimensions of standard wired precast concrete block supports.

Length	Width	Height
2 inches	2 inches	3/4 inch
2	2	1
2	2	1 1/2
2	2	2
3	3	3

[15]U.S. Department of Commerce, Wire Bar Supports for Reinforced Concrete Construction, Washington, D.C., 1966.

TABLE 2-19. Recommended dimensions for 180-degree bends.

Bar Size	D	A Inches	B Inches
3	6d	5	3
4	6d	6	4
5	6d	7	5
6	6d	8	6
7	6d	10	7
8	6d	11	8
9	8d	15	11 1/4
10	8d	17	12 3/4
11	8d	19	14 1/4
14	10d	26	20 1/2
18	10d	35	27

FIGURE 2-6

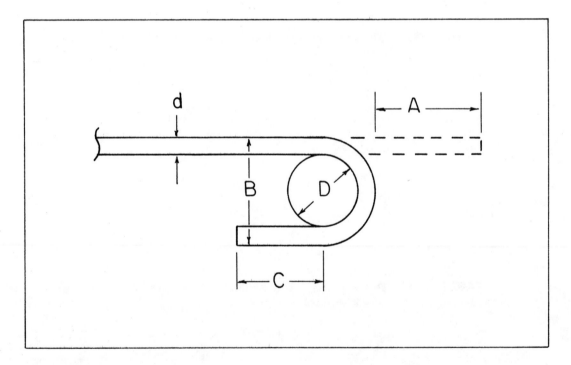

Embedding of Reinforcing Bars

Industry standards for protection of reinforcing bars are shown in Table 2–20[16].

---

[16]Ibid.

TABLE 2-20. Protection of embedded bars.

Location of Reinforcing Bars	Thickness of Concrete Protection	
	Inches	Centimeters
Sides and bottoms of footings cast against earth	3	7.5
Cured concrete exposed to action of weather or ground; #6 bars and larger	2	5
Cured concrete exposed to action of weather or ground; #5 bars and smaller	1 1/2	3.8
Overall reinforcement in columns	1 1/2	3.8
Bottom and sides of beams and girders	1 1/2	3.8
Bottoms and sides of joists	3/4	2
Bottoms of floor slabs	3/4	2
Slabs not exposed directly to weather or ground	3/4	2
From faces of walls not exposed directly to weather or ground	3/4	2
At upper face of beam or girder not exposed directly to weather or ground	1 1/2	3.8
From upper face of slab or joist not exposed directly to weather or ground	3/4	2

BRICK AND TILE[17]

Nominal Modular Sizes: Industry standards that include thickness of mortar joint on three sides

Table 2–21 lists names, dimensions and, for rapid estimating, the smallest number of courses whose height adds to an integral number of inches. In general, mortar joint thicknesses are 1/4 inch for glazed brick and structural facing tile, 3/8 or 1/2 inch for facing brick and unglazed facing tile, and 1/2 inch for building brick and structural tile.

Table 2–22 gives dimensions of full-size units of structural clay load-bearing wall tile.

For structural clay non-load-bearing tile, Table 2–23 gives functional names and dimensions for industry standard models.

Structural clay floor tile, Table 2–24, are given in specified dimensions.

---

[17]Structural Clay Products Institute, Technical Notes on Brick and Tile Construction (Number 10a), Washington D.C., 1963. © Structural Clay Products Institute, 1520 Eighteenth Street NW, Washington 200–36 D.C.

TABLE 2-21. Nominal modular sizes of brick.

Unit Designation	Thickness in	Thickness cm	Face Height in	Face Height cm	Face Length in	Face Length cm	Modular Coursing
Modular	4	10.2	2 2/3	6.8	8	20.3	3 courses = 8 inches
Engineer	4	10.2	3 1/5	8.1	8	20.3	5 courses = 16 inches
Economy	4	10.2	4	10.2	8	20.3	1 course = 4 inches
Double	4	10.2	5 1/3	13.5	8	20.3	3 courses = 16 inches
Roman	4	10.2	2	5.1	12	30.5	1 course = 2 inches
Norman	4	10.2	2 2/3	6.8	12	30.5	3 courses = 8 inches
Norwegian	4	10.2	3 1/5	8.1	12	30.5	5 courses = 16 inches
King Norman	4	10.2	4	10.2	12	30.5	1 course = 4 inches
Norman Economy	4	10.2	4	10.2	12	30.5	1 course = 4 inches
General	4	10.2	4	10.2	12	30.5	1 course = 4 inches
Utility	4	10.2	4	10.2	12	30.5	1 course = 4 inches
Triple	4	10.2	5 1/3	13.5	12	30.5	3 courses = 16 inches
"SCR brick"*	6	15.3	2 2/3	6.8	12	30.5	3 courses = 8 inches

*Reg. U.S. Pat. Off., SCPRF

TABLE 2-22. Structural clay load-bearing wall tile.

Thickness		Face Height		Face Length	
in	cm	in	cm	in	cm
4	10.2	5 1/3	13.5	12	30.5
4	10.2	8	20.3	8	20.3
4	10.2	8	20.3	12	30.5
4	10.2	12	30.5	12	30.5
6	15.3	5 1/3	13.5	12	30.5
6	15.3	8	20.3	12	30.5
6	15.3	12	30.5	12	30.5
8	20.3	5 1/3	13.5	8	20.3
8	20.3	8	20.3	12	30.5
8	20.3	8	20.3	16	40.6
8	20.3	12	30.5	12	30.5
10	25.4	8	20.3	12	30.5
10	25.4	12	30.5	12	30.5
12	30.5	12	30.5	12	30.5

TABLE 2-24. Structural clay floor tile.

Thickness		Width		Length	
in	cm	in	cm	in	cm
4	10.2	12	30.5	11½	29.2
4	10.2	12	30.5	12	30.5
5	12.7	12	30.5	11½	29.2
5	12.7	12	30.5	12	30.5
6	15.3	12	30.5	11½	29.2
6	15.3	12	30.5	12	30.5
8	20.3	12	30.5	11½	29.2
8	20.3	12	30.5	12	30.5
10	25.4	12	30.5	11½	29.2
10	25.4	12	30.5	12	30.5

TABLE 2-23. Structural clay non-load-bearing tile.

	Thickness		Face Height		Face Length	
	in	cm	in	cm	in	cm
Partition tile	4	10.2	12	30.5	12	30.5
Partition tile	6	15.3	12	30.5	12	30.5
Partition tile	8	20.3	12	30.5	12	30.5
Partition tile	10	25.4	12	30.5	12	30.5
Furring tile, solid	2*	5.1	12	30.5	12	30.5
Furring tile, solid	3*	7.6	12	30.5	12	30.5
Furring tile, split	1½*	3.8	12	30.5	12	30.5
Furring tile, split	2*	5.1	12	30.5	12	30.5

*Specified thickness; does not include mortar

TABLE 2-25. Unglazed structural clay facing tile.

Finish	Thickness		Face Height		Face Length	
	in	cm	in	cm	in	cm
smooth	4	10.2	4	10.2	8	20.3
smooth	4	10.2	4	10.2	12	30.5
smooth	4	10.2	5 1/3	13.5	8	20.3
smooth	4	10.2	5 1/3	13.5	12	30.5
smooth	4	10.2	8	20.3	8	20.3
smooth	4	10.2	8	20.3	12	30.5
smooth	4	10.2	8	20.3	16	40.6
smooth	4	10.2	12	30.5	12	30.5
textured	4	10.2	4	10.2	8	20.3
textured	4	10.2	4	10.2	12	30.5
textured	4	10.2	5 1/3	13.5	8	20.3
textured	4	10.2	5 1/3	13.5	12	30.5
textured	4	10.2	8	20.3	8	20.3
textured	4	10.2	8	20.3	12	30.5
textured	4	10.2	8	20.3	16	40.6
textured	4	10.2	12	30.5	12	30.5
smooth	6	15.3	4	10.2	8	20.3
smooth	6	15.3	4	10.2	12	30.5
smooth	6	15.3	5 1/3	13.5	8	20.3
smooth	6	15.3	5 1/3	13.5	12	30.5
smooth	6	15.3	8	20.3	8	20.3
smooth	6	15.3	8	20.3	12	30.5
smooth	6	15.3	8	20.3	16	40.6
smooth	6	15.3	12	30.5	12	30.5
textured	6	15.3	4	10.2	8	20.3
textured	6	15.3	4	10.2	12	30.5
textured	6	15.3	5 1/3	13.5	8	20.3
textured	6	15.3	5 1/3	13.5	12	30.5
textured	6	15.3	8	20.3	8	20.3
textured	6	15.3	8	20.3	12	30.5
textured	6	15.3	8	20.3	16	40.6
textured	6	15.3	12	30.5	12	30.5
smooth	8	20.3	4	10.2	8	20.3
smooth	8	20.3	4	10.2	12	30.5
smooth	8	20.3	5 1/3	13.5	8	20.3
smooth	8	20.3	5 1/3	13.5	12	30.5
smooth	8	20.3	8	20.3	8	20.3
smooth	8	20.3	8	20.3	12	30.5
smooth	8	20.3	8	20.3	16	40.6
smooth	8	20.3	12	30.5	12	30.5
textured	8	20.3	4	10.2	8	20.3
textured	8	20.3	4	10.2	12	30.5
textured	8	20.3	5 1/3	13.5	8	20.3
textured	8	20.3	5 1/3	13.5	12	30.5
textured	8	20.3	8	20.3	8	20.3
textured	8	20.3	8	20.3	12	30.5
textured	8	20.3	8	20.3	16	40.6
textured	8	20.3	12	30.5	12	30.5

TABLE 2-26. Glazed ceramic brick and structural facing tile.

Series	Thickness		Face Height		Face Length	
	in	cm	in	cm	in	cm
6T	4	10.2	5 1/3	13.5	12	30.5
6T	6	15.3	5 1/3	13.5	12	30.5
6T	8	20.3	5 1/3	13.5	12	30.5
4D	4	10.2	5 1/3	13.5	8	20.3
4D	6	15.3	5 1/3	13.5	8	20.3
4D	8	20.3	5 1/3	13.5	8	20.3
8W	4	10.2	8	20.3	16	40.6
4S (brick)	4	10.2	2 2/3	6.8	8	20.3

Nominal dimensions of structural clay unglazed facing tile are given in Table 2–25. These tiles are available in both smooth and textured natural finishes.

Glazed ceramic brick and structural facing tile are detailed in Table 2–26. These units are standardized with nominal dimensions.

Estimating Materials[18]

Tables 2–27 through 2–30 provide convenient estimates of brick, tile, and mortar quantities that will remain in finished walls; waste and breakage factors should be brought in after all other calculations are completed. One suggested rule is to add 2 percent to net tile quantities and 5 percent to brick. Add 10 percent to mortar estimates for brick and side-construction tile, and 20 percent for end-construction tile.

When bonds with full headers are used with a brick wall, net quantities estimated should be increased by the factors shown in Table 2–31. This table is applicable only to those bricks whose lengths are twice their bed depths.

Table 2–32 has two applications: where backup tiles are used, and for general conversion of tile to equivalent brick.

MORTAR

Types of Mortar[19]

Table 2–33 lists designations and applications for the various types of mortar.

Sand[20]

Table 2–34 gives ASTM standards for sand used as aggregate in mortar.

---

[18]Structural Clay Products Institute, Technical Notes on Brick and Tile Construction (Number 10), Washington, D.C. © 1961 Structural Clay Products Institute, 1520 Eighteenth Street NE, Washington 6 D.C.
[19]Structural Clay Products Institute, Technical Notes on Brick and Tile Construction (Number 8), Washington, D.C. © 1961 Structural Clay Products Institute 1520 Eighteenth Street NW, Washington 6 D.C.
[20]Ibid.

Nominal Brick Size in Inches			Brick Per Sq Ft of Wall	Cubic Feet of Mortar Per 100 Sq Ft of Wall			Cubic Feet of Mortar Per 1000 Brick		
				Joint Thickness			Joint Thickness		
h	t	l		¼ in.	⅜ in.	½ in.	¼ in.	⅜ in.	½ in.
2⅔ x 4 x 8			6.750	3.81	5.47	6.95	5.65	8.10	10.30
3⅕ x 4 x 8			5.625	3.34	4.79	6.10	5.94	8.52	10.84
4 x 4 x 8			4.500	——	4.12	5.24	——	9.15	11.65
5⅓ x 4 x 8			3.375	——	3.44	4.34	——	10.19	12.87
2 x 4 x 12			6.000	——	6.43	8.20	——	10.72	13.67
2⅔ x 4 x 12			4.500	3.52	5.06	6.46	7.82	11.24	14.35
3 x 4 x 12			4.000	——	4.60	5.87	——	11.51	14.68
3⅕ x 4 x 12			3.750	3.04	4.37	5.58	8.11	11.66	14.89
4 x 4 x 12			3.000	2.56	3.69	4.71	8.54	12.29	15.70
5⅓ x 4 x 12			2.250	——	3.00	3.84	——	13.34	17.05
2⅔ x 6 x 12			4.500	——	7.85	10.15	——	17.45	22.55
3⅕ x 6 x 12			3.750	——	6.79	8.77	——	18.10	23.39
4 x 6 x 12			3.000	——	5.72	7.40	——	19.07	24.67

TABLE 2-27. Estimates of brick and mortar requirements for walls without headers.

Nominal Tile Face Size in Inches		Tile Per Sq Ft of Wall	Cubic Feet of Mortar Per 100 Sq Ft of Wall			Cubic Feet of Mortar Per 1000 Units		
			Joint Thickness			Joint Thickness		
h	l		¼ in.	⅜ in.	½ in.	¼ in.	⅜ in.	½ in.
5⅓ x 8		3.375	1.28	1.90	2.51	3.79	5.62	7.43
8 x 8		2.250	1.03	1.53	2.02	4.56	6.78	8.97
4 x 12		3.000	1.37	2.03	2.69	4.56	6.78	8.97
5⅓ x 12		2.250	1.11	1.66	2.19	4.94	7.36	9.74
8 x 12		1.500	——	1.28	1.69	——	8.52	11.28
12 x 12		1.000	0.69	1.03	1.36	6.87	10.25	13.60
8 x 16		1.125	0.77	1.15	1.53	6.87	10.25	13.60
12 x 16		0.750	0.60	0.90	1.19	8.03	11.99	15.91

Note: This table is based on the assumption that both head and bed joints consist of two, separated, 1-in. wide joints.

TABLE 2-28. Estimates of tile and mortar requirements for vertical-cell tile.

Nominal Tile Face Size in Inches			Tile Per Sq Ft of Wall	Cubic Feet of Mortar Per 100 Sq Ft of Wall			Cubic Feet of Mortar Per 1000 Tile		
				Joint Thickness			Joint Thickness		
t	h	l		¼ in.	⅜ in.	½ in.	¼ in.	⅜ in.	½ in.
4 x	5⅓ x	8	3.375	1.96	2.85	3.68	5.81	8.45	10.90
4 x	8 x	8	2.250	1.48	2.16	2.80	6.58	9.60	12.44
4 x	4 x	12	3.000	2.28	3.30	4.25	7.60	11.01	14.18
4 x	5⅓ x	12	2.250	1.80	2.61	3.36	7.98	11.59	14.95
4 x	6 x	12	2.000	1.63	——	——	8.17	——	——
4 x	8 x	12	1.500	——	1.91	2.47	——	12.75	16.49
4 x	12 x	12	1.000	0.99	1.45	1.88	9.91	14.49	18.81
4 x	8 x	16	1.125	1.23	1.79	2.31	10.92	15.87	20.54
6 x	5⅓ x	8	3.375	2.74	4.02	5.24	8.13	11.92	15.53
6 x	5⅓ x	12	2.250	2.58	3.78	4.93	11.45	16.80	21.89
6 x	6 x	12	2.000	2.33	——	——	11.65	——	——
6 x	8 x	12	1.500	——	2.69	3.52	——	17.96	23.44
6 x	12 x	12	1.000	——	1.97	2.58	——	19.69	25.75
8 x	4 x	12	3.000	4.36	6.43	8.42	14.54	21.43	28.07
8 x	5⅓ x	12	2.250	3.36	4.95	6.49	14.93	22.01	28.84
8 x	8 x	12	1.500	——	3.47	4.56	——	23.17	30.38
8 x	12 x	12	1.000	——	2.49	3.27	——	24.90	32.70
8 x	12 x	16	0.750	——	2.36	3.10	——	31.52	41.38
10 x	12 x	12	1.000	——	3.01	3.96	——	30.11	39.64
12 x	8 x	12	1.500	——	5.04	6.29	——	33.58	41.96
12 x	12 x	12	1.000	——	3.53	4.66	——	35.32	46.59

Note: This table is based on the assumption that head joints consist of two, separated, 1-in. wide joints and that full bed joints are actual wall thickness.

TABLE 2-29. Estimates of tile and mortar requirements for horizontal-cell tile with full bed joints.

TABLE 2-30. Estimates of tile and mortar requirements for horizontal-cell tile with divided bed joints and multishell and cored-shell vertical-cell tile.

Nominal Tile Face Size in Inches		Tile Per Sq Ft of Wall	Cubic Feet of Mortar Per 100 Sq Ft of Wall			Cubic Feet of Mortar Per 1000 Tile		
			Joint Thickness			Joint Thickness		
h	l		¼ in.	⅜ in.	½ in.	¼ in.	⅜ in.	½ in.
5⅓ x	8	3.375	2.06	3.07	4.07	6.10	9.10	12.06
4 x	12	3.000	2.41	3.60	4.77	8.03	11.99	15.91
5⅓ x	12	2.250	1.89	2.83	3.75	8.42	12.57	16.69
6 x	12	2.000	1.72	——	——	8.61	——	——
8 x	12	1.500	——	2.06	2.73	——	13.73	18.23
12 x	12	1.000	——	1.55	2.05	——	15.46	20.54
12 x	16	0.750	——	1.42	1.89	——	18.93	25.17

Note: This table is based on the assumption that head joints consist of two, separated, 1-in. wide joints and that bed joints are two, separated, 2-in. wide joints.

TABLE 2-31. Bond correction factors for walls of Table 2-27.

Bond	Correction Factor*
Full headers every 5th course only.................	1/5
Full headers every 6th course only.................	1/6
Full headers every 7th course only.................	1/7
English bond (full headers every 2nd course).........	1/2
Flemish bond (alternate full headers and stretchers every course).......................	1/3
Flemish headers every 6th course..................	1/18
Flemish cross bond (Flemish headers every 2nd course).................................	1/6
Double-stretcher, garden wall bond................	1/5
Triple-stretcher, garden wall bond.................	1/7

TABLE 2-32. Brick and tile equivalents.

Nominal Tile Size			Equivalent Brick Units	
t	h	l	2⅔ by 4 by 8	4 by 4 by 8
4 x	4	x 12	2.25	1.50
4 x	5⅓	x 12	3.00	2.00
4 x	8	x 12	4.50	3.00
4 x	12	x 12	6.75	4.50
8 x	4	x 12	4.50	3.00
8 x	5⅓	x 12	6.00	4.00
8 x	8	x 12	9.00	6.00
8 x	12	x 12	13.50	9.00
12 x	12	x 12	20.25	13.50

TABLE 2-33.   Types of mortar.

Designation	General Application Rules	Applications
Type M	Maximum compressive strength	Unreinforced masonry below grade and in contact with earth—foundations, retaining walls, walks, sewers, manholes
Type N	Medium strength, general purpose	Above-grade use in parapet walls, chimneys, and exterior walls subject to severe exposure
Type O	Interior non-load-bearing	Non-load-bearing masonry or load-bearing walls of solid masonry where pressive stresses below 100 psi and exposure not severe
Type S	Maximum bond	When mortar adhesion is the sole bonding agent between facing and backing, for reinforced masonry, and for unreinforced masonry when maximum flexural strength required

TABLE 2-34.   Gradation limits of sand used as aggregate for mortar.

Sieve Size	Natural Sand	Manufactured Sand
4	100	100
8	95–100	95–100
16	70–100	70–100
30	40–75	40–75
50	10–35	20–40
100	2–15	10–25
200	—	0–10

Component Proportions (Based on 1 cubic unit of mortar for each cubic unit of damp loose sand in the mixture[21])

In Table 2–35 any volumetric unit can be used as long as it is used for all items in a column. Proportioning by volume is generally used because it is more convenient, although proportioning by weight is more accurate. Table 2–36 gives quantities in pounds to yield one cubic foot of mortar.

---

[21]Structural Clay Products Institute, Technical Notes on Brick and Tile Construction (Number 10), Washington, D.C. © 1961 Structural Clay Products Institute, 1520 Eighteenth Street NW, Washington 6 D.C.

TABLE 2-35. Mortar component proportions by cubic unit.

	M 1:1/4:3	S 1:1/2:4-1/2	N 1:1:6	O 1:2:9
Cement	0.333	0.222	0.167	0.111
Lime	0.083	0.056	0.167	0.222
Sand	1.000	1.000	1.000	1.000

TABLE 2-36. Mortar component quantities in pounds.

	M 1:1/4:3	S 1:1/2:4-1/2	N 1:1:6	O 1:2:9
Cement	31.33	20.89	15.67	10.44
Lime	3.33	2.22	6.67	8.89
Sand	80.00	80.00	80.00	80.00

BRICK MASONRY WALLS[22]

When "With Inspection" is mentioned in the following tables, this excerpt from paragraph 1.3.1 of the referenced document is applicable:

. . . shall be inspected by an engineer or architect, preferably the one responsible for the design, or by a competent representative responsible to him. Such inspection shall be of a nature as to determine, in general, that the construction and workmanship are in accordance with the contract drawings and specifications.

External Non-Load-Bearing Walls (of non-reinforced brick masonry)

Table 2–37 gives height- or length-to-thickness ratio as a function of design wind pressure, based on the following assumptions:

- walls are simply supported without openings or other interruptions
- weight of wall is neglected
- allowable flexural tensile stresses (see Table 2–39) apply, increased by 33 1/3 percent for wind.

Quantities in the body of this table give the ratio h/t where *h* is the clear span (height or length) between lateral supports and *t* is actual wall thickness. Ratios given for a design wind pressure of 5 psf are applicable to partitions only.

To adapt Table 2–37 to cavity walls having wythes of equal thickness and built with the same units and mortar, consider *t* to have a value equal to 1.41 times the actual thickness of one wythe.

---

[22]Structural Clay Products Institute, Building Code Requirements for Engineered Brick Masonry, McLean, Virginia, 1969. Copyright August 1969.

TABLE 2-37. Lateral support ratios for non-load-bearing brick masonry walls.

Design Wind Pressure, psf	Without Inspection				With Inspection			
	Vertical Span		Horizontal Span		Vertical Span		Horizontal Span	
	N Mortar	S or M Mortar	N Mortar	S or M Mortar	N Mortar	S or M Mortar	N Mortar	S or M Mortar
5	31	35	44	50	38	43	54	61
10	22	25	31	35	27	30	38	43
15	18	20	25	29	22	25	31	35
20	15	18	22	25	19	21	27	30
25	14	16	20	22	17	19	24	27
30	13	14	18	20	15	17	22	25
35	12	13	16	19	14	16	20	23
40	11	12	15	18	13	15	19	21
45	10	12	14	17	13	14	18	20
50	10	11	14	16	12	14	17	19

Load-Bearing Walls: Allowable stresses based on assumed value of compressive strength when tests not conducted

Formula

$$f_m' = A(400 + Bf_b')$$

where: f_m' = assumed compressive strength of masonry at 28 days, in pounds per square inch

A = 2/3 without inspection

 = 1.0 with inspection

B = 0.2 for type N mortar

 = 0.25 for type S mortar

 = 0.3 for type M mortar

f_b' = average compressive strength of brick, in pounds per square inch, but not to exceed 14,000 psi (value provided by supplier of brick).

TABLE 2-38. Assumed compressive strength of brick.

Compressive Strength of Units, psi	Assumed Compressive Strength of Brick Masonry f'_m, psi					
	Without Inspection			With Inspection		
	Type N Mortar[b]	Type S Mortar[b]	Type M Mortar[b][c]	Type N Mortar[b]	Type S Mortar[b]	Type M Mortar[b][c]
14,000 plus	2140	2600	3070	3200	3900	4600
12,000	1870	2270	2670	2800	3400	4000
10,000	1600	1930	2270	2400	2900	3400
8,000	1340	1600	1870	2000	2400	2800
6,000	1070	1270	1470	1600	1900	2200
4,000	800	930	1070	1200	1400	1600
2,000	530	600	670	800	900	1000

Table 2–38 has been prepared from this formula for bricks that are most likely to be used in construction. Walls of other bricks can either be interpolated from the table or calculated from the formula.

Example

What compressive strength should be assumed for a wall of 5000 psi bricks bonded with type N mortar if there is no inspection?

Solution

$$f_m' = \frac{2}{3}(400 + (0.2)5000)$$
$$= 933 \text{ pounds per square inch}$$

Allowable Stresses

For general design work, Table 2–39 presents various stresses which are SCPI minimums.

Example

Calculate shear stress for the wall of the previous example.

Solution

From the table:

$$v_m = 0.5\sqrt{f_m'}$$

where f_m' has been evaluated in the previous example.

$$v_m = 0.5\sqrt{933}$$
$$= 15.3 \text{ pounds per square inch}$$

Since this value is less than the maximum of 28 psi indicated in Table 2–39, it is the allowable shear stress.

Table 2–40 presents allowable stresses for reinforced brick masonry. Design of brick masonry with reinforcing involves variables too numerous and complex to summarize in a handbook; therefore, this table should be considered as a source of preliminary information. Complete design manuals should be consulted for final design calculations.

Bolts and Anchors

For bolts and anchors solidly embedded in mortar or grout, Table 2–41 gives allowable shear stress in pounds.

WOOD[23]

Selection of the proper wood for a certain application is difficult because availability, price, preference, and other factors vary significantly with location. Therefore, this section

---

[23]Unless otherwise indicated, information on wood is from Department of the Army, Military Handbook Lumber and Allied Products, Washington, D.C., 1958.

TABLE 2-39. Allowable stresses in non-reinforced brick masonry.

Description		Allowable Stresses, psi	
		Without Inspection [a]	With Inspection [a]
Compressive, Axial [b]			
Walls	f_m	$0.20f'_m$	$0.20f'_m$
Columns	f_m	$0.16f'_m$	$0.16f'_m$
Compressive, Flexural [b]			
Walls	f_m	$0.32f'_m$	$0.32f'_m$
Columns	f_m	$0.26f'_m$	$0.26f'_m$
Tensile, Flexural [e] [f]			
Normal to bed joints [b]			
M or S mortar	f_t	24	36
N mortar	f_t	19	28
Parallel to bed joints [e]			
M or S mortar	f_t	48	72
N mortar	f_t	37	56
Shear [g]			
M or S mortar	v_m	$0.5\sqrt{f'_m}$, but not to exceed 40	$0.5\sqrt{f'_m}$, but not to exceed 80
N mortar	v_m	$0.5\sqrt{f'_m}$, but not to exceed 28	$0.5\sqrt{f'_m}$, but not to exceed 56
Bearing			
On full area	f_m	$0.25f'_m$	$0.25f'_m$
On one-third area or less [d]	f_m	$0.375f'_m$	$0.375f'_m$
Modulus of Elasticity [h]	E_m	$1000f'_m$, but not to exceed 2,000,000 psi	$1000f'_m$, but not to exceed 3,000,000 psi
Modulus of Rigidity [h]	E_v	$400f'_m$, but not to exceed 800,000 psi	$400f'_m$, but not to exceed 1,200,000 psi

TABLE 2-40. Allowable stresses in reinforced brick masonry.

Description		Allowable Stresses, psi	
		Without Inspection [a]	With Inspection [a]
Compressive, Axial			
Walls	f_m	$0.25f'_m$	$0.25f'_m$
Columns [b]	f_m	$0.20f'_m$	$0.20f'_m$
Compressive, Flexural			
Walls and beams	f_m	$0.40f'_m$	$0.40f'_m$
Columns [b]	f_m	$0.32f'_m$	$0.32f'_m$
Shear			
No shear reinforcement			
Flexural Members [c]	v_m	$0.7\sqrt{f'_m}$, but not to exceed 25	$0.7\sqrt{f'_m}$, but not to exceed 50
Shear Walls [d]	v_m	$0.5\sqrt{f'_m}$, but not to exceed 50	$0.5\sqrt{f'_m}$, but not to exceed 100
With shear reinforcement taking entire shear			
Flexural Members [c]	v	$2.0\sqrt{f'_m}$, but not to exceed 60	$2.0\sqrt{f'_m}$, but not to exceed 120
Shear Walls [d]	v	$1.5\sqrt{f'_m}$, but not to exceed 75	$1.5\sqrt{f'_m}$, but not to exceed 150
Bond			
Plain bars	u	53	80
Deformed bars	u	107	160
Bearing			
On full area	f_m	$0.25f'_m$	$0.25f'_m$
On one-third area or less [e]	f_m	$0.375f'_m$	$0.375f'_m$
Modulus of Elasticity [f]	E_m	$1000f'_m$, but not to exceed 2,000,000 psi	$1000f'_m$, but not to exceed 3,000,000 psi
Modulus of Rigidity [f]	E_v	$400f'_m$, but not to exceed 800,000 psi	$400f'_m$, but not to exceed 1,200,000 psi

TABLE 2-41.   Allowable shear on bolts and anchors.

Bolt or Anchor Diameter, in.	Minimum Embedment, in.[b]	Allowable Shear, lb	
		Without Inspection [c]	With Inspection [c]
$\frac{1}{4}$	4	180	270
$\frac{3}{8}$	4	270	410
$\frac{1}{2}$	4	370	550
$\frac{5}{8}$	4	500	750
$\frac{3}{4}$	5	730	1100
$\frac{7}{8}$	6	1000	1500
1	7	1230	1850
$1\frac{1}{8}$	8	1500	2250

will generally give figures for several species rather than pick any single product as optimum for an application.

Characteristics of Species

Table 2–42 lists relative strengths of various species in several modes (bending, compressive, etc). It can be seen that no one type of wood is strongest in all modes, although hickory comes close. However, selection of wood cannot be made on a basis of relative strength alone; it may be more economical to use a larger quantity of a wood with less relative strength. In addition, total optimization may depend on other factors such as shrinkage and workability.

Table 2–43 shows that if size stability is important, hickory loses some of its advantage. Table 2–44 gives recommended moisture content for wood items at time of installation. These values of moisture will result in a minimum of shrinking and swelling under weather and heating conditions expected for the area indicated. When applied to dwellings, Table 2–44 should not be used if a radiant heating system is to be installed.

Size Standards

Finished softwoods have been standardized in the industry at dimensions as given in Table 2–45. Some new size standards now in effect[24] are given in Table 2–46, where dry lumber is defined as being 19 percent or less in moisture content. A general rule is that lumber changes approximately 1 percent in size for each 4 percent change in moisture content, and reaches stability at approximately 15 percent under normal use conditions.

---

[24]Western Wood Products Association, Portland, Oregon, Catalog A—Product Use Manual.

TABLE 2-42. Relative strengths and densities of various species.

Name of species	Weight per cubic foot at 12 percent moisture content	Composite strength values				
		Bending strength	Compressive strength (endwise)	Stiffness	Hardness	Shock resistance
1	2	3	4	5	6	7
	Lb.	*Comparative fig.*	*Comparative fig.*	*Comparative fig.*	*Comparative fig.*	*Comparative fig.*
HARDWOODS						
Ash, commercial white (av. of 4 species)	41	110	106	161	108	139
Birch, sweet	46	116	105	206	104	157
Cottonwood, eastern	28	61	63	122	36	72
Elm, American	36	84	74	129	66	126
Elm, rock	44	106	97	147	104	190
Gum, red	34	85	78	148	61	106
Hickories, pecan and true (av. of 8 species)	50	135	122	184	142	279
Maple, sugar	44	114	104	178	115	137
Oaks, commercial red and white (av. of 15 species).	45	100	92	161	105	134
Tupelo, water	35	82	86	127	77	80
Yellow poplar	28	76	72	151	44	76
SOFTWOODS						
Cedar, western red	23	60	75	108	38	52
Cedar, southern white	23	53	60	93	35	51
Cypress	32	79	93	139	52	72
Douglas fir (coast type)	34	90	104	185	58	86
Douglas fir (Mountain type)	30	75	83	142	52	66
Fir, white (av. of 4 species)	26	72	76	141	41	66
Hemlock, eastern	28	72	79	121	51	67
Hemlock, west coast	29	74	85	145	50	73
Larch, western	36	97	106	179	63	107
Pine, longleaf	41	103	115	186	71	109
Pine, shortleaf	38	87	92	161	56	96
Pine, Idaho	27	68	76	145	34	66
Pine, ponderosa	28	64	69	113	41	57
Redwood	30	82	102	136	54	66
Spruces (av. of red, white, Sitka)	28	71	74	136	42	71

TABLE 2-43. Shrinkage factors.

Species	Shrinkage (percent of dimensions when green)								
	Dried to 20 percent moisture content [1]			Dried to 6 percent moisture content [2]			Dried to 0 percent moisture content		
	Radial	Tangential	Volumetric	Radial	Tangential	Volumetric	Radial	Tangential	Volumetric
	Percent	Percent	Percent	Percent	Percent	Percent	Percent	Percent	Percent
SOFTWOODS									
Cedar:									
Western red	0.8	1.7	2.3	1.9	4.0	5.4	2.4	5.0	6.8
Incense [1]	1.1	1.7	2.5	2.6	4.2	6.1	3.3	5.2	7.6
Cypress	1.3	2.1	3.5	3.0	5.0	8.4	3.8	6.2	10.5
Douglas fir:									
Coast type	1.7	2.6	3.9	4.0	6.2	9.4	5.0	7.8	11.8
Mountain type	1.2	2.1	3.5	2.9	5.0	8.5	3.6	6.2	10.6
Fir, white	1.1	2.4	3.3	2.6	5.7	7.8	3.2	7.1	9.8
Hemlock:									
Eastern	1.0	2.3	3.2	2.4	5.4	7.8	3.0	6.8	9.7
West Coast	1.4	2.6	4.0	3.4	6.3	9.5	4.3	7.9	11.9
Larch, western	1.4	2.7	4.4	3.4	6.5	10.6	4.2	8.1	13.2
Pine:									
Idaho white	1.4	2.5	3.9	3.3	5.9	9.4	4.1	7.4	11.8
Lodgepole	1.5	2.2	3.8	3.6	5.4	9.2	4.5	6.7	11.5
Northern white	0.8	2.0	2.7	1.8	4.8	6.6	2.3	6.0	8.2
Norway (red)	1.5	2.4	3.8	3.7	5.8	9.2	4.6	7.2	11.5
Ponderosa	1.3	2.1	3.2	3.1	5.0	7.7	3.9	6.3	9.6
Southern yellow longleaf	1.7	2.5	4.1	4.1	6.0	9.8	5.1	7.5	12.2
Sugar	1.0	1.9	2.6	2.3	4.5	6.3	2.9	5.6	7.9
Redwood (old-growth)	0.9	1.5	2.3	2.1	3.5	5.4	2.6	4.4	6.8
Spruce:									
Engelmann	1.1	2.2	3.5	2.7	5.3	8.3	3.4	6.6	10.4
Sitka	1.4	2.5	3.8	3.4	6.0	9.2	4.3	7.5	11.5
HARDWOODS									
Ash, white	1.6	2.6	4.5	3.8	6.2	10.7	4.8	7.8	13.4
Aspen, quaking	1.2	2.2	3.8	2.8	5.4	9.2	3.5	6.7	11.5
Basswood	2.2	3.1	5.3	5.3	7.4	12.6	6.6	9.3	15.8
Birch, yellow	2.4	3.1	5.6	5.8	7.4	13.4	7.2	9.2	16.7
Hickory, shagbark	2.3	3.3	5.6	5.6	8.0	13.4	7.0	10.0	16.7
Locust, black	1.5	2.4	3.4	3.7	5.8	8.2	4.6	7.2	10.2
Maple, sugar	1.6	3.2	5.0	3.9	7.6	11.9	4.9	9.5	14.9
Oak, northern red	1.3	2.7	4.5	3.2	6.6	10.8	4.0	8.2	13.5
Oak, white	1.8	3.0	5.3	4.2	7.2	12.6	5.3	9.0	15.8
Yellow poplar	1.3	2.4	4.1	3.2	5.7	9.8	4.0	7.1	12.3

[1] These shrinkage values have been taken as one-third the shrinkage to the ovendry condition as given in the last three columns of this table.

[2] These shrinkage values have been taken as four-fifths of the shrinkage to the ovendry condition as given in the last three columns.

TABLE 2-44. Recommended moisture content at time of installation.[1]

Use of lumber	Moisture content for—[2]					
	Dry southwestern States		Damp southern coastal States		Remainder of the United States	
	Average	Individual pieces	Average	Individual pieces	Average	Individual pieces
	Percent	Percent	Percent	Percent	Percent	Percent
Interior finish woodwork and softwood flooring.	6	4–9	11	8–13	8	5–10
Hardwood flooring	6	5–8	10	9–12	7	6–9
Siding, exterior trim, sheathing, and framing.[3]	9	7–12	12	9–14	12	9–14

[1] Applicable to dwellings with heating systems other than floor radiant-heating systems.

[2] If the average is within ±1 percent of the optimum and the moisture content values of all the pieces fall within the prescribed range, the entire lot will probably be satisfactory.

[3] Framing lumber of higher moisture content is commonly used in ordinary construction because material of the moisture content specified may not be available except on special order.

TABLE 2-45. Summary of American Standard thicknesses and widths[1] for softwood yard lumber.

Item	Thicknesses		Widths	
	Nominal	Minimum dressed	Nominal	Minimum dressed
	Inches	*Inches*	*Inches*	*Inches*
Finish: Select or common	2 $\frac{3}{8}$	$\frac{5}{16}$	2	1 $\frac{5}{8}$
	2 $\frac{1}{2}$	$\frac{7}{16}$	3	2 $\frac{5}{8}$
	2 $\frac{5}{8}$	$\frac{9}{16}$	4	3 $\frac{1}{2}$
	2 $\frac{3}{4}$	$\frac{11}{16}$	5	4 $\frac{1}{2}$
	1	$\frac{13}{16}$	6	5 $\frac{1}{2}$
	1 $\frac{1}{4}$	1 $\frac{1}{16}$	7	6 $\frac{1}{2}$
	1 $\frac{1}{2}$	1 $\frac{5}{16}$	8	7 $\frac{1}{4}$
	1 $\frac{3}{4}$	1 $\frac{7}{16}$	9	8 $\frac{1}{4}$
	2	1 $\frac{5}{8}$	10	9 $\frac{1}{4}$
	2 $\frac{1}{2}$	2 $\frac{1}{8}$	11	10 $\frac{1}{4}$
	3	2 $\frac{5}{8}$	12	11 $\frac{1}{4}$
	3 $\frac{1}{2}$	3 $\frac{1}{8}$	14	13
	4	3 $\frac{1}{2}$	16	15
Bevel siding	2 $\frac{1}{2}$	$\frac{7}{16}$ butt, $\frac{3}{16}$ tip	4	3 $\frac{1}{2}$
	2 $\frac{9}{16}$	$\frac{12}{16}$ butt, $\frac{3}{16}$ tip	5	4 $\frac{1}{2}$
	2 $\frac{5}{8}$	$\frac{9}{16}$ butt, $\frac{3}{16}$ tip	6	5 $\frac{1}{2}$
	2 $\frac{3}{4}$	$\frac{11}{16}$ butt, $\frac{3}{16}$ tip	8	7 $\frac{1}{4}$
	1	$\frac{3}{4}$ butt, $\frac{3}{16}$ tip	10	9 $\frac{1}{4}$
			12	11 $\frac{1}{4}$
Bungalow siding	2 $\frac{3}{4}$	$\frac{11}{16}$ butt, $\frac{3}{16}$ tip	8	7 $\frac{1}{4}$
			10	9 $\frac{1}{4}$
			12	11 $\frac{1}{4}$
Rustic and drop siding (shiplapped, $\frac{3}{8}$-inch lap)	2 $\frac{5}{8}$	$\frac{9}{16}$	4	3 $\frac{1}{8}$
	1	$\frac{3}{4}$	5	4 $\frac{1}{8}$
			6	5 $\frac{1}{16}$
Rustic and drop siding (shiplapped, $\frac{1}{2}$-inch lap)	2 $\frac{5}{8}$	$\frac{9}{16}$	4	3
	1	$\frac{3}{4}$	6	5
			8	6 $\frac{13}{16}$
			10	8 $\frac{13}{16}$
			12	10 $\frac{13}{16}$
Rustic and drop siding (D & M)	2 $\frac{5}{8}$	$\frac{9}{16}$	4	3 $\frac{1}{4}$
	1	$\frac{3}{4}$	5	4 $\frac{1}{4}$
			6	5 $\frac{3}{16}$
			8	6 $\frac{13}{16}$
			10	8 $\frac{13}{16}$
Flooring	2 $\frac{3}{8}$	$\frac{5}{16}$	2	1 $\frac{1}{2}$
	2 $\frac{1}{2}$	$\frac{7}{16}$	3	2 $\frac{3}{8}$
	2 $\frac{5}{8}$	$\frac{9}{16}$	4	3 $\frac{1}{4}$
	1	$\frac{25}{32}$	5	4 $\frac{1}{4}$
	1 $\frac{1}{4}$	1 $\frac{1}{16}$	6	5 $\frac{3}{16}$
	1 $\frac{1}{2}$	1 $\frac{5}{16}$		
Ceiling	2 $\frac{3}{8}$	$\frac{5}{16}$	3	2 $\frac{3}{8}$
	2 $\frac{1}{2}$	$\frac{7}{16}$	4	3 $\frac{1}{4}$
	2 $\frac{5}{8}$	$\frac{9}{16}$	5	4 $\frac{1}{4}$
	2 $\frac{3}{4}$	$\frac{11}{16}$	6	5 $\frac{3}{16}$
Partition	1	$\frac{23}{32}$	3	2 $\frac{3}{8}$
			4	3 $\frac{1}{4}$
			5	4 $\frac{1}{4}$
			6	5 $\frac{3}{16}$

See footnotes at end of table.

TABLE 2-45. cont.

Item	Thicknesses		Widths	
	Nominal	Minimum dressed	Nominal	Minimum dressed
	Inches	*Inches*	*Inches*	*Inches*
Stepping	1	25/32	8	7¼
	1¼	1 1/16	10	9¼
	1½	1 5/16	12	11¼
	2	1⅝		
Boards [3]	1	25/32	2	1⅝
	1¼	1 1/16	3	2⅝
	1½	1 5/16	4	3⅝
			5	4⅝
			6	5½
			7	6½
			8	7½
			9	8½
			10	9½
			11	10½
			12	11½
			14	13½
			16	15½
Shiplap, ⅜-inch lap	1	25/32	4	3⅛
			6	5⅛
			8	7⅛
			10	9⅛
			12	11⅛
			14	13⅛
			16	15⅛
Shiplap, ½-inch lap	1	25/32	4	3
			6	5
			8	7
			10	9
			12	11
			14	13
			16	15
Center matched ¼-inch tongue	1	25/32	4	3¼
	1¼	1 1/16	6	5 3/16
	1½	1 5/16	8	7
			10	9
			12	11
Dimension, plank, and joist [4]	2	1⅝	2	1⅝
	2½	2⅛	3	2⅝
	3	2⅝	4	3⅝
	3½	3⅛	6	5½
	4	3⅝	8	7½
			10	9½
			12	11½
			14	13½
			16	15½
			18	17½
Timbers	[5] 5	½ off	[6] 5	½ off
Factory flooring, heavy roofing, decking and sheet piling.[4]	2	1⅝	4	[7] 3
	2½	2⅛	6	[7] 5
	3	2⅝	8	[8] 7
See footnotes at end of table.	4	3⅝	10	[8] 9
	5	4⅝	12	[8] 11

[1] The thicknesses apply to all widths and the widths to all thicknesses except as modified. In tongue-and-grooved flooring and in tongue-and-grooved shiplapped ceiling of 5/16-, 7/16-, and 9/16-inch dressed thicknesses, the tongue or lap shall be three-sixteenths inch wide, with the overall widths three-sixteenths inch wider than the face widths shown. In all other worked lumber of dressed thickness 11/16 to 1 5/16 inches, the tongue shall be one-fourth inch wide or wider in tongue-and-grooved lumber, and the lap three-eighths inch wide or wider in shiplapped lumber, and the overall widths shall be not less than the dressed face widths shown, plus the width of the tongue lap.

[2] For nominal thicknesses under 1 inch, the board measure count is based on the nominal surface dimensions (width by length). With these exceptions, the nominal thicknesses and widths in this table are the same as the board measure or count sizes.

[3] In some regions lumber thicker than 1½ inches is graded according to board rules. When proper provision is made for this in the applicable grading rules, such lumber may be regarded as American standard lumber.

[4] In worked lumber of nominal thicknesses of 2 inches and over, the tongue shall be three-eighths inch wide in tongued-and-grooved lumber and the lap one-half inch wide in shiplapped lumber, with the overall widths three-eighths inch and one-half inch wider, respectively, than the face widths shown above.

[5] And thicker.

[6] And wider.

[7] Face width when shiplapped; when tongued and grooved the face width is one-eighth inch greater; when grooved for splines the face width is one-half inch greater.

[8] Face width when shiplapped or tongued and grooved; when grooved for splines the face width is one-half inch greater.

TABLE 2-46. New grading sizes.

New Sizes

Nominal Size	Unseasoned	Dry
2 × 2	1 9/16 × 1 9/16	1 1/2 × 1 1/2
2 × 3	1 9/16 × 2 9/16	1 1/2 × 2 1/2
2 × 4	1 9/16 × 3 9/16	1 1/2 × 3 1/2
2 × 6	1 9/16 × 5 5/8	1 1/2 × 5 1/2
2 × 8	1 9/16 × 7 1/2	1 1/2 × 7 1/4
2 × 10	1 9/16 × 9 1/2	1 1/2 × 9 1/4
2 × 12	1 9/16 × 11 1/2	1 1/2 × 11 1/4
1 × 2	25/32 × 1 9/16	3/4 × 1 1/2
1 × 3	25/32 × 2 9/16	3/4 × 2 1/2
1 × 4	25/32 × 3 9/16	3/4 × 3 1/2
1 × 6	25/32 × 5 5/8	3/4 × 5 1/2
1 × 8	25/32 × 7 1/2	3/4 × 7 1/4
1 × 10	25/32 × 9 1/2	3/4 × 9 1/4
1 × 12	25/32 × 11 1/2	3/4 × 11 1/4

Hardwood lumber is usually sold rough rather than dressed, but for those pieces that are sold surfaced, dressed thicknesses are as shown in Table 2–47. There are no fixed thicknesses for the piece as a whole corresponding to the various nominal thicknesses in which softwood lumber is usually sold.

TABLE 2-47. Hardwood dressed thicknesses.

Rough, inches	Surfaced two sides, inches	Rough, inches	Surfaced two sides, inches
3/8	3/16	1 1/2	1 5/16
1/2	5/16	2	1 3/4
5/8	7/16	2 1/2	2 1/4
3/4	9/16	3	2 3/4
1	15/16	3 1/2	3 1/4
1 1/4	1 1/16	4	3 3/4

Board Foot Measure

Formula

$$B = \frac{T(W)L}{12}$$

where: B = volume in board feet
T = thickness in inches
W = width in inches
L = length in feet

Example

How many board feet will a 2 × 12 which is 12 feet long contain?

Solution

$$B = \frac{2(12)12}{12}$$

$$= 24 \text{ board feet}$$

Table 2–48 is a tabulation of board feet in various pieces of standard size.

TABLE 2-48. Number of board feet in various sizes of lumber.

Nominal cross section	Footage tally for length of—					
	8 feet	10 feet	12 feet	14 feet	16 feet	18 feet
Inches	*Board feet*	*Board feet*	*Board feet*	*Board feet*	*Board feet*	*Board feet*
1 x 3	2	2½	3	3½	4	4½
1 x 4	2⅔	3⅓	4	4⅔	5⅓	6
1 x 6	4	5	6	7	8	9
1 x 8	5⅓	6⅔	8	9⅓	10⅔	12
1 x 10	6⅔	8⅓	10	11⅔	13⅓	15
1 x 12	8	10	12	14	16	18
1½ x 4	4	5	6	7	8	9
1½ x 6	6	7½	9	10½	12	13½
1½ x 8	8	10	12	14	16	18
1½ x 10	10	12½	15	17½	20	22½
1½ x 12	12	15	18	21	24	27
2 x 4	5⅓	6⅔	8	9⅓	10⅔	12
2 x 6	8	10	12	14	16	18
2 x 8	10⅔	13⅓	16	18⅔	21⅓	24
2 x 10	13⅓	16⅔	20	23⅓	26⅔	30
2 x 12	16	20	24	28	32	36
3 x 4	8	10	12	14	16	18
3 x 6	12	15	18	21	24	27
3 x 8	16	20	24	28	32	36
3 x 10	20	25	30	35	40	45
3 x 12	24	30	36	42	48	54
4 x 4	10⅔	13⅓	16	18⅔	21⅓	24
4 x 6	16	20	24	28	32	36
4 x 8	21⅓	26⅔	32	37⅓	42⅔	48
4 x 10	26⅔	33⅓	40	46⅔	53⅓	60
4 x 12	32	40	48	56	64	72
6 x 6	24	30	36	42	48	54
6 x 7	28	35	42	49	56	63
6 x 8	32	40	48	56	64	72
6 x 10	40	50	60	70	80	90
6 x 12	48	60	72	84	96	108
7 x 9	42	52½	63	73½	84	94½
8 x 8	42⅔	43⅓	64	74⅔	85⅓	96
8 x 10	53⅓	66⅔	80	93⅓	106⅔	120
8 x 12	64	80	96	112	128	144

Selection of Species

Although Table 2–49 groups species specifically for use in constructing containers, it also includes a definition of the characteristics of each group so that the user can adapt the table to other applications.

TABLE 2-49. Grouping by some important characteristics.

Group 1 includes the lighter and softer woods of both the softwoods and hardwoods. Group 1 woods are comparatively free from splits during nailing; they have moderate nail-holding power, moderate strength as a beam, and moderate shock-resisting capacity. They are soft, light in weight, easy to work, hold their shape well after manufacture; and, as a rule, are easy to dry.

Group 1 includes the following woods:

Aspen, bigtooth	Fir, Pacific silver
Aspen, quaking	Fir, white
Basswood, American	Magnolia
Buckeye, yellow	Pine, northern white
Butternut	Pine, jack
Cedar, Alaska-yellow	Pine, lodgepole
Cedar, northern white	Pine, ponderosa
Cedar, Port Orford	Pine, red
Cedar, western red	Pine, sugar
Chestnut, American	Pine, Idaho white
Cottonwood, black	Redwood
Cottonwood, eastern	Spruce, Engelmann
Cypress	Spruce, red
Fir, subalpine	Spruce, Sitka
Fir, balsam	Spruce, white
Fir, California red	Willow, black
Fir, grand	Willow, western black
Fir, noble	Yellow-poplar

Group 2 consists entirely of the heavier softwoods, which have a pronounced difference in hardness between the springwood (the lighter colored portion of each annual ring) and summerwood (the darker portion of the annual ring). They have greater nail-holding power than Group 1 woods, but greater tendency to split in nailing, since both nail-holding and splitting increase with hardness. The hard bands of summerwood sometimes have a tendency to deflect nails and cause them to run out at the side of the board.

Group 2 woods are—

Douglas fir	Pine, pitch
Hemlock, eastern	Pine, pond
Hemlock, west coast	Pine, shortleaf
Larch, western	Pine, slash
Pine, loblolly	Pine, table mountain
Pine, longleaf	Tamarack

Group 3 woods are hardwoods of medium density. These woods have about the same nail-holding power and strength as a beam as the Group 2 woods, but are less inclined to split or shatter under impact. These are the most useful woods for box ends and cleats. They also furnish most of the rotary-cut veneer for wire-bound and plywood boxes.

Group 3 includes—

Ash, black	Red and sap gum
Ash, pumpkin	Sycamore
Elm, American or white	Tupelo
Maple, soft	

Group 4 is made up of dense hardwood species. These species have great shock-resisting capacity and nail-holding power, but are hard to drive nails into and have more tendency to split at the nails than any of the other groups of woods, since they are our hardest and heaviest domestic woods. They are, however, especially useful where high nail-holding power is required, for blocking and skids, and many of them make excellent rotary-cut veneer for wire-bound and plywood boxes.

Group 4 woods are—

Ash, white	Hickory
Beech	Maple, hard
Birch	Oaks
Elm, rock	Pecan
Hackberry	

TABLE 2-50. How various defects occur in different common grades of boards.

Grade factor	Occurrence in grade			
	No. 1 C	No. 2 C	No. 3 C	No. 4 C
Intergrown knot_____	Frequent occurrence; medium sizes.	Other defects more important.	Other defects more important.	Other defects more important.
Encased knot ___ __	Frequent occurrence; medium sizes.	Frequent occurrence; large sizes.	Other defects more important.	Other defects more important.
Spiked knot _____	Minor occurrence; small sizes.	Limited occurrence; medium sizes.	Frequent occurrence; large sizes.	Heavy occurrence; large sizes.*
Decayed knot _____	Minor occurrence; small sizes.	Limited occurrence; medium sizes.	Frequent occurrence; large sizes.	Heavy occurrence; large sizes.*
Knot hole _____	Minor occurrence; small sizes.	Limited occurrence; medium sizes.	Frequent occurrence; large sizes.	Heavy occurrence; large sizes.*
Decay_____	None _____	Limited occurrence; medium sizes.	Frequent occurrence; large sizes.	Heavy occurrence; large sizes.*

* Within the limits that the piece constitutes a usable board.

Common grades

The presence of defects such as knots and decay determines the grade. Table 2–50 describes, in a qualitative way, the allowable occurrence of various defects in Common Grades 1C through 4C.

Plywood

Species of wood used in making veneers for plywood have been classified into five groups, as shown in Table 2–51[25] based on modulus of elasticity.

TABLE 2-51. Classification of species for plywood veneers.

Group 1	Group 2	
Apitong	Cedar, Port Orford	Maple, Black
Birch, Yellow	Cypress	Meranti
Sweet	Douglas Fir 2	Mersawa
Douglas Fir 1	Fir, California Red	Mengkulang
Kapur	Grand	Pine, Pond
Kerying	Noble	Red
Larch, Western	Pacific Silver	Western White
Maple, Sugar	White	Virginia
Pine, Caribbean	Hemlock, Western	Poplar, Yellow
Southern	Lauan, Red	Spruce, Red
Loblolly	Tangile	Sitka
Longleaf	White	Sweet Gum
Slash	Almon	Tamarack
Tanoak	Bagtikan	
	Mayapis	

[25]American Plywood Association, Plywood Design Specification, Tacoma, Washington. © Copyright 1966 American Plywood Association.

Group 3	Group 4	Group 5
Alder, Red	Aspen, Bigtooth	Basswood
Cedar, Alaska	Quaking	Fir, Balsam
Hemlock, Eastern	Birch, Paper	Poplar, Balsam
Pine, Jack	Cedar, Incense	
Lodgepole	Western Red	
Ponderosa	Cativo	
Spruce	Fir, Subalpine	
Redwood	Pine, Sugar	
Spruce, Black	Eastern White	
Eastern	Poplar, Western	
Engelmann		
Red		
White		

Minimum bending radius[26]

The radii shown in Table 2–52 have been found to be appropriate minimums for mill-run panels of the thicknesses shown, bent dry. Shorter radii can be developed by selecting for bending areas that are free of knots and short grain, and/or by wetting or steaming (exterior glue recommended).

TABLE 2-52. Minimum Bending Radii in feet.

Panel Thickness	Across Grain	Parallel to Grain
1/4″	2	5
5/16″	2	6
3/8″	3	8
1/2″	6	12
5/8″	8	16
3/4″	12	20

Fasteners[27]

Table 2–53 shows ultimate test loads (maximum load carried by the plywood under test, at actual failure). Each load must be reduced by a factor appropriate to the intended use. A load factor of 2 is appropriate for many product-design applications; load factors of around 4 or 5 are often used for permanent structural applications.

Plywood veneer grades[28]

The grade of veneer is described by a letter as follows:

A Smooth and paintable. Neatly made repairs permissible. Also used for natural finish in less demanding applications.

---

[26]American Plywood Association, Plywood "How-to" Book, Tacoma, Washington. © Copyright 1971 American Plywood Association.
[27]American Plywood Association, Plywood for Industrial Uses, © 1972.
[28]Ibid.

B Solid surface veneer. Circular repair plugs and tight knots permitted.

C Knotholes to 1 inch. Occasional knotholes 1/2″ larger permitted providing total width of all knots and knotholes within a specified section does not exceed certain limits. Limited splits permitted. Minimum veneer permitted in Exterior-type plywood.

C$_{plgd}$ Improved C veneer with splits limited to 1/8″ in width and knotholes and borer holes limited 1/4″ by 1/2″.

D Permits knots and knotholes to 2–1/2″ in width and 1/2″ larger under certain specified limits. Limited splits permitted.

TABLE 2-53. Fastener loads.

Fastener Loads

NAILS	Ultimate Lateral Loads in Douglas fir lumber (lb. per common nail) (1) (2)			
Plywood Thickness	6d	8d	10d	16d
5/16″	275	305		
3/8″	275	340		
1/2″		350	425	
5/8″		350	425	445
3/4″			410	445

(1) Assume 3/8″ edge distance.
(2) For galvanized casing nails, multiply tabulated values by 0.6.

SCREWS	Ultimate Withdrawal Loads (2) (lb. per screw)					
Penetration into Plywood (1)	Size of Wood Screw					
	6	7	8	9	10	12
3/8″	150	165	180	195		
1/2″	200	220	240	260	280	
5/8″	250	275	300	325	350	395
3/4″	300	330	360	390	420	475

(1) Screws driven perpendicular to face of panel.
(2) Values may be increased one-fourth for sheet metal screws.

STAPLES	Ultimate Loads (1) (2) (lb. per staple)	
Penetration Into Lumber	Lateral Load	Withdrawal Load
3/4″	160	100
1″	180	150
1-1/4″	200	200
1-1/2″	220	

(1) Values are for 3/8″ and thicker plywood, 16 gage galvanized staples with 7/16″ crown, driven into Douglas fir lumber.
(2) Some plastic coated staples may provide higher values.

BOLTS	Ultimate Loads at listed angle between plywood face grain and load direction (lb. per bolt) (1) (2)					
Plywood Thickness	1/2″ Bolt			3/4″ Bolt		
	0°	45°	90°	0°	45°	90°
5/16″			2400			
1/2″	4740	6200	4570	7800	6720	6900
5/8″	5400	5400	4320	8070	7720	6900
3/4″	5280	3500	5630	7920	7270	8650
13/16″						8820

(1) Values are for plywood gussets on both sides of 2-1/2″ Douglas fir lumber with bolt loaded in double shear.
(2) To develop loads tabulated, plywood end distance is six times bolt diameter, "D" for 0 to 45 degrees, and 8D for 90 degrees; edge distance is 3D for 0, and 6D for 45 degrees and 90 degrees. Reduce loads proportionately for reduced end distances. Minimum end distance is 3D for 0 and 45 degrees, 4D for 90 degrees.

Grade use guide[29]

Table 2–54 gives application and availability information for appearance and engineered grades of plywood.

---

[29]Ibid.

TABLE 2-54. Grade use guide to plywood.

	Use these terms when you specify plywood (1)	Description and Most Common Uses	Typical Grade-trademarks	Face	Back	Inner Plys	Most Common Thicknesses (inch) (3)
APPEARANCE GRADES (1)(2) — Interior type	A-B INT-DFPA	For interior applications where appearance of one side is less important and two smooth solid surfaces are necessary. Built-ins, cabinets, furniture, partitions.		A	B	D	1/4 3/8 1/2 5/8 3/4
	A-D INT-DFPA	For interior uses where appearance of only one side is important. Paneling, built-ins, shelving, partitions, flow-racks, die-cut parts, templates.		A	D	D	1/4 3/8 1/2 5/8 3/4
	B-D INT-DFPA	Interior utility panel for use where one smooth side is required. Good for backing, sides of built-ins, shelving, slipsheets, separator boards, and bins.		B	D	D	1/4 3/8 1/2 5/8 3/4
Exterior type	A-C EXT-DFPA (4)	Exterior use where appearance of only one side is important. Siding, soffits, fences, structural uses, boxcar and truck lining, tanks, trays, commercial refrigerators.		A	C	C	1/4 3/8 1/2 5/8 3/4
	B-C EXT-DFPA (4)	An outdoor utility panel for work buildings, boxcar and truck linings, containers, tanks, agricultural equipment.		B	C	C	1/4 3/8 1/2 5/8 3/4
	HDO EXT-DFPA (4)	Exterior type High Density Overlaid plywood with hard, semi-opaque resin-fiber overlay. Abrasion resistant. Painting not ordinarily required. For concrete forms, cabinets, counter tops, signs, and tanks.		A or B	A or B	C Plgd	5/16 3/8 1/2 5/8 3/4
	MDO EXT-DFPA (4)	Exterior type Medium Density Overlaid with smooth, opaque, resin-fiber overlay heat-fused to one or both panel faces. Ideal base for paint. Recommended for siding, built-ins, signs, and displays.		B	B or C	C or C Plgd	5/16 3/8 1/2 5/8 3/4
	303® SIDING EXT-DFPA	Grade designation covers proprietary plywood products for exterior siding, fencing, etc., with special surface treatment such as V-groove, channel groove, rough-sawn. Stud spacing shown on grade stamp.		(5)	C	C	3/8 1/2 5/8
	TEXTURE 1-11® EXT-DFPA	Exterior type, sanded or unsanded, shiplapped edges with parallel grooves 1/4" deep, 3/8" wide. Grooves 2" or 4" o.c. Available in 8' and 10' lengths and MDO. For siding, accent paneling, fencing, displays.		C or btr.	C	C	5/8
ENGINEERED GRADES (6) — Interior type	STANDARD C-D INT-DFPA (2)(7)	Unsanded sheathing grade for wall and roof sheathing, subflooring; limited-exposure crates, containers, pallets. Also available with exterior glue. Specify STANDARD with exterior glue for moderate temporary exposure. For permanent exposure to weather or moisture, only Exterior-type plywood is suitable.		C	D	D	5/16 3/8 1/2 5/8 3/4 7/8
	STRUCTURAL I C-D INT-DFPA	Unsanded structural grade where plywood strength properties are of maximum importance. For containers, pallets, bins. Made only with exterior glue. Limited to Group 1 species for face, back and inner plys.		C	D	D	5/16 3/8 1/2 5/8 3/4
	UNDERLAYMENT INT-DFPA (2)(7)	For underlayment or combination subfloor-underlayment under resilient floor coverings, carpeting. Sanded or touch-sanded as specified.		C Plgd	D	C & D	1/4 3/8 1/2 5/8 3/4
	C-D PLUGGED INT-DFPA (2)(7)	For utility built-ins, backing for wall and ceiling tile. Not a substitute for UNDERLAYMENT. Ply beneath face permits D grade veneer. Also for cable reels, walkways, separator boards. Unsanded or touch-sanded as specified.		C Plgd	D	D	5/16 3/8 1/2 5/8 3/4
	2·4·1 INT-DFPA (7)(8)	Combination subfloor-underlayment. Quality base for resilient floor coverings, carpeting, wood strip flooring. Use 2·4·1 with exterior glue in areas subject to excessive moisture. Unsanded or touch-sanded as specified.		C Plgd	D	C & D	(available 1-1/8" or 1-1/4")
Exterior type	C-C EXT-DFPA (2)	Unsanded grade with waterproof bond for subflooring and roof decking, siding on service buildings; crating, pallets, pallet bins, cable reels.		C	C	C	5/16 3/8 1/2 5/8 3/4 7/8
	UNDERLAYMENT C-C PLUGGED EXT-DFPA (2) or C-C PLUGGED EXT-DFPA (2)	For underlayment or combination subfloor-underlayment under resilient floor coverings where excessive moisture conditions may be present. Also for refrigerated or controlled atmosphere rooms, for pallets, fruit pallet bins, reusable cargo containers, tanks, boxcar and truck floors and linings. Sanded or touch-sanded as specified.		C Plgd	C	C or Special C	1/4 3/8 1/2 5/8 3/4
	B-B PLYFORM EXT-DFPA	Concrete form grade with high re-use factor. Sanded both sides. Edge-sealed and mill-oiled unless otherwise specified. Special restrictions on species. Also available in HDO.		B	B	C	5/8 3/4

NOTES:
(1) Sanded both sides except where decorative or other surfaces specified.
(2) Available in Group 1, 2, 3, 4, or 5 unless otherwise specified.
(3) Standard 4 x 8' panel sizes; other sizes available.
(4) Also available in STRUCTURAL I (face, back and inner plys limited to Group 1 species).
(5) C or better for 5 plys; C-Plugged or better for 3-ply panels.
(6) All grades except PLYFORM available tongue-and-grooved in panels 1/2" and thicker.
(7) Also available with exterior glue.
(8) Available in Group 1, 2 or 3 only.

TABLE 2-55. Plywood Pallets.

Load-span tables—unsanded plywood

Two-Way-Entry Pallet—Suggested Maximum Uniform Load (lbs. per sq. ft.)
(Face grain perpendicular to stringers)

Identification Index	Thickness Available	Span in Inches (S)							Factor for Structural I**
		16	18	20	22	24	30	36	
		Suggested Uniform Load (lbs. per sq. ft.)*							
24/0	⅜″ ½″	335	265	215	175	150	95	65	1.21
30/12	⅝″	540	430	345	285	240	155	105	—
32/16	½″ ⅝″	500	395	320	265	225	145	100	1.27
36/16	¾″	685	540	440	360	305	195	135	—
42/20	⅝″ ¾″ ⅞″	770	610	495	405	340	220	150	1.16
48/24	¾″ ⅞″	980	775	630	520	435	280	195	1.15

*To find total allowable pallet loads, multiply table values by pallet area (sq. ft.)
**When Structural I panels are used, multiply allowable loads in table by factor indicated.

Nine-Block Four-Way-Entry Pallet
Suggested Total Maximum Uniform Load (Total Pallet Area)
9 Blocks, 4″ x 6″ bearing area per block. Plywood face grain and block length parallel to long dimension.

Pallet Size (in)	42/20 Std. ⅝″ - ¾″ - ⅞″	48/24 Std. ¾″ - ⅞″	42/20 Struct. I ⅝″	48/24 Struct. I ¾″
32 x 40	3400	6000	5400	7800
36 x 36	2600	4600	4200	7500
36 x 42	3100	5400	4900	8200
32 x 48	4100	5300	4800	6100
42 x 42	2500	4500	4100	7200
36 x 48	3500	6000	5400	6900
40 x 48	3100	5400	4900	7600

Large Size Nine-Block Pallets—Suggested Total Maximum Uniform Load
9 Blocks, 6″ x 6″ bearing area per block. Plywood face grain and block length parallel to long dimension.

Pallet Size	42/20 Std. ⅝″ - ¾″ - ⅞″	48/24 Std. ¾″ - ⅞″	42/20 Struct. I ⅝″	48/24 Struct. I ¾″
48 x 48	2700	4800	4300	7700
48 x 60	3400	6000	5400	6900
48 x 72	3800	4800	4400	5600

Load-span tables—sanded plywood

Two-Way-Entry Pallet—Suggested Maximum Uniform Load (lbs per sq. ft.)
(Face grain perpendicular to stringers)

Thickness	Span in Inches (S)						
	16	18	20	22	24	30	36
	Suggested Uniform Load (lbs. per sq. ft.)						
⅜″	340	280	220	185	150	95	65
½″	510	420	325	280	225	145	100
⅝″	675	555	430	370	300	190	135
¾″	855	705	545	470	380	245	170
1″	1375	1180	880	755	610	390	270
2•4•1 (1⅛″)	1875	1480	1200	990	835	535	370

Nine-Block Four-Way-Entry Pallet—
Suggested Total Maximum Uniform Load (Total Pallet Area)
9 Blocks, 4″ x 6″ bearing area per block. Plywood face grain and block length parallel to long dimension.

Pallet Size	Sanded Plywood Thickness			
	⅝″	¾″	1″	2•4•1 (1⅛″)
32 x 40	4100	5900	8300	8200
36 x 36	3100	5400	8300	8300
36 x 42	3700	6200	8300	8200
32 x 48	3600	4600	7400	8200
42 x 42	3000	5200	8300	8200
36 x 48	4100	5200	8300	8200
40 x 48	3700	5800	8300	8200

Large Size Nine-Block Pallet—Suggested Total Maximum Uniform Load
9 Blocks, 6″ x 6″ bearing area per block. Plywood face grain and block length parallel to long dimension.

Pallet Size	Sanded Plywood Thickness			
	⅝″	¾″	1″	2•4•1 (1⅛″)
48 x 48	3200	5600	9800	9800
48 x 60	4100	5200	8400	9800
48 x 72	3300	4200	6800	9200

General Note: Except for 2•4•1, all sanded tables apply to Group 1 plywood only. Where Groups 2, 3 or 4 plywood are used, the table values should be modified by the following percentages:
Group 2 or 3: 73% of table value. — Group 4: 61% of table value.
Suggested Loads for 2•4•1 apply to all Groups.

Pallets[30]

Table 2–55 gives span and dimension information for design of pallets with plywood surfaces. This information is based on the assumption of an odd number of laminations, with grain direction alternated.

Section properties of plywood[31]

For engineering of structures, section properties are given in Tables 2–54 and 2–55. These figures are based on 12-inch widths and have been adjusted to account for reduced effectiveness of plys with grain perpendicular to applied stress.

Table 2–55 is used when face plys are of the same species group as inner plys, and includes Structural I and II, Marine Exterior, and all grades using Group 4 stresses. Table 2–54 includes all other Product Standard grades, and is used when face plys are of different species group than the inner plys.

Concrete forms of plywood[32]

Recommended design pressures for plywood when used in forms for placing concrete are given in Table 2–56. These values are based on concrete of 150 pounds per cubic foot. They are derived from test data and should be considered as general guidelines only, since they are subject to numerous variables.

TABLE 2-56. Suggested concrete design pressures.

Rate of Placement (ft/hr)	Vibrated		Unvibrated	
	At 50°F	At 70°F	At 50°F	At 70°F
2	510	400	460	360
3	690	530	620	480
4	870	660	780	590
5	1050	790	950	710
6	1230	920	1110	830
7	1410	1050	1270	950
8	1470	1090	1320	980
9	1520	1130	1370	1020

---

[30]Ibid.

[31]American Plywood Association, Plywood Design Specification, Tacoma, Washington.©Copyright 1966 American Plywood Association.

[32]American Plywood Association, Guide to Plywood for Concrete Forms, Tacoma, Washington. © 1967 American Plywood Association.

TABLE 2-57. Recommended preservatives and retentions for ties, lumber, piles, poles, and posts.

Product	Minimum net retention of—(Pounds per cubic foot)				
	Coal-tar creosote (TT-W-556)	Creosote-coal tar solution (TT-W-566)	Creosote-petroleum solution (TT-W-568)	Pentachlorophenol, 5 percent in petroleum[1] (TT-W-570)	Copper naphthenate (0.75 percent copper metal) in petroleum[1] (AWPA P8)
Ties (crossties, switch ties, and bridge ties) -----	8	8	9		
Lumber, and structural timbers:					
For use in coastal waters:					
Douglas fir (coast type) lumber and timbers.	14	14			
Southern yellow pine lumber and timbers	20	20			
For use in fresh water, in contact with ground or for important structural members not in contact with ground or water.	10	10	12	10	10
For other use not in contact with ground or water.	6	6	7	6	6
Piles:					
For use in coastal waters:					
Douglas fir (coast type) ----------	[2]17	[2]17			
Southern yellow pine--------	[2]20	[2]20			
For land or fresh water use--------	12	12	14	12	
Poles (utility and building) ----------	8,[3]10			8,[3]10	8,[3]10
Posts (round, fence) ----------	6	6	7	6	6

[1] Until Federal Specifications on these solutions become available, the petroleum oils conforming to American Wood-Preserver's Association P9 should be used. The heavy oil in AWPA P9 is recommended for the treatment of poles, posts, and other timbers to be used in contact with the ground or fresh water. Special petroleum solvents, as well as conditioning of the wood after treatment, are necessary when cleanliness and paintability of the treated wood is required.

[2] Retention determined by assay of borings.

[3] Higher retention is required for poles over 37.5 inches in circumference (measured 6 feet from the butt) and for all poles used under severe service conditions.

Steel and Aluminum

CHAPTER 3

STEEL

Classifications and Properties[1,2]

Some basic mechanical properties of typical structural steels are given in Table 3–1.

Shapes, Dimensions and Loading[3]

American Standard Beams are designated by a section number, which is the letter S followed by the overall beam depth in inches. Table 3–2 shows dimension and loading information for American Standard Beams of A36 steel. To determine allowable loads for A572 Grade 50 steel, multiply the loads in Table 3–2 by 1.38.

American Standard Channels are designated by a section number, which is the letter C followed by the overall depth in inches. Table 3–3 shows dimension and loading information for American Standard Channels of A36 steel.

Wide Flange Beams are designated by a section number composed of the letter W followed by a number, which is usually the whole number part of the beam depth. Table 3–4 includes a column of actual depths. This table presents dimension and loading information for Wide Flange Beams of A36 steel; to determine allowable loads for A572 Grade 50 steel, multiply loads in the table by the indicated conversion factor.

Section W4 has a flange slope of 1/4 in 12; all other sections have parallel flanges.

ALUMINUM[4]

Industry standards for identifying and classifying aluminum and alloys use a four-

---

[1]Bethlehem Steel Corporation, Modern Steels for Construction—a Selection Guide (Booklet 2489), Bethlehem, Pa., 1968.

[2]Bethlehem Steel Corporation, Chemical Composition and Mechanical Properties Structural Steel Shapes and Piling (Folder 2439-A), Bethlehem, Pa.

[3]Bethlehem Steel Corporation, Cards 2715 and 2716, Bethlehem, Pa.

[4]The Aluminum Association, Engineering Data for Aluminum Structures, New York, 1969.

TABLE 3-1. Mechanical properties of some steels.

Designation		Product	ASTM Group or pounds per foot	Minimum Yield Point (psi)	Tensile Strength	Endurance Limit (Percent of tensile strength)
ASTM A36		Shapes	Groups 1–5	36,000	58,000 to 80,000	60
		Plates	To 8 incl	36,000	58,000 to 80,000	60
		Plates	Over 8 to 15 incl	32,000	58,000 to 80,000	60
		Bars	To 4 incl	36,000	58,000 to 80,000	60
ASTM A283	Grade A	Plates	To 15	24,000	45,000 to 55,000	
	Grade B	Plates	To 15	27,000	50,000 to 60,000	
	Grade C	Plates	To 15	30,000	55,000 to 65,000	
	Grade D	Plates	To 15	33,000	60,000 to 72,000	
ASTM A440		Shapes	Groups 1 and 2	50,000	70,000 min	50
		Shapes	Group 3	46,000	67,000 min	50
		Shapes	Group 4 (to 426 lb/ft incl)	42,000	63,000 min	50
		Plates and bars	To 3/4 incl	50,000	70,000 min	50
		Plates and bars	Over 3/4 to 1 1/2 incl	46,000	67,000 min	50
		Plates and bars	Over 1 1/2 to 4 incl	42,000	63,000 min	50
ASTM A441		Shapes	Groups 1 and 2	50,000	70,000 min	60
		Shapes	Group 3	46,000	67,000 min	60

	Form	Size	Yield	Tensile	
	Shapes	Groups 4 and 5	42,000	63,000 min	60
	Plates and bars	To 3/4 incl	50,000	70,000 min	60
	Plates and bars	Over 3/4 to 1 1/2 incl	46,000	67,000 min	60
	Plates and bars	Over 1 1/2 to 4 incl	42,000	63,000 min	60
	Plates	Over 4 to 8 incl	40,000	60,000 min	60
ASTM A572 Grade 42			42,000	60,000 min	60
Grade 45			45,000	60,000 min	60
Grade 50			50,000	65,000 min	60
Grade 55			55,000	70,000 min	50 to 60
Grade 60			60,000	75,000 min	50
Grade 65			65,000	80,000 min	50
ASTM A242 Type 1	Shapes	Groups 1 and 2	50,000	70,000 min	60 to 75
	Shapes	Group 3	46,000	67,000 min	60 to 75
	Shapes	Groups 4 and 5	42,000	63,000 min	60 to 75
	Plates and bars	To 3/4 incl	50,000	70,000 min	60 to 75
	Plates and bars	Over 3/4 to 1 1/2 incl	46,000	67,000 min	60 to 75
	Plates and bars	Over 1 1/2 to 4 incl	42,000	63,000 min	60 to 75

TABLE 3-2. American Standard beams.

Section Number	Weight	Flange	Web	½ Web	C	K	Grip	Conv. Factor	SAFE LOAD IN TONS FOR SPAN IN FEET																REACTION IN KIPS		
									6	8	10	12	14	16	18	20	22	24	26	28	30	32	34	36	Maximum Web Shear	Crippling 3½" Brg.	Crippling 1" Add. Brg.
S24	120	8	13/16	7/16	1/2	1 15/16	1 1/8	1.38		251	201	168	144	126	112	101	91	84	77	72	67	63	59	56	278	117	21.5
	105.9	7 7/8	5/8	5/16	3/8	1 15/16	1 1/8	1.38		218	188	156	134	117	104	94	85	78	72	67	63	59	55	52	218	92	16.9
	100	7 1/4	3/4	3/8	7/16	1 5/8	7/8	1.38		198	158	132	113	99	88	79	72	66	61	57	53	50	47	44	260	103	20.2
	90	7 1/8	5/8	5/16	3/8	1 5/8	7/8	1.38		186	149	124	106	93	83	75	68	62	57	53	50	47	44	42	217	86	16.8
	79.9	7	1/2	1/4	5/16	1 5/8	7/8	1.38		174	139	116	100	87	78	70	63	58	54	50	47	44	41	39	174	69	13.5
S20	95	7 1/4	13/16	7/16	1/2	1 3/4	7/8	1.38	214	160	128	107	92	80	71	64	58	54	49	46	43	40	38	36	232	113	21.6
	85	7	11/16	5/16	3/8	1 3/4	15/16	1.38		150	120	100	86	75	67	60	55	50	46	43	40	38	36	34	189	93	17.6
	75	6 3/8	5/8	5/16	3/8	1 9/16	13/16	1.38	169	127	101	84	72	63	56	51	46	42	39	36	34	32	30	28	186	88	17.3
	65.4	6 1/4	1/2	1/4	5/16	1 9/16	3/4	1.38	145	117	94	78	67	59	52	47	43	39	36	34	31	29	28	26	145	68	13.5
S18	70	6 1/4	3/4	3/8	7/16	1 3/8	11/16	1.38	136	102	82	68	58	51	46	41	37	34	32	29	27	26	24	23	186	94	19.2
	54.7	6	1/2	1/4	5/16	1 3/8	11/16	1.38	118	89	71	59	51	44	40	36	32	30	27	26	24	22	21	20	120	61	12.4
S15	50	5 5/8	9/16	5/16	3/8	1 1/4	9/16	1.38	86	64	52	43	37	32	29	26	24	22	20	19	17	16			120	71	14.9
	42.9	5 1/2	7/16	1/4	5/16	1 1/4	9/16	1.38	79	59	47	40	34	30	26	24	22	20	18	17	16	15			89	53	11.1
S12	50	5 1/2	11/16	3/8	7/16	1 5/16	11/16	1.38	67	51	40	34	29	25	23	20	19	17							120	89	18.5
	40.8	5 1/4	1/2	1/4	5/16	1 5/16	5/8	1.38	60	45	36	30	26	23	20	18	17	15							80	60	12.4
	35	5 1/8	7/16	1/4	5/16	1 1/8	1/2	1.38	51	38	30	25	22	19	17	15	14	13							74	53	11.6
	31.8	5	3/8	3/16	1/4	1 1/8	1/2	1.38	48	36	29	24	21	18	16	15	13	12							61	44	9.5
S10	35	5	5/8	5/16	3/8	1	1/2	1.38	39	29	23	20	17	15	13	12									86	72	16.0
	25.4	4 5/8	5/16	3/16	1/4	1	1/2	1.38	33	25	20	16	14	12	11	10									45	38	8.4
S8	23	4 1/8	7/16	1/4	5/16	7/8	7/16	1.38	21	16	13	11	9	8											51	*	11.9
	18.4	4	5/16	1/8	3/16	7/8	7/16	1.38	19	14	11	10	8	7											31	*	7.3
S7	20	3 7/8	7/16	1/4	5/16	13/16	3/8	1.38	16	12	10	8	7												46	*	12.2
	15.3	3 5/8	1/4	1/8	3/16	13/16	3/8	1.38	14	11	8	7	6												25	*	6.8
S6	17.25	3 5/8	1/2	1/4	5/16	3/4	3/8	1.38	12	9	7	6													40.5	*	12.6
	12.5	3 3/8	1/4	1/8	3/16	3/4	5/16	1.38	10	7	6	5													20	*	6.2
S5	14.75	3 1/4	1/2	1/4	5/16	11/16	5/16	1.38	8	6	5														35.8	*	13.3
	10	3	1/4	1/8	3/16	11/16	5/16	1.38	6	5	4														15.2	*	5.7
S4	9.5	2 3/4	5/16	3/16	1/4	5/8	5/16	1.38	5	4															18.9	*	8.8
	7.7	2 5/8	3/16	1/8	3/16	5/8	5/16	1.38	4	3															11.0	*	5.1
S3	7.5	2 1/2	3/8	3/16	1/4	9/16	1/4	1.38	3																15.2	*	9.4
	5.7	2 3/8	3/16	1/8	3/16	9/16	1/4	1.38	3																7.4	*	4.6

All American Standard Beams are compact and have a flange slope of 2 in 12.

* Exceeds Maximum Web Shear

TABLE 3-3. American Standard channels.

Section Number	Weight	Flange	Web	½ Web	C	K	Grip	Gage	Safe load in tons for span in feet: 6	8	10	12	14	16	18	20	22	24	Reaction in kips: Maximum Web Shear	Crippling: 3½″ Brg.	Crippling: 1″ Add. Brg.
C 15	50	3¾	¾	⅜	13/16	1 5/16	⅝	2¼	66	49	39	33	28	25	22	20	18	16	156	93	19.3
	40	3½	9/16	¼	⅝	1 5/16	⅝	2	56	42	34	28	24	21	19	17	15	14	113	68	14.0
	33.9	3⅜	7/16	3/16	½	1 5/16	⅝	2	51	38	31	26	22	19	17	15	14	13	87	52	10.8
C 12	30	3⅛	½	¼	9/16	1 1/16	½	1¾	33	25	20	16	14	12	11	10	9	8	89	63	13.8
	25	3	⅜	3/16	7/16	1 1/16	½	1¾	29	22	18	15	13	11	10	9	8	7	67	48	10.4
	20.7	3	5/16	⅛	⅜	1 1/16	½	1¾	26	20	16	13	11	10	9	8	7	6	49	34	7.6
C 10	30	3	11/16	5/16	¾	15/16	7/16	1¾	25	19	15	13	11	10	9	8	7	6	98	81	18.2
	25	2⅞	9/16	¼	⅝	15/16	7/16	1¾	22	17	13	11	10	8	7	6.5	6	5.5	76	63	14.2
	20	2¾	⅜	3/16	7/16	15/16	7/16	1½	19	14	12	10	8	7	6.5	6	5.5	5	55	45	10.2
	15.3	2⅝	¼	⅛	5/16	15/16	7/16	1½	16	12	10	8	7	6	5.5	5	4.5	4	35	29	6.5
C 9	20	2⅝	7/16	¼	½	⅞	7/16	1½	17	12	10	8	7	6	5.5	5	4.5		58	53	12.1
	15	2½	5/16	⅛	⅜	⅞	7/16	1⅜	14	10	8	7	6	5	4.5	4	3.5		37	34	7.7
	13.4	2⅜	¼	⅛	5/16	⅞	⅜	1⅜	13	10	7.5	6.5	5.5	5	4.5	4	3.5		30	27	6.2
C 8	18.75	2½	½	¼	9/16	13/16	⅜	1½	13	10	8	6.5	5.5	5	4.5	4			56	*	13.1
	13.75	2⅜	5/16	⅛	⅜	13/16	⅜	1⅜	11	8	6.5	5.5	4.5	4	3.5	3			35	35	8.2
	11.5	2¼	¼	⅛	5/16	13/16	⅜	1⅜	10	7.5	6	5	4.5	4	3.5	3			26	26	5.9
C 7	14.75	2¼	7/16	3/16	½	13/16	⅜	1¼	9.5	7	5.5	4.5	4	3.5	3				43	*	11.3
	12.25	2¼	5/16	3/16	⅜	13/16	⅜	1¼	8.5	6.5	5	4	3.5	3	2.5				32	*	8.5
	9.8	2⅛	¼	⅛	5/16	13/16	⅜	1¼	7.5	5.5	4.5	3.5	3.1	2.8	2.5				21	*	5.7
C 6	13.0	2⅛	7/16	¼	½	¾	5/16	1⅜	7	5.5	4	3.5	3						38	*	11.8
	10.5	2	5/16	3/16	⅜	¾	⅜	1⅛	6	4.5	3.5	3	2.5						27.3	*	8.5
	8.2	1⅞	3/16	⅛	¼	¾	5/16	1⅛	5.5	4	3	2.5	2						17.4	*	5.4
C 5	9.0	1⅞	5/16	3/16	⅜	11/16	5/16	1⅛	4.3	3.2	2.5	2.1							23.6	*	8.8
	6.7	1¾	3/16	⅛	¼	11/16	5/16	1⅛	3.7	2.8	2.2	1.9							13.8	*	5.1
C 4	7.25	1¾	5/16	3/16	⅜	⅝	5/16	1	2.8	2.1	1.7								18.6	*	8.6
	5.4	1⅝	3/16	⅛	¼	⅝	¼	1	2.3	1.8	1.4								10.4	*	4.9
C 3	6.0	1⅝	⅜	3/16	7/16	⅝	5/16	⅞	1.7	1.3									15.5	*	9.6
	5.0	1½	¼	⅛	5/16	⅝	¼	⅞	1.5	1.1									11.2	*	7.0
	4.1	1⅜	3/16	⅛	¼	⅝	¼	⅞	1.4	1.0									7.4	*	4.6

TABLE 3-4. Wide-flange beams.

Section Number	Weight	Depth	Flange	Web	½ Web	Non-Compact	Conv. Factor	18	20	22	24	26	28	30	32	34	36	38	40	42	44	Maximum Web Shear	Crippling 3½" Brg.	Crippling 1" Add. Brg.
	300	36 3/4	16 5/8	15/16	1/2		1.38	491	442	402	369	340	316	295	277	260	246	233	221	211	201	503	161	25.5
	280	36 1/2	16 5/8	7/8	7/16		1.38	459	413	375	344	318	295	275	258	243	229	217	206	197	188	468	148	23.9
	260	36 1/4	16 1/2	7/8	7/16		1.38	423	381	346	317	293	272	254	238	224	212	200	190	181	173	444	138	22.8
	245	36	16 1/2	13/16	7/16		1.38	397	357	325	298	275	255	238	223	210	199	188	179	170	163	419	129	21.7
	230	35 7/8	16 1/2	3/4	3/8		1.38	372	334	304	279	257	239	223	209	197	186	176	167	159	152	398	121	20.7
W36	194	36 1/2	12 1/8	3/4	3/8		1.38	295	266	242	221	204	190	177	166	156	148	140	133	127	121	407	117	20.8
	182	36 3/8	12 1/8	3/4	3/8		1.38	276	249	226	207	191	178	166	156	146	138	131	124	119	113	382	109	19.6
	170	36 1/8	12	11/16	3/8		1.38	258	232	211	193	178	166	155	145	137	129	122	116	111	106	357	100	18.4
	160	36	12	5/8	5/16		1.38	241	217	197	181	167	155	145	136	128	120	114	108	103	99	341	95	17.6
	150	35 7/8	12	5/8	5/16	+	1.38	224	201	183	168	155	144	134	-126	119	112	106	101	96	92	325	90	16.9
	135	35 1/2	12	5/8	5/16	+	1.25	195	176	160	146	135	126	117	110	103	98	93	88	84	80	308	83	16.1
	240	33 1/2	15 7/8	13/16	7/16		1.38	361	325	295	271	250	232	217	203	191	180	171	162	155	148	403	133	22.4
	220	33 1/4	15 3/4	3/4	3/8		1.38	329	296	270	247	228	212	198	185	175	165	156	148	141	135	374	122	20.9
	200	33	15 3/4	11/16	3/8		1.38	298	268	244	223	206	192	179	168	158	149	141	134	128	122	342	110	19.3
W33	152	33 1/2	11 5/8	5/8	5/16		1.38	216	195	177	162	150	139	130	122	115	108	103	98	93	89	308	92	17.1
	141	33 1/4	11 1/2	5/8	5/16		1.38	199	179	163	149	138	128	119	112	105	100	94	90	85	81	292	86	16.3
	130	33 1/8	11 1/2	9/16	5/16		1.38	180	162	147	135	125	116	108	101	95	90	85	81	77	74	278	81	15.7
	118	32 7/8	11 1/2	9/16	5/16	+	1.25	159	144	131	120	110	103	96	90	85	80	76	72	68	65	264	76	15.0
	210	30 3/8	15 1/8	3/4	3/8		1.38	289	260	237	217	200	186	174	163	153	145	137	130	124	118	341	122	20.9
	190	30 1/8	15	11/16	3/8		1.38	261	235	213	196	181	168	157	147	138	130	124	117	112	107	310	109	19.2
	172	29 7/8	15	5/8	5/16		1.38	235	212	192	176	163	151	141	132	125	118	111	106	101	96	284	98	17.7
W30	132	30 1/4	10 1/2	5/8	5/16		1.38	169	152	138	127	117	109	102	95	90	85	80	76	73	69	270	86	16.6
	124	30 1/8	10 1/2	9/16	5/16		1.38	158	142	129	118	109	102	95	89	84	79	75	71	68	65	256	81	15.8
	116	30	10 1/2	9/16	5/16		1.38	146	131	119	110	101	94	88	82	77	73	69	66	63	60	245	77	15.2
	108	29 7/8	10 1/2	9/16	5/16	+	1.38	133	120	109	100	92	86	80	75	71	67	63	60	57	55	237	74	14.8
	99	29 5/8	10 1/2	1/2	1/4	+	1.25	120	108	98	90	83	77	72	68	64	60	57	54	52	49	224	69	14.1
	177	27 1/4	14 1/8	3/4	3/8		1.38	219	197	179	165	152	141	132	123	116	110	104	99	94	90	287	110	19.6
	160	27 1/8	14	11/16	5/16		1.38	198	178	162	148	137	127	119	111	105	99	94	89	85	81	258	99	17.8
	145	26 7/8	14	5/8	5/16		1.38	179	161	147	135	124	115	108	101	95	90	85	81	77	74	234	88	16.2
W27	114	27 1/4	10 1/8	9/16	5/16		1.38	133	120	109	100	92	86	80	75	71	67	63	60	57	55	225	79	15.4
	102	27 1/8	10	1/2	1/4		1.38	119	107	97	89	82	76	71	67	63	59	56	54	51	49	203	71	14.0
	94	26 7/8	10	1/2	1/4	+	1.38	108	97	89	81	75	70	65	61	57	54	51	49	46	44	191	65	13.2
	84	26 3/4	10	7/16	1/4	+	1.25	94	85	77	71	65	61	57	53	50	47	45	43	41	39	179	61	12.5
	160	24 3/4	14 1/8	11/16	5/16		1.38	184	166	151	138	127	118	111	104	98	92	87	83	79	75	235	97	17.7
	145	24 1/2	14	5/8	5/16	+	1.38	166	149	136	124	115	107	100	93	88	83	79	75	71	68	216	88	16.4
	130	24 1/4	14	9/16	5/16	+	1.25	147	133	121	110	102	95	88	83	78	74	70	66	63	60	199	80	15.3
W24	120	24 1/4	12 1/8	9/16	5/16		1.38	133	120	109	100	92	86	80	75	71	67	63	60	57	55	196	78	15.0
	110	24 1/8	12	1/2	1/4	+	1.38	122	110	100	92	85	79	73	69	65	61	58	55	53	50	179	71	13.8
	100	24	12	7/16	1/4	+	1.25	111	100	91	83	77	71	67	62	59	56	53	50	48	46	163	64	12.6
	94	24 1/4	9	1/2	1/4		1.38	98	89	81	74	68	63	59	55	52	49	47	44	42	40	182	69	13.9
	84	24 1/8	9	1/2	1/4		1.38	87	79	72	66	61	56	53	49	46	44	42	40	38	36	164	62	12.7
	76	23 7/8	9	7/16	1/4		1.38	78	70	64	59	54	50	47	44	42	39	37	35	34	32	153	56	11.9
	68	23 3/4	9	7/16	1/4	+	1.25	68	61	56	51	47	44	41	39	36	34	32	31	29	28	143	53	11.2

All sections have parallel flanges.

TABLE 3-4. cont.

Section Number	Weight	Depth	Flange	Web	½ Web	Non-Compact	Conv. Factor	6	8	10	12	14	16	18	20	22	24	26	28	30	Maximum Web Shear	Crippling 3½" Brg.	Crippling 1" Add. Brg.
	66	10 3/8	10 1/8	7/16	1/4		1.38		69	59	49	42	37	33	30	27	25	23	21	20	69	59	12.3
	60	10 1/4	10 1/8	7/16	1/4		1.38		62	54	45	39	34	30	27	25	23	21	19	18	62	53	11.2
	54	10 1/8	10	3/8	3/16	‡	1.25		54	49	41	35	30	27	24	22	20	19	18		54	46	9.9
	49	10	10	5/16	3/16	†	1.36			40	34	29	25	22	20	18	17				49	42	9.2
	45	10 1/8	8	3/8	3/16	‡	1.38		49	40	33	28	25	22	20	18					51	44	9.5
	39	10	8	5/16	3/16	‡	1.25		42	34	28	24	21	19	17						46	39	8.6
	33	9 3/4	8	5/16	3/16	†	1.36		32	26	22	19	16	15	13						41	35	7.9
W10	29	10 1/4	5 3/4	5/16	3/16		1.38	41	31	25	21	18	16	14	13						43	34	7.8
	25	10 1/8	5 3/4	1/4	1/8	‡	1.38	35	27	21	18	15	13	12	11						37	29	6.8
	21	9 7/8	5 3/4	1/4	1/8	‡	1.25	29	22	17	15	13	11	10	9						34	27	6.5
	19	10 1/4	4	1/4	1/8		1.38	25	19	15	12.5	10.8	9.4	8.4	7.5						37.2	28.3	6.8
	17	10 1/8	4	1/4	1/8	‡	1.38	22	16	13	11.0	9.3	8.1	7.2	6.5						35.2	26.7	6.5
	15	10	4	1/4	1/8	‡	1.25	18	14	11	9.2	7.9	6.9	6.2	5.5						33.4	25.2	6.2
	11.5	9 7/8	4	3/16	1/8	†	1.36	13	9.6	7.7	6.4	5.5	4.8	4.3	3.9						25.8	19.4	4.9
	35	8 1/8	8	5/16	3/16	‡	1.25		31	25	21	18	16	14	13	11					37	37	8.5
	31	8	8	5/16	3/16	†	1.36		25	20	17	14	13	11	10						33	*	7.8
	28	8	6 1/2	5/16	1/8	‡	1.38	32	24	20	16	14	12								33	33	7.7
	24	7 7/8	6 1/2	1/4	1/8	‡	1.25	28	21	17	14	12	10								28	*	6.6
W8	20	8 1/8	5 1/4	1/4	1/8	‡	1.38	23	17	14	11	10	9								29	28	6.7
	17	8	5 1/4	1/4	1/8	‡	1.25	19	14	11	9	8	7								27	26	6.2
	15	8 1/8	4	1/4	1/8	‡	1.38	16	12	9.5	7.9	6.8	5.9								28.8	27.3	6.6
	13	8	4	1/4	1/8	‡	1.25	13.2	9.9	7.9	6.6	5.7	5								26.7	25.2	6.2
	10	7 7/8	4	3/16	1/8	†	1.36	9.5	7.2	5.7	4.8	4.1	3.5								19.5	18.4	4.6
	25	6 3/8	6 1/8	5/16	3/16	‡	1.38	23	17	14	11	10	9	8.5	7.5	6.5					30	*	8.6
	20	6 1/4	6	1/4	1/8	‡	1.25	18	14	11	9	7.5	6.5	6							23	*	7.0
	15.5	6	6	1/4	1/8	†	1.36	13	10	7.5	6										21	*	6.5
W6	16	6 1/4	4	1/4	1/8		1.38	13.5	10.1	8.1	6.8										23.6	*	7.0
	12	6	4	1/4	1/8		1.38	9.7	7.3	5.8	4.9										20	*	6.2
	8.5	5 7/8	4	3/16	1/8	†	1.36	6.2	4.7	3.7	3.1										14.4	*	4.6

† Indicates non-compact shape in A36 and A572, Gr. 50.

‡ Indicates non-compact shape in A572, Gr. 50.

* Exceeds maximum web shear

TABLE 3-4. cont.

Section Number	Weight	Depth	Flange	Web	½ Web Non-Compact	Conv. Factor	14	16	18	20	22	24	26	28	30	32	34	36	38	40	Maximum Web Shear	Crippling 3½" Brg.	Crippling 1" Add. Brg.
W24	61	23 3/4	7	7/16	1/4	1.38	74	65	58	52	47	43	40	37	35	32	31	29	27	26	144	52.3	11.3
	55	23 1/2	7	3/8	3/16	1.38	65	57	51	46	41	38	35	33	30	28	27	25	24	23	135	48.1	10.7
	142	21 1/2	13 1/8	11/16	3/8	1.38	182	159	141	127	116	106	98	91	85	80	75	71	67	64	205	96	17.8
	127	21 1/4	13	9/16	5/16 +	1.38	163	142	127	114	104	95	88	81	76	71	67	63	60	57	181	83	15.9
	112	21	13	1/2	1/4 +	1.25	143	125	111	100	91	83	77	72	67	63	59	56	53	50	160	73	14.2
	96	21 1/8	9	9/16	5/16	1.38	113	99	88	79	72	66	61	57	53	50	47	44	42	40	176	79	15.5
	82	20 7/8	9	1/2	1/4	1.38	96	84	75	67	61	56	52	48	45	42	40	38	36	34	151	67	13.5
W21	73	21 1/4	8 1/4	7/16	1/4	1.38	86	76	67	61	55	50	47	43	40	38	36	34	32	30	140	59	12.3
	68	21 1/8	8 1/4	7/16	1/4	1.38	80	70	62	56	51	47	43	40	38	35	33	31	30	28	132	55	11.6
	62	21	8 1/4	3/8	3/16 +	1.38	72	63	56	51	46	42	39	36	34	32	30	28	27	26	122	51	10.8
	55	20 3/4	8 1/4	3/8	3/16 +	1.25	63	55	49	44	40	37	34	32	30	28	26	25	23	22	113	46	10.1
	49	20 7/8	6 1/2	3/8	3/16	1.38	53	47	41	37	34	31	29	27	25	23	22	21	19.6	18.7	111	45.3	9.9
	44	20 5/8	6 1/2	3/8	3/16	1.38	46	41	36	33	30	27	25	23	22	20	19.2	18.1	17.2	16.3	104	41.7	9.4
	114	18 1/2	11 7/8	5/8	5/16	1.38	126	110	98	88	80	74	68	63	59	55	52	49	47		159	83	16.1
	105	18 3/8	11 3/4	9/16	5/16	1.38	116	101	90	81	74	68	62	58	54	51	48	45	43		147	77	15.0
	96	18 1/8	11 3/4	1/2	1/4	1.38	106	92	82	74	67	62	57	53	49	46	44	41	39		135	69	13.8
	85	18 3/8	8 7/8	1/2	1/4	1.38	89	78	70	63	57	52	48	45	42	39	37	35	33		140	71	14.2
	77	18 1/8	8 3/4	1/2	1/4	1.38	81	71	63	57	52	47	44	41	38	36	34	32	30		125	63	12.8
	70	18	8 3/4	7/16	1/4	1.38	74	64	57	52	47	43	40	37	34	32	30	29	27		114	57	11.8
W18	64	17 7/8	8 3/4	3/8	3/16	1.38	67	59	52	47	43	39	36	34	31	30	28	26	25		104	52	10.9
	60	18 1/4	7 1/2	7/16	3/16	1.38	62	54	48	43	39	36	33	31	29	27	26	24	23		110	53	11.2
	55	18 1/8	7 1/2	3/8	3/16	1.38	56	49	44	40	36	33	30	28	26	25	23	22	21		102	49	10.5
	50	18	7 1/2	3/8	3/16 +	1.38	51	45	40	36	33	30	28	26	24	23	21	20	19		93	44	9.7
	45	17 7/8	7 1/2	5/16	3/16 +	1.25	45	40	35	32	29	27	25	23	21	20	19	18	17		87	41	9.0
	40	17 7/8	6	5/16	3/16	1.38	39	34	30	27	25	23	21	19.5	18.2	17.1	16.1	15.1	14.4	13.7	82	37.9	8.5
	35	17 3/4	6	5/16	3/16	1.38	33	29	26	23	21	19.3	17.8	16.6	15.5	14.5	13.6	12.9	12.2	11.6	76	34.7	8.0
	96	16 3/8	11 1/2	1/2	1/4	1.38	95	83	74	67	61	56	51	48	45	42	39				127	74	14.4
	88	16 1/8	11 1/2	1/2	1/4	1.38	87	76	67	61	55	51	47	43	41	38	36				118	68	13.6
	78	16 3/8	8 5/8	1/2	1/4	1.38	73	64	57	51	47	43	40	37	34	32	30				125	71	14.3
	71	16 1/8	8 1/2	1/2	1/4	1.38	66	58	52	47	42	39	36	33	31	29	28				114	64	13.1
	64	16	8 1/2	7/16	1/4	1.38	60	52	47	42	38	35	32	30	28	26	25				103	58	12.0
W16	58	15 7/8	8 1/2	7/16	1/4	1.38	54	47	42	38	34	32	29	27	25	24	22				94	52	11.0
	50	16 1/4	7 1/8	3/8	3/16	1.38	46	41	36	33	30	27	25	23	22	20	19				90	47	10.3
	45	16 1/8	7	3/8	3/16	1.38	42	36	32	29	27	24	23	21	20	18	17				81	43	9.3
	40	16	7	5/16	3/16	1.38	37	32	29	26	24	22	20	19	17	16	15				71	37	8.3
	36	15 7/8	7	5/16	3/16 +	1.25	32	28	25	23	21	19	18	16	15	14	13				69	36	8.1
	31	15 7/8	5 1/2	1/4	1/8	1.38	27	24	21	19	17	16	14.5	13.5	12.5	11.8					63.2	32.9	7.4
	26	15 5/8	5 1/2	1/4	1/8 +	1.25	22	19	17	15.3	14	12.7	11.7	10.9	10.2	9.5					56.7	29.1	6.8
	119	14 1/2	14 5/8	9/16	5/16 + ‡	1.25	108	95	84	76	69	63	59	54	51	48	45	42	40		120	78	15.4
	111	14 3/8	14 5/8	9/16	5/16 +	1.25	101	88	79	71	64	59	54	51	47	44	42	39	37		113	73	14.6
W14	103	14 1/4	14 5/8	1/2	1/4 †	1.36	86	75	67	60	55	50	46	43	40	38	36	34	32		102	66	13.4
	95	14 1/8	14 1/2	7/16	1/4 †	1.36	79	69	62	55	50	46	43	40	37	35	33				95	61	12.6
	87	14	14 1/2	7/16	1/4 †	1.36	73	64	57	51	46	42	39	36	34	32					85	55	11.3

REACTION IN KIPS

TABLE 3-4. cont.

Section Number	Weight	Depth	Flange	Web	½ Web	Non-Compact	Conv. Factor	6	8	10	12	14	16	18	20	22	24	26	28	30	32	Maximum Web Shear	3½″ Brg.	1″ Add. Brg.
	84	14 1/8	12	7/16	1/4	+‡	1.25				87	75	66	58	53	48	44	41	38	35		93	59	12.2
	78	14	12	7/16	1/4	+	1.25				80	69	61	54	49	44	41	38	35	33		87	56	11.6
	74	14 1/4	10 1/8	7/16	1/4		1.38			90	75	64	56	50	45	41	38	35	32	30		93	59	12.2
	68	14	10	7/16	1/4	+	1.38			82	68	59	52	46	41	38	35	32	30	28		85	54	11.3
	61	13 7/8	10	3/8	3/16	+	1.25			74	61	53	46	41	37	34	31	29	27	25		76	48	10.2
	53	14	8	3/8	3/16		1.38			62	52	45	39	35	31	29	26	24	22	21		75	47	10.0
	48	13 3/4	8	5/16	3/16	+	1.38			56	47	40	35	31	28	26	24	22	20	19		68	43	9.2
W14	43	13 5/8	8	5/16	3/16	+	1.25			50	42	36	32	28	25	23	21	20	18	17		61	38	8.3
	38	14 1/8	6 3/4	5/16	3/16	+	1.38		55	44	37	31	28	25	22	20	18	17	16	15		64	38	8.5
	34	14	6 3/4	5/16	3/16	‡	1.25		49	39	33	28	25	22	20	18	16	15	14	13		58	34	7.7
	30	13 7/8	6 3/4	1/4	1/8	+	1.25		42	34	28	24	21	19	17	15	14	13	12	11		54	32	7.3
	26	13 7/8	5	1/4	1/8	+	1.38	47	35	28	23	20	17.5	15.5	14	12.7	11.7	10.8	10	9.3		51.4	30.1	6.9
	22	13 3/4	5	1/4	1/8	+	1.25	39	29	23	19	16.5	14.4	12.8	11.5	10.5	9.6	8.9	8.3	7.7		45.8	26.8	6.2
	85	12 1/2	12 1/8	1/2	1/4	+‡	1.25				77	66	58	52	47	42	39	36	33	31	29	90	65	13.4
	79	12 3/8	12 1/8	1/2	1/4	+	1.25				72	61	54	48	43	39	36	33	31	28	27	84	61	12.7
	72	12 1/4	12	7/16	1/4	†	1.36			72	60	51	45	40	36	33	30	28	26	24		76	55	11.6
	65	12 1/8	12	3/8	3/16	†	1.36			65	54	46	41	36	33	30	27	25				69	49	10.5
	58	12 1/4	10	3/8	3/16	+‡	1.25			63	52	45	39	35	31	29	26					63	46	9.7
	53	12	10	3/8	3/16	+	1.25			57	47	41	36	32	29	26	24					60	44	9.3
	50	12 1/4	8 1/8	3/8	3/16		1.38		65	52	43	37	33	29	26	24	22					66	48	10.0
W12	45	12	8	5/16	3/16		1.38		58	47	39	34	29	26	24	21	20					59	43	9.1
	40	12	8	5/16	1/8	+	1.25		51	42	35	30	26	23	21	19	18					51	37	7.9
	36	12 1/4	6 5/8	5/16	1/8		1.38		46	37	31	26	23	21	19	17	16					54	37	8.2
	31	12 1/8	6 1/2	1/4	1/8		1.38		40	32	27	23	20	18	16	15	13					46	31	7.2
	27	12	6 1/2	1/4	1/8	+	1.25		34	28	23	20	17	15	14	13	12					42	28	6.5
	22	12 1/4	4	1/4	1/8		1.38	34	25	20	17	14.5	12.6	11.3	10.1	9.2	8.5					46.4	29.8	7.0
	19	12 1/8	4	1/4	1/8		1.38	29	21	17	14.3	12.3	10.7	9.5	8.6	7.8	7.2					42.3	27.1	6.5
	16.5	12	4	1/4	1/8	+	1.25	23	18	14	11.7	10	8.8	7.8	7	6.4	5.9					40.0	25.6	6.2
	14	11 7/8	4	3/16	1/8	†	1.36	18	13.5	10.9	9.1	7.8	6.8	6.1	5.5	5	4.5					34.5	21.9	5.4

REACTION IN KIPS — Crippling

digit number, followed by a hyphen, a letter, and a one-, two-, or three-digit number. The first of the four digits indicates the major alloying element according to the following code:

		Alloy Number
Aluminum*		1xxx
	Major Alloying Element**	
Copper		2xxx
Manganese		3xxx
Silicon		4xxx
Magnesium		5xxx
Magnesium and Silicon		6xxx
Zinc		7xxx
Other Element		8xxx
Unused Series		9xxx

*Aluminum content is a minimum of 99.00%

**Standard limits for alloying elements and impurities are expressed to the following significance:

Less than 1/1000 percent	0.000x
1/1000 to 1/100 percent	0.00x
1/100 to 1/10 percent	
Unalloyed aluminum made by a refining process	0.0xx
Alloys and unalloyed aluminum not made by a refining process	0.0x
1/10 through 1/2 percent	0.xx
Over 1/2 percent	0.x, x.x, etc.

The second digit indicates alloy modifications; a zero in this position indicates the original alloy, and 1 through 9 are assigned consecutively as modifications are made.

The last two of the four digits identify the alloy within a group.

Temper is indicated by a letter and digits following the hyphen. The more usual temper designations are:

O—Annealed, recrystallized wrought products the softest temper of wrought products

H—Strain hardened wrought products

H12, H14, H16, H18—Indicates strain hardened only—Quarter, half, three-quarters, and full hard respectively.

H111—Indicates products which are strain hardened less than the amount required for a controlled H11 temper (1/8 hard).

H112—Indicates products which acquire some temper from shaping processes not having special control over the amount of strain-hardening or thermal treatment, but for which there are mechanical property limits or mechanical property testing is required.

H22, H24, H26, H28—Indicates strain-hardened and then partially annealed—Quarter, half, three-quarters, and full hard respectively.

H32, H34, H36, H38—Indicates strain-hardened and then stabilized—Quarter, half, three-quarters, and full hard respectively.

H311—Indicates products which are strain-hardened less than the amount required for a controlled H31 temper. (1/8 hard).

H321—Indicates products that are strain-hardened less than the amount required for a controlled H32 temper.

H323 and H343—Indicate products of alloys containing more than 4% magnesium that are specially fabricated to have acceptable resistance to stress-corrosion cracking.

T—Thermally treated to produce stable tempers other than O or H. Applies to products which are thermally treated, with or without supplementary strain-hardening, to produce stable tempers. The T is always followed by one or more digits. Some of these are:

T3—Solution heat-treated and then cold worked. Applies to products which are cold worked to improve strength or in which the effect of cold work in flattening or straightening is recognized in applicable specifications.

T4—Solution heat-treated and naturally aged to a substantially stable condition. Applies to products which are not cold worked after solution heat-treatment, or in which the effect of cold work in

flattening or straightening may not be recognized in applicable specifications.

T5—Cooled from an elevated temperature shaping process and then artificially aged. Applied to products which are cooled from an elevated temperature shaping process, such as casting or extrusion, and then artificially aged to improve mechanical properties or dimensional stability or both.

T6—Solution heat-treated and then artificially aged. Applies to products which are not cold worked after solution heat treatment, or in which the effect of cold work in flattening or straightening may not be recognized in applicable specifications.

T651—Stress-relieved by stretching from 1/2% to 3% depending upon the product after solution heat treatment.

T6510—Products having no further straightening after stretching.

T6511—Products that may receive minor straightening after stretching to comply with standard tolerances.

T7—Solution heat-treated and stabilized.

T8—Solution heat-treated, cold worked, and then artificially aged.

T9—Solution heat-treated, artificially aged, and then cold worked.

Composition, Applications, and Properties

Table 3–5 gives nominal composition, commercial forms, and typical applications for basic alloys. For some of the more popular alloys, details on characteristics are given in Table 3–6, as a function of temper. Mechanical properties for alloys, identified by their alloy number and temper, are given in Table 3–7.

TABLE 3-5. Composition and applications of aluminum alloys.

ALLOY DESIGNATION	NOMINAL COMPOSITION, %	COMMERCIAL FORMS a	CHARACTERISTICS b					TYPICAL APPLICATIONS
			Corrosion Resistance	Machinability	Weldability c	Maximum Strength d	Annealed Strength e	
EC	99.45 Al min	STEPBW	A-A	D-C	A-A	27	10	Electrical conductors
1060	99.60 Al min	STW	—	—	—	20	10	Chemical equipment; railroad tank cars
1100	99.00 Al min, 0.12 Cu	STEBWFO	A-A	D-C	A-A	24	13	Sheet metal work; spun hollow ware
1145	99.45 Al min	SO	A-A	D-C	A-A	28	12	Foil; light sheet metal work
2011	5.5 Cu, 0.5 Bi, 0.5 Pb	BW	C-C	A-A	D-D	60	—	Screw machine products
2014	4.4 Cu, 0.8 Si, 0.8 Mn, 0.4 Mg	STEBF	C-C	B-B	B-C	70	27	Truck frames; aircraft structures
2017	4.0 Cu, 0.5 Mn, 0.5 Mg	BW	C	B	B-C	62	26	Screw machine products, fittings
2018	4.0 Cu, 0.6 Mg, 2.0 Ni	F	C	B	B-C	61	—	Aircraft engine cylinder heads and pistons
2024	4.5 Cu, 0.6 Mn, 1.5 Mg	STPEBW	C-C	B-B	B-B	75	27	Truck wheels; screw machine products; aircraft structures
2025	4.5 Cu, 0.8 Si, 0.8 Mn	F	C-D	B-B	B-B	58	25	Forgings; aircraft propellers
2117	2.5 Cu, 0.3 Mg	WB	C	C	B-C	43	—	Rivets and redraw rod
2218	4.0 Cu, 1.5 Mg, 2.0 Ni	F	C	B	B-C	48	—	Jet engine impellers and rings
2219	6.3 Cu, 0.3 Mn, 0.10 V, 0.15 Zr	SEF	B	B	A	70	25	Structural use at high temperatures (to 600 F); high-strength weldments
2618	2.3 Cu, 1.6 Mg, 1.0 Ni, 1.1 Fe	F	C	B	B-C	64	—	Aircraft engines (temperatures to 450 F)
3003	1.2 Mn, 0.12 Cu	All forms	A-A	D-C	A-A	30	16	Cooking utensils; chemical equipment; pressure vessels; sheet metal work; builder's hardware
3004	1.2 Mn, 1.0 Mg	S	A-A	D-C	A-A	41	26	Sheet metal work; storage tanks
4032	12.2 Si, 0.9 Cu, 1.1 Mg, 0.9 Ni	F	C-D	D-C	B-C	55	—	Pistons
4043	5.0 Si	W	—	—	—	—	—	Welding wire
4343	7.5 Si	SW	—	—	—	—	—	Brazing sheet and wire
5005	0.8 Mg	SWO	A-A	D-C	A-A	30	18	Appliances and utensils; architectural; electrical conductor
5050	1.4 Mg	STPO	A-A	D-C	A-A	32	21	Builders' hardware, refrigerator trim and coiled tubes
5052	2.5 Mg, 0.25 Cr	STBWPO	A-A	D-C	A-A	42	28	Sheet metal work; hydraulic tube; appliances
5056	5.2 Mg, 0.1 Mn, 0.10 Cr	BW	A-C	D-C	A-A	63	42	Cable sheating; rivets for magnesium; screen wire; zippers
5083	4.5 Mg, 0.7 Mn, 0.15 Cr	SEBF	A-C	D-C	A-B	52	42	Unfired, welded pressure vessels; marine, auto and aircraft; cryogenics; TV towers, drilling rigs; transportation equipment; missile components
5086	4.0 Mg, 0.5 Mn, 0.15 Cr	SETP	A-C	D-C	A-B	50	38	
5154	3.5 Mg, 0.25 Cr	STPEBW	A-A	D-C	A-A	48	35	Welded structures; storage tanks; pressure vessels; salt-water service
5252	2.5 Mg, 0.25 Cr	S	A-A	D-C	A-A	39	28	Automobile trim
5356	5.0 Mg, 0.1 Mn, 0.10 Cr	W	—	—	—	—	—	Welding wire
5454	2.7 Mg, 0.8 Mn, 0.10 Cr	STPEB	A-A	D-C	A-A	44	36	Welded structures and pressure vessels; marine service
5456	5.1 Mg, 0.8 Mn, 0.10 Cr	SEP	A-B	D-C	A	56	45	High-strength welded structures; storage tanks; pressure vessels; marine applications
5657	0.8 Mg	S	A-A	D-C	A-A	32	19	Anodized auto and appliance trim
6053	0.7 Si, 1.3 Mg, 0.25 Cr	BW	A-B	C	B-C	42	16	Wire and rod for rivets
6061	0.6 Si, 1.0 Mg, 0.25 Cu, 0.20 Cr	STPEBWF	A-A	B-C	A-A	45	18	Heavy-duty structures where corrosion resistance needed; truck and marine; railroad cars, furniture, pipelines
6063	0.4 Si, 0.7 Mg	TPE	A-A	D-C	A-A	42	13	Pipe railing; furniture, architectural extrusions
6066	1.3 Si, 1.1 Mg, 1.0 Cu, 0.9 Mn	TPEBF	B-C	D-B	A-A	57	22	Forgings and extrusions for welded structures
6101	0.5 Si, 0.6 Mg	TPEB	A-B	B-C	A-B	32	14	High-strength bus conductors
6151	1.0 Si, 0.6 Mg, 0.25 Cr	F	A-B	C	A-B	48	—	Moderate-strength intricate forgings for machine and auto parts
6262	0.6 Si, 1.0 Mg, 0.25 Cu, 0.09 Cr, 0.6 Pb, 0.6 Bi	WB	A-A	A-A	B-B	58	—	Screw machine products
6463	0.4 Si, 0.7 Mg	E	A-A	D-C	A-A	35	22	Architectural and trim extrusions
7001	7.4 Zn, 2.1 Cu, 3.0 Mg, 0.30 Cr	TEB	C	B	D	98	32	High-strength structures
7039	4.0 Zn, 0.2 Mn, 2.7 Mg, 0.20 Cr	S	A-C	B	D	60	32	Welded cryogenic and missile applications
7072	1.0 Zn	S	A-A	D-C	A-A	74	13	Fin stock
7075	5.6 Zn, 1.6 Cu, 2.5 Mg, 0.30 Cr	STEBWF	C	B	D	83	33	Aircraft and other structures; keys
7079	4.3 Zn, 0.6 Cu, 0.2 Mn, 3.3 Mg, 0.20 Cr	EFS	C	B	D	78	32	Structural parts for aircraft
7178	6.8 Zn, 2.0 Cu, 2.7 Mg, 0.30 Cr	STEP	C	B	D	88	33	Aircraft and other structural uses

a B—bar or rod; E—extrusions; F—forgings or forging stock; O—foil; P—pipe; S—sheet or plate; T—tube; W—wire.

b Relative ratings in decreasing order of merit—A, B, C, D. Where applicable, ratings for both annealed and hardest tempers are given (for example, A-C).

c Weldability: A—generally weldable; B—weldable with special techniques for specific applications; C—limited weldability; D—not weldable. Ratings are given for arc welding. Gas welding and brazeability ratings are the same or differ by only one; exceptions are most of the 2000 and 7000 series alloys.

d Typical maximum tensile strength in kips per square inch, for fully work-hardened condition or heat-treated to highest strength level. (Multiply by 0.703 to convert to kilograms per square millimeter.)

e Typical annealed tensile strength in kips per square inch. (Multiply by 0.703 to convert to kilograms per square millimeter.)

TABLE 3-6. Typical characteristics.

ALLOY AND TEMPER	RESISTANCE TO CORROSION	WORKABILITY (COLD)	MACHINABILITY	BRAZEABILITY	WELDABILITY			FORGEABILITY
					GAS	ARC	RESISTANCE SPOT & STEAM	
EC-0	A	A	D	A	A	A	B	—
-H12	A	A	D	A	A	A	A	—
-H14	A	A	C	A	A	A	A	—
-H16	A	B	C	A	A	A	A	—
-H19	A	C	C	A	A	A	A	—
1100-0	A	A	D	A	A	A	B	A
-H12	A	A	D	A	A	A	A	A
-H14	A	A	C	A	A	A	A	A
-H16	A	B	C	A	A	A	A	A
-H18	A	C	C	A	A	A	A	A
2011-T3	C	C	A	D	D	D	B	—
-T8	C	D	A	D	D	D	B	—
2014-T4	C	C	B	D	D	B	B	C
-T6	C	D	B	D	D	B	B	C
2017-T4	C	C	B	D	D	B	B	—
2018-T61	C	—	B	D	D	B	B	C
2024-T3	C	C	B	D	D	B	B	—
-T4	C	C	B	D	D	B	B	—
-T36	C	D	B	D	D	B	B	—
2117-T4	C	B	C	D	D	B	B	—
2218-T72	C	—	B	D	—	B	—	D
3003-0	A	A	D	A	A	A	B	A
-H12	A	A	D	A	A	A	A	A
-H14	A	B	C	A	A	A	A	A
-H16	A	C	C	A	A	A	A	A
-H18	A	C	C	A	A	A	A	A
3004-0	A	A	D	B	B	A	B	—
-H32	A	B	D	B	B	A	A	—
-H34	A	B	C	B	B	A	A	—
-H36	A	C	C	B	B	A	A	—
-H38	A	C	C	B	B	A	A	—
5005-0	A	A	D	B	A	A	B	—
-H12	A	A	D	B	A	A	A	—
-H14	A	B	C	B	A	A	A	—
-H16	A	C	C	B	A	A	A	—
-H18	A	C	C	B	A	A	A	—
-H32	A	A	D	B	A	A	A	—
-H34	A	B	C	B	A	A	A	—
-H36	A	C	C	B	A	A	A	—
-H38	A	C	C	B	A	A	A	—

ALLOY AND TEMPER	RESISTANCE TO CORROSION	WORKABILITY (COLD)	MACHINABILITY	BRAZEABILITY	WELDABILITY			FORGEABILITY
					GAS	ARC	RESISTANCE SPOT & STEAM	
5050-0	A	A	D	B	A	A	B	—
-H32	A	B	D	B	A	A	A	—
-H34	A	B	C	B	A	A	A	—
-H36	A	C	C	B	A	A	A	—
-H38	A	C	C	B	A	A	A	—
5052-0	A	A	D	C	A	A	B	—
-H32	A	B	C	D	A	A	A	—
-H34	A	B	C	C	A	A	A	—
-H36	A	C	C	C	A	A	A	—
-H38	A	C	C	C	A	A	A	—
5056-0	A	A	D	D	C	A	B	—
-H38	C	C	C	D	C	A	A	—
5086-0	A	A	D	D	C	A	B	—
-H32	A	B	D	D	C	A	A	—
-H34	B	B	C	D	C	A	A	—
-H36	B	C	C	D	C	A	A	—
-H38	B	C	C	D	C	A	A	—
5154-0	A	A	D	D	C	A	B	—
-H32	A	B	D	D	C	A	A	—
-H34	A	B	C	D	C	A	A	—
-H36	A	C	C	D	C	A	A	—
-H38	A	C	C	D	C	A	A	—
-H112	A	B	D	D	C	A	A	—
6061-0	A	A	D	A	A	A	B	—
-T4	A	C	C	A	A	A	A	—
-T6	A	C	C	A	A	A	A	—
6063-0	A	A	D	A	A	A	B	—
-T1†	A	B	C	A	A	A	A	—
-T4	A	B	C	A	A	A	A	—
-T5	A	B	C	A	A	A	A	—
-T6	A	C	C	A	A	A	A	—
-T83	A	C	C	A	A	A	A	—
-T831	A	C	C	A	A	A	A	—
-T832	A	C	C	A	A	A	A	—
6066-0	B	B	D	A	A	A	B	—
-T4	B	C	B	A	A	A	A	—
-T6	B	C	B	A	A	A	A	—
7001-T6	C	D	B	D	D	D	B	D
7075-T6	C	D	B	D	D	D	B	—

* Resistance to Corrosion, Workability (Cold), Machinability and Forgeability ratings A, B, C and D are relative ratings in decreasing order of merit.

Weldability and Brazeability ratings A, B, C and D are relative ratings defined as follows:

A. Generally weldable by all commercial procedures and methods.

B. Weldable with special technique or on specific applications which justify preliminary trials or testing to develop welding procedure and weld performance.

C. Limited weldability because of crack sensitivity or loss in resistance to corrosion, and all mechanical properties.

D. No commonly used welding methods have so far been developed.

† Formerly designated T42.

TABLE 3-7. Mechanical properties for some wrought aluminum alloys.

Values Are Given in Units of ksi (1000 lb/in ^{2})

| Alloy And Temper | Product* | Thickness Range* in. | TENSION | | COM-PRES-SION | SHEAR | | BEARING | | Compressive Modulus of Elasticity‡ |
			F_{tu}† ksi	F_{ty}† ksi	F_{cy} ksi	F_{su} ksi	F_{sy} ksi	F_{bu} ksi	F_{by} ksi	E ksi
1100-H12	Sheet, Plate	All	14	11	10	9	6.5	28	18	10,100
-H14	Rolled Rod & Bar	All	16	14	13	10	8	32	21	10,100
	Drawn Tube									
2014-T6	Sheet	0.040-0.249	66	58	59	40	33	125	93	10,900
-T651	Plate	0.250-2.000	67	59	58	40	34	127	94	10,900
-T6,T6510**	Extrusions	All	60	53	55	35	31	114	85	10,900
-T6,T651	Rolled Rod & Bar Drawn Tube	All	65	55	53	38	32	124	88	10,900
Alclad 2014-T6	Sheet	0.020-0.039	63	55	56	38	32	120	88	10,800
-T6	Sheet	0.040-0.249	64	57	58	39	33	122	91	10,800
-T651	Plate	0.250-0.499	64	57	56	39	33	122	91	10,800
3003-H12	Sheet & Plate	0.017-2.000	17	12	10	11	7	34	19	10,100
-H14	Sheet & Plate	0.009-1.000	20	17	14	12	10	40	25	10,100
-H16	Sheet	0.006-0.162	24	21	18	14	12	46	31	10,100
-H18	Sheet	0.006-0.128	27	24	20	15	14	49	34	10,100
3003-H12	Drawn Tube	All	17	12	10	11	7	34	19	10,100
-H14	Drawn Tube	All	20	17	16	12	10	40	25	10,100
-H16	Drawn Tube	All	24	21	19	14	12	46	31	10,100
-H18	Drawn Tube	All	27	24	21	15	14	49	34	10,100
Alclad 3003-H12	Sheet & Plate	0.017-2.000	16	11	9	10	6.5	32	18	10,100
-H14	Sheet & Plate	0.009-1.000	19	16	13	12	9	38	24	10,100
-H16	Sheet	0.006-0.162	23	20	17	14	12	44	30	10,100
-H18	Sheet	0.006-0.128	26	23	19	15	13	47	32	10,100
Alclad 3003-H14	Drawn Tube	0.010-0.500	19	16	15	12	9	38	24	10,100
-H18	Drawn Tube	0.010-0.500	26	23	20	15	13	47	32	10,100
3004-H32	Sheet & Plate	0.017-2.000	28	21	18	17	12	56	36	10,100
-H34	Sheet & Plate	0.009-1.000	32	25	22	19	14	64	40	10,100
-H36	Sheet	0.006-0.162	35	28	25	20	16	70	45	10,100
3004-H34	Drawn Tube	0.018-0.450	32	25	24	19	14	64	40	10,100
-H36	Drawn Tube	0.018-0.450	35	28	27	20	16	70	45	10,100
Alclad 3004-H32	Sheet	0.017-0.249	27	20	17	16	12	54	34	10,100
-H34	Sheet	0.009-0.249	31	24	21	18	14	62	38	10,100
-H36	Sheet	0.006-0.162	34	27	24	19	16	68	43	10,100
-H14	Sheet	0.009-0.249	32	26	22	19	15	64	39	10,100
-H16	Sheet	0.006-0.162	35	30	26	20	17	66	45	10,100
-H131,H241,H341	Sheet	0.024-0.050	31	26	22	18	15	62	39	10,100
-H151,H261,H361	Sheet	0.024-0.050	34	30	26	19	17	66	45	10,100
3005-H25	Sheet	0.013-0.050	26	22	20	15	13	49	35	10,100
5005-H12	Sheet & Plate	0.018-2.000	18	14	13	11	8	34	22	10,100
-H14	Sheet & Plate	0.009-1.000	21	17	15	12	10	40	25	10,100
-H16	Sheet	0.006-0.162	24	20	18	14	12	48	30	10,100
-H32	Sheet & Plate	0.017-2.000	17	12	11	11	7	34	20	10,100
-H34	Sheet & Plate	0.009-1.000	20	15	14	12	8.5	40	24	10,100
-H36	Sheet	0.006-0.162	23	18	16	13	11	48	29	10,100

TABLE 3-7. cont.

Alloy And Temper	Product*	Thickness Range* in.	TENSION		COM-PRES-SION	SHEAR		BEARING		Compressive Modulus of Elasticity‡
			F_{tu}† ksi	F_{ty}† ksi	F_{cy} ksi	F_{su} ksi	F_{sy} ksi	F_{bu} ksi	F_{by} ksi	E ksi
5050-H32	Sheet	0.017-0.249	22	16	14	14	9	44	27	10,100
-H34	Sheet	0.009-0.249	25	20	18	15	12	50	32	10,100
-H32	Rolled Rod & Bar Drawn Tube	All	22	16	15	13	9	44	27	10,100
-H34	Rolled Rod & Bar Drawn Tube	All	25	20	19	15	12	50	32	10,100
5052-H32	Sheet & Plate	All	31	23	21	19	13	60	39	10,200
-H34	Rolled Rod & Bar Drawn Tube	All	34	26	24	20	15	65	44	10,200
-H36	Sheet	0.006-0.162	37	29	26	22	17	70	46	10,200
5083-H111	Extrusions	up thru 0.500	40	24	21	24	14	78	41	10,400
-H111	Extrusions	0.501 and over	40	24	21	23	14	78	38	10,400
-H321	Sheet & Plate	0.188-1.500	44	31	26	26	18	84	53	10,400
-H323	Sheet	0.051-0.249	45	34	32	26	20	88	58	10,400
-H343	Sheet	0.051-0.249	50	39	37	29	23	95	66	10,400
-H321	Plate	1.501-3.000	41	29	24	24	17	78	49	10,400
5086-H111	Extrusions	up thru 0.500	36	21	18	21	12	70	36	10,400
-H111	Extrusions	0.501 and over	36	21	18	21	12	70	34	10,400
-H112	Plate	0.250-0.499	36	18	17	22	10	72	31	10,400
-H112	Plate	0.500-1.000	35	16	16	21	9	70	28	10,400
-H112	Plate	1.001-2.000	35	14	15	21	8	70	28	10,400
-H112	Plate	2.001-3.000	34	14	15	21	8	68	28	10,400
-H32	Sheet & Plate	All	40	28	26	24	16	78	48	10,400
-H34	Drawn Tube	All	44	34	32	26	20	84	58	10,400
5154-H38	Sheet	0.006-0.128	45	35	33	24	20	81	56	10,300
5454-H111	Extrusions	up thru 0.500	33	19	16	20	11	64	32	10,400
-H111	Extrusions	0.501 and over	33	19	16	19	11	64	30	10,400
-H112	Extrusions	up thru 5.000	31	12	13	19	7	62	24	10,400
-H32	Sheet & Plate	0.020-2.000	36	26	24	21	15	70	44	10,400
-H34	Sheet & Plate	0.020-1.000	39	29	27	23	17	74	49	10,400
5456-H111	Extrusions	up thru 0.500	42	26	22	25	15	82	44	10,400
-H111	Extrusions	0.501 and over	42	26	22	24	15	82	42	10,400
-H112	Extrusions	up thru 5.000	41	19	20	24	11	82	38	10,400
-H321	Sheet & Plate	0.188-1.250	46	33	27	27	19	87	56	10,400
-H321	Plate	1.251-1.500	44	31	25	25	18	84	53	10,400
-H321	Plate	1.501-3.000	41	29	25	25	17	82	49	10,400
-H323	Sheet	0.051-0.249	48	36	34	28	21	94	61	10,400
-H343	Sheet	0.051-0.249	53	41	39	31	24	101	70	10,400
6005-T5	Extrusions	up thru 0.500	38	35	35	24	20	80	56	10,100
6061-T6,T651	Sheet & Plate	0.010-4.000	42	35	35	27	20	88	58	10,100
-T6,T6510**	Extrusions	up thru 3.000	38	35	35	24	20	80	56	10,100
-T6,T651	Rolled Rod & Bar	up thru 8.000	42	35	35	27	20	88	56	10,100
-T6	Drawn Tube	0.025-0.500	42	35	35	27	20	88	56	10,100
-T6	Pipe	up thru 0.999	42	35	35	27	20	88	56	10,100
-T6	Pipe	over 0.999	38	35	35	24	20	80	56	10,100
6063-T5	Extrusions	up thru 0.500	22	16	16	13	9	46	26	10,100
-T5	Extrusions	over 0.500	21	15	15	12	8.5	44	24	10,100
-T6	Extrusions, Pipe	All	30	25	25	19	14	63	40	10,100
6351-T5	Extrusions	up thru 1.00	38	35	35	24	20	80	56	10,100

* Most product and thickness ranges are taken from The Aluminum Association's 1968-1969 edition of "Aluminum Standards and Data."

† F_{tu} and F_{ty} are minimum specified values (except for Alclad 3004-H14, -H16 and F_{ty} for Alclad 3003-H18) other strength properties are corresponding minimum expected values.

‡ For deflection calculations an average modulus of elasticity is used; numerically this is 100 ksi lower than the values in this column.

** Values also apply to -T6511 temper.

TABLE 3-8. Standard I-beams.

—ALUMINUM ASSOCIATION STANDARD I-BEAMS— DIMENSIONS, AREAS, WEIGHTS AND SECTION PROPERTIES

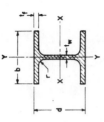

Size		Area* in.²	Weight† lb/ft	Flange Thickness t_f in.	Web Thickness t_w in.	Fillet Radius R in.	Section Properties‡					
Depth d in.	Width b in.						Axis X-X			Axis Y-Y		
							I in.⁴	S in.³	r in.	I in.⁴	S in.³	r in.
3.00	2.50	1.392	1.637	0.20	0.13	0.25	2.24	1.49	1.27	0.52	0.42	0.61
3.00	2.50	1.726	2.030	0.26	0.15	0.25	2.71	1.81	1.25	0.68	0.54	0.63
4.00	3.00	1.965	2.311	0.23	0.15	0.25	5.62	2.81	1.69	1.04	0.69	0.73
4.00	3.00	2.375	2.793	0.29	0.17	0.25	6.71	3.36	1.68	1.31	0.87	0.74
5.00	3.50	3.146	3.700	0.32	0.19	0.30	13.94	5.58	2.11	2.29	1.31	0.85
6.00	4.00	3.427	4.030	0.29	0.19	0.30	21.99	7.33	2.53	3.10	1.55	0.95
6.00	4.00	3.990	4.692	0.35	0.21	0.30	25.50	8.50	2.53	3.74	1.87	0.97
7.00	4.50	4.932	5.800	0.38	0.23	0.30	42.89	12.25	2.95	5.78	2.57	1.08
8.00	5.00	5.256	6.181	0.35	0.23	0.30	59.69	14.92	3.37	7.30	2.92	1.18
8.00	5.00	5.972	7.023	0.41	0.25	0.30	67.78	16.94	3.37	8.55	3.42	1.20
9.00	5.50	7.110	8.361	0.44	0.27	0.30	102.02	22.67	3.79	12.22	4.44	1.31
10.00	6.00	7.352	8.646	0.41	0.25	0.40	132.09	26.42	4.24	14.78	4.93	1.42
10.00	6.00	8.747	10.286	0.50	0.29	0.40	155.79	31.16	4.22	18.03	6.01	1.44
12.00	7.00	9.925	11.672	0.47	0.29	0.40	255.57	42.60	5.07	26.90	7.69	1.65
12.00	7.00	12.153	14.292	0.62	0.31	0.40	317.33	52.89	5.11	35.48	10.14	1.71

* Areas listed are based on nominal dimensions.
† Weights per foot are based on nominal dimensions and a density of 0.098 pound per cubic inch which is the density of alloy 6061.

‡ I = moment of inertia; S = section modulus; r = radius of gyration.

TABLE 3-9. Standard channels.

aluminum association channels and I-beams/**structural shapes**

**—ALUMINUM ASSOCIATION STANDARD CHANNELS—
DIMENSIONS, AREAS, WEIGHTS
AND SECTION PROPERTIES**

| Size | | Area* | Weight† | Flange Thick-ness | Web Thick-ness | Fillet Radius | Section Properties ‡ | | | | | | |
| Depth d in. | Width b in. | in.² | lb/ft | t_f in. | t_w in. | R in. | Axis X-X | | | Axis Y-Y | | | |
							I in.⁴	S in.³	r in.	I in.⁴	S in.³	r in.	x in.
2.00	1.00	0.491	0.577	0.13	0.13	0.10	0.288	0.288	0.766	0.045	0.064	0.303	0.298
2.00	1.25	0.911	1.071	0.26	0.17	0.15	0.546	0.546	0.774	0.139	0.178	0.397	0.471
3.00	1.50	0.965	1.135	0.20	0.13	0.25	1.41	0.94	1.21	0.22	0.22	0.47	0.49
3.00	1.75	1.358	1.597	0.26	0.17	0.25	1.97	1.31	1.20	0.42	0.37	0.55	0.62
4.00	2.00	1.478	1.738	0.23	0.15	0.25	3.91	1.95	1.63	0.60	0.45	0.64	0.65
4.00	2.25	1.982	2.331	0.29	0.19	0.25	5.21	2.60	1.62	1.02	0.69	0.72	0.78
5.00	2.25	1.881	2.212	0.26	0.15	0.30	7.88	3.15	2.05	0.98	0.64	0.72	0.73
5.00	2.75	2.627	3.089	0.32	0.19	0.30	11.14	4.45	2.06	2.05	1.14	0.88	0.95
6.00	2.50	2.410	2.834	0.29	0.17	0.30	14.35	4.78	2.44	1.53	0.90	0.80	0.79
6.00	3.25	3.427	4.030	0.35	0.21	0.30	21.04	7.01	2.48	3.76	1.76	1.05	1.12
7.00	2.75	2.725	3.205	0.29	0.17	0.30	22.09	6.31	2.85	2.10	1.10	0.88	0.84
7.00	3.50	4.009	4.715	0.38	0.21	0.30	33.79	9.65	2.90	5.13	2.23	1.13	1.20
8.00	3.00	3.526	4.147	0.35	0.19	0.30	37.40	9.35	3.26	3.25	1.57	0.96	0.93
8.00	3.75	4.923	5.789	0.41	0.25	0.35	52.69	13.17	3.27	7.13	2.82	1.20	1.22
9.00	3.25	4.237	4.983	0.35	0.23	0.35	54.41	12.09	3.58	4.40	1.89	1.02	0.93
9.00	4.00	5.927	6.970	0.44	0.29	0.35	78.31	17.40	3.63	9.61	3.49	1.27	1.25
10.00	3.50	5.218	6.136	0.41	0.25	0.35	83.22	16.64	3.99	6.33	2.56	1.10	1.02
10.00	4.25	7.109	8.360	0.50	0.31	0.40	116.15	23.23	4.04	13.02	4.47	1.35	1.34
12.00	4.00	7.036	8.274	0.47	0.29	0.40	159.76	26.63	4.77	11.03	3.86	1.25	1.14
12.00	5.00	10.053	11.822	0.62	0.35	0.45	239.69	39.95	4.88	25.74	7.60	1.60	1.61

* Areas listed are based on nominal dimensions.
† Weights per foot are based on nominal dimensions and a density of 0.098 pound per cubic inch which is the density of alloy 6061.

‡ I = moment of inertia; S = section modulus; r = radius of gyration.

Structural Shapes

Because of the extrusion process used to manufacture aluminum structurals, a series of new standard I-beams and channels, optimized for aluminum's properties, has been established by the industry. Standard shapes have straight flanges, and dimension proportions have been changed from the conventional shapes, which were patterned after familiar steel shapes.

Tables 3–8 and 3–9 give data on Aluminum Association Standard I-beams and Standard channels.

Some conventional shapes are given in the next series of tables. Table 3–10 shows American Standard I-beams and Table 3–11 shows American Standard channels. Wide-flange H-beams are shown in Table 3–12.

Some special channels are detailed in Table 3–13 along with an indication of normal availability from warehouse stocks.

Dissimilar Metals: Minimizing damage from battery action

Because they are the most active, metals near the top of Table 3–14 will be the negative pole and will be more likely to form stable compounds. When it is not practicable to avoid contact between dissimilar metals, the one that is most difficult to replace should be selected from lower on the list than the other. For example, if a threaded stud and a nut are to be used, one aluminum and the other copper, the latter material should be used for the stud because it is likely that the aluminum part will corrode away in time and the nut will be easier to replace.

The closer to each other the metals are in the table, the slower will be the action.

TABLE 3-14. Electromotive series.

Potassium	Nickel
Sodium	Tin
Barium	Lead
Strontium	Hydrogen
Calcium	Copper
Magnesium	Arsenic
Aluminum	Bismuth
Manganese	Antimony
Zinc	Mercury
Chromium	Silver
Cadmium	Palladium
Iron	Platinum
Cobalt	Gold

TABLE 3-10. American Standard I-beams.

american standard I-beams/**structural shapes**

—I-BEAMS—AMERICAN STANDARD

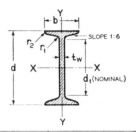

Size									Axis X-X			Axis Y-Y		
Depth d in.	Weight lb/ft	Width b in.	Web Thickness t_w in.	Area in²	Avg Flange Thickness in.	r_1 in.	r_2 in.	d_1 in.	I in.⁴	S in.³	r in.	I in.⁴	S in.³	r in.
* 3	1.96	2.330	0.170	1.67	0.257	0.27	0.10	1¾	2.52	1.68	1.23	0.46	0.39	0.52
3	2.25	2.411	0.251	1.91	0.257	0.27	0.10	1¾	2.71	1.80	1.19	0.51	0.42	0.52
* 3	2.59	2.509	0.349	2.21	0.257	0.27	0.10	1¾	2.93	1.95	1.15	0.59	0.47	0.52
* 4	2.64	2.660	0.190	2.25	0.289	0.29	0.11	2¾	6.06	3.03	1.64	0.76	0.57	0.58
* 4	3.28	2.796	0.326	2.79	0.289	0.29	0.11	2¾	6.79	3.39	1.56	0.90	0.65	0.57
* 5	3.43	3.000	0.210	2.92	0.323	0.31	0.13	3½	12.26	4.90	2.05	1.21	0.81	0.64
5	4.23	3.137	0.347	3.60	0.323	0.31	0.13	3½	13.69	5.48	1.95	1.41	0.90	0.63
* 5	5.10	3.284	0.494	4.34	0.323	0.31	0.13	3½	15.22	6.09	1.87	1.66	1.01	0.62
* 6	4.30	3.330	0.230	3.66	0.355	0.33	0.14	4½	22.08	7.36	2.46	1.82	1.09	0.71
* 6	5.10	3.443	0.343	4.34	0.355	0.33	0.14	4½	24.11	8.04	2.36	2.04	1.19	0.69
6	5.96	3.565	0.465	5.07	0.355	0.33	0.14	4½	26.31	8.77	2.28	2.31	1.30	0.68
7	5.27	3.660	0.250	4.48	0.389	0.35	0.15	5¼	36.69	10.48	2.86	2.63	1.44	0.77
* 7	6.05	3.755	0.345	5.15	0.389	0.35	0.15	5¼	39.40	11.26	2.77	2.88	1.53	0.75
7	6.92	3.860	0.450	5.88	0.389	0.35	0.15	5¼	42.40	12.12	2.69	3.17	1.64	0.73
* 8	6.35	4.000	0.270	5.40	0.421	0.37	0.16	6¼	57.55	14.39	3.27	3.73	1.86	0.83
8	7.96	4.171	0.441	6.77	0.421	0.37	0.16	6¼	64.85	16.21	3.10	4.31	2.07	0.80
* 8	8.81	4.262	0.532	7.49	0.421	0.37	0.16	6¼	68.73	17.18	3.03	4.66	2.19	0.79
9	7.51	4.330	0.290	6.38	0.453	0.39	0.17	7	85.90	19.09	3.67	5.09	2.35	0.89
* 10	8.76	4.660	0.310	7.45	0.487	0.41	0.19	8	123.39	24.68	4.07	6.78	2.91	0.95
10	10.37	4.797	0.447	8.82	0.487	0.41	0.19	8	134.81	26.96	3.91	7.50	3.13	0.92
10	12.10	4.944	0.594	10.29	0.487	0.41	0.19	8	147.06	29.41	3.78	8.36	3.38	0.90
* 12	10.99	5.000	0.350	9.35	0.538	0.45	0.21	9¾	218.13	36.35	4.83	9.35	3.74	1.00
12	12.09	5.078	0.428	10.28	0.538	0.45	0.21	9¾	229.36	38.23	4.72	9.87	3.89	0.98
12	14.08	5.250	0.460	11.97	0.653	0.56	0.28	9¼	272.15	45.36	4.77	13.54	5.16	1.06
12	15.56	5.355	0.565	13.23	0.653	0.56	0.28	9¼	287.27	47.88	4.66	14.50	5.42	1.05
12	17.28	5.477	0.687	14.70	0.653	0.56	0.28	9¼	304.84	50.81	4.56	15.71	5.74	1.03

* Standard shapes normally available from warehouse stocks.

TABLE 3-11. American Standard channels.

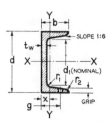

Size		Width b	Web Thickness t_w	Area	Avg Flange Thickness	r_1	r_2	d_1	Axis X-X			Axis Y-Y			
Depth d in.	Weight lb/ft	in.	in.	in.²	in.	in.	in.	in.	I in⁴	S in³	r in.	I in⁴	S in³	r in.	x in.
* 3	1.42	1.410	0.170	1.20	0.270	0.27	0.10	1¾	1.66	1.10	1.17	0.20	0.20	0.40	0.44
3	1.48	1.427	0.187	1.26	0.270	0.27	0.10	1¾	1.69	1.13	1.16	0.21	0.21	0.41	0.44
* 3	1.73	1.498	0.258	1.47	0.270	0.27	0.10	1¾	1.85	1.24	1.12	0.25	0.23	0.41	0.44
3	1.95	1.560	0.320	1.66	0.270	0.27	0.10	1¾	1.99	1.33	1.10	0.28	0.25	0.41	0.45
* 3	2.07	1.596	0.356	1.76	0.270	0.27	0.10	1¾	2.07	1.38	1.08	0.31	0.27	0.42	0.46
* 4	1.85	1.580	0.180	1.57	0.293	0.28	0.11	2¾	3.83	1.92	1.56	0.32	0.28	0.45	0.46
* 4	2.16	1.647	0.247	1.84	0.293	0.28	0.11	2¾	4.19	2.10	1.51	0.37	0.31	0.45	0.45
* 4	2.50	1.720	0.320	2.13	0.293	0.28	0.11	2¾	4.58	2.29	1.47	0.43	0.34	0.45	0.46
* 5	2.32	1.750	0.190	1.97	0.317	0.29	0.11	3¾	7.49	3.00	1.95	0.48	0.38	0.49	0.48
* 5	3.11	1.885	0.325	2.64	0.317	0.29	0.11	3¾	8.90	3.56	1.83	0.63	0.45	0.49	0.48
* 5	3.97	2.032	0.472	3.38	0.317	0.29	0.11	3¾	10.43	4.17	1.76	0.81	0.53	0.49	0.51
* 6	2.83	1.920	0.200	2.40	0.340	0.30	0.12	4½	13.12	4.37	2.34	0.69	0.49	0.54	0.51
* 6	3.00	1.945	0.225	2.55	0.340	0.30	0.12	4½	13.57	4.52	2.31	0.73	0.51	0.54	0.51
* 6	3.63	2.034	0.314	3.09	0.340	0.30	0.12	4½	15.18	5.06	2.22	0.87	0.56	0.53	0.50
* 6	4.48	2.157	0.437	3.82	0.340	0.30	0.12	4½	17.39	5.80	2.13	1.05	0.64	0.52	0.51
7	3.38	2.090	0.210	2.87	0.364	0.31	0.13	5½	21.27	6.08	2.72	0.97	0.63	0.58	0.54
* 7	3.54	2.110	0.230	3.01	0.364	0.31	0.13	5½	21.84	6.24	2.69	1.01	0.64	0.58	0.54
* 7	4.23	2.194	0.314	3.60	0.364	0.31	0.13	5½	24.24	6.93	2.60	1.17	0.70	0.57	0.52
* 7	5.10	2.299	0.419	4.33	0.364	0.31	0.13	5½	27.24	7.78	2.51	1.38	0.78	0.56	0.53
7	5.96	2.404	0.524	5.07	0.364	0.31	0.13	5½	30.25	8.64	2.44	1.59	0.86	0.56	0.55
* 8	4.25	2.290	0.250	3.62	0.387	0.32	0.13	6¼	33.85	8.46	3.06	1.40	0.81	0.62	0.56
* 8	4.75	2.343	0.303	4.04	0.387	0.32	0.13	6¼	36.11	9.03	2.99	1.53	0.85	0.61	0.55
* 8	5.62	2.435	0.395	4.78	0.387	0.32	0.13	6¼	40.04	10.01	2.90	1.75	0.93	0.61	0.55
* 8	6.48	2.527	0.487	5.51	0.387	0.32	0.13	6¼	43.96	10.99	2.82	1.98	1.01	0.60	0.57
* 9	4.60	2.430	0.230	3.92	0.409	0.33	0.14	7¼	47.68	10.60	3.49	1.75	0.96	0.67	0.60
9	5.19	2.485	0.285	4.41	0.409	0.33	0.14	7¼	51.02	11.34	3.40	1.93	1.01	0.66	0.59
* 9	6.91	2.648	0.448	5.88	0.409	0.33	0.14	7¼	60.92	13.54	3.22	2.42	1.17	0.64	0.58
9	8.65	2.812	0.612	7.35	0.409	0.33	0.14	7¼	70.89	15.75	3.11	2.94	1.34	0.63	0.61
* 10	5.28	2.600	0.240	4.49	0.434	0.34	0.14	8¼	67.37	13.47	3.87	2.28	1.16	0.71	0.63
10	6.91	2.739	0.379	5.88	0.434	0.34	0.14	8¼	78.95	15.79	3.66	2.81	1.32	0.69	0.61
* 10	8.64	2.886	0.526	7.35	0.434	0.34	0.14	8¼	91.20	18.24	3.52	3.36	1.48	0.68	0.62
10	10.37	3.033	0.673	8.82	0.434	0.34	0.14	8¼	103.45	20.69	3.43	3.95	1.66	0.67	0.65
* 12	7.41	2.960	0.300	6.30	0.498	0.38	0.17	10	131.84	21.97	4.57	3.99	1.76	0.80	0.69
* 12	8.64	3.047	0.387	7.35	0.498	0.38	0.17	10	144.37	24.06	4.43	4.47	1.89	0.78	0.67
* 12	10.37	3.170	0.510	8.82	0.498	0.38	0.17	10	162.08	27.01	4.29	5.14	2.06	0.76	0.67
12	12.10	3.292	0.632	10.29	0.498	0.38	0.17	10	179.65	29.94	4.18	5.82	2.24	0.75	0.69
* 15	11.71	3.400	0.400	9.96	0.647	0.50	0.24	12⅜	314.76	41.97	5.62	9.63	3.11	0.90	0.79
* 15	17.28	3.716	0.716	14.70	0.647	0.50	0.24	12⅜	403.64	53.82	5.24	12.53	4.30	0.92	0.80

* Standard shapes normally available from warehouse stocks.

structural shapes/wide flange sections

—WIDE-FLANGE SECTIONS—H-BEAMS

TABLE 3-12. Wide-flange H-beams.

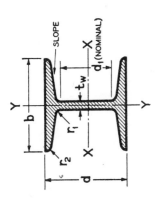

Size Nominal Depth and Width	Weight lb/ft	Actual Depth d in.	Actual Width b in.	Web Thickness t_w in.	Area in.²	Slope	Avg Flange Thickness in.	r_1 in.	r_2 in.	d_1 in.	Axis X-X I in.⁴	S in.³	r in.	Axis Y-Y I in.⁴	S in.³	r in.
2 x 2	0.78	2.00	2.000	0.094	0.664	0	0.125	0.125	0.125	1½	0.481	0.481	0.85	0.154	0.154	0.48
2 x 2	1.43	2.00	2.000	0.188	1.217	1:11.4	0.232	0.188	0.094	1⅛	0.782	0.782	0.80	0.275	0.275	0.47
2½ x 2	1.80	2.50	2.000	0.250	1.529	1:7	0.247	0.250	0.125	1⅜	1.453	1.162	0.97	0.292	0.292	0.44
*4 x 4	4.76	4.00	4.000	0.313	4.05	1:11.3	0.370	0.313	0.145	2⅜	10.80	5.40	1.63	3.52	1.76	0.93
*5 x 5	6.49	5.00	5.000	0.313	5.52	1:13.6	0.415	0.313	0.165	3⅜	23.94	9.58	2.08	7.73	3.09	1.18
*6 x 4	4.16	6.00	4.000	0.230	3.54	0	0.279	0.250	0	4⅞	21.75	7.25	2.48	2.98	1.49	0.92
*6 x 6	5.40	6.00	6.000	0.240	4.59	0	0.269	0.250	0	4⅞	30.17	10.06	2.56	9.69	3.23	1.45
*6 x 6	7.85	6.00	5.933	0.250	6.68	1:15.6	0.451	0.313	0.180	4⅜	44.25	14.75	2.57	14.02	4.67	1.45
6 x 6	8.30	6.00	6.000	0.313	7.06	1:15.6	0.451	0.313	0.180	4⅜	45.37	15.12	2.54	14.49	4.83	1.43
6 x 6	9.18	6.00	6.125	0.438	7.81	1:15.6	0.451	0.313	0.180	4⅜	47.62	15.87	2.47	15.49	5.16	1.41
*8 x 5¼	5.90	8.00	5.250	0.230	5.02	0	0.308	0.320	0	6¾	56.73	14.18	3.36	7.44	2.83	1.22
*8 x 6½	8.32	8.00	6.500	0.245	7.08	0	0.398	0.400	0	6⅜	84.15	21.04	3.44	18.23	5.61	1.61
*8 x 8	10.72	8.00	8.000	0.288	9.12	0	0.433	0.400	0	6⅜	109.66	27.41	3.47	36.97	9.24	2.01
*8 x 8	11.24	8.00	7.938	0.313	9.55	1:18.9	0.458	0.313	0.179	6¼	113.33	28.33	3.45	33.87	8.47	1.88
8 x 8	11.82	8.00	8.000	0.375	10.05	1:18.9	0.458	0.313	0.179	6¼	115.97	28.99	3.40	34.73	8.68	1.86
8 x 8	12.99	8.00	8.125	0.500	11.05	1:18.9	0.458	0.313	0.179	6¼	121.31	30.33	3.31	36.50	9.13	1.82
*10 x 5¾	7.30	9.90	5.750	0.240	6.21	0	0.340	0.312	0	8½	106.74	21.56	4.15	10.77	3.75	1.32

* Standard shapes normally available from warehouse stocks.

TABLE 3-13. Special channels.

—SPECIAL CHANNELS

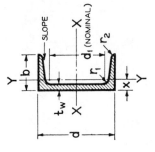

| Size | | | | | | Avg Flange Thick-ness | | | | Axis X-X | | | Axis Y-Y | | | |
Depth d in.	Weight lb/ft	Width b in.	Web Thick-ness t_w in.	Area in.²	Slope	in.	r_1 in.	r_2 in.	d_1 in.	I in.⁴	S in.³	r in.	I in.⁴	S in.³	r in.	x in.
*3	2.24	2.000	0.250	1.90	1:12.1	0.320	0.250	0	1¾	2.61	1.74	1.17	0.68	0.52	0.60	0.68
*3	2.70	2.000	0.375	2.30	0	0.375	0.188	0.375	1⅞	2.89	1.92	1.12	0.78	0.59	0.58	0.67
*4	3.32	2.500	0.318	2.82	1:34.9	0.344	0.375	0.125	2⅜	6.84	3.42	1.56	1.62	0.95	0.76	0.81
5	3.10	2.875	0.188	2.64	1:10.7	0.312	0.250	0.094	3½	11.20	4.48	2.06	1.91	0.96	0.85	0.89
5	4.74	2.500	0.500	4.03	0	0.375	0.375	0.250	3½	13.37	5.35	1.82	1.94	1.08	0.69	0.71
*5	5.82	2.875	0.438	4.95	1:9.8	0.562	0.250	0.094	3	18.13	7.25	1.91	3.57	1.87	0.85	0.96
*6	5.77	3.000	0.500	4.91	0	0.375	0.375	0.250	4½	24.05	8.02	2.21	3.52	1.61	0.85	0.81
*6	5.93	3.500	0.375	5.04	1:49.6	0.442	0.480	0.420	4	28.22	9.41	2.37	5.58	2.31	1.05	1.09
*8	6.59	3.000	0.380	5.60	1:14.43	0.468	0.550	0.220	5¾	54.15	13.54	3.11	4.10	1.88	0.86	0.81
*8	7.86	3.500	0.425	6.68	1:28.5	0.524	0.525	0.375	5¾	63.76	15.94	3.09	7.06	2.84	1.03	1.01
*10	8.58	3.500	0.375	7.30	1:9	0.544	0.625	0.188	7½	109.62	21.92	3.88	7.19	2.80	0.99	0.93
*10	9.32	3.563	0.438	7.93	1:9	0.544	0.625	0.188	7½	114.87	22.97	3.81	7.73	2.93	0.99	0.92
*10	10.05	3.625	0.500	8.55	1:9	0.544	0.625	0.188	7½	120.03	24.01	3.75	8.25	3.04	0.98	0.91

* Standard shapes normally available from warehouse stocks.

Security
Provisions

CHAPTER 4

This chapter begins with a segregation of occupancies according to fire hazards, as defined by the National Fire Protection Association for the purpose of sprinkler installation. After covering sprinklers, fire doors and related subjects, we will move into security considerations, and then a few items for some special types of occupancies.

FIRE PREVENTION AND FIRE FIGHTING

Reprinting here of the innumerable codes, local and national, that define occupancies by the related fire hazard would make only a small part of the chapter applicable to each reader. Instead, one national definition has been selected: that which the National Fire Protection Association has prepared specifically for sprinkler installations.[1] Occupancies in the following lists are "such as," rather than all-inclusive.

Light Hazard

The Light Hazard class should include those properties where the amount and combustibility of the contents is low, and there is no obstruction to sprinkler distribution. This class excludes mercantiles, warehouse and manufacturing occupancies and includes only occupancies such as:

Apartments	Libraries, except Large Stack
Asylums	Room Areas
Churches	Museums
Clubs	Nursing, Convalescent and Care Homes
Colleges and Universities	Office Buildings
Dormitories	Prisons
Dwellings	Public Buildings
Hospitals	Rooming Houses
Hotels	Schools
Institutions	Tenements

---

[1]Information for these sections on sprinkler systems is from: National Fire Protection Association, Installation of Sprinker Systems (NFPA No. 13), Boston, Massachusetts. Copyright © 1969.

Ordinary Hazard: (Group 1)

This group of the ordinary hazard class includes those properties where combustibility is low, with no flammable liquids or other quick burning materials, stock piles do not exceed 6 to 8 feet and other factors are favorable. Following are some examples of types of properties generally falling into this group:

Abrasive Works	Fur Processing
Automobile Garages	Glass and Glass Products Factories
Bakeries	Ice Manufacturing
Beverage Manufacturing	Laundries
Bleacheries	Macaroni Factories
Boiler Houses	Millinery Manufacturing Plants
Bottling Works	Restaurants
Breweries	Slaughterhouses
Brick, Tile and Clay Products	Smelters
Canneries	Steel Mills
Cement Plants	Theatres and Auditoriums
Dairy Products Mfg. and Processing	Watch and Jewelry Manufacturing
Electric Generating Stations	Waterworks Pumping Stations
Foundries	Wineries

Ordinary Hazard: (Group 2)

This group of the ordinary hazard class includes those properties where combustibility of contents and ceiling heights are generally less favorable than those listed in Group No. 1, but there are only minor amounts of flammable liquids and essentially no obstruction. Examples of types of properties generally falling into this group are:

Cereal Mills	*Lithographing
Chemical Works—Ordinary	*Machine Shops
Clothing Factories	*Mercantiles
*Cold Storage Warehouses	*Metal Working
Confectionery Products Mfg.	Pharmaceutical Manufacturing
Cotton and Woolen Mills	Printing and Publishing
**Distilleries	Rope, Cordage and Twine Factories
Dye and Print Works	Shoe Factories
Grain Elevators, Tanks and Warehouses	Storage Buildings (having low factors of combustibility and obstruction)
*Leather Goods Manufacturing	Sugar Refining
Libraries, Large Stack Room Areas	Tanneries
	Textile Knitting and Weaving Mills
	Tobacco Products Manufacturing

Ordinary Hazard: (Group 3)

This group of the ordinary hazard class includes those properties where features of combustibility of contents, ceiling heights and obstruction are unfavorable, separately or jointly. Following are some examples of the type of property falling into this group:

*Feed Mills
*Flour Mills
Paper and Pulp Mills
Paper Process Plants
Piers and Wharves

**Tire Manufacturing and Storage Warehouses (Paper, household furniture, paint, department store, etc.)
**Whiskey Warehouses

Extra Hazard

This class includes only those buildings or portions of buildings housing occupancies where the hazard is severe as determined by the authority having jurisdiction. These occupancies include such as:

**Aircraft Hangars
Chemical Works—Extra Hazard
Cotton Picker and Opening Operations
Explosives and Pyrotechnic Manufacturing

Linseed Oil Mills
Oil Refineries
**Pyroxylin Plastic Mfg. and Processing
Shade Cloth Manufacturing
Solvent Extracting
Varnish Works

Linoleum and Oilcloth Manufacturing
and other occupancies involving processing, mixing, storage and dispensing flammable and/or combustible liquids.

For general information, Table A–26 gives explosive and related information on many industrial chemicals.

SPRINKLER SYSTEMS

Water Supply Requirements

The National Fire Protection Association manual on sprinklers emphasizes that final specifications for this topic must be based on experienced judgment; therefore, the information supplied here is to be considered only a guide for preliminary planning. Table 4–1 is a guide to water supply requirements, where quantitative listings are used wherever they have been established nationally.

Pressure Tank: Formula for air pressure in tank

When a pressure tank is used, minimum allowable capacities are 2000 gallons for light hazard occupancy and 3000 gallons for ordinary hazard Groups 1 and 2. Other occupancies are not specified in the national requirements, but are referred to the authority having jurisdiction.

---

*Under conditions favorable to the individual property, and with special permission of the authority having jurisdiction, this class may, in some cases, qualify under the immediately preceding group.
**Nation Fire Protection Association has separately published standards relating to water supply requirements for this class.

Formula

$$P = \frac{30}{A} - 15 + 0.434\,\frac{H}{A}$$

where: P = pressure in pounds on the gauge
A = proportion of tank occupied by air
H = height of highest sprinkler above tank bottom
= 0 if tank is located above highest sprinkler

Example

The bottom of a pressure tank is 20 feet lower than the highest sprinkler in the system. What pressure is required if the tank is to be kept 2/3 full of water (1/3 air)?

$$P = \frac{30}{0.333} - 15 + 0.434\,\frac{20}{0.333}$$

$$= 101 \text{ pounds per square inch}$$

TABLE 4-1. Guide to water supply requirements for sprinkler systems.

Occupancy Classification	Minimum Residual Pressure Required Under the Roof (See Note 1)	Minimum Acceptable Flow at Base of Riser (See Note 2)	Duration in Minutes
LIGHT HAZARD	15 psi	500–750 gpm (See Note 3)	60
ORDINARY HAZARD (GROUP 1)	15 psi or higher	500–1000 gpm	60–100
ORDINARY HAZARD (GROUP 2)	15 psi or higher	500–1500 gpm	60–100
ORDINARY HAZARD (GROUP 3)	Pressure and flow requirements for sprinklers and hose streams to be determined by authority having jurisdiction.		60–120
GENERAL STORAGE WAREHOUSES,			
HIGH RISE BUILDINGS,			
WOODWORKERS	Pressure and flow requirements for sprinklers and hose streams to be determined by authority having jurisdiction.		
EXTRA HAZARD	Pressure and flow requirements for sprinklers and hose streams to be determined by authority having jurisdiction.		

NOTES:

1. The pressure required at the base of the sprinkler riser(s) shall be the residual pressure required under the roof plus the pressure required to reach this elevation.

2. The lower figure is the minimum flow ordinarily acceptable for recognition as a supply to a sprinkler system. The higher flow should normally suffice for all cases under each group unless adverse conditions are present.

3. The requirement may be reduced to 250 gpm if building is limited in area or if building (including roof) is noncombustible construction.

Light Hazard Installations

Not more than eight sprinklers should be used on branch lines on either side of a cross main. Table 4–2 shows the number of sprinklers allowed for various pipe sizes, except as follows:

- Each large area requiring more than 100 sprinklers and without subdividing partitions (not necessarily fire walls) should be supplied by feed mains or risers sized for ordinary hazard occupancies.

- Where sprinklers are installed above and below a ceiling and such sprinklers are supplied from a common set of branch lines, such branch lines should not exceed 8 sprinklers above and 8 below the ceiling on either side of the cross main. Pipe sizing through 2 1/2 inch should be as shown in Table 4–3.

TABLE 4-2. Light hazard sprinkler installation.

Steel		Copper	
1 in. pipe........	2 sprinklers	1 in. tube........	2 sprinklers
1¼ in. pipe........	3 sprinklers	1¼ in. tube........	3 sprinklers
1½ in. pipe........	5 sprinklers	1½ in. tube........	5 sprinklers
2 in. pipe........	10 sprinklers	2 in. tube........	12 sprinklers
2½ in. pipe........	30 sprinklers	2½ in. tube........	40 sprinklers
3 in. pipe........	60 sprinklers	3 in. tube........	65 sprinklers
3½ in. pipe........	100 sprinklers	3½ in. tube........	115 sprinklers
4 in. pipe...	*	4 in. tube...	*

TABLE 4-3. Light hazard sprinklers installed above and below ceiling.

**Number of Sprinklers
Above and Below**

Steel		Copper	
1 in.............	2 sprinklers	1 in.............	2 sprinklers
1¼ in.............	4 sprinklers	1¼ in.............	4 sprinklers
1½ in.............	7 sprinklers	1½ in.............	7 sprinklers
2 in.............	15 sprinklers	2 in.............	18 sprinklers
2½ in.............	50 sprinklers	2½ in.............	65 sprinklers

Example

A 2 1/2-inch steel pipe, which is permitted to supply 30 sprinklers in one fire area, may supply a total of 50 sprinklers where not over 30 sprinklers are above or below the ceiling. Where the total number above and below the ceiling exceeds 50, the pipe supplying more than 50 sprinklers should be increased to 3 inch and sized thereafter according to Table 4–2 for the number of sprinklers above or below the ceiling, whichever is larger.

Ordinary Hazard Installations

Not more than eight sprinklers should be used on branch lines on either side of a cross main. Table 4–4 shows the number of sprinklers allowed for various pipe sizes, except as follows:

- If the distance between sprinklers on a branch exceeds 12 feet or if the distance between branch lines exceeds 12 feet, Table 4–5 is used to determine the number of sprinklers.

---

*The area served by any one 4-inch pipe or tube size on any one floor of one fire section shall not exceed 52,000 square feet.

TABLE 4-4. Ordinary hazard sprinkler installation.

Steel		Copper	
1 in. pipe	2 sprinklers	1 in. tube	2 sprinklers
1¼ in. pipe	3 sprinklers	1¼ in. tube	3 sprinklers
1½ in. pipe	5 sprinklers	1½ in. tube	5 sprinklers
2 in. pipe	10 sprinklers	2 in. tube	12 sprinklers
2½ in. pipe	20 sprinklers	2½ in. tube	25 sprinklers
3 in. pipe	40 sprinklers	3 in. tube	45 sprinklers
3½ in. pipe	65 sprinklers	3½ in. tube	75 sprinklers
4 in. pipe	100 sprinklers	4 in. tube	115 sprinklers
5 in. pipe	160 sprinklers	5 in. tube	180 sprinklers
6 in. pipe	275 sprinklers	6 in. tube	300 sprinklers
8 in. pipe	*	8 in. tube	*

* The area served by any one 8-inch pipe or tube size on any one floor of one fire section shall not exceed 52,000 square feet except that for solid piled storage in excess of 15 feet in height or palletized or rack storage in excess of 12 feet the area served by any one 8-inch pipe or tube size shall not exceed 40,000 square feet. Where single systems serve both such storage and Ordinary Hazard areas, storage area covered shall not exceed 40,000 square feet and total area covered shall not exceed 52,000 square feet.

TABLE 4-5. Ordinary hazard sprinkler installation where distances exceed 12 feet.

Steel		Copper	
2½ in. pipe	15 sprinklers	2½ in. tube	20 sprinklers
3 in. pipe	30 sprinklers	3 in. tube	35 sprinklers
3½ in. pipe	60 sprinklers	3½ in. tube	65 sprinklers

TABLE 4-6. Ordinary hazard sprinklers installed above and below ceiling.

	Number of Sprinklers Above and Below		
Steel		Copper	
1 in.	2 sprinklers	1 in.	2 sprinklers
1¼ in.	4 sprinklers	1¼ in.	4 sprinklers
1½ in.	7 sprinklers	1½ in.	7 sprinklers
2 in.	15 sprinklers	2 in.	18 sprinklers
2½ in.	30 sprinklers	2½ in.	40 sprinklers
3 in.	60 sprinklers	3 in.	65 sprinklers

Where sprinklers are installed above and below a ceiling and such sprinklers are supplied from a common set of branch lines, such branch lines should not exceed 8 sprinklers above and 8 below the ceiling on either side of the cross main. Pipe sizing through 3 inch should be as shown in Table 4–6.

TABLE 4-7. Extra hazard sprinkler installation.

Steel		Copper	
1 in. pipe.......	1 sprinkler	1 in. tube.......	1 sprinkler
1¼ in. pipe.......	2 sprinklers	1¼ in. tube.......	2 sprinklers
1½ in. pipe.......	5 sprinklers	1½ in. tube.......	5 sprinklers
2 in. pipe.......	8 sprinklers	2 in. tube.......	8 sprinklers
2½ in. pipe.......	15 sprinklers	2½ in. tube.......	20 sprinklers
3 in. pipe.......	27 sprinklers	3 in. tube.......	30 sprinklers
3½ in. pipe.......	40 sprinklers	3½ in. tube.......	45 sprinklers
4 in. pipe.......	55 sprinklers	4 in. tube.......	65 sprinklers
5 in. pipe.......	90 sprinklers	5 in. tube.......	100 sprinklers
6 in. pipe.......150 sprinklers		6 in. tube.......170 sprinklers	
8 in. pipe...	*	8 in. tube...	*

* The area served by any one 8-inch pipe or tube size on any one floor of one fire section shall not exceed 25,000 square feet.

Extra Hazard Installations

Not more than six sprinklers should be used on branch lines on either side of a cross main. Table 4-7 is a guide to the number of sprinklers, assuming there are no unusual features to be considered.

Sprinkler Heads[2]

Many types of standard sprinkler heads are available, and manufacturers also have a line of products specially designed by their engineering departments. Some sprinklers designed for installation against a wall, or in a corner, have specially selected spray patterns. Descriptions of some representative sprinklers follow.

Standard upright sprinkler

This type distributes water at a 180-degree angle, especially for area coverage. It is intended for installation where exposed piping is not objectionable.

Standard pendent sprinkler

A pendent sprinkler mounts below its supply pipe and therefore is intended where piping is concealed or where exposed piping is close to the overhead. Covers a floor area approximately 16 feet in diameter.

Large orifice sprinkler

This sprinkler is intended for the same situations as standard upright or pendent sprinklers. However, discharge of approximately 140 percent more water at the same pressure makes the large orifice sprinkler better suited for locations where high density is required or where residual water pressure is low.

---

[2]The Viking Corporation, Sprinkler System Guide, Form 2026, Michigan, 1970.

Small orifice sprinkler

This type is also intended for the same situations as standard upright or pendent sprinklers. However, smaller discharge of water for any given pressure makes the small orifice sprinkler better suited for locations where low density is required or where residual water pressure is high.

Flush sprinkler

The sprinkler body is above the ceiling; only the link projects below. When link fuses, deflector drops into position held by chains, and water spray is delivered with uniform coverage.

Side wall sprinkler

This type is designed for horizontal installation along side walls or exposed beams in corridors, hallways, and small rooms where structural or other conditions do not readily permit standard sprinkler installations.

Table 4–8 gives some temperature information applicable to the sprinklers just mentioned.

TABLE 4-8. Typical sprinkler operation.

Classification	Available Fusing point	Use where temperature does not exceed
Ordinary	160 F	100 F
Intermediate	212 F	150 F
High	280 F	225 F
Extra High	360 F	300 F

Suspension by Rods

Table 4–9 summarizes the various dimensions associated with using rod hangers for sprinkler-supply pipes. The columns headed BOLT and LAG SCREW indicate the minimum size of such fasteners when used with an eye rod on the side of a beam. The last two columns show minimum thickness of plank and minimum width of lower face of beams or joists in which lag screw rods are used.

Suspension by "U" Hooks

Table 4–10 gives minimum sizes of rods from which "U" hooks are formed, plus dimensions of screws for mounting.

Ceiling Flanges

When pipes are supported through ceiling flanges attached to wooden structural members, fastener dimensions are obtained from Table 4–11.

TABLE 4-9.   Rod hangers for sprinkler supply pipes.

Pipe size, inches	Diameter of rod, inches	Bolt diameter, inches	Lag screw dimensions, inches	Plank thickness, inches	Beam width, inches
2	3/8	3/8	3/8 × 2 1/2	3	2
2 1/2	1/2	1/2	1/2 × 3	4	2
3	1/2	1/2	1/2 × 3	4	2
3 1/2	1/2	1/2	1/2 × 3	4	2
4	5/8	1/2	1/2 × 3	4	3
5	5/8	1/2	1/2 × 3	4	3
6	3/4	1/2	1/2 × 3	4	4
8	7/8	5/8	5/8 × 3	*	*

*Lag screw rods should not be used to support pipes larger than 6 inches.

TABLE 4-10.   "U" hook pipe supports.

Pipe size, inches	"U" hook rod diameter, inches	Dimensions, inches drive screw	lag screw
To 2	5/16	#16 × 2	
2 1/2	3/8		3/8 × 2 1/2
3	3/8		3/8 × 2 1/2
3 1/2	7/16		3/8 × 2 1/2
4	7/16		1/2 × 3
5	1/2		1/2 × 3
6	5/8		1/2 × 3
8	3/4		5/8 × 3

TABLE 4-11.   Fasteners for ceiling flanges.

Pipe size, inches	2-screw flanges	3-screw flanges		4-screw flanges	
	Wood screw	Wood screw	Lag screw	Wood screw	Lag screw
To 2	#18 × 1 1/2	#18 × 1 1/2		#18 × 1 1/2	
2 1/2			3/8 × 2		3/8 × 1 1/2
3			3/8 × 2		3/8 × 1 1/2
3 1/2			3/8 × 2		3/8 × 1 1/2
4			1/2 × 2		1/2 × 2
5			1/2 × 2		1/2 × 2
6			1/2 × 2		1/2 × 2
8			5/8 × 2		5/8 × 2

FIRE DOORS

Fire Door Classifications

Doors for containing fires are classified by the National Fire Protection Association as shown in Table 4–12.[3] The Underwriters' Laboratories label will contain information shown in the Time Rating and Temperature Rise columns. The topic of fire doors is one that points up the value of complete early planning so as to avoid the use of non-standard doors that will not have the label. This information is given for purposes of insurance compliance, rather than building codes, as indicated by the following quotations:[4]

> Maximum insurance premium credits and satisfactory fire protection are only effective when approved and labeled fire doors are mounted with approved and labeled fire door hardware.

> Doors that are either notched, mortised, beveled or rabbeted are not standard and cannot bear the Underwriters' label. Certificates of Inspection indicating that doors are otherwise built according to standard details, can be furnished for notched doors if requested.

and another manufacturer gives a similar caution notice:[5]

> Openings calling for a Class A, B, C, or D Underwriters' label must not be in excess of 120 sq. ft. in area or more than 12 ft. wide or high. However, when the opening is in excess of that size, but does not exceed 24 ft. in width or height, Akbar equipment can be furnished with a special certificate indicating compliance with all fire door requirements.

SAFES AND VAULTS

The industry[6] has attempted to eliminate misunderstanding by establishing some definitions that are compatible with usage by associated agencies. When the terms, "burglary," "fire door," and others are used in this chapter, they will have the following meanings:

Burglary. Forceable entry after premises are closed.

Robbery. Violence or the threat of violence used against an individual with the intent of taking property or other valuables.

Fire door. A door that acts as a flame barrier but does not necessarily have the insulation or fit for providing a heat barrier.

Fire-insulated door. A door that provides a heat barrier for time periods as specified in tables to follow.

---

[3]National Fire Protection Association, Installation of Fire Doors and Windows, (NFPA No. 80), © 1970, Boston, Massachusetts, 1968.

[4]Richards-Wilcox, Fire Doors and Hardware, Catalog A-420-R5, Illinois. Copyright © Richards-Wilcox Division, Hupp Inc., 1969, 1972.

[5]Kinnear Corporation, Kinnear Fire Doors, Bulletin 135, Columbus, Ohio. p. 4.

[6]Safe Manufacturers National Association, Incorporated, 366 Madison Avenue, New York, New York, 10017.

TABLE 4-12

Classification	Time Rating (as shown on label)		Temperature Rise (as shown on label)	Permissible Glass Area
3 Hour fire doors (A) are for use in openings in walls separating buildings or dividing a single building into fire areas.	3 Hr.	(A)	30 min. 250F. Max	None
	3 Hr.	(A)	30 min. 450F. Max	Permitted
	3 Hr.	(A)	30 min. 650F. Max	
	3 Hr.	(A)	*	
1-1/2 Hour fire doors (B) and (D) are for use In openings in 2 Hour enclosures of vertical communication through buildings (stairs, elevators, etc.) or in exterior walls which are subject to severe fire exposure from outside of the building. 1 Hour fire doors (B) are for use in openings in 1 Hour enclosures of vertical communication through buildings (stairs, elevators, etc.).	1-1/2 Hr.	(B)	30 min. 250F. Max	Up to 100 square inches per door
	1-1/2 Hr.	(B)	30 min. 450F. Max	
	1-1/2 Hr.	(B)	30 min. 650F. Max	
	1-1/2 Hr.	(B)	*	
	1 Hr.	(B)	30 min. 250F. Max	
	1-1/2 Hr.	(D)	30 min. 250F. Max	None
	1-1/2 Hr.	(D)	30 min. 450F. Max	Permitted
	1-1/2 Hr.	(D)	30 min. 650F. Max	
	1-1/2 Hr.	(D)	*	
3/4 Hour fire doors (C) and (E) are for use In openings in corridor and room partitions or In exterior walls which are subject to moderate fire exposure from outside of the building.	3/4 Hr.	(C)	**	Up to 1296 square inches per light
	3/4 Hr.	(E)	**	Up to 720 square inches per light

*The labels do not record any temperature rise limits. This means that the temperature rise on the unexposed face of the door at the end of 30 minutes of test is in excess of 850° F.

**Temperature--Rise is not recorded for 3/4 hr. doors.

Burglary and Robbery Resistive Equipment[7]

Table 4–13 lists characteristics that have been standardized throughout the industry. The industry stresses the difference between record safes designed to protect records from fire, and money chests designed to protect valuables from burglary. Table 4–14 lists SMNA equipment which is labeled as fire-resistive, and includes a summary of the test features.

Fire Resistive Vaults[8]

This section provides some figures for estimating weights and loads for a completely fire-resistive enclosure that is to be constructed in a non-fire-resistive building. The vault to be considered here is a ground-supported type (supported from the ground up, and independent of building members).

---

[7]Safe Manufacturers National Association, "What SMNA Labels Mean in Protection Against Losses by Fire," Robbery and Burglary, New York.

[8]The Mosler Safe Company, "How to Construct Fire Resistive Vaults," Specification FP 2221–570, Ohio.

TABLE 4-13. Burglary- and robbery-resistive labeled equipment.

SMNA SPEC	GROUP	UL LABEL	DESIGN FEATURES DOOR	WALL	LOCK	CASUALTY UNDERWRITERS INSURANCE CLASSIFICATION † MERCANTILE SAFE POLICY	BROAD FORM
UB-1	U1	TXTL60	1½"S ⊙	1"S, P	C	I	G
UB-1	U2	TRTL60	1½"S ⊙	1"S, P	C	I	G
UB-1	U4	TRTL30	1½"S ⊙	1"S, P	C	H	G
UB-1	U5	TL30	1½"S ⊙	1"S, P	C	F	F
UB-1	U6	TL15	1½"S ⊙ ▭	1"S, P	C	ER	ER
B-1	1	TX60*	1½"S ⊙	1½"S, SC	C	H	G
B-1	1	TR60*	1½"S ⊙	1½"S, SC	C	H	G
B-1	1	X60*	1½"S ⊙	1½"S, SC	C	F	F
B-1	2	**	1½"S ⊙	1"S, SC, CH	C	E	E
B-1	3	**	1½"S ⊙	1"S, SC	C	E	E
B-1	3	TR30*	1½"S ⊙	1"S, SC	C	F	F
B-1	4	**	1½"S ⊙	1"S, P	C	E	E
B-1	4	TR30*	1½"S ⊙	1"S	C	F	F
B-1	5	**	1½"S ▭	1"S, P	C	E	E
B-1	6		1"S ⊙ ▭	½"S, SC or P	C	C	C
R-1	6		1"S ▭	½"S, SC or P	C	C	C
R-1	8		1"S ⊙ ▭	½"S	KL	***	—
R-1	9		½"S ⊙ ▭	¼"S	KL	***	—
R-1	9		½"S ⊙ ▭	¼"S	C	B	B
R-1	10		NMT		C	B	B
R-1	10		NMT		KL	None	—
M-12		Deposit Slot Accessible From Exterior of Container, Steel Construction.					

CODE:
B — Burglary-Resistive
R — Robbery-Resistive
C — Combination Lock
KL — Key Lock
M — Deposit Chute
P — Plate

S — Steel
SC — Steel Casting
CH — Case Hardened
TL — Tool-Resistive
TR — Torch and Tool-Resistive

TX — Explosives and Tool-Resistive
U — Underwriter's Laboratories
UL — Underwriter's Laboratories
UL — Burglary

▭ —Rectangular Door
⊙ — Round Door

UL No.'s—Minutes (TX60, for example indicates Tool and Explosive Resistant for 60 Minutes)

NMT—No Minimum Thickness

† — National Bureau of Casualty Underwriters, and Mutual Insurance Rating Bureau

* — No longer manufactured

** — UL Label for relocking device only; SMNA label for unit

*** — Coverage available if SMNA-labeled

NOTE:
Burglary-Resistive equipment is designed of laminated or solid steel. "Laminated Steel" is defined as two or more sheets of steel, with the facing surface bonded together with no other material between the sheets. It is designed to prevent burglaries, which are defined as forceable entry after premises are closed.

Robbery-Resistive equipment is designed to protect property in the possession of the custodian. Such equipment includes robbery-resistive safes, cages, alarms, bullet proof glass, and others. Robbery is defined as violence or the threat of violence used against an individual with the intent of taking property or other valuables.

TABLE 4-14. Fire-resistive labeled equipment.

PRODUCT CLASSIFICATION	SMNA SPEC.	SMNA CLASS.	UL EQUIV.	PRODUCT DESIGN AND TEST FEATURES
Fire-Insulated Safe	F 1-D	A	A	4 Hour Tested Fire-Resistive Safe (With Impact Test)
Fire-Insulated Safe	F 1-D	B	B	2 Hour Tested Fire-Resistive Safe (With Impact Test)
Fire-Insulated Safe	F 1-D	C	C	1 Hour Tested Fire-Resistive Safe (With Impact Test)
Fire-Insulated Record Container	F 1-D	C	C	1 Hour Tested Fire-Resistive Container (With Impact Test)
Fire-Insulated Safe	F 1-ND	D	D	1 Hour Tested Fire-Resistive Safe (Without Impact Test)
Fire-Insulated Ledger Tray	F 1-D	C	C	1 Hour Tested Fire-Resistive Ledger Tray (With Impact Test)
Fire-Insulated Container	F 2-ND	E	E	½ Hour Tested Fire-Resistive Container (Without Impact Test)
Fire-Insulated Container	F 2-ND	D	D	1 Hour Tested Fire-Resistive Container (Without Impact Test)
Fire-Insulated Container	F 2-ND	2 Hour	B	2 Hour Tested Fire-Resistive Container (Without Impact Test)
Fire-Insulated Vault Door	F 3	2 Hour	2 Hour	2 Hour Tested Fire-Resistive Vault Door
Fire-Insulated Vault Door	F 3	4 Hour	4 Hour	4 Hour Tested Fire-Resistive Vault Door
Fire-Insulated Vault Door	F 3	6 Hour	6 Hour	6 Hour Tested Fire-Resistive Vault Door
Fire-Insulated File Room Door	F 4	1 Hour	1 Hour	1 Hour Tested Fire-Resistive File or Storage Room Door
Fire-Insulated Record Container Data Processing Safe	F 2-D*	Class 150	Class 150	2 Hour or 4 Hour Fire-Resistive Data Processing Safe

NOTE:

Class A	protects paper records from damage by fire (2,000°F) up to 4 hours.
Class B	protects paper records from damage by fire (1,850°F) up to 2 hours.
Class C and D	protects paper records from damage by fire (1,700°F) up to 1 hour.
Class E	protects paper records from damage by fire (1,550°F) up to ½ hour.
Class 150	protects EDP records from damage by fire and humidity for rated period.
The Drop (or Impact) **Test:**	The Drop (or Impact) Test is used to determine whether or not the fire-resistance of a product would be impaired by being dropped 30 feet while still hot. Fire-resistant equipment is designed specifically to resist fire, and consists of a metal shell filled with a fire-resistant insulation.

* Impact tested unloaded.

Table 4–15[9] gives suggested minimum thickness of walls, where bricks are assumed to be sand-lime type, American Standard ASA-78.1–1942, and hollow units are assumed to be hollow load-bearing concrete masonry units, American Standard ASA79.1–1942, or a hollow wall of bricks. This table is constructed from the top; for a six-story building only the first six lines would apply.

Under the same conditions, the floor of a ground-supported vault would be a minimum of 6 inches thick and the roof a minimum of 8 inches. If vaults are built in a tier, the slab between them is not considered a roof, and is designed only for structural considerations. All dimensions given here are minimums and should be increased if they are not sufficient for live loads, impact loads and other considerations.

TABLE 4-15. Suggested minimum thickness of walls for ground-supported vaults.

Class of wall	Reinforced Concrete (6 hour)	(4 hour)	(2 hour)	Brick (6 hour)	(4 hour)	(2 hour)	Hollow Units (2 hour)
Floor—counting from top down			Thickness of Wall, Inches				
Top	10	8	6	12	12	8	8
2nd from top	10	8	8	12	12	12	12
3rd from top	10	10	10	12	12	12	12
4th from top	12	10	10	16	16	16	16
5th from top	12	12	12	16	16	16	16
6th from top	12	12	12	16	16	16	16
7th from top	12	12	12	16	16	16	16
8th from top	12	12	12	16	16	16	16
9th from top	12	12	12	16	16	16	16
10th from top	14	12	12	16	16	16	16

Burglary-Resistive Vaults[10]

One of the arrangements for reinforcing steel in concrete consists of sheets of heavy-gage expanded metal. To meet Insurance Rating Board Classification 5R, the concrete wall, ceilings, and floors are 12 inches thick with expanded metal sheets located 2 1/2 inches from all inside and outside surfaces (2 grid system). Classes 6R or 9R require 18 inch concrete thickness and 3 sheets of expanded metal reinforcing (3 grid system) located in the middle and 2 inches from each surface.

Tables 4–16 and 4–17 are load tables (pounds per square foot) for the 2 grid system and the 3 grid system respectively. Concrete is assumed to have an ultimate strength of 3000 pounds per square inch, and calculations are based on uniformly applied loads.

---

[9]National Fire Protection Association, "Protection of Records," (NFPA No. 232), Boston, Massachusetts. Copyright © 1970.

[10]Wheeling Corrugating Company, Wheeling Grid-Crete, WC-383-R1, Wheeling, West Virginia.

To estimate other building requirements, consider the 12-inch wall to weigh 154 pounds per square foot, and the 18-inch wall 230 pounds per square foot.

TABLE 4-16. **Load table for 2-grid system to meet Insurance Rating Board Classification 5R.**

Clear Span (feet)	Total Load	Live Load
10	1841	1687
11	1521	1367
12	1306	1152
13	1089	935
14	939	785
15	818	664
16	719	565
17	637	483
18	568	414
19	510	356
20	460	306

TABLE 4-17. **Load table for 3-grid system to meet Insurance Rating Board Classifications 6R and 9R.**

Clear Span (Feet)	Total Load	Live Load
10	3960	3730
11	3273	3043
12	2750	2520
13	2343	2113
14	2021	1791
15	1760	1530
16	1547	1317
17	1370	1140
18	1222	992
19	1097	867
20	990	760
21	898	668
22	818	588
23	749	519
24	688	458
25	634	404

Note: It is not recommended that live loads in excess of 1250 pounds per square foot be used.

Electrical Power—
Design and Installation

CHAPTER 5

General concepts are covered first, followed by tables of codes and application information. Although some organizations are using "hertz" to mean "cycles per second," this book will use the latter (or its abbreviation *cps*) because its self-descriptive nature makes confusion impossible regardless of which term an individual prefers.

GENERAL CONCEPTS

Ohm's Law (for DC and for AC where voltage and current are in phase)

Formula

$$E = IR$$

where: E = voltage in volts
I = current in amperes
R = resistance in ohms
Multiplying prefixes such as kilo- or micro- can be used as long as they are used consistently with all three factors.

Example

How much resistance does a wire have if there is a difference of 2 volts between its ends, and 5 amperes are flowing through it?

Solution

Rearranging the Ohm's Law equation to solve for R gives

$$R = \frac{E}{I}$$

and the given values are substituted

$$R = \frac{2}{5}$$

$$= 0.4 \text{ ohm}$$

127

Ohm's Law (for AC circuits)

Formula

$$Z = \frac{E}{I}$$

where: Z = effective impedance in ohms or other consistent units
E = voltage in volts or other consistent units
I = current in amperes or other consistent units

Example

What is the impedance of a transformer winding if 115 VAC applied across it causes 10 amperes to flow?

Solution

$$Z = \frac{115}{10}$$
$$= 11.5 \text{ ohms}$$

Power

$$P = EI \cos \theta$$

where: P = power in watts or other consistent units
E = voltage in volts or other consistent units
I = current in amperes or other consistent units
θ = phase angle between current and voltage
$\quad = 0$ if circuit is purely resistive
$\cos \theta$ = power factor
$\quad = 1$ if circuit is purely resistive

Example

Because of heavy inductive loads in a plant, there is a 30 degree angle between voltage and current when 100 amperes is drawn at 220 volts. How much power is dissipated?

Solution

Substituting (after evaluating cos 30°) gives

$$P = 220(100)0.866$$
$$= 19052 \text{ watts}$$

Nomogram for Voltage, Current, Resistance, Power (assuming unity power factor)

The scales of Figure 5–1 are all mutually compatible: a straight line drawn through the figure connects, on all scales, values which agree with the equations just presented. One way to use such a nomogram is to place a pencil point on a value that is not a variable in the situation at hand (such as 115 volts) and then rotate a straightedge about that point, noting combinations of the other three variables that are consistent.

FIGURE 5-1

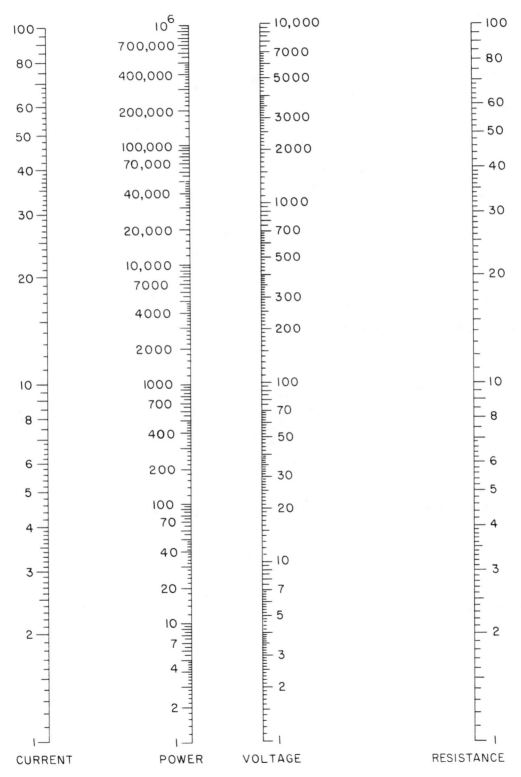

CURRENT POWER VOLTAGE RESISTANCE

No units are shown in Figure 5–1. All scales can be assumed to be in basic units (volts, amperes, etc.) and their ranges can be extended by multiplying all scales by a power of ten. The same result is achieved by applying the same prefix (milli-, mega-, etc.) to all scales.

Converting Between AC Descriptive Units

Table 5–1 gives conversion factors between pairs of the four common methods of describing AC amplitudes.

TABLE 5-1.   AC conversion factors.

Given Unit	Meaning	Desired Unit			
		Average	RMS	Peak	Peak to Peak
Average	Integrated mean value	1.0	1.11	1.57	1.274
RMS	Same power as DC of equal voltage	0.90	1.0	1.414	2.828
Peak	Baseline to extreme	0.637	0.707	1.0	2.000
Peak to peak	Between extremes	0.32	0.354	0.500	1.0

Star Connection: Figure 5-2

Formulas

$$E_{\text{line}} = 1.73 E_{\text{phase}}$$
$$I_{\text{line}} = I_{\text{phase}}$$

Example

What voltage will appear between phases if each phase generates 115 volts?

Solution

$$E_{\text{line}} = 1.73(115)$$
$$= 200 \text{ volts}$$

Delta Connection: Figure 5-3

Formulas

$$E_{\text{line}} = E_{\text{phase}}$$
$$I_{\text{line}} = 1.73 I_{\text{phase}}$$

Example

If all phases are loaded to draw 50 amperes, what current will flow in each phase?

Solution

Rearranging to solve for I_{phase} and substituting yields

$$I_{\text{phase}} = \frac{50}{1.73}$$

$$= 28.8 \text{ amperes}$$

FIGURE 5-2

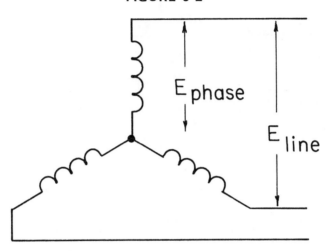

FIGURE 5-3

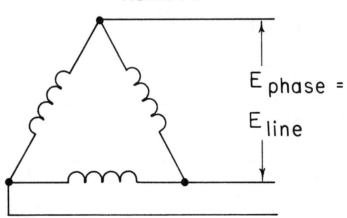

Summary of Equations[1]

Table 5–2 presents a summary of basic equations for electricity, arranged in various useful forms.

---

[1]General Electric Company, Calculation Data, CM-662, Bridgeport, Conn., 1964, p. 4.

TABLE 5-2. Summary of equations.

Desired Data	Alternating Current			Direct Current
	Single Phase	Two Phase Four Wire†	Three Phase	
Kilowatts	$\dfrac{I\,E\cos\theta}{1000}$	$\dfrac{2\,I\,E\cos\theta}{1000}$	$\dfrac{1.73\,I\,E\cos\theta}{1000}$	$\dfrac{I\,E}{1000}$
Kilovolt-amperes	$\dfrac{I\,E}{1000}$	$\dfrac{2\,I\,E}{1000}$	$\dfrac{1.73\,I\,E}{1000}$	$\dfrac{I\,E}{1000}$
Horsepower Output	$\dfrac{I\,E\cos\theta\times\text{Eff.}}{746}$	$\dfrac{2\,I\,E\cos\theta\times\text{Eff.}}{746}$	$\dfrac{1.73\,I\,E\cos\theta\times\text{Eff.}}{746}$	$\dfrac{I\,E\times\text{Eff.}}{746}$
Amperes When Horsepower Is Known	$\dfrac{hp\times746}{E\cos\theta\times\text{Eff.}}$	$\dfrac{hp\times746}{2\,E\cos\theta\times\text{Eff.}}$	$\dfrac{hp\times746}{1.73\,E\cos\theta\times\text{Eff.}}$	$\dfrac{hp\times746}{E\times\text{Eff.}}$
Amperes When Kilowatts Are Known	$\dfrac{kw\times1000}{E\cos\theta}$	$\dfrac{kw\times1000}{2\,E\cos\theta}$	$\dfrac{kw\times1000}{1.73\,E\cos\theta}$	$\dfrac{kw\times1000}{E}$
Amperes When Kilovolt-amperes Are Known	$\dfrac{kva\times1000}{E}$	$\dfrac{kva\times1000}{2\,E}$	$\dfrac{kva\times1000}{1.73\,E}$	$\dfrac{kva\times1000}{E}$
e_r When $e_s,\ I_s,\ \cos\theta$ Are Known	$\sqrt{e_s^2 - I^2(X\cos\theta \mp R\sin\theta)^2} - I\,(R\cos\theta \pm X\sin\theta)$			$e_s - IR$
e_s When $e_r,\ I_s,\ \cos\theta$ Are Known	$\sqrt{(e_r\cos\theta + IR)^2 + (e_r\sin\theta + IX)^2}$			$e_r + IR$

† In two-phase three-wire circuits, the current in the common conductor is 1.41 times that in either phase conductor.

NOTATION

$\cos\theta$ = Power factor of load
E = Volts between conductors
e = Volts to neutral
Eff. = Efficiency of motor

e_r = Volts at receiving end
e_s = Volts at sending end
I = Line current amperes
R = Resistance in ohms to neutral
$\sin^2\theta$ = $1 - \cos^2\theta$
X = Reactance in ohms to neutral
Where double signs, such as $\mp$ or $\pm$ are shown, use upper one for lagging and lower one for leading power factor.

Electric Shock: Current which causes animal hearts to fibrilate

This formula has a correlation factor of 0.913 on a least-squares fit of experimental data. Evidence indicates that the formula is equally valid for predicting human tolerance.

Formula

$$I = 1.415W + 18.254$$

where: I = current of 3 second duration which just causes heart fibrilation, in milliamperes
W = animal weight, in pounds

Example

Would a current-limiting device be satisfactory for protecting human life if it allowed a maximum of 210 milliamperes to flow?

Solution

Substituting an average weight of 150 pounds in the equation gives

$$I = 1.415(150) + 18.254$$
$$= 230.5 \text{ milliamperes}$$

The proposed current is only 10 percent less than this value—definitely not a sufficient safety factor, even for a person of average weight.

INSTALLATION RULES

Working Clearance[2]: Working space measured from exposed live parts or from enclosure front

Table 5–3 shows required clear distance. An exception to working clearance requirements is allowed in back of assemblies such as dead-front switchboards or control centers when there are no renewable or adjustable parts on the back, such as fuses and switches, and all connections are accessible from locations other than the back.

TABLE 5-3. Minimum working clearance, feet.

	*Condition**		
Voltage to Ground	*1*	*2*	*3*
0–150	2 1/2	2 1/2	3
151–600	2 1/2	3 1/2	4

*Condition 1: exposed live part on one side and no live or grounded part on the other side of the working space or exposed live parts on both sides effectively guarded by suitable wood or other insulating materials; insulated wire or insulated bus bars operating at not more than 300 volts not considered live parts.

[2]National Fire Protection Association, National Electrical Code, NFPA No. 70–1971, Boston, Mass., p. 16. Copyright © 1971.

Condition 2: exposed live parts on one side and grounded parts on the other side; concrete, brick, or tile walls considered as grounded.

Condition 3: exposed live parts on both sides of the work space (not guarded as provided in Condition 1) with the operator between.

Service Drop Clearance[3] (up to 600 volts)

Service drops over ground areas must be provided with clearances as shown in Table 5–4.

TABLE 5-4. Service drop clearances over ground areas.

Type of Ground Area	Clearance, feet
Finished grade	10
Sidewalks	10
Platform or projection	10
Commercial areas not subject to trucks	12
Commercial parking lots not subject to trucks	12
Drive-in establishments not subject to trucks	12
Commercial areas subject to trucks	15
Parking lots subject to trucks	15
Agricultural areas	15
Public streets, alleys, roads	18
Driveways on other than residential property	18

Conductors: Characteristics and applications

Table 5–5[4] lists some basic properties of wires. When conductors larger than Number 4/0 are used with AC, resistances in Table 5–5 should be multiplied by the factors given in Table 5–6[5] to correct for skin effect. Maximum allowable continuous current[6] for ambient temperatures up to 30°C (86°F) is given in Tables 5–7 and 5–8 for copper conductors and in Tables 5–9 and 5–10 for aluminum conductors. In higher ambients, currents should be derated by the factors given in Table 5–11.

[3]Ibid., p. 44.
[4]General Electric Company, Conductor Data CM-644, Bridgeport, Conn., 1964, p. 5.
[5]National Fire Protection Association, National Electrical Code, NFPA No. 70–1971, Boston, Mass., p. 488. Copyright © 1971.
[6]Ibid., pp. 114–118.

TABLE 5-5. Properties of conductors.

*American Wire Gage (Awg) Working Table (U.S. Bureau of Standards)

Gage No. Awg	Nom. Diam in Mils	Circular Mils	Square Inches	Maximum Ohms per 1000 Ft at 25 C (77 F)	Approx. Lb per 1000 Ft
0000	460	211600	.1662	.0500	641
000	410	167800	.1318	.0630	508
00	365	133100	.1045	.0795	403
0	325	105600	.08291	.100	320
1	289	83690	.06573	.126	253
2	258	66360	.05212	.159	201
3	229	52620	.04133	.201	159
4	204	41740	.0328	.253	126
5	182	33090	.0260	.320	100
6	162	26240	.0206	.403	79.4
7	144	20820	.0164	.508	63.0
8	128	16510	.0130	.640	50.0
9	114	13090	.0103	.808	39.6
10	102	10380	.008155	1.02	31.4
11	91	8230	.00646	1.29	24.9
12	81	6530	.00513	1.62	19.8
13	72	5180	.00407	2.04	15.7
14	64	4110	.00323	2.57	12.4
15	57	3260	.00256	3.24	9.87
16	51	2580	.00203	4.10	7.81
17	45	2050	.00161	5.15	6.21
18	40	1620	.00128	6.51	4.92
19	36	1290	.00101	8.21	3.90
20	32	1020	.000804	10.3	3.10
21	28.5	812	.000638	13.0	2.46
22	25.3	640	.000503	16.5	1.94
23	22.6	511	.000401	20.7	1.55
24	20.1	404	.000317	26.2	1.22
25	17.9	320	.000252	33.0	.970
26	15.9	253	.000199	41.8	0.765
27	14.2	202	.000158	52.4	0.610
28	12.6	159	.000125	66.6	0.481
29	11.3	128	.000100	82.8	0.387
30	10.0	100	.0000785	106	0.303
31	8.9	79.2	.0000622	134	0.240
32	8.0	64.0	.0000503	165	0.194
33	7.1	50.4	.0000396	210	0.153
34	6.3	39.7	.0000312	266	0.120
35	5.6	31.4	.0000246	337	0.0949
36	5.0	25.0	.0000196	423	0.0757
37	4.5	20.2	.0000159	522	0.0613
38	4.0	16.0	.0000126	661	0.0480
39	3.5	12.2	.0000096	863	0.0371
40	3.1	9.61	.0000076	1100	0.0291

Comparative wire gage table giving a comparison of the Brown & Sharpe, or American (Awg); the Birmingham (Bwg); and the British Standard (Bsg) wire gages

Awg	Bwg	Bsg	Awg	Bwg	Bsg
4/0	4/0	6/0	.4600	.454	.464
	3/0	5/0	.4096	.425	.432
3/0		4/0			.400
2/0	2/0	3/0	.3648	.380	.372
1/0	1/0	2/0		.340	.348
		1/0	.3249		.324
	1	1			.300
1	2	2	.2893	.284	.276
2	3	3	.2576	.259	.252
3	4	4	.2294	.238	.232
	5	5		.220	.212
4	6	6	.2043	.203	.192
5	7	7	.1819	.180	.176
6	8	8	.1620	.165	.160
7	9	9	.1443	.148	.144
8	10	10	.1285	.134	.128
9	11	11	.1144	.120	.116
10	12	12	.1019	.109	.104
11	13	13	.0907	.095	.092
12	14	14	.0808	.083	.080
13	15	15	.0720	.072	.072
14	16	16	.0641	.065	.064
15	17	17	.0571	.058	.056
16	18	18	.0508	.049	.048
17	19	19	.0453	.042	.040
18		20	.0403		.036
19	20		.0359	.035	
20	21	21	.0320	.032	.032
21	22	22	.0285	.028	.028
22	23	23	.0253	.025	.024
23	24	24	.0226	.022	.022
24	25	25	.0201	.020	.020
25	26	26	.0179	.018	.018
26	27	27	.0159	.016	.0164
27	28	28	.0152	.014	.0148
	29	29		.013	.0136
28	30	30	.0126	.012	.0124
29		31	.0113		.0116
		32			.0108
30	31	33	.0100	.010	.0100
31	32	34	.0089	.009	.0092
32	33	35	.0080	.008	.0084
33	34	36	.0071	.007	.0076
		37			.0068
34		38	.0063		.0060
35		39	.0056		.0052
36	35	40	.0050	.005	.0048
37		41	.0045		.0044
38	36	42	.0040	.004	.0040
39		43	.0035		.0036
		44			.0032
40		45	.0031		.0028

†Bare concentric cables of standard annealed copper (U.S. Bureau of Standards)

Size Awg or MCM	Maximum Ohms per 1000 Ft at 25 C (77 F) Std. Str.	Approx Lb per 1000 Ft	Standard Strands No. of Wires	Nom. Diam of Wires in Mils	Flexible Strands No. of Wires	Nom. Diam of Wires in Mils	Nom. Outside Diam in Mils
3000	.00363	9349	169	133.2	217	117.6	2000
2500	.00436	7794	127	140.3	169	121.6	1820
2000	.00539	6176	127	125.5	169	108.8	1630
1750	.00616	5403	127	117.4	169	101.8	1530
1700	.00634	5249	127	115.7	169	100.3	1500
1500	.00719	4632	91	128.4	127	108.7	1410
1250	.00863	3859	91	117.2	127	99.2	1290
1200	.00899	3703	91	114.8	127	97.2	1260
1000	.0108	3086	61	128.0	91	104.8	1150
950	.0114	2933	61	124.8	91	102.2	1120
900	.0120	2780	61	121.5	91	99.4	1090
850	.0127	2622	61	118.0	91	96.6	1060
800	.0135	2469	61	114.5	91	93.8	1030
750	.0144	2316	61	110.9	91	90.8	1000
700	.0154	2160	61	107.1	91	87.7	965
650	.0166	2006	61	103.2	91	84.5	930
600	.0180	1850	61	99.2	91	81.2	893
550	.0196	1700	61	95.0	91	77.7	855
500	.0216	1542	37	116.2	61	90.5	814
450	.0240	1390	37	110.3	61	85.9	773
400	.0270	1236	37	104.0	61	81.0	729
350	.0308	1080	37	97.3	61	75.7	681
300	.0360	925	37	90.0	61	70.1	631
250	.0431	772	37	82.2	61	64.0	576
0000	.0509	653	19	105.5	37	75.6	529
000	.0642	518	19	94.0	37	67.3	471
00	.0811	411	19	83.7	37	60.0	420
0	.102	326	19	74.5	37	53.4	374
1	.129	259	19	66.4	37	47.6	333
2	.162	205	7	97.4	19	59.1	296
3	.205	162	7	86.7	19	52.6	263
4	.259	129	7	77.2	19	46.9	234
5	.326	102	7	68.8	19	41.7	208
6	.410	80.9	7	61.2	19	37.2	186
7	.519	64.2	7	54.5	19	33.1	166
8	.654	51	7	48.6	19	29.5	148
10	1.039	32	7	38.5	19	23.4	117
12	1.652	20	7	30.5	19	18.5	92
14	2.626	12.7	7	24.2	19	14.7	73
16	4.176	8	7	19.2	19	11.7	58

* The fundamental resistivity used in calculating the table is the International Annealed Copper Standard viz., 0.15328 ohm-g/m² at 20 C. The temperature coefficient for this particular resistivity at 20 C = 0.00393, or at 0 C = 0.00427. However, the temperature coefficient is proportional to the conductivity and hence the change of resistivity per degree C is a constant, 0.000597 ohm-g/m². The "constant mass" temperature coefficient of any sample is a

$$\times t = \frac{0.000597 + 0.000005}{\text{resistivity in ohms-g/m}^2 \text{ at } t \text{ degree C}}$$

The density is 8.89 grams per cubic centimeter.

The values given in the table are only for annealed copper of the standard resistivity. The user of the table must apply the proper correction for copper of any other resistivity. Hard drawn copper may be taken as about 2.5 per cent higher resistivity than annealed copper.

Ohms per mile, or pounds per mile, may be obtained by multiplying the respective values above by 5.28.

† Resistance at T degrees above or below 25 C = R (at 25 degrees) (1 + 0.00385 [T-25]).

The values given for ohms per 1000 feet and pounds per 1000 feet are 2 per cent greater than for a solid rod of cross section equal to the total cross section of the wires of the cable.

Resistivity of pure copper at 20 C = 0.15328 ohms per g/m².

TABLE 5-7. Allowable ampacities of up to 3 insulated copper conductors in raceway.

Size	Temperature Rating of Conductor							
AWG MCM	60°C (140°F) TYPES RUW (14-2), T, TW	75°C (167°F) TYPES RH, RHW, RUH (14-2), THW, THWN, XHHW	85°C (185°F) TYPES V, MI	90°C (194°F) TYPES TA, TBS, SA, AVB, SIS, FEP, FEPB, RHH, THHN, XHHW**	110°C (230°F) TYPES AVA, AVL	125°C (257°F) TYPES AI (14-8), AIA	200°C (392°F) TYPES A (14-8), AA, FEP*, FEPB*	250°C (482°F) TYPE TFE (Nickel or nickel-coated copper only)
14	15	15	25	25†	30	30	30	40
12	20	20	30	30†	35	40	40	55
10	30	30	40	40†	45	50	55	75
8	40	45	50	50	60	65	70	95
***6	55	65	70	70	80	85	95	120
***4	70	85	90	90	105	115	120	145
***3	80	100	105	105	120	130	145	170
***2	95	115	120	120	135	145	165	195
***1	110	130	140	140	160	170	190	220
***0	125	150	155	155	190	200	225	250
***00	145	175	185	185	215	230	250	280
000	165	200	210	210	245	265	285	315
0000	195	230	235	235	275	310	340	370
250	215	255	270	270	315	335	...	...
300	240	285	300	300	345	380	...	...
350	260	310	325	325	390	420	...	...
400	280	335	360	360	420	450	...	...
500	320	380	405	405	470	500	...	...
600	355	420	455	455	525	545	...	...
700	385	460	490	490	560	600	...	...
750	400	475	515	500	580	620	...	...
800	410	490	515	515	600	640	...	...
900	435	520	555	555	600	...	...	...
1000	455	545	585	585	680	730	...	...
1250	495	590	645	645	...	...	...	...
1500	520	625	700	700	785	...	...	...
1750	545	650	735	735	...	...	...	...
2000	560	665	775	775	840	...	...	...

* Special use only
** For dry locations only.

*** For 3-wire, single-phase residential services, the allowable ampacity of RH, RHH, RHW, THW and XHHW copper conductors shall be for sizes No. 4-100 Amp., No. 3-110 Amp., No. 2-125 Amp., No. 1-150 Amp., No. 1/0-175 Amp., and No. 2/0-200 Amp.

† The ampacities for Types FEP, FEPB, RHH, THHN, and XHHW conductors for sizes AWG 14, 12 and 10 shall be the same as designated for 75°C conductors in this Table.

TABLE 5-6. Multiplying factors for converting DC resistance to 60 cycle AC resistance.

Size	Multiplying Factor			
	For Nonmetallic Sheathed Cables in Air or Nonmetallic Conduit		For Metallic Sheathed Cables or all Cables in Metallic Raceways	
	Copper	Aluminum	Copper	Aluminum
Up to 3 AWG	1.	1.	1.	1.00
2	1.	1.	1.01	1.00
1	1.	1.	1.01	1.00
0	1.001	1.000	1.02	1.00
00	1.001	1.001	1.03	1.00
000	1.002	1.001	1.04	1.01
0000	1.004	1.002	1.05	1.01
250 MCM	1.005	1.002	1.06	1.02
300 MCM	1.006	1.003	1.07	1.02
350 MCM	1.009	1.004	1.08	1.03
400 MCM	1.011	1.005	1.10	1.04
500 MCM	1.018	1.007	1.13	1.06
600 MCM	1.025	1.010	1.16	1.08
700 MCM	1.034	1.013	1.19	1.11
750 MCM	1.039	1.015	1.21	1.12
800 MCM	1.044	1.017	1.22	1.14
1000 MCM	1.067	1.026	1.30	1.19
1250 MCM	1.102	1.040	1.41	1.27
1500 MCM	1.142	1.058	1.53	1.36
1750 MCM	1.185	1.079	1.67	1.46
2000 MCM	1.233	1.100	1.82	1.56

TABLE 5-8. Allowable ampacities of single insulated copper conductor in air.

Size	60°C (140°F)	75°C (167°F)	85°C (185°F)	90°C (194°F)	110°C (230°F)	125°C (257°F)	200°C (392°F)	250°C (482°F)	
AWG MCM	TYPES RUW (14-2), T, TW	TYPES RH, RHW, RUH (14-2), THW, THWN, XHHW	TYPES V, MI	TYPES TA, TBS, SA, AVB, SIS, FEP, FEPB, RHH, THHN, XHHW**	TYPES AVA, AVL	TYPES AI (14-8), AIA	TYPES A (14-8), AA, FEP*, FEPB*	TYPE TFE (Nickel or nickel-coated copper only)*	Bare and Covered Conductors
14	20	20	30	30†	40	40	45	60	30
12	25	25	40	40†	50	50	55	80	40
10	40	40	55	55†	65	70	75	110	55
8	55	65	70	70	85	90	100	145	70
6	80	95	100	100	120	125	135	210	100
4	105	125	135	135	160	170	180	285	130
3	120	145	155	155	180	195	210	335	150
2	140	170	180	180	210	225	240	390	175
1	165	195	210	210	245	265	280	450	205
0	195	230	245	245	285	305	325	545	235
00	225	265	285	285	330	355	370	605	275
000	260	310	330	330	385	410	430	725	320
0000	300	360	385	385	445	475	510	850	370
250	340	405	425	425	495	530	…	…	410
300	375	445	480	480	555	590	…	…	460
350	420	505	530	530	610	655	…	…	510
400	455	545	575	575	665	710	…	…	555
500	515	620	660	660	765	815	…	…	630
600	575	690	740	740	855	910	…	…	710
700	630	755	815	815	940	1005	…	…	780
750	655	785	845	845	980	1045	…	…	810
800	680	815	880	880	1020	1085	…	…	845
900	730	870	940	940	…	…	…	…	905
1000	780	935	1000	1000	1165	1240	…	…	965
1250	890	1065	1130	1130	1450	…	…	…	…
1500	980	1175	1260	1260	…	…	…	…	1215
1750	1070	1280	1370	1370	1715	…	…	…	…
2000	1155	1385	1470	1470	…	…	…	…	1405

* Special use only.

** For dry locations only

† The ampacities for Types FEP, FEPB, RHH, THHN, and XHHW conductors for sizes AWG 14, 12 and 10 shall be the same as designated for 75°C conductors in this Table.

TABLE 5-9. Allowable ampacities of up to 3 insulated aluminum conductors in raceway.

Size	60°C (140°F)	75°C (167°F)	85°C (185°F)	90°C (194°F)	110°C (230°F)	125°C (257°F)	200°C (392°F)
AWG MCM	TYPES RUW (12-2), T, TW	TYPES RH, RHW, RUH (12-2), THW, THWN, XHHW	TYPES V, MI	TYPES TA, TBS, SA, AVB, SIS, RHH, THHN, XHHW**	TYPES AVA, AVL	TYPES AI (12-8), AIA	TYPES A (12-8), AA
12	15	15	25	25†	25	30	30
10	25	25	30	30†	35	40	45
8	30	40	40	40	45	50	55
6	40	50	55	55	60	65	75
4	55	65	70	70	80	90	95
3	65	75	80	80	95	100	115
2	75	90	95	95	105	115	130
1	85	100	110	110	125	135	150
0	100	120	125	125	150	160	180
00	115	135	145	145	170	180	200
000	130	155	165	165	195	210	225
0000	155	180	185	185	215	245	270
250	170	205	215	215	250	270	…
300	190	230	240	240	275	305	…
350	210	250	260	260	310	335	…
400	225	270	290	290	335	360	…
500	260	310	330	330	380	405	…
600	285	340	370	370	425	440	…
700	310	375	395	395	455	485	…
750	320	385	405	405	470	500	…
800	330	395	415	415	485	520	…
900	355	425	455	455	560	600	…
1000	375	445	480	480	…	…	…
1250	405	485	530	530	650	…	…
1500	435	520	580	580	…	…	…
1750	455	545	615	615	705	…	…
2000	470	560	650	650	…	…	…

* For 3-wire, single-phase residential services, the allowable ampacity of RH, RHH, RHW, THW, and XHHW conductors shall be for sizes No. 2-100 Amp., No. 1-110 Amp., No. 1/0-125 Amp., No. 2/0-150 Amp., No. 3/0-175 Amp., and No. 4/0-200 Amp.

** For dry locations only.

† The ampacities for Types RHH, THHN, and XHHW conductors for sizes AWG 12 and 10 shall be the same as designated for 75°C conductors in this Table.

TABLE 5-10. Allowable ampacities of single insulated aluminum conductor in air.

Size	Temperature Rating of Conductor.							
AWG MCM	60°C (140°F)	75°C (167°F)	85°C (185°F)	90°C (194°F)	110°C (230°F)	125°C (257°F)	200°C (392°F)	
	TYPES RUW (12-2), T, TW	TYPES RH, RHW, RUH (12-2), THW, THWN, XHHW	TYPES V, MI	TYPES TA, TBS, SA, AVB, SIS, RHH, THHN, XHHW*	TYPES AVA, AVL	TYPES AI (12-8), AIA	TYPES A (12-8), AA	Bare and Covered Conductors
12	20	20	30	30 †	40	40	45	30
10	30	30	45	45 †	50	55	60	45
8	45	55	55	55	65	70	80	55
6	60	75	80	80	95	100	105	80
4	80	100	105	105	125	135	140	100
3	95	115	120	120	140	150	165	115
2	110	135	140	140	165	175	185	135
1	130	155	165	165	190	205	220	160
0	150	180	190	190	220	240	255	185
00	175	210	220	220	255	275	290	215
000	200	240	255	255	300	320	335	250
0000	230	280	300	300	345	370	400	290
250	265	315	330	330	385	415	....	320
300	290	350	375	375	435	460	....	360
350	330	395	415	415	475	510	....	400
400	355	425	450	450	520	555	....	435
500	405	485	515	515	595	635	....	490
600	455	545	585	585	675	720	....	560
700	500	595	645	645	745	795	....	615
750	515	620	670	670	775	825	....	640
800	535	645	695	695	805	855	....	670
900	580	700	750	750	....	....	....	725
1000	625	750	800	800	930	990	....	770
1250	710	855	905	905	....	....	....	....
1500	795	950	1020	1020	1175	....	....	985
1750	875	1050	1125	1125	....	....	....	....
2000	960	1150	1220	1220	1425	....	....	1165

* For dry locations only.
† The ampacities for Types RHH, THHN, and XHHW conductors for sizes AWG 12 and 10 shall be the same as designated for 75°C conductors in this Table.

TABLE 5-11.   Correction factors for Tables 5-7 through 5-10.

Temperature Rating of Conductor

C	F	60°C (140°F)	75°C (167°F)	85°C (185°F)	90°C (194°F)	110°C (230°F)	125°C (257°F)	200°C (392°F)
40	104	.82	.88	.90	.90	.94	.95	—
45	113	.71	.82	.85	.85	.90	.92	—
50	122	.58	.75	.80	.80	.87	.89	—
55	131	.41	.67	.74	.74	.83	.86	—
60	140	—	.58	.67	.67	.79	.83	.91
70	158	—	.35	.52	.52	.71	.76	.87
75	167	—	—	.43	.43	.66	.72	.86
80	176	—	—	.30	.30	.61	.69	.84
90	194	—	—	—	—	.50	.61	.80
100	212	—	—	—	—	—	.51	.77
120	248	—	—	—	—	—	—	.69
140	284	—	—	—	—	—	—	.59

Tables 5–7 and 5–9, for up to three conductors, can be used for larger numbers of conductors by applying derating factors from Table 5–12.

TABLE 5-12.   Factors for derating Tables 5-7 and 5-9.

Number of Conductors	Derating Factor
4 to 6	.80
7 to 24	.70
25 to 42	.60
43 and above	.50

Table 5–13[7] gives capacity in amperes for some of the more common sizes of copper bus bars.

Conduit Sizes[8]

The sum of cross-sectional areas of conductors in a conduit should not be more than the values indicated in Table 5–14.

---

[7]Underwriters' Laboratories, Inc., Power Outlets (UL231), Chicago, Ill., 1970, p. 37.
[8]National Fire Protection Association, National Electrical Code, NFPA No. 70–1971, Boston, Mass., pp. 408ff. Copyright © 1971.

TABLE 5-13. Ampacity of bus bars.

Width of Bus Bar in Inches	Bus-Bar Thicknesses In Inches											
	3/64	0.051 No. 16 AWG	1/16	0.064 No. 14 AWG	5/64	0.081 No. 12 AWG	3/32	1/8	5/32	3/16	7/32	1/4
3/8	18	19	23	24	29	30	35	47	59	70	82	94
7/16	21	22	27	28	34	35	41	55	68	82	96	109
1/2	23	26	31	32	39	41	47	63	78	94	109	125
9/16	26	29	35	36	44	46	53	70	88	105	123	141
5/8	29	32	39	40	49	51	59	78	98	117	137	156
11/16	32	35	43	44	54	56	64	86	108	129	150	172
3/4	35	38	47	48	59	61	70	94	117	141	164	188
7/8	41	45	55	56	68	71	82	109	137	164	191	—
1	47	51	63	64	78	81	94	125	156	188	—	—
1 1/8	53	57	70	72	88	91	105	141	176	—	—	—
1 1/4	59	64	78	80	98	101	117	156	195	—	—	—
1 3/8	64	70	86	88	102	111	129	172	—	—	—	—

Belt Width, Inches	CARRYING IDLERS						RETURN IDLERS
	Weight of Material Conveyed Pounds Per Cubic Foot						
	30	50	75	100	150	200	
14	5½	5	5	5	4½	4½	10
16	5½	5	5	5	4½	4½	10
18	5½	5	5	5	4½	4½	10
20	5½	5	4½	4½	4	4	10
24	5	4½	4½	4	4	4	10
30	5	4½	4½	4	4	4	10
36	5	4½	4	4	3½	3½	10
42	4½	4½	4	3½	3	3	10
48	4½	4	4	3½	3	3	10
54	4½	4	3½	3½	3	3	10
60	4	4	3½	3	3	3	10
66	4	4	3½	3	3	2½	8
72	4	3½	3½	3	2½	2½	8

Note: In the shaded area, for more severe applications particulary for 35° and 45° idlers, the maximum allowable idler loading may be surpassed. In questionable cases consult REX CHAINBELT.

TABLE 5-14.   Allowable conduit area occupied by conductors.

| | *Percent* Area of Conduit or Tubing | | | | |
| | Number of Conductors | | | | |
	1	2	3	4	Over 4
All conductor types except lead-covered (new or rewiring)	53	31	40	40	40
Lead-covered conductors	53	31	40	40	40

Note: See Table 5–16 for number of conductors all of the same size in trade sizes of conduit 1/2 inch through 6 inch.

As an aid in evaluating conduits and percentage fill, Table 5–15 shows worked-out areas and percentages for various standard conduits. If the conductors in a conduit are all one size, Table 5–16 can be used to determine the allowable number. Table 5–17 shows maximum numbers of fixture wires allowed in trade size conduit or tubing. Dimensions of lead-covered types of conductor are covered in Table 5–18.

Conduit Bends[9]

Table 5–19 gives minimum radius for any field bend, except that tighter bends are allowed for conductors without lead sheath when bent on a single-operation bending machine designed for the purpose. Table 5–20 gives minimum radius for these conditions.

TABLE 5-15.   Cross-sectional areas of conduits.

| | | Area—Square Inches | | | | | | | | |
| | | | Not Lead Covered | | | Lead Covered | | | | |
Trade Size	Internal Diameter Inches	Total 100%	2 Cond. 31%	Over 2 Cond. 40%	1 Cond. 53%	1 Cond. 55%	2 Cond. 30%	3 Cond. 40%	4 Cond. 38%	Over 4 Cond. 35%
½	.622	.30	.09	.12	.16	.17	.09	.12	.11	.11
¾	.824	.53	.16	.21	.28	.29	.16	.21	.20	.19
1	1.049	.86	.27	.34	.46	.47	.26	.34	.33	.30
1¼	1.380	1.50	.47	.60	.80	.83	.45	.60	.57	.53
1½	1.610	2.04	.63	.82	1.08	1.12	.61	.82	.78	.71
2	2.067	3.36	1.04	1.34	1.78	1.85	1.01	1.34	1.28	1.18
2½	2.469	4.79	1.48	1.92	2.54	2.63	1.44	1.92	1.82	1.68
3	3.068	7.38	2.29	2.95	3.91	4.06	2.21	2.95	2.80	2.58
3½	3.548	9.90	3.07	3.96	5.25	5.44	2.97	3.96	3.76	3.47
4	4.026	12.72	3.94	5.09	6.74	7.00	3.82	5.09	4.83	4.45
4½	4.506	15.94	4.94	6.38	8.45	8.77	4.78	6.38	6.06	5.56
5	5.047	20.00	6.20	8.00	10.60	11.00	6.00	8.00	7.60	7.00
6	6.065	28.89	8.96	11.56	15.31	15.89	8.67	11.56	10.98	10.11

[9]Ibid., p. 142.

TABLE 5-16. Maximum number of conductors in trade sizes of conduit or tubing.

Type Letters	Conductor Size AWG, MCM	½	¾	1	1¼	1½	2	2½	3	3½	4	4½	5	6
TW, T, RUH, RUW, XHHW (14 thru 8)	14	9	15	25	44	60	99	142						
	12	7	12	19	35	47	78	111	171					
	10	5	9	15	26	36	60	85	131	176				
	8	3	5	8	14	20	33	47	72	97	124			
RHW and RHH (without outer covering), THW	14	6	10	16	29	40	65	93	143	192				
	12	4	8	13	24	32	53	76	117	157				
	10	4	6	11	19	26	43	61	95	127	163			
	8	1	4	6	11	15	25	36	56	75	96	121	152	
TW, T, THW, RUH (6 thru 2), RUW (6 thru 2), FEPB (6 thru 2), RHW and RHH (without outer covering)	6	1	2	4	7	10	16	23	36	48	62	78	97	141
	4	1	1	3	5	7	12	17	27	36	47	58	73	106
	3	1	1	2	4	6	10	15	23	31	40	50	63	91
	2	1	1	2	4	5	9	13	20	27	34	43	54	78
	1		1	1	3	4	6	9	14	19	25	31	39	57
	0		1	1	2	3	5	8	12	16	21	27	33	49
	00		1	1	1	3	5	7	10	14	18	23	29	41
	000		1	1	1	2	4	6	9	12	15	19	24	35
	0000			1	1	1	3	5	7	10	13	16	20	29
	250			1	1	1	2	4	6	8	10	13	16	23
	300			1	1	1	2	3	5	7	9	11	14	20
	350				1	1	1	3	4	6	8	10	12	18
	400				1	1	1	2	4	5	7	9	11	16
	500					1	1	1	3	4	6	7	9	14
	600					1	1	1	3	4	5	6	7	11
	700					1	1	1	2	3	4	5	7	10
	750					1	1	1	2	3	4	5	6	9

TABLE 5-16. cont.

Type Letters	Conductor Size AWG, MCM	½	¾	1	1¼	1½	2	2½	3	3½	4	4½	5	6
THWN,	14	13	24	39	69	94	154							
	12	10	18	29	51	70	114	164						
	10	6	11	18	32	44	73	104	160					
	8	3	6	10	19	26	42	60	93	125	160			
THHN, FEP (14 thru 2), FEPB (14 thru 8), XHHW (4 thru 500MCM)	6	1	4	6	11	15	26	37	57	76	98	125	154	
	4	1	2	4	7	9	16	22	35	47	60	75	94	137
	3	1	1	3	6	8	13	19	29	39	51	64	80	116
	2	1	1	3	5	7	11	16	25	33	43	54	67	97
	1			1	3	5	8	12	18	25	32	40	50	72
	0		1	1	3	4	7	10	15	21	27	33	42	61
	00		1	1	2	3	6	8	13	17	22	28	35	51
	000		1	1	1	3	5	7	11	14	18	23	29	42
	0000		1	1	1	2	4	6	9	12	15	19	24	35
	250			1	1	1	3	4	7	10	12	16	20	28
	300			1	1	1	3	4	6	8	11	13	17	24
	350			1	1	1	2	3	5	7	9	12	15	21
	400				1	1	1	3	5	6	8	10	13	19
	500				1	1	1	2	4	5	7	9	11	16
	600					1	1	1	3	4	5	7	9	13
	700					1	1	1	3	4	5	6	8	11
	750					1	1	1	2	3	4	5	6	11
XHHW	6	1	3	5	9	13	21	30	47	63	81	102	128	185
	600					1	1	1	3	4	5	7	9	13
	700					1	1	1	3	4	5	6	7	11
	750					1	1	1	2	3	4	5	6	10

TABLE 5-16. cont.

Type Letters	Conductor Size AWG, MCM	½	¾	1	1¼	1½	2	2½	3	3½	4	4½	5	6
RHW,	14	3	6	10	18	25	41	58	90	121	155			
	12	3	5	9	15	21	35	50	77	103	132			
	10	2	4	7	13	18	29	41	64	86	110	138		
	8	1	2	4	8	10	17	25	39	52	67	84	105	152
RHH	6	1	1	2	5	6	11	15	24	32	41	51	64	93
	4	1	1	1	3	5	8	12	18	24	31	39	50	72
(with	3	1	1	1	3	4	7	10	16	22	28	35	44	63
outer	2		1	1	3	4	6	9	14	19	24	31	38	56
covering)	1		1	1	1	3	5	7	11	14	18	23	29	42
	0		1	1	1	2	4	6	9	12	16	20	25	37
	00			1	1	1	3	5	8	11	14	18	22	32
	000			1	1	1	3	4	7	9	12	15	19	28
	0000				1	1	2	4	6	8	10	13	16	24
	250				1	1	1	3	5	6	8	11	13	19
	300				1	1	1	3	4	5	7	9	11	17
	350				1	1	1	2	4	5	6	8	10	15
	400				1	1	1	1	3	4	6	7	9	14
	500				1	1	1	1	3	4	5	6	8	11
	600					1	1	1	2	3	4	5	6	9
	700					1	1	1	1	3	3	4	6	8
	750						1	1	1	3	3	4	5	8

TABLE 5-17. Maximum number of fixture wires in trade size of conduit or tubing.

Conduit Trade Size (Inches)	½			¾			1			1¼			1½			2		
Wire Types	18	16	14	18	16	14	18	16	14	18	16	14	18	16	14	18	16	14
PTF, PTFF, PGFF, PGF, PFF, PF	23	18	14	40	31	24	65	50	39	115	90	70	157	122	95	257	200	156
TFFN, TFN	19	15		34	26		55	43		97	76		132	104		216	169	
SF-1	16			29			47			83			114			186		
SFF-1, FF-1, FFH-1	15			26			43			76			104			169		
CF	13	10	8	23	18	14	38	30	23	66	53	40	91	72	55	149	118	90
TF	11	10		20	18		32	30		57	53		79	72		129	118	
RFH-1, RF-1	11			20			32			57			79			129		
TFF	11	10		20	17		32	27		56	49		77	66		126	109	
AF	11	9	7	19	16	12	31	26	20	55	46	36	75	63	49	123	104	81
SFF-2	9	7	6	16	12	10	27	20	17	47	36	30	65	49	42	106	81	68
SF-2	9	8	6	16	14	11	27	23	18	47	40	32	65	55	43	106	90	71
FF-2, FFH-2	9	7		15	12		25	19		44	34		60	46		99	75	
RFH-2	7	5		12	10		20	16		36	28		49	38		80	62	
RF-2	7	6		12	10		20	16		36	29		49	40		80	65	

TABLE 5-18. Dimensions of lead-covered conductors, types RL, RHL, and RUL.

Size AWG-MCM	Single Conductor		Two Conductor		Three Conductor	
	Diam. Inches	Area Sq. Ins.	Diam. Inches	Area Sq. Ins.	Diam. Inches	Area Sq. Ins.
14	.28	.062	.28 x .47	.115	.59	.273
12	.29	.066	.31 x .54	.146	.62	.301
10	.35	.096	.35 x .59	.180	.68	.363
8	.41	.132	.41 x .71	.255	.82	.528
6	.49	.188	.49 x .86	.369	.97	.738
4	.55	.237	.54 x .96	.457	1.08	.916
2	.60	.283	.61 x 1.08	.578	1.21	1.146
1	.67	.352	.70 x 1.23	.756	1.38	1.49
0	.71	.396	.74 x 1.32	.859	1.47	1.70
00	.76	.454	.79 x 1.41	.980	1.57	1.94
000	.81	.515	.84 x 1.52	1.123	1.69	2.24
0000	.87	.593	.90 x 1.64	1.302	1.85	2.68
250	.98	.754	....	.....	2.02	3.20
300	1.04	.85	....	.....	2.15	3.62
350	1.10	.95	....	.....	2.26	4.02
400	1.14	1.02	....	.....	2.40	4.52
500	1.23	1.18	....	.....	2.59	5.28

The above cables are limited to straight runs or with nominal offsets equivalent to not more than two quarter bends.

Note — No. 14 to No. 8, solid conductors: No. 6 and larger, stranded conductors. Data for 30-mil insulation not yet compiled.

TABLE 5-19. Minimum radius in inches of ordinary conduit bends.

Size of Conduit (inches)	Conductors without lead sheath	Conductors with lead sheath
1/2	4	6
3/4	5	8
1	6	11
1 1/4	8	14
1 1/2	10	16
2	12	21
2 1/2	15	25
3	18	31
3 1/2	21	36
4	24	40
4 1/2	27	45
5	30	50
6	36	61

TABLE 5-20. Minimum radius in inches of special conduit bends.

Size of Conduit (inches)	Radius to Center of Conduit
1/2	4
3/4	4 1/2
1	5 3/4
1 1/4	7 1/4
1 1/2	8 1/4
2	9 1/2
2 1/2	10 1/2
3	13
3 1/2	15
4	16
4 1/2	20
5	24
6	30

TABLE 5-21. Maximum spacing for conductor supports in vertical raceway.

				Aluminum	Copper
No. 18		to No. 8	not greater than	100 feet	100 feet
No. 6		to No. 0	not greater than	200 feet	100 feet
No. 00		to No. 0000	not greater than	180 feet	80 feet
211,601	CM	to 350,000 CM	not greater than	135 feet	60 feet
350,001	CM	to 500,000 CM	not greater than	120 feet	50 feet
500,001	CM	to 750,000 CM	not greater than	95 feet	40 feet
	Above	750,000 CM	not greater than	85 feet	35 feet

Vertical Raceways[10]

Table 5–21 gives maximum spacing between clamps or other strain reliefs that are required in vertical raceways.

Branch Circuits[11]

A branch circuit having two or more outlets is restricted to supplying not more than the loads indicated in Table 5–22, where the term "fixed" recognizes cord connections when otherwise permitted.

---

[10]Ibid., p. 94.
[11]Ibid., p. 28.

TABLE 5-22.   Branch circuit descriptions.

Branch Circuit Size	Maximum Load
15 ampere and 20 ampere	Lighting units and/or appliances. The rating of any portable appliance not to exceed 80 percent of the branch circuit rating. The total rating of fixed appliances not to exceed 50 percent of the branch circuit rating when lighting units or portable appliances are also supplied.
30 ampere	Fixed lighting units with heavy duty lampholders in other than dwelling occupancies; or appliances in any occupancy. Rating of any one portable or stationary appliance not to exceed 24 amperes.
40 ampere	Fixed lighting units with heavy duty lampholders in other than dwelling occupancies; or fixed cooking appliances; or infra-red heating units
50 ampere	Fixed lighting units with heavy duty lampholders in other than dwelling occupancies; or fixed cooking appliances; or infra-red heating units

For raceways or cables with the following type wires:

FEP	FEPB	RUW	SA	T
TW	RH	RUH	RHW	RHH
THHN	THW	THWN	XHHW	

Table 5–23 shows minimum size wire and other requirements for various services.

TABLE 5-23.   Branch circuit requirements.

CIRCUIT RATING	15 amp.	20 amp.	30 amp.	40 amp.	50 amp.
CONDUCTORS: (Min. size)					
Circuit wires*	14	12	10	8	6
Taps	14	14	14	12	12
OVERCURRENT PROTECTION	15	20	30	40	50
OUTLET DEVICES:					
Lampholders permitted	any type	any type	heavy duty	heavy duty	heavy duty
Receptacle rating	15 max	15 or 20	30	40 or 50	50
MAXIMUM LOAD	15	20	30	40	50

*These ampacities are for copper conductors where derating is not required.

TABLE 5-24. Minimum size of grounding conductor in grounded system.

Size of Largest Service-Entrance Conductor or Equivalent for Parallel Conductors		Size of Grounding Electrode Conductor	
Copper	Aluminum or Copper-Clad Aluminum	Copper	Aluminum or Copper-Clad Aluminum
2 or smaller	0 or smaller	8	6
1 or 0	2/0 or 3/0	6	4
2/0 or 3/0	4/0 or 250 MCM	4	2
Over 3/0 thru 350 MCM	Over 250 MCM thru 500 MCM	2	0
Over 350 MCM thru 600 MCM	Over 500 MCM thru 900 MCM	0	3/0
Over 600 MCM thru 1100 MCM	Over 900 MCM thru 1750 MCM	2/0	4/0
Over 1100 MCM	Over 1750 MCM	3/0	250 MCM

Where there are no service-entrance conductors, the grounding electrode conductor size shall be determined by the equivalent size of the largest service-entrance conductor required for the load to be served.

TABLE 5-25. Minimum size of grounding conductor in ungrounded system.

Size of Largest Service-Entrance Conductor or Equivalent for Parallel Conductors		Size of Grounding Electrode Conductor			
Copper	Aluminum or Copper-Clad Aluminum	Copper	Aluminum or Copper-Clad Aluminum	Conduit or Pipe	Electrical Metallic Tubing
2 or smaller	0 or smaller	8	6	½	½
1 or 0	2/0 or 3/0	6	4	½	1
2/0 or 3/0	4/0 or 250 MCM	4	2	¾	1¼
Over 3/0 thru 350 MCM	Over 250 MCM thru 500 MCM	2	0	¾	1¼
Over 350 MCM thru 600 MCM	Over 500 MCM thru 900 MCM	0	3/0	1	2
Over 600 MCM thru 1100 MCM	Over 900 MCM thru 1750 MCM	2/0	4/0	1	2
Over 1100 MCM	Over 1750 MCM	3/0	250 MCM	1	2

Where there are no service-entrance conductors the grounding electrode conductor size shall be determined by the equivalent size of the largest service-entrance conductor required for the load to be served.

Grounding Conductors[12]

For most grounded systems the minimum size of grounding conductor is given in Table 5–24. In an ungrounded system the minimum size of conductor for grounding a service raceway, the metal sheath or armor of a service cable, and service equipment is given in Table 5–25. Minimum conductor sizes for grounding of equipment are given in Table 5–26.

TABLE 5-26. **Minimum size of conductor for grounding equipment.**

Rating or Setting of Automatic Overcurrent Device in Circuit Ahead of Equipment, Conduit, etc. not exceeding Amperes	Copper Wire No.	Aluminum or Copper-Clad Aluminum Wire No.
15	14	12
20	12	10
30	10	8
40	10	8
60	10	8
100	8	6
200	6	4
400	3	1
600	1	2/0
800	0	3/0
1000	2/0	4/0
1200	3/0	250 MCM
1600	4/0	350 MCM
2000	250 MCM	400 MCM
2500	350 MCM	500 MCM
3000	400 MCM	600 MCM
4000	500 MCM	800 MCM
5000	700 MCM	1000 MCM
6000	800 MCM	1200 MCM

Voltage Drop: Due to finite resistance of conductor

Formula

$$V = \frac{R_{1000}(2L)I}{1000}$$

where: V = difference in volts between supply and load ends of conductor
R_{1000} = resistance per 1000 feet of conductor, in ohms (see Table 5–5)
L = length of conductor, in feet
I = current flowing through conductor, in amperes

---

[12]Ibid., p. 82.

Example

A three ampere load is supplied by 200 feet of number 16 wire from a 115-volt source. What voltage appears at the load?

Solution

Table 5–5 shows that number 16 wire has a resistance of 4.10 ohms per 1000 feet. Substituting in the equation gives

$$V = \frac{4.10(2)200(3)}{1000}$$

$$= 5 \text{ volts}$$

and the load will be supplied with

$$115 - 5 = 110 \text{ volts}$$

Heating, Cooling and Ventilation

CHAPTER 6

Heat from Electrical Appliances

Table 6–1[1] lists the rate at which heat units are added to the environment by electrical appliances.

TABLE 6-1. Heat from electrical appliances.

General lights and heating	3.4 BTU/hr/watt	860 Cal/hr/watt
2650 watt toaster	9100 BTU/hr	2300 Kcal/hr
5000 watt toaster	19,000 BTU/hr	4800 Kcal/hr
Hair dryer	2000 BTU/hr	510 Kcal/hr
Motor less than 2 HP	3600 BTU/hr/HP	910 Kcal/hr/HP
Motor over 3 HP	3000 BTU/hr/HP	760 Kcal/hr/HP

Heat from Gas Appliances

Table 6–2[2] lists the rate at which heat units are added to the environment by gas appliances.

TABLE 6-2. Heat from gas appliances.

Restaurant range, 4 burners and oven	100,000 BTU/hr	25,300 Kcal/hr
Steam table (per square foot of top surface)	2,000	510
Restaurant coffee urn	10,000	2,530
Enclosed steak broiler	60,000	15,200
Two-inch diameter burner	10,000	2,530
Four-inch diameter burner	15,000	3,800
Five-inch diameter burner	25,000	63,000
Dish warmer (per square foot of shelf)	600	152
Hair dryer	3,000	760
Clothes pressing machine	17,000 BTU/hr	4,300 Kcal/hr
Per cubic foot of natural gas	1,000 BTU	253 Kcal
Per cubic foot of mixed gas	850 BTU	215 Kcal
Per cubic foot of mfgd gas	535 BTU	136 Kcal

---

[1]The Trane Company, Trane Air Conditioning Manual, La Crosse, Wisconsin, 1955, 3–14 and 3–15.
[2]Ibid., Table 3–16.

Heat from Occupants

Table 6–3[3] gives the rate at which heat units are added to the building's environment by people in various activities.

TABLE 6-3.   Heat generated by occupants of building.

	Typical Application	BTU per Hour
Seated, at rest	theatre, matinee	330
	evening	350
Seated, very light work	office, hotel	400
Moderately active office work		450
Standing, light work, slow walk	department store	450–500
Sedentary work	restaurant	550
Light bench work	factory	750
Moderate dancing		850
Brisk walking, moderate heavy work		1000
Bowling, heavy work		1450

Distribution of Heating

Table 6–4 shows, for a typical American city, percentages of annual heating costs that can be expected to occur in each month.

TABLE 6-4.   Percent of annual heating costs.

Month	%	Month	%	Month	%
January	19	May	5	September	1
February	17	June	—	October	6
March	14	July	—	November	12
April	9	August	—	December	17

Temperature of Air Supply

Formula

$$T_s = \frac{H_s}{1.1A}$$

where: T_s = change required in dry-bulb temperature of air supply, °F

H_s = sensible heat loss of room, BTU/hour

A = air supply, cubic feet per minute

---

[3]American Society of Heating, Refrigeration and Air Conditioning Engineers, Inc., ASHRAE Guide and Data Book, N.Y., 1965, p. 518.

Example

How many degrees must the air be heated if it is supplied at 15 CFM to a room with sensible heat loss of 500 BTU per hour?

Solution

$$T_s = \frac{500}{1.1(15)}$$
$$= 30.3 \text{ degrees Fahrenheit}$$

Heat Required to Warm Air: Compensation for sensible heat loss

Formula

$$H_i = .018A_i(T_i - T_o)$$

where: H_s = heat necessary for warming infiltrated air to room temperature, BTU/hour

A_i = infiltrated air, CFM

T_i = indoor air temperature, °F

T_o = outdoor air temperature, °F

Example

At what rate must heat be added to air infiltrating at 15 CFM if indoor and outdoor temperatures are 72 and 40 degrees respectively?

Solution

$$H_i = .018 \, (15) \, (72 - 40)$$
$$= 8.64 \text{ BTU/hour}$$

Heat Conducted Through Wall

Formula

$$H = WU \, (T_i - T_o)$$

where: H = heat conducted through wall, BTU/hour

W = area of wall surface, square feet

U = coefficient of heat transmission of wall material,

$$\frac{\text{BTU/hour}}{\text{ft}^2 \text{ of surface/degree of temperature difference}}$$

T_i = indoor temperature near wall, °F

T_o = outdoor temperature, °F

Example

At what rate will heat be lost through a wall of 300 square feet if its coefficient of heat transmission is 0.9 and temperatures are 72 degrees inside and 40 outside?

Solution

$$H = 300 \ (0.9) \ (72 - 40)$$
$$= 8640 \ \text{BTU/hour}$$

Floor Heat Loss: Slab floor on grade

Formula

$$H_f = FC \ (T_i - T_o)$$

where: H_f = heat loss due to slab floor on grade, BTU/hour
F = floor perimeter, feet
C = conduction coefficient
$\quad$ = 0.81 with no edge insulation
$\quad$ = 0.55 with edge insulation
T_i = indoor temperature
T_o = outdoor temperature

Example

How much heat would be lost due to slab floor whose perimeter is 180 feet if there is no edge insulation, and temperatures are 72 inside and 40 outside?

Solution

$$H_f = 180 \ (0.55) \ (72 - 40)$$
$$= 3168 \ \text{BTU/hour}$$

Spot Temperature (On surface that separates two temperatures)

Formula

$$T_x = \frac{U_2}{U_1} \ (T_o - T_i) + T_i$$

where: T_x = temperature on interface surface, °F
U_2 = coefficient of heat flow of surface material
U_1 = 1.46 for vertical surface
$\quad$ = 1.63 for horizontal surface if heat flow is upward
$\quad$ = 1.08 for horizontal surface if heat flow is downward
T_o = outdoor air temperature, °F
T_i = indoor air temperature, °F

Example

What will the temperature be on the floor of a cantilevered room if the floor material has heat flow coefficient of 0.5 and the air is 72 degrees inside and 40 degrees outside?

Solution

$$T_x = \frac{0.5}{1.08} \ (40 - 72) + 72$$
$$= 57.2 \ \text{degrees Fahrenheit}$$

Rate of Transferring Heat to Surface (from airstream)

Formula

$$H_t = SU(T_a - T_s)$$

where: H_t = rate of heat transfer, BTU/hour
S = area of surface, square feet
U = coefficient of heat transfer
T_s = temperature of surface, °F
T_a = temperature of airstream, °F

Example

At what rate is heat removed from a 90 degree airstream that moves across 100 square feet of a wall whose temperature is 57 degrees, if the coefficient of heat transfer is 0.87?

Solution

$$H_t = 100 \ (0.8)(90 - 57)$$
$$= 2640 \ \text{BTU/hour}$$

Infiltration Through Walls (due to wind)

Table 6–5[4] gives infiltration, in units of cubic feet per (square feet) (hour), as a function of wall material and wind velocity.

TABLE 6-5. Infiltration through walls.

Wall Material	Wind velocity, mph					
	5	10	15	20	25	30
Brick 8 1/2″—plain	2	4	8	12	19	23
—plastered, 2 coats gypsum	.02	.04	.07	.11	.16	.24
13″ —plain	1	4	7	12	16	21
—plastered, 2 coats gypsum	.01	.01	.03	.04	.07	.10
—furring, lath, 2 coats gypsum plaster	.03	.10	.21	.36	.53	.72
Frame wall, lath, 3 coats gypsum plaster	.03	.07	.13	.18	.23	.26

Infiltration Through Cracks

Table 6–6[5] gives cubic feet of infiltration per foot of crack per hour as a function of wind velocity and construction.

---

[4]Ibid., p. 460.
[5]Ibid., p. 459.

TABLE 6-6. Infiltration through cracks.

		Wind Velocity mph					
		5	10	15	20	25	30
Double-hung wood sash windows (unlocked)	around frame in masonry wall, not caulked	3	8	14	20	27	35
	caulked	1	2	3	4	5	6
	around frame in wood frame construction	2	6	11	17	23	30
	total for average window, 1/16″ crack and 3/64″ clearance. Includes wood frame leakage, not weatherstripped	7	21	39	59	80	104
	weatherstripped	4	13	24	36	49	63
Double-hung metal windows	Not weather-stripped, locked	20	45	70	96	125	154
	unlocked	20	47	74	104	137	170
	Weather-stripped, unlocked	6	19	32	46	60	76
Rolled section steel sash windows	Industrial pivoted 1/16″ crack	52	108	176	244	304	372
	Architectural projected 1/32″ crack	15	36	62	86	112	139
	3/64″	20	52	88	116	152	182
	Residential casement 1/64″	6	18	33	47	60	74
	1/32″	14	32	52	76	100	128
	Heavy casement section, projected, 1/64″ crack	3	10	18	26	36	48
	1/32″	8	24	38	54	72	92
Hollow metal, vertically pivoted window		30	88	145	186	221	242

Heat Loss from Pipes

Table 6–7[6] gives rate of heat transfer (BTU per hour per foot) from pipe to surrounding air.

TABLE 6-7. Heat loss from pipes.

Pipe size, inches	Hot water, 180°F bare	Hot water, 180°F insulated	Steam, 227°F bare	Steam, 227°F insulated
1/2	65	22	100	33
3/4	75	25	120	38
1	95	28	145	43
1 1/4	115	33	180	49
1 1/2	130	36	200	54
2	160	42	250	63
2 1/2	185	48	295	73
3	220	53	350	85
4	280	68	440	103

Heat Transfer from Ducts[7]

Formula

$$Q_s = \frac{T_o - T_a}{\dfrac{L_1}{k_1} + \dfrac{L_2}{k_2} + R_s} \qquad \text{(flat surfaces)}$$

$$= \frac{T_o - T_a}{\dfrac{r_s \, l_n \dfrac{R_1}{R_0}}{k_1} + \dfrac{r_s \, l_n \dfrac{R_2}{R_0}}{k_2} + R_s} \quad \text{(for cylindrical surfaces)}$$

where: Q_s = rate of heat transfer per square foot of outer surface of insulation, BTU/ hour per square foot

T_o = temperature of inner surface of insulation, °F

T_a = temperature of ambient air, °F

L_1, etc. = thickness of insulation layer, inches

k_1, etc. = 0.24 to 0.35 for blankets and felts

    = 0.32 to 0.57 for asbestos products

    = 0.23 to 0.40 for most boards and blocks

    = 0.50 for insulating cements

R_s = surface resistance, (hour) (ft²) (°F) per BTU

r_s = outer radius of insulation, inches

R_1, etc. = outer radius of intermediate layers of insulation, inches

R_0 = inner radius of insulation, inches

---

[6]Trane, op. cit., Table 3–17.
[7]ASHRAE, op. cit., p. 451.

Example

At what rate will heat be lost from a rectangular duct carrying 95 degree air through 40 degree ambient if there is a half-inch blanket over one inch of asbestos? Assume a surface resistance of 0.57.

Solution

Assume top-of-the-range values for k coefficients.

$$Q_s = \frac{95 - 40}{\dfrac{1}{0.57} + \dfrac{0.5}{0.35} + 0.57}$$

$$= 14.7 \text{ BTU per hour per square foot}$$

Air Flow Required (to maintain a specified temperature difference)

Formula

$$A = \frac{H}{1.08\ (T_i - T_o)}$$

where: A = air flow, cubic feet per minute
H = heat losses, BTU/hour
T_i = indoor temperature
T_o = outdoor temperature

Example

How much air is required to maintain a building at 72°F if 200 BTU/hour must be replaced and outside air is 40°F?

Solution

$$A = \frac{2000}{1.08\ (72 - 40)}$$

$$= 57.8 \text{ cubic feet per minute}$$

Ventilation due to Wind (flow restricted by inlet only)

Formula

$$A = 88ICV$$

where: A = air flow due to wind, cubic feet per minute
I = inlet opening, square feet
C = Correction for angle between wind and inlet opening
$\quad$ = 0.5 to 0.6 if perpendicular to wind
$\quad$ = 0.25 to 0.35 if diagonal to wind
V = velocity of wind, miles per hour

Example

How much air will flow due to a wind of 12 mph if inlets totaling 6 square feet are set diagonal to the wind?

Solution

Use the average value of angle correction, 0.30.

$$A = 88 \ (6) \ 0.30 \ (12)$$
$$= 1900 \text{ cubic feet per minute}$$

Stack Effect: Air flow due to temperature difference

Formula

$$A = kI \ \sqrt{v(T_i - T_o)}$$

where: A = air flow, cubic feet per minute

k = effectiveness of inlet and outlet, varies from 9.4 when entire opening is available, to 7.2

I = inlet or outlet opening, square feet

v = vertical distance between inlet and outlet, feet

T_i = average indoor temperature over distance v, °F

T_o = outdoor temperature

Example

How much ventilation will occur due to the stack effect if the outlet is 10 feet above the inlet, indoor temperature averages 72°F, outdoor temperature is 40°F, and the outlet opening of two square feet is fully effective?

Solution

$$A = 9.4(2) \ \sqrt{10(72 - 40)}$$
$$= 336 \text{ cubic feet per minute}$$

Cooling Requirements: BTU/hour/cfm of outside air

Table 6–8[8] gives cooling load requirements for ventilating air, based on design outdoor wet-bulb temperature and wet-bulb temperature of conditioned room.

---

[8]Trane, op. cit., Table 3–20.

TABLE 6-8. Cooling load requirements.

Design Outdoor Wet-Bulb Temperature	Wet-bulb temperature of conditioned room									
	69	68	67	66	65	64	63	62	61	60
80	44.7	48.2	51.7	55.1	58.5	61.7	64.9	68.0	71.1	74.1
79	40.1	43.7	47.2	50.6	53.9	57.2	60.4	63.5	66.6	69.5
78	35.7	39.2	42.7	46.1	49.5	52.7	55.9	59.0	62.1	65.1
77	31.3	34.9	38.3	41.8	45.1	48.3	51.5	54.7	57.7	60.7
76	27.1	30.7	34.1	37.5	40.7	44.1	47.3	50.5	53.5	56.5
75	23.0	26.5	30.0	33.4	36.7	40.0	43.2	46.3	49.4	52.3
74	18.9	22.5	25.9	29.3	32.7	35.9	39.1	42.3	45.3	48.3
73	14.9	18.5	22.0	25.4	28.7	32.0	35.2	38.3	41.4	44.3
72	11.1	14.6	18.1	21.5	24.8	28.1	31.3	34.4	37.5	40.5

Outdoor Air Requirements

Table 6–9[9] gives air requirements for various types of occupancies.

TABLE 6-9. Outdoor air requirements.

Occupancy	Smoking	CFM/person Rec.	Min.	Min. CFM/ft² of Floor
Meeting Rooms	Heavy	50	30	1.25
Corridors				.25
Department Stores	None	71/2	5	.05
Department Stores	Considerable	10	71/2	
Factories	None	10	71/2	.10
Garages				1.00
Hotel Rooms	Heavy	30	25	.33
Restaurant Kitchen				4.00
Laboratory	Some	20	15	
Office, General	Some	15	10	.25
Office, Private	None	25	15	.25
Office, Private	Considerable	30	25	.25
Restaurant, Cafeteria	Considerable	12	10	
Restaurant, Dining room	Considerable	15	12	

[9]ASHRAE, op. cit., p. 495.

Piping and Fluid Flow

CHAPTER 7

This chapter covers, first, distribution of liquids and gases through pipes and tubing, then, characteristics and installation of pipes and tubing.

CHARACTERISTICS OF FLUIDS

Pressure Volume Relationship: Boyle's Law for perfect gas

Formula

$$P_1 V_1 = P_2 V_2$$

where: P_1 = pressure at volume V_1
P_2 = pressure at volume V_2

Example

One cubic foot of a gas is under 20 psi pressure. What will the pressure be if the gas is compressed to 3/4 cubic foot?

Solution

Solve for P_2

$$P_2 = \frac{P_1 V_1}{V_2}$$

and substitute given values

$$P_2 = \frac{20(1)}{3/4}$$
$$= 27 \text{ psi}$$

Pressure-Temperature Relationship: Charles' Law for constant volume

Formula

$$\frac{P_1}{T_1} = \frac{P_2}{T_2}$$

where: P_1 = pressure at temperature T_1
       P_2 = pressure at temperature T_2

Example

What will the resultant pressure be if a sealed container of gas at 100°F and 16 psi is heated to 190°F?

Solution

Solve for P_2 and substitute

$$P_2 = \frac{P_1 T_2}{T_1}$$
$$= \frac{16(190)}{100}$$
$$= 30.4 \text{ psi}$$

Volume-Temperature Relationship: Charles' Law for constant pressure

Formula

$$\frac{V_1}{T_1} = \frac{V_2}{T_2}$$

Example

If 15 cubic feet of gas at 80°F is heated to 130°F, what volume should it occupy in order to keep the pressure unchanged?

Solution

Solve for V_2 and substitute

$$V_2 = \frac{V_1 T_2}{T_1}$$
$$= \frac{15(130)}{80}$$
$$= 24.4 \text{ cubic feet}$$

Velocity Head: Kinetic energy due to motion of fluid through conduit

Formula

$$H_v = \frac{V^2}{2g}$$

where: H_v = velocity head in feet
       V = velocity of flow in feet per second
       g = 32.2 feet per second^2

Example

How much velocity head will result from fluid flowing at 17 feet per second?

Solution

$$H_v = \frac{17^2}{2(32.2)}$$
$$= 4.5 \text{ feet}$$

Total Head

Formula

$$H_t = H_v + H_s + \frac{P}{D}$$

where: H_t = total head in feet
H_v = velocity head (q.v.) in feet
H_s = static head
P = fluid pressure in pounds per square foot
D = fluid density in pounds per cubic foot

Example

How much total head will result from a system which has a velocity head of 12 feet and a static head of 16 feet if fluid of 59 pounds per cubic foot is under a 300 pounds per square foot pressure?

Solution

$$H_t = 12 + 16 + \frac{300}{59}$$
$$= 33 \text{ feet}$$

STRESS, PRESSURE, FLOW

Tangential Stress: Hoop stress on walls of pipe

Formula

$$S = \frac{pd}{2T}$$

where: S = tangential stress, pounds per square inch
p = internal pressure of fluid, pounds per square inch
d = internal diameter of pipe, inches
t = wall thickness of pipe, inches

Example

Under how much hoop stress will a pipe be if it has internal diameter of 1.12 inches, wall thickness of 0.065 inch, and carries fluid at 36 pounds per square inch?

Solution

$$S = \frac{36(1.12)}{2(.065)}$$
$$= 310 \text{ pounds per square inch}$$

Longitudinal Stress: Cylinder with closed end

Formula

$$S = \frac{pd^2}{4T(d+t)}$$

where: S = longitudinal stress, pounds per square inch
p = internal pressure of fluid, pounds per square inch
d = internal diameter of pipe, inches
t = wall thickness of pipe, inches

Example

How much longitudinal stress will be applied to the walls of a capped 1.12-inch inside diameter pipe if it holds fluid at 36 pounds per square inch? Wall thickness if .065 inch.

Solution

$$S = \frac{36(1.12)^2}{4(.065)(1.12+.065)}$$
$$= 147 \text{ pounds per square inch}$$

Bursting Force: Tending to separate two halves of a sphere

Formula

$$F = 0.786\, d^2 p$$

where: F = bursting force, pounds
d = inside diameter, inches
p = internal pressure, pounds per square inch

Example

What will the bursting force of a hydraulic accumulator be if it has an internal diameter of 24 inches and is pressurized at 90 pounds per square inch?

Solution

$$F = 0.786(24)^2 90$$
$$= 35,100 \text{ pounds}$$

Discharge Through Orifice: Theoretical value

Formula

$$Q = A\sqrt{2gh}$$

where: Q = flow of liquid in cubic feet per second
A = cross-sectional area of opening, square inches
g = 32.2 feet per second
h = pressure head, feet

Example

What quantity of liquid will flow through an orifice of 0.430 square inch cross-section if it is acted on by a head of 28 feet?

Solution

$$Q = 0.430 \sqrt{2(32.2)28}$$
$$= 18.23 \text{ cubic feet per second}$$

Pressure Drop: As a function of fluid velocity

Formula

$$d_p = \frac{fwLV^2}{193\,d}$$

where: d_p = pressure drop in round pipe, pounds per square inch
    f = friction factor obtained from manufacturer of pipe, usually between .001 and 1.0
    w = fluid density, pounds per cubic foot
    L = length of pipe over which pressure drop is effective, feet
    V = velocity of fluid flow, feet per second

Example

By how much will the pressure drop over a length of 10 feet if fluid of 65 pounds per cubic foot is flowing at 17 feet per second through pipe of 1.12 inch inside diameter? Assume a friction factor of .03.

Solution

$$d_p = \frac{.03(65)10(17)^2}{193(1.12)}$$
$$= 26 \text{ pounds per square inch}$$

Pressure Drop: As a function of flow rate

Formula

$$d_p = .00086 \frac{fwLF_g^2}{d^5}$$
$$= 174 \frac{fwLF_f^2}{d^5}$$

where: f = friction factor obtained from manufacturer of pipe, usually between .001 and 1.0
    w = fluid density, pounds per cubic foot
    F_g = fluid flow rate, gallons per minute
    F_f = fluid flow rate, cubic feet per second
    other quantities are as in pressure drop as a function of fluid velocity

Example

How much pressure will be dropped if, in the preceding example, fluid was flowing at 100 gallons per minute?

Solution

$$d_p = .00086 \, \frac{.03(65)10(100)^2}{1.12^5}$$

$$= 85 \text{ pounds per square inch}$$

Flow Rate of Steam

Formula

$$W_{fs} = \sqrt{\frac{d_p d^6 w}{360L(d + 3.6)}}$$

    where: W_{fs} = steam conducted through pipe, pounds per hour
                 d_p = pressure drop in pipe, pounds per square inch
                 d = inside diameter of pipe, inches
                 w = density of steam, pounds per cubic foot
                 L = length of pipe over which pressure drop is noted, feet

Example

At what rate will steam at 2 pounds per cubic foot be conducted through 100 feet of pipe which has 1.12 inch inside diameter if there is a pressure drop of 5 pounds per square inch along the pipe?

Solution

$$W_{fs} = \sqrt{\frac{5(1.12)^6 2}{360(100) \, (1.12 + 3.6)}}$$

$$= .0108 \text{ pounds per hour}$$

Flow Rate of Water

Formula

$$F_g = 4.32 \sqrt{\frac{p_d d^2}{fL}}$$

$$F_w = .0096 \sqrt{\frac{p_d d^5}{fL}}$$

    where: F_g = fluid flow rate, gallons per minute
                F_w = fluid flow rate, cubic feet per second
                p_d = pressure drop in pipe, pounds per square inch
                d = inside diameter of pipe, inches
                f = friction factor obtained from manufacturer of pipe, usually between .001
                    and 1.0
                L = length of pipe over which pressure drop is noted, feet

Example

How many gallons per minute will flow from a pipe of 1.12 inch inside diameter if the friction factor is .03 and the pressure drops 0.9 pounds per square inch over 100 feet of length?

Solution

$$F_g = 4.32 \sqrt{\frac{0.9(1.12)^2}{.03(100)}}$$

$$= 8.4 \text{ gallons per minute}$$

Velocity of Sewage Flow, open Channel

Formula

$$V = \frac{1.486}{n} (A/P)^{0.67} S^{0.5}$$

where: V = velocity of sewage flow in feet per second
  n = coefficient which is a function of channel surfaces; see Table 7–1
  A = wetted area
  P = wetted perimeter
  S = hydraulic gradient in feet per thousand

TABLE 7-1. Values of *n*.

Surfaces of channel		n
Very smooth timber		.009
Very smooth pipe		.010
Smooth masonry or brickwork		.012
Ordinary concrete conduits		.012
Vitrified clay pipe		.015
Ordinary brick conduit		.015
Rough brick conduit		.017
Smooth earth	.020 to	.035
Rough channels with vegetation growth	.030 to	.050

Example

What rate of flow can be expected through an ordinary concrete open channel with wetted area of 5 1/4 square feet and wetted perimeter of 12 1/2 feet if the hydraulic gradient is .02?

Solution

$$V = \frac{1.486}{.012} (5.25/12.5)^{0.67}(.02)^{0.5}$$

$$= 10.4 \text{ feet per second}$$

INSTALLATION

Thickness of Cast-Iron Pipe

Formula

$$t = \frac{d(p + p_h)}{2S} + \frac{0.28}{d^{0.15}}$$

where: t = wall thickness of pipe, inches
   d = inside diameter of pipe, inches
   p = internal pressure of fluid (static,) pounds per square inch
   P_h = water hammer, pounds per square inch
   S = allowable unit stress, pounds per square inch

Example

What wall thickness should be specified for cast iron pipe of 4 inch inside diameter that is to conduct fluid at 36 pounds per square inch static pressure with an expected water hammer of 10 pounds per square inch? Assume allowable unit stress of 50,000 pounds per square inch.

Solution

$$t = \frac{1.12(36 + 10)}{2(50,000)} + \frac{0.28}{1.12^{0.15}}$$
$$= 0.28 \text{ inch}$$

Bending Round Tubing Without Mandrel: Guideline for low scrap losses

Formula

$$R = 1.551 \frac{(D^2 - d^2)}{D - d}$$

where: R = minimum center line bend radius for tubing up to 2 1/2″ o.d. bent up to
   90° and tubing over 2 1/2″ bent up to 75°
   D = outside diameter of tubing
   d = inside diameter of tubing

Example

For tubing of 1.125 outside diameter and 1.067 inside diameter, what should the minimum bend radius be?

Solution

$$R = 1.551 \frac{(1.125^2 - 1.067^2)}{1.125 - 1.067}$$
$$= 3.4 \text{ inches}$$

Distance Between Bends[1]

Formula

$$L = 2(D) \quad \text{—if bends are in the same plane}$$
$$L = 3(D) \quad \text{—if bends are in different planes}$$

where: D = outside diameter

Example

How much distance should be allowed between bends in one plane if tubing of 2 1/4 outside diameter is used?

Solution

$$L = 2(2\ 1/4)$$
$$= 4\ 1/2 \text{ inches between bends}$$

Distance from End of Tube[2]: To maintain true diameter at end

Formula

$$L = 2(D)$$

Example

How much length should be allowed from the theoretical end of the first bend and the tubing's end if tubing of 7/8 outside diameter is used?

Solution

$$L = 2(7/8)$$
$$= 1\ 3/4 \text{ inches}$$

Developed Length of Bend[3]

Formula

$$L = .0175\ RA$$

where: L = developed length on centerline
R = bend radius to centerline of tubing
A = degree of bend

Example

What is the developed length of a 40 degree bend on a 7 1/2 inch radius?

---

[1]Welded Steel Tube Institute, Incorporated, "Handbook of Welded Steel Tubing," Cleveland Ohio, p. 81. Copyright 1967 by Welded Steel Tube Institute, Incorporated.
[2]Ibid., p. 81.
[3]Ibid., p. 84.

Solution

$$L = (.0175)7.5(40)$$
$$= 5.24$$

Weight of Round Tubing (hot finished or cold drawn)

Formula

$$W = 2.67(D^2 - d^2)L$$

where: W = total weight, pounds
D = outside diameter, inches
d = inside diameter, inches
L = length of tubing, feet

Example

What would be the weight of 75 feet of tubing with an outside diameter of 0.438 and an inside diameter of 0.420?

Solution

$$W = 2.67(0.438^2 - 0.420^2)75$$
$$= 3.2 \text{ pounds}$$

Elevators and Conveyors

CHAPTER 8

This chapter covers movement of people and materials by means of hydraulic elevators, traction elevators, and various types of conveyors.

ELEVATORS, GENERAL

Elevator Buffers: Rated speed not over 200 feet per minute

Spring buffers required[1] under car and counterweight should be provided with space for the following strokes:

Rated Car Speed in Feet per Minute	Stroke in Inches
100 or less	1 1/2
101 to 150	2 1/2
151 to 200	4

Elevator Buffers: Rated speed over 200 feet per minute[2]

Formula

$$S = \frac{(1.15V)^2}{19320}$$

where: S = minimum allowable stroke, inches
V = rated car speed, feet per second

Example

How much room must be provided for buffer stroke when rated elevator speed is 400 feet per minute?

---

[1]The American Society of Mechanical Engineers, "American National Standard Safety Code for Elevators, Dumbwaiters, Escalators, and Moving Walks." New York, N.Y., Copyright © 1971, by The American Society of Mechanical Engineers.
[2]Ibid.

Solution

$$S = \frac{((1.15)(400))^2}{19320}$$
$$= 10.9 \text{ inches}$$

Buffer Reaction[3]

Formula

$$R = 2W\left(1 + \frac{v^2}{2gS}\right)$$

where: R = reaction of oil buffer or of spring buffer which does not fully compress, pounds
W = weight of car plus rated load, pounds
v = speed of car at impact, feet per second
g = 32.2 feet per second per second
S = buffer stroke, feet

Example

If the elevator in the preceding example has a gross weight of 10,000 pounds, determine building structure requirements for buffer reaction.

Solution

$$R = 2(10,000)\left(1 + \frac{400^2}{2(32.2)11}\right)$$
$$= 35,000 \text{ pounds}$$

Minimum Rated Load, Passenger Elevators[4]: (for given platform size)

Formula

$W = 0.667A^2 + 66.7A$ (inside net platform area not more than 50 square feet)
$W = 0.0467A^2 + 125A - 1367$ (inside net platform area more than 50 square feet)
where: W = minimum rated load, pounds
A = inside net platform area, square feet

Example

What is the minimum rated load for a passenger elevator with net inside dimensions of 10 feet by 10 feet (100 square feet)?

Solution

Substituting directly into the second equation gives:
$$W = 0.0467(100)^2 + 125(100) - 1367$$
$$= 11,600 \text{ pounds}$$

---

[3]Ibid.
[4]Ibid.

Minimum Rated Load, Freight Elevators[5] (for given platform size)

Table 8–1 gives minimum rated loads for freight elevators.

TABLE 8-1. Minimum rated load for freight elevators.

Class	Class Description	Minimum rated load
A	General freight loading	50 pounds per square foot of inside net platform area
B	Motor-vehicle loading	30 pounds per square foot of inside net platform area
C1	Industrial truck loading; truck carried on elevator	Actual load (including truck) but not less than 50 pounds per square foot of inside net platform area
C2	Industrial truck loading; truck not carried on elevator	Actual load but not less than 50 pounds per square foot of inside net platform area
C3	Other loading with heavy concentrations where truck is not used	Actual load but not less than 50 pounds per square foot of inside net platform area

Car Top Clearance[6] (when elevator is at top landing)

Overhead clearance must meet *both* of two conditions: a minimum distance between car crosshead and nearest obstruction (dimension a), and a minimum distance between any equipment located on top of the car and nearest obstruction (dimension c).

Formulas: when dimension b does not exceed 24 inches, including cars with no sheave or other equipment in or on crosshead

$$c_{min} = a$$

$$a_{min} = e + d + 24 + \frac{g}{2} \text{ (buffer not partially compressed)}$$

$$a_{min} = d' + 24 + \frac{g}{2} \quad \text{(spring-return-type oil buffer partially compressed)}$$

Formulas: when dimension b exceeds 24 inches

$$c_{min} = a - b$$

$$a_{min} = e + d + b + \frac{g}{2} \text{ (buffer not partially compressed)}$$

$$a_{min} = d' + b + \frac{g}{2} \quad \text{(spring-return-type oil buffer partially compressed)}$$

---

[5]Ibid.
[6]Ibid.

where: a = distance from top of car crosshead to nearest obstruction directly above it, inches

b = distance which car sheave or other equipment mounted in or on car crosshead projects above crosshead, inches

c = distance from top of any equipment located on top of car to nearest obstruction directly above it, inches

d = stroke of counterweight oil or spring buffer, inches

d' = uncompressed portion of spring-return-type counterweight oil buffer stroke, inches

e = bottom runby of counterweight, inches

g = depends on the type of buffer and its use; for preliminary planning, use calculated value of stroke

Example

An elevator will run at 625 feet per minute, no equipment is mounted on the car crosshead, and the counterweight has an eight-inch runby when the car is level with the top terminal landing. What overhead clearances must be provided?

Solution

Elevator engineers will determine precise values for the variables, but for the Plant Engineer's preliminary look at clearances that must be provided, it is sufficient to let $d = g$ = stroke. Substituting 625 feet per minute in the equation previously given for stroke gives 24 inches, which will now be substituted in the equation for a; that result will in turn be used in the equation for c.

$$a_{\min} = 8 + 24 + 24 + \frac{24}{2}$$

   = 68 inches clearance above crosshead

$$c_{\min} = 68 - 2$$

   = 66 inches clearance above equipment mounted on car top

Counterweight Top Clearance[7] (when car is at bottom landing)

Formula

$$f_{\min} = h + i + 6 + \frac{g}{2} \qquad \text{(buffer not partially compressed)}$$

$$f_{\min} = i' + 6 + \frac{g}{2} \qquad \text{(spring-return-type oil buffer partially compressed)}$$

where: f = distance from top of counterweight frame (or top of sheave if there is one) to nearest obstruction directly above

h = bottom car runby

i = stroke of car oil or spring buffer

i' = uncompressed portion of car oil buffer when car is level with bottom terminal landing

---

[7]Ibid.

> $g =$ depends on the type of buffer and its use; for preliminary planning, use calculated value of stroke

Example

An installation with 2:1 roping is rated at 225 feet per minute. What clearance must be provided above the counterweight sheave if the car has a 10-inch runby?

Solution

Substituting 225 feet per minute in the equation previously given for stroke gives 3.5 inches, which will now be substituted in the equation for f_{min}. Since there is a runby, the buffer is not partially compressed and the first equation applies.

$$f_{min} = 10 + 3.5 + 6 + \frac{3.5}{2}$$
$$= 21.25 \text{ inches}$$

HYDRAULIC ELEVATORS

An economic analysis will generally favor hydraulic elevators for buildings with rise of about 65 feet (usually 7 floors) or less. One of the main advantages of this type elevator is flexibility; the power unit can be located where convenient and the piqing can be run as required.

Cylinder: Minimum wall thickness for housing the plunger[8]

Formula

$$t = \frac{pd}{2S}$$

where: $t =$ thickness of wall, inches
$p =$ working pressure, pounds per square inch
$d =$ internal diameter, inches
$S =$ design stress, pounds per square inch (12,000 psi maximum for mild steel and 1/5 the ultimate strength for other metals)

Example

Working pressure is 300 pounds per square inch, internal diameter is 14 inches, and the cylinder material is high mild steel (use 12,000 psi). What will the minimum cylinder wall thickness be?

Solution

$$t = \frac{300(14)}{2(12,000)}$$
$$= 0.175 \text{ inch}$$

---

[8]Ibid.

Piping[9] (for working pressures over 250 psi)

Formula

$$t = \frac{pD}{2S} + C$$

where: t = minimum thickness of pipe wall, inches
p = working pressure, pounds per square inch
D = outside diameter of pipe, inches
S = allowable stress, pounds per square inch (1/5 of ultimate strength)
C = 0.05 for threaded pipe up to 3/8 inch
= depth of thread for threaded pipe over 3/8 inch
= depth of groove for grooved pipe
= 0.0 for other pipe of unreduced thickness

Example

A hydraulic elevator installation works with 360 psi. Its connecting pipes will be of 1/2 inch outside diameter, inside diameter not more than 3/8 inch, and having an allowable stress of 1200 psi. What minimum wall thickness will be allowed for this pipe?

Solution

$$t = \frac{360(0.5)}{2(1200)}$$
$$= 0.125 \text{ inch}$$

Typical Hydraulic Elevator Installations[10]

This section describes some pre-engineered elevator installations to show what is typically recommended for various situations in buildings to seven floors.

Passenger elevators

Table 8–2 gives some dimensions for standard installations in a few typical applications. The vertical opening at each floor is 7'0" and the cylinder hole is equal to total elevator travel plus 6'0".

TABLE 8-2. Hydraulic passenger elevators.

	Small Office	*Average Hotel or Office*		*Large Store or Office*
	Capacity in pounds			
	2000	2500	3000	3500
Platform Width	6'-4"	7'-0"	7'-0"	7'-0"
Platform Depth	4'-5"	5'-0"	5'-6"	6'-2"
Door Width	3'-0"	3'-6"	3'-6"	3'-10"
Hoistway Width	7'-8"	8'-4"	8'-4"	8'-4"
Hoistway Depth	5'-2"	5'-9"	6'-3"	6'-11"

[9]Ibid.
[10]Dover Corporation, Elevator Division, "Oildraulic and Traction Elevator Planning Guide," Memphis, Tennessee. Copyright 1967, Dover Corporation.

	Speed in Feet Per Minute			
	75	100	150	200
Top Landing to Overhead	12'–0''	12'–0''	12'–0''	12'–0'
Bottom Landing to Pit Floor	4'–0''	4'–0''	4'–0''	4'–0''

Hospital elevators

The dimensional characteristic that sets hospital elevators apart is a relatively large depth-to-width ratio. It is also more common in such installations to have cars with an entrance at both front and rear, even though both doors may not be used at all floors. The vertical opening is typically 7'0'' in height, and the cylinder hole is equal to total travel plus 6'0''.

Table 8–3 gives some planning dimensions for standard installations in a few typical applications. Hoistway depth is defined here as between rough sills if there is a double entrance, or from sill to back wall if there is a single entrance. For total wall-to-wall hoistway depth, add 5 1/2 inches to value given for a single-door model; add 11 inches for a double-door model.

TABLE 8-3. Hydraulic hospital elevators.

	3500 Pound Capacity		4000 Pound Capacity	
	Single Entrance Car	Double Entrance Car	Single Entrance Car	Double Entrance Car
Platform Width	5'–4''	5'–4''	5'–8''	5'–8''
Platform Depth	8'–4''	8'–9 1/2''	8'–8''	9'–1 1/2''
Door Width	3'–8''	3'–8''	4'–0''	4'–0''
Hoistway Width	6'–10''	6'–10''	7'–4''	7'–4''
Hoistway Depth	8'–10''	9'–2''	9'–2''	9'–6''
	Speed in Feet per Minute			
	75	100	150	200
Top Landing to Overhead	12'–0''	12'–0''	12'–0''	12'–6''
Bottom Landing Pit Floor	4'–0''	4'–0''	4'–0''	4'–0''

Freight elevators

By using vertical bi-parting doors, freight elevators present a wide opening for easy loading. Vertical opening is typically 7'0'' for light duty installations and 8'0'' for heavy duty.

Table 8–4 gives some planning dimensions for standard installations of light duty and heavy duty freight elevators. Hoistway depth as given in the table assumes a single-entrance model installed in a building with sufficient floor height for the type of door used; two inches should be added for double-entrance models. If floor heights are low, an additional 1 3/4 inches should be added for single-entrance models and an additional 3 1/2 inches for double-entrance models.

TABLE 8-4. Hydraulic freight elevators.

	Light Duty			*Heavy Duty (Power Truck)*		
	Capacity in Pounds					
	2500	5000	7500	5000	7500	10000
Platform Width	5'–4''	8'–4''	8'–4''	8'–4''	8'–4''	8'–4''
Platform Depth	7'–0''	10'–0''	12'–0''	10'–0''	12'–0''	14'–0''
Opening Width	5'–0''	8'–0''	8'–0''	8'–0''	8'–0''	8'–0''
Hoistway Width	7'–2''	10'–2''	10'–2''	10'–2''	10'–2''	10'–4''
Hoistway Depth	7'–8''	10'–8''	12'–8''	10'–8''	12'–8''	14'–8''
	Speed in Feet per Minute					
	25	50	75	100	150	200
Top Landing to Overhead, 7' door	14'–0''	14'–0''	14'–0''	14'–0''	14'–0''	14'–0''
Top Landing to Overhead, 8' door	15'–0''	15'–0''	15'–0''	15'–0''	15'–0''	15'–0''
Bottom Landing to to Pit Floor	4'–6''	4'–6''	4'–6''	4'–6''	4'–6''	4'–6''

TRACTION AND DRUM ELEVATORS[11]

Hoist Ropes (at least 3 required on traction elevator)

Formula

$$f = \frac{S(N)}{W}$$

where: f = safety factor applied to selection of ropes
       S = manufacturer's rated breaking strength of one rope
      N = number of runs of rope under load—for multiple roping this figure is equal to the number of ropes times the roping multiple
     W = maximum static load imposed on all car ropes with the car at its rated load at any position in hoistway

Table 8–5 gives *minimum* safety factors. Table values are to be compared to the factor found by equation, and whichever is larger should be used.

---

[11]The American Society of Mechanical Engineers, "American National Standard Safety Code for Elevators, Dumbwaiters, Escalators, and Moving Walks." New York, N.Y., Copyright © 1971, by The American Society of Mechanical Enginers.

Example

Given that a passenger elevator with 1:1 roping is rated at 100 feet per minute, what safety factor will apply if 3 ropes with manufacturer's rating of 7500 pounds each is planned?

Solution

$$f = \frac{7500(3)}{3000}$$
$$= 7.5$$

In Table 8–5 the minimum safety factor for a passenger elevator rated at 100 feet per minute is 7.95 and, since it is larger than the value just calculated, should be used.

TABLE 8-5.   Hoist rope minimum safety factors.

Rope Speed in Feet Per Minute	Minimum Factor of Safety Passenger	Freight	Rope Speed in Feet Per Minute	Minimum Factor of Safety Passenger	Freight
50	7.60	6.65	700	11.00	9.80
75	7.75	6.85	750	11.15	9.90
100	7.95	7.00	800	11.25	10.00
125	8.10	7.15	850	11.35	10.10
150	8.25	7.30	900	11.45	10.15
175	8.40	7.45	950	11.50	10.20
200	8.60	7.65	1000	11.55	10.30
225	8.75	7.75	1050	11.65	10.35
250	8.90	7.90	1100	11.70	10.40
300	9.20	8.20	1150	11.75	10.45
350	9.50	8.45	1200	11.80	10.50
400	9.75	8.70	1250	11.80	10.50
450	10.00	8.90	1300	11.85	10.55
500	10.25	9.15	1350	11.85	10.55
550	10.45	9.30	1400	11.90	10.55
600	10.70	9.50	1450	11.90	10.55
650	10.85	9.65	1500	11.90	10.55

Typical Traction Elevator Installations[12]

This section describes some pre-engineered elevator installations to demonstrate typical recommendations for various situations in high-rise buildings. In general, high-rise is defined as exceeding seven floors.

Passenger elevators

Tables 8–6 and 8–7 give some planning dimensions for standard installations in a

---

[12]Dover Corporation, op. cit.

few typical applications. The vertical opening at each floor is 7'0" and the minimum floor-to-ceiling dimension of overhead machine room is 7'6".

TABLE 8-6. Traction passenger elevators.

	Small Office	Average Hotel or Office		Large Store or Office
	Capacity in Pounds			
	2000	2500	3000	3500
Platform Width	6'4"	7'0"	7'0"	7'0"
Platform Depth	4'5"	5'0"	5'6"	6'2"
Door Width	3'0"	3'6"	3'6"	3'10"
Hoistway Width	7'8"	8'4"	8'4"	8'4"
Hoistway Depth	6'2"	6'9"	7'3"	7'11"

Hospital elevators

Table 8–8 gives some dimensions for planning of standard installations in a few typical applications. In each instance, the vertical opening on all floors is 7'0" and the minimum floor-to-ceiling dimension of overhead machine room is 7'6". Hoistway depth is defined here as between rough sills if there is a double entrance, or from sill to back wall if there is a single entrance. For total wall-to-wall hoistway depth, add 5 1/2 inches to the dimension given for a single-door model; add 11 inches for a double-door model.

Freight elevators

Vertical opening of freight elevator doors is typically 7'0" for light duty installations and 8'0" for heavy duty installations. Table 8–9 gives some dimensions for standard installations of light duty and heavy duty freight elevators. Hoistway depth as given in the table assumes a single-entrance model installed in a building with sufficient floor height for the type of door used; two inches should be added for double entrance models. If floor heights are low an additional 1 3/4 inches should be added for single-entrance models and an additional 3 1/2 inches for double-entrance models.

POWERED CONVEYORS—BULK MATERIALS, CONTINUOUS HANDLING[13]

In this arrangement, lumpy or powdered material is carried directly on a belt that is supported by roller stations that consist of one horizontal and two angled idlers, forming the belt into a trough.

---

[13]Rex Chainbelt Inc., "Rex Components and Products for Power Transmission and Material Handling," Milwaukee, Wisconsin, pp. 559–636. Copyright 1969, Rex Chainbelt Inc.

TABLE 8-7. Minimum pit, overhead, and machine room dimensions for passenger elevators.

		Speed in Feet Per Minute				
		100–150	200–350	400–500	500	600	700
2000 pounds	Machine Room Depth	12'0"	12'0"	13'0"			
	Top Landing to Overhead	16'4"	16'10"	17'8"			
	Bottom Landing to Pit Floor	5'4"	5'0"	6'6"			
2500 pounds	Machine Room Depth	13'0"	13'0"	13'0"	16'0"	16'0"	16'0"
	Top Landing to Overhead	16'4"	16'10"	17'8"	21'0"	18'10"	20'0"
	Bottom Landing to Pit Floor	5'4"	5'0"	6'6"	9'4"	9'4"	10'0"
3000 pounds	Machine Room Depth	13'0"	14'0"	24'0"	16'0"	16'0"	16'0"
	Top Landing to Overhead	16'4"	16'10"	17'8"	21'0"	18'10"	20'0"
	Bottom Landing to Pit Floor	5'4"	5'0"	6'6"	9'4"	9'4"	10'0"
3500 pounds	Machine Room Depth	13'0"	14'0"	14'0"	17'0"	17'0"	17'0"
	Top Landing to Overhead	16'4"	16'10"	17'8"	23'0"	18'0"	20'0"
	Bottom Landing to Pit Floor	5'4"	5'0"	6'6"	9'4"	9'4"	10'0"

TABLE 8-8. Traction hospital elevators.

	3500 Pound Capacity		4000 Pound Capacity	
	Single Entrance Car	Double Entrance Car	Single Entrance Car	Double Entrance Car
Platform Width	5'4''	5'4''	5'8''	5'8''
Platform Depth	8'4''	8'9 1/2''	8'8''	9'1 1/2''
Door Width	3'8''	3'8''	4'0''	4'0''
Hoistway Width	7'5''	7'9''	7'9''	7'9''
Hoistway Depth	8'10''	9'2''	9'2''	9'6''

		Speed in Feet Per Minute			
		100–200	250–350	400–450	500
3500 pounds	Machine Room Depth	12'0''	12'0''	12'0''	18'0''
	Top Landing to Overhead	16'8''	18'0''	19'0''	22'0''
	Bottom Landing to Pit Floor	5'4''	5'0''	6'6''	9'4''
4000 pounds	Machine Room Depth	12'6''	12'6''	12'6''	18'0''
	Top Landing to Overhead	16'8''	18'0''	19'0''	22'6''
	Bottom Landing to Pit Floor	5'4''	5'0''	6'6''	9'4''

TABLE 8-9. Traction freight elevators.

	Light Duty			Heavy Duty (Power Truck)		
	Capacity in Pounds					
	2500	5000	7500	5000	7500	10000
Platform Width	5'4''	8'4''	8'4''	8'4''	8'4''	8'4''
Platform Depth	7'0''	10'0''	12'0''	10'0''	12'0''	14'0''
Opening Width	5'0''	8'0''	8'0''	8'0''	8'0''	8'0''
Hoistway Width	7'4''	10'4''	10'4''	10'8''	11'0''	11'0''
Hoistway Depth	7'8''	10'8''	12'8''	10'8''	12'8''	14'8''

	Speed in Feet Per Minute			
	50	75	100	200
Top Landing to Overhead, 7′ door	17′0″	17′0″	17′0″	17′0″
Top Landing to Overhead, 8′ door	17′6″	17′6″	17′6″	17′6″
Bottom Landing to Pit Floor	5′6″	5′6″	5′6″	5′6″

Minimum Possible Belt Width: First step in design iteration

Table 8–10 is used for several determinations in this section. First, enter the table at whichever of the four columns on the right best describes the material, and note minimum belt width in the left-most column.

Maximum Recommended Belt Speed

Check the symbols at the bottom of Table 8–10 and select the one that closest describes the material to be handled. For the minimum belt width as determined in the previous step, note the belt speed in the heading of the column in which the applicable symbol appears. An installation should not run continuously at maximum speed and therefore the final design can be expected to use a speed between 100 and 200 feet per minute less than this maximum.

Capacity (relative to 100 pounds per cubic foot)

Formula

$$C_{rel} = \frac{(100)C_{req}}{D}$$

where: C_{rel} = capacity of system relative to 100 pounds per cubic foot
C_{req} = required capacity in tons per hour
D = density of material to be conveyed in pounds per cubic foot

Example

What is the relative capacity of a system carrying anthracite coal at 60 pounds per cubic foot if it is required that 750 tons be handled each hour?

Solution

$$C_{rel} = \frac{(100)750}{60}$$
$$= 1250$$

The significance of this quantity will be shown as a system is designed in examples to follow.

TABLE 8-10. Belt capacity for 20 degree troughing idlers.

Belt Width Inches	Surcharge Angle Degrees	Cross Sectional Area Square Feet	50	100	150	200	250	300	350	400	500	600	700	800	10% Lumps—90% Fines 20° Surcharge	10% Lumps—90% Fines 30° Surcharge	All Lumps—No Fines 20° Surcharge	All Lumps—No Fines 30° Surcharge
	0	.049	7	15	22	29	37	44	51■	59◆	74●	88	103	118				
	5	.060	9	18	27	36	45	54	63■	72◆	90●	108	126	144				
14	10	.071	11	21	32	43	53	64	75■	85◆	107●	128	149	170	4	2	3	1½
	20	.093	14	28	42	56	70	84	98■	112◆	140●	167	195	223				
	25	.105	16	32	47	63	79	95	110■	126◆	158●	189	221	252				
	30	.116	17	35	52	70	87	104	122■	139◆	174●	209	244	278				
	0	.068	10	20	31	41	51	61	71■	82◆	102●	122	143	163				
	5	.082	12	25	37	49	62	74	86■	98◆	123●	148	172	197				
16	10	.097	15	29	44	58	73	87	102■	116◆	146●	175	204	233	5	2½	3	1½
	20	.127	19	38	57	76	95	114	133■	152◆	191●	229	267	305				
	25	.143	21	43	64	86	107	129	150■	172◆	215●	257	300	343				
	30	.159	24	48	72	95	119	143	167■	191◆	239●	286	334	382				
	0	.090	14	27	41	54	68	81	95■	108◆	135●	162	189	216				
	5	.109	16	33	49	65	82	98	114■	131◆	164●	196	229	262				
18	10	.128	19	38	58	77	96	115	134■	154◆	192●	230	269	307	6	3	4	2
	20	.168	25	50	76	101	126	151	176■	202◆	252●	302	353	403				
	25	.188	28	56	85	113	141	169	197■	226◆	282●	338	395	451				
	30	.209	31	63	94	125	157	188	219■	251◆	314●	376	439	502				
	0	.115	17	35	52	69	86	104	121■	138◆	173●	207	242	276				
	5	.139	21	42	63	83	104	125	146■	167◆	209●	250	292	334				
20	10	.163	24	49	73	98	122	147	171■	196◆	245●	293	342	391	6	3½	4	2
	20	.213	32	64	96	128	160	192	224■	256◆	320●	383	447	511				
	25	.239	36	72	108	143	179	215	251■	287◆	359●	430	502	574				
	30	.266	40	80	120	160	200	239	279■	319◆	399●	479	559	638				
	0	.174	26	52	78	104	131	157	183	209	261■	313◆	365●	418				
	5	.209	31	63	94	125	157	188	219	251	314■	376◆	439●	502				
24	10	.246	37	74	111	148	185	221	258	295	369■	443◆	517●	590	8	4	5	2½
	20	.321	48	96	144	193	241	289	337	385	482■	578◆	674●	770				
	25	.360	54	108	162	216	270	324	378	432	540■	648◆	756●	864				
	30	.399	60	120	180	240	299	359	419	479	599■	718◆	838●	958				
	0	.285	43	86	128	171	214	257	299	342	428■	513◆	599●	684				
	5	.342	51	103	154	205	257	308	359	410	513■	616◆	718●	821				
30	10	.402	60	121	181	241	302	361	422	482	603■	724◆	844●	965	10	5	6	3
	20	.523	78	157	235	314	392	471	549	628	785■	941◆	1098●	1255				
	25	.586	88	176	264	352	440	527	615	703	879■	1055◆	1231●	1406				
	30	.649	97	195	292	389	487	584	681	779	974■	1168◆	1363●	1558				
	0	.423	63	127	190	254	317	381	444	508	635■	761◆	888●	1015				
	5	.508	76	152	229	305	381	457	533	610	762■	914◆	1067●	1219				
36	10	.596	89	179	268	358	447	536	626	715	894■	1073◆	1252●	1430	12	6	7	3½
	20	.774	116	232	348	464	581	697	813	929	1161■	1393◆	1625●	1858				
	25	.867	130	260	390	520	650	780	910	1040	1301■	1561◆	1821●	2081				
	30	.961	144	288	432	577	721	865	1009	1153	1442■	1730◆	2018●	2306				
	0	.589	88	177	265	353	442	530	618	707	884	1060■	1237◆	1414●				
	5	.706	106	212	318	424	530	635	741	847	1059	1271■	1483◆	1694●				
42	10	.829	124	249	373	497	622	746	870	995	1244	1492■	1741◆	1990●	14	7	8	4
	20	1.074	161	322	483	644	806	967	1128	1289	1611	1933■	2255◆	2578●				
	25	1.204	181	361	542	722	903	1084	1264	1445	1806	2167■	2528◆	2890●				
	30	1.333	200	400	600	800	1000	1200	1400	1600	2000	2399■	2799◆	3199●				
	0	.782	117	235	352	469	587	704	821	938	1173	1408■	1642◆	1877●				
	5	.937	141	281	422	562	703	843	984	1124	1406	1687■	1968◆	2249●				
48	10	1.099	165	330	495	659	824	989	1154	1319	1649	1978■	2308◆	2638●	16	8	10	5
	20	1.424	214	427	641	854	1068	1282	1495	1709	2136	2563■	2990◆	3418●				
	25	1.595	239	479	718	957	1196	1436	1675	1914	2393	2871■	3350◆	3828●				
	30	1.765	265	530	794	1059	1324	1589	1853	2118	2648	3177■	3707◆	4236●				
	0	1.002	150	301	451	601	752	902	1052	1202	1503	1804■	2104◆	2405●				
	5	1.201	180	360	540	721	901	1081	1261	1441	1802	2162■	2522◆	2882●				
54	10	1.407	211	422	633	844	1055	1266	1477	1688	2111	2533■	2955◆	3377●	18	9	11	5½
	20	1.823	273	547	820	1094	1367	1641	1914	2188	2735	3281■	3828◆	4375●				
	25	2.040	306	612	918	1224	1530	1836	2142	2448	3060	3672■	4284◆	4896●				
	30	2.259	339	678	1017	1355	1694	2033	2372	2711	3389	4066■	4744◆	5422●				
	0	1.250	188	375	563	750	938	1125	1313	1500	1875	2250■	2625◆	3000●				
	5	1.497	225	449	674	898	1123	1347	1572	1796	2246	2695■	3144◆	3593●				
60	10	1.753	263	526	789	1052	1315	1578	1841	2104	2630	3155■	3681◆	4207●	20	10	12	6
	20	2.270	341	681	1022	1362	1703	2043	2384	2724	3405	4086■	4767◆	5448●				
	25	2.540	381	762	1143	1524	1905	2286	2667	3048	3810	4572■	5334◆	6096●				
	30	2.813	422	844	1266	1688	2110	2532	2954	3376	4220	5063■	5907◆	6751●				
	0	1.525	229	458	686	915	1144	1373	1601	1830	2288	2745■	3203◆	3660●				
	5	1.825	274	548	821	1095	1369	1643	1916	2190	2738	3285■	3833◆	4380●				
66	10	2.138	321	641	962	1283	1604	1924	2245	2566	3207	3848■	4490◆	5131●	22	11	13	6½
	20	2.767	415	830	1245	1660	2075	2490	2905	3320	4151	4981■	5811◆	6641●				
	25	3.095	464	929	1393	1857	2321	2786	3250	3714	4643	5571■	6500◆	7428●				
	30	3.428	514	1028	1543	2057	2571	3085	3599	4114	5142	6170■	7199◆	8227●				
	0	1.826	274	548	822	1096	1370	1643	1917	2191	2739	3287■	3835◆	4382●				
	5	2.187	328	656	984	1312	1640	1968	2296	2624	3281	3937■	4593◆	5249●				
72	10	2.560	384	768	1152	1536	1920	2304	2688	3072	3840	4608■	5376◆	6144●	24	12	14	7
	20	3.313	497	994	1491	1988	2485	2982	3479	3976	4970	5963■	6957◆	7951●				
	25	3.710	557	1113	1670	2226	2783	3339	3896	4452	5565	6678■	7791◆	8904●				
	30	4.103	615	1231	1846	2462	3077	3693	4308	4924	6155	7385■	8616◆	9847●				

CAPACITY—SHORT TONS (2000 Lbs.) PER HOUR—100 POUNDS PER CUBIC FOOT MATERIAL. BELT SPEED—FEET PER MINUTE▲

MAXIMUM LUMP SIZE LARGEST DIMENSION—INCHES

▲ Maximum Suggested Belt Speeds
  Grain or other Free Flowing, Non Abrasive Materials●●●
  Coal, Damp Clay, Soft Ores, Overburden and Earth, Fine Crushed Stone◆◆◆
  Heavy, Hard, Sharp Edged Ore, Coarse Crushed Stone■■■

▲ Suggested Belt Speeds for Other Conditions
  Fine, Dry, Dusty or Fluffy Material 100-200 FPM Maximum
  Fragile Materials where degradation is harmful 150-250 FPM Maximum
  Wet Materials or materials which tend to cling to belt 300 FPM Min.

Optimum Belt Width and Trough Angle

After the actual belt speed has been selected, move down that column of Table 8–10 to the first entry that is larger than C_{rel} just calculated. Moving down the column in this manner will in effect examine successively larger belt sizes. For each belt size, only the capacity that is in the row with the correct surcharge angle should be considered. When an entry larger than C_{rel} has been located, look to the left-most column and note the optimum belt width for use with 20-degree troughing idlers.

Enter Table 8–11 and 8–12 at the same belt speed and move down the columns in the same way to values which exceed C_{rel}. Those tables will show optimum belt width for 35-degree and 45-degree troughing angles respectively.

The three pairs of capacity and width values can now be compared. Usually the arrangement that requires the least belt width will be selected as being the most economical installation. The final step is to compare the selected belt width with the minimum that was determined in the first step, and make final selection of whichever is larger.

Example

Anthracite coal, weighing 60 pounds per cubic foot and consisting of lumps up to 8 inches (representing not more than 10 percent by volume) and finer material, forms a surcharge angle of 20 degrees. A belt is to be selected to move at least 750 tons per hour.

Solution

In Table 8–10, fourth column from the end, note that a lump size of 8 inches requires a minimum belt width of 24 inches. Then, at the foot of the same table, note that coal is represented by a diamond symbol and in the 24-inch belt rows the diamond symbol is found under a maximum speed of 600 feet per minute. It is therefore reasonable to design the conveyor for a constant speed of 500 feet per minute.

Next, use the given values of 750 tons per hour and 60 pounds per cubic foot in the equation for C_{rel}. It was previously found that this computation yields 1250 tons per hour.

In each table, under the 500 feet per minute column heading, the first capacities in a 20-degree surcharge angle row which exceed 1250 tons per hour are:

- 20 degree idlers, 42″ belt, 1611 tons per hour
- 35 degree idlers, 36″ belt, 1472 tons per hour
- 45 degree idlers, 36″ belt, 1590 tons per hour

The 45-degree idler arrangement provides the largest capacity with least belt width and, since it is larger than the minimum recommended for moving 8-inch lumps, that arrangement will be selected.

Idler Roller Spacing

Carrying idlers, those that support the belt during the part of the run when it is carrying a load, should be spaced as shown in Table 8–13.

TABLE 8-11. Belt capacity for 35 degree troughing angle.

CAPACITY—SHORT TONS (2000 Lbs.) PER HOUR—100 POUNDS PER CUBIC FOOT MATERIAL

BELT SPEED—FEET PER MINUTE▲

Belt Width Inches	Surcharge Angle Degrees	Cross Sectional Area Square Feet	50	100	150	200	250	300	350	400	500	600	700	800
14	0	.079	12	24	36	47	59	71	83■	95♦	119•	142	166	190
	5	.088	13	26	40	53	66	79	92■	106♦	132•	158	185	211
	10	.098	15	29	44	59	74	88	103■	118♦	147•	176	206	235
	20	.117	18	35	53	70	88	105	123■	140♦	176•	211	246	281
	25	.128	19	38	58	77	96	115	134■	154♦	192•	230	269	307
	30	.138	21	41	62	83	104	124	145■	166♦	207•	248	290	331
16	0	.109	16	33	49	65	82	98	114■	131♦	164•	196	229	262
	5	.122	18	37	55	73	92	110	128■	146♦	183•	220	256	293
	10	.135	20	41	61	81	101	122	142■	162♦	203•	243	284	324
	20	.161	24	48	72	97	121	145	169■	193♦	242•	290	338	386
	25	.175	26	53	79	105	131	158	184■	210♦	263•	315	368	420
	30	.189	28	57	85	113	142	170	198■	227♦	284•	340	397	454
18	0	.144	22	43	65	86	108	130	151■	173♦	216•	259	302	346
	5	.161	24	48	72	97	121	145	169■	193♦	242•	290	338	386
	10	.178	27	53	80	107	134	160	187■	214♦	267•	320	374	427
	20	.212	32	64	95	127	159	191	223■	254♦	318•	382	445	509
	25	.231	35	69	104	139	173	208	243■	277♦	347•	416	485	554
	30	.249	37	75	112	149	187	224	261■	299♦	374•	448	523	598
20	0	.184	28	55	83	110	138	166	193■	221♦	276•	331	386	442
	5	.205	31	62	92	123	154	185	215■	246♦	308•	369	431	492
	10	.226	34	68	102	136	170	203	237■	271♦	339•	407	475	542
	20	.270	41	81	122	162	203	243	284■	324♦	405•	486	567	648
	25	.293	44	88	132	176	220	264	308■	352♦	440•	527	615	703
	30	.316	47	95	142	190	237	284	332■	379♦	474•	569	664	758
24	0	.278	42	83	125	167	209	250	292	334	417■	500♦	584•	667
	5	.309	46	93	139	185	232	278	324	371	464■	556♦	649•	742
	10	.341	51	102	153	205	256	307	358	409	512■	614♦	716•	818
	20	.406	61	122	183	244	305	365	426	487	609■	731♦	853•	974
	25	.441	66	132	198	265	331	397	463	529	662■	794♦	926•	1058
	30	.475	71	143	214	285	356	428	499	570	713■	855♦	998•	1140
30	0	.456	68	137	205	274	342	410	479	547	684■	821♦	958•	1094
	5	.506	76	152	228	304	380	455	531	607	759■	911♦	1063•	1214
	10	.558	84	167	251	335	419	502	586	670	837■	1004♦	1172•	1339
	20	.663	99	199	298	398	497	597	696	796	995■	1193♦	1392•	1591
	25	.718	108	215	323	431	539	646	754	862	1077■	1292♦	1508•	1723
	30	.773	116	232	348	464	580	696	812	928	1160■	1391♦	1623•	1855
36	0	.676	101	203	304	406	507	608	710	811	1014■	1217♦	1420•	1622
	5	.750	113	225	338	450	563	675	788	900	1125■	1350♦	1575•	1800
	10	.827	124	248	372	496	620	744	868	992	1241■	1489♦	1737•	1985
	20	.981	147	294	441	589	736	883	1030	1177	1472■	1766♦	2060•	2354
	25	1.062	159	319	478	637	797	956	1115	1274	1593■	1912♦	2230•	2549
	30	1.143	171	343	514	686	857	1029	1200	1372	1715■	2057♦	2400•	2743
42	0	.940	141	282	423	564	705	846	987	1128	1410	1692■	1974•	2256•
	5	1.043	156	313	469	626	782	939	1095	1252	1565	1877■	2190•	2503•
	10	1.148	172	344	517	689	861	1033	1205	1378	1722	2066■	2411•	2755•
	20	1.361	204	408	612	817	1021	1225	1429	1633	2042	2450■	2858•	3266•
	25	1.473	221	442	663	884	1105	1326	1547	1768	2210	2651■	3093•	3535•
	30	1.585	238	476	713	951	1189	1427	1664	1902	2378	2853■	3329•	3804•
48	0	1.249	187	375	562	749	937	1124	1311	1499	1874	2248■	2623•	2998•
	5	1.383	207	415	622	830	1037	1245	1452	1660	2075	2489■	2904•	3319•
	10	1.523	228	457	685	914	1142	1371	1599	1828	2285	2741■	3198•	3655•
	20	1.804	271	541	812	1082	1353	1624	1894	2165	2706	3247■	3788•	4330•
	25	1.952	293	586	878	1171	1464	1757	2050	2342	2928	3514■	4099•	4685•
	30	2.100	315	630	945	1260	1575	1890	2205	2520	3150	3780■	4410•	5040•
54	0	1.600	240	480	720	960	1200	1440	1680	1920	2400	2880■	3360•	3840•
	5	1.771	266	531	797	1063	1328	1594	1860	2125	2657	3188■	3719•	4250•
	10	1.950	293	585	878	1170	1463	1755	2048	2340	2925	3510■	4095•	4680•
	20	2.309	346	693	1039	1385	1732	2078	2424	2771	3464	4156■	4849•	5542•
	25	2.498	375	749	1124	1499	1874	2248	2623	2998	3747	4496■	5246•	5995•
	30	2.686	403	806	1209	1612	2015	2417	2820	3223	4029	4835■	5641•	6446•
60	0	1.992	299	598	896	1195	1494	1793	2092	2390	2988	3586■	4183•	4781•
	5	2.208	331	662	994	1325	1656	1987	2318	2650	3312	3974■	4637•	5299•
	10	2.430	365	729	1094	1458	1823	2187	2552	2916	3645	4374■	5103•	5832•
	20	2.876	431	863	1294	1726	2157	2588	3020	3451	4314	5177■	6040•	6902•
	25	3.111	467	933	1400	1867	2333	2800	3267	3733	4667	5600■	6533•	7466•
	30	3.345	502	1004	1505	2007	2509	3011	3512	4014	5018	6021■	7025•	8028•
66	0	2.430	365	729	1094	1458	1823	2187	2552	2916	3645	4374■	5103•	5832•
	5	2.692	404	808	1211	1615	2019	2423	2827	3230	4038	4846■	5653•	6461•
	10	2.962	444	889	1333	1777	2222	2666	3110	3554	4443	5332■	6220•	7109•
	20	3.506	526	1052	1578	2104	2630	3155	3681	4207	5259	6311■	7363•	8414•
	25	3.791	569	1137	1706	2275	2843	3412	3981	4549	5687	6824■	7961•	9098•
	30	4.076	611	1223	1834	2446	3057	3668	4280	4891	6114	7337■	8560•	9782•
72	0	2.922	438	877	1315	1753	2192	2630	3068	3506	4383	5260■	6136•	7013•
	5	3.225	484	968	1451	1935	2419	2903	3386	3870	4838	5805■	6773•	7740•
	10	3.547	532	1064	1596	2128	2660	3192	3724	4256	5321	6385■	7449•	8513•
	20	4.197	630	1259	1889	2518	3148	3777	4407	5036	6296	7555■	8814•	10073•
	25	4.538	681	1361	2042	2723	3404	4084	4765	5446	6807	8168■	9530•	10891•
	30	4.879	732	1464	2196	2927	3659	4391	5123	5855	7319	8782■	10246•	11710•

Note: A Minimum Speed of at least 300 FPM is recommended for proper discharge.

▲ Maximum Suggested Belt Speeds
Grain or other Free Flowing, Non Abrasive Materials•••
Coal, Damp Clay, Soft Ores, Overburden and Earth, Fine Crushed Stone♦♦♦
Heavy, Hard, Sharp Edged Ore, Coarse Crushed Stone■■■

▲ Suggested Belt Speeds for Other Conditions
Fine, Dry, Dusty or Fluffy Material 100-200 FPM Maximum
Fragile Materials where degradation is harmful 150-250 FPM Maximum
Wet Materials or materials which tend to cling to belt 300 FPM Min.

TABLE 8-12. Belt capacity for 45 degree troughing angle.

Belt Width Inches	Surcharge Angle Degrees	Cross Sectional Area Square Feet	CAPACITY—SHORT TONS (2000 Lbs.) PER HOUR—100 POUNDS PER CUBIC FOOT MATERIAL BELT SPEED—FEET PER MINUTE▲											
			50	100	150	200	250	300	350	400	500	600	700	800
14	0	.093	14	28	42	56	70	84	98▪	112♦	140•	167	195	223
	5	.102	15	31	46	61	77	92	107▪	122♦	153•	184	214	245
	10	.110	17	33	50	66	83	99	116▪	132♦	165•	198	231	264
	20	.128	19	38	58	77	96	115	134▪	154♦	192•	230	269	307
	25	.139	21	42	63	83	104	125	146▪	167♦	209•	250	292	334
	30	.146	22	44	66	88	110	131	153▪	175♦	219•	263	307	350
16	0	.129	19	39	58	77	97	116	135▪	155♦	194•	232	271	310
	5	.140	21	42	63	84	105	126	147▪	168♦	210•	252	294	336
	10	.152	23	46	68	91	114	137	160▪	182♦	228•	274	319	365
	20	.175	26	53	79	105	131	158	184▪	210♦	263•	315	368	420
	25	.188	28	56	85	113	141	169	197▪	226♦	282•	338	395	451
	30	.200	30	60	90	120	150	180	210▪	240♦	300•	360	420	480
18	0	.170	26	51	77	102	128	153	179♦	204♦	255•	306	357	408
	5	.185	28	56	83	111	139	167	194▪	222♦	278•	333	389	444
	10	.200	30	60	90	120	150	180	210▪	240♦	300•	360	420	480
	20	.230	35	69	104	138	173	207	242▪	276♦	345•	414	483	552
	25	.246	37	74	111	148	185	221	258▪	295♦	369•	443	517	590
	30	.262	39	79	118	157	197	236	275▪	314♦	393•	472	550	629
20	0	.217	33	65	98	130	163	195	228▪	260♦	326•	391	456	521
	5	.236	35	71	106	142	177	212	248▪	283♦	354•	425	496	566
	10	.254	38	76	114	152	191	229	267▪	305♦	381•	457	533	610
	20	.293	44	88	132	176	220	264	308▪	352♦	440•	527	615	703
	25	.313	47	94	141	188	235	282	329▪	376♦	470•	563	657	751
	30	.333	50	100	150	200	250	300	350▪	400♦	500•	599	699	799
24	0	.327	49	98	147	196	245	294	343	392	491▪	589♦	687•	785
	5	.355	53	107	160	213	266	320	373	426	533▪	639♦	746•	852
	10	.383	57	115	172	230	287	345	402	460	575▪	689♦	804•	919
	20	.440	66	132	198	264	330	396	462	528	660▪	792♦	924•	1056
	25	.470	71	141	212	282	353	423	494	564	705▪	846♦	987•	1128
	30	.499	75	150	225	299	374	449	524	599	749▪	898♦	1048•	1198
30	0	.536	80	161	241	322	402	482	563	643	804▪	965♦	1126•	1286
	5	.580	87	174	261	348	435	522	609	696	870▪	1044♦	1218•	1392
	10	.625	94	188	281	375	469	563	656	750	938▪	1125♦	1313•	1500
	20	.716	107	215	322	430	537	644	752	859	1074▪	1289♦	1504•	1718
	25	.764	115	229	344	458	573	688	802	917	1146▪	1375♦	1604•	1834
	30	.812	122	244	365	487	609	731	853	974	1218▪	1462♦	1705•	1949
36	0	.795	119	239	358	477	596	716	835	954	1193▪	1431♦	1670•	1908
	5	.860	129	258	387	516	645	774	903	1032	1290▪	1548♦	1806•	2064
	10	.926	139	278	417	556	695	833	972	1111	1389▪	1667♦	1945•	2222
	20	1.060	159	318	477	636	795	954	1113	1272	1590▪	1908♦	2226•	2544
	25	1.131	170	339	509	679	848	1018	1188	1357	1697▪	2036♦	2375•	2714
	30	1.201	180	360	540	721	901	1081	1261	1441	1802▪	2162♦	2522•	2882
42	0	1.106	166	332	498	664	830	995	1161	1327	1659	1991▪	2323♦	2654•
	5	1.194	179	358	537	716	896	1075	1254	1433	1791	2149▪	2507♦	2866•
	10	1.286	193	386	579	772	965	1157	1350	1543	1929	2315▪	2701♦	3086•
	20	1.471	221	441	662	883	1103	1324	1545	1765	2207	2648▪	3089♦	3530•
	25	1.568	235	470	706	941	1176	1411	1646	1882	2352	2822▪	3293♦	3763•
	30	1.665	250	500	749	999	1249	1499	1748	1998	2498	2997▪	3497♦	3996•
48	0	1.467	220	440	660	880	1100	1320	1540	1760	2201	2641▪	3081♦	3521•
	5	1.584	238	475	713	950	1188	1426	1663	1901	2376	2851▪	3326♦	3802•
	10	1.705	256	512	767	1023	1279	1535	1790	2046	2558	3069▪	3581♦	4092•
	20	1.848	277	554	832	1109	1386	1663	1940	2218	2772	3326▪	3881♦	4435•
	25	2.076	311	623	934	1246	1557	1868	2180	2491	3114	3737▪	4360♦	4982•
	30	2.204	331	661	992	1322	1653	1984	2314	2645	3306	3967▪	4628♦	5290•
54	0	1.877	282	563	845	1126	1408	1689	1971	2252	2816	3379▪	3942♦	4505•
	5	2.028	304	608	913	1217	1521	1825	2129	2434	3042	3650▪	4259♦	4867•
	10	2.182	327	655	982	1309	1637	1964	2291	2618	3273	3928▪	4582♦	5237•
	20	2.493	374	748	1122	1496	1870	2244	2618	2992	3740	4487▪	5235♦	5983•
	25	2.656	398	797	1195	1594	1992	2390	2789	3187	3984	4781▪	5578♦	6374•
	30	2.819	423	846	1269	1691	2114	2537	2960	3383	4229	5074▪	5920♦	6766•
60	0	2.340	351	702	1053	1404	1755	2106	2457	2808	3510	4212▪	4914♦	5616•
	5	2.527	379	758	1137	1516	1895	2274	2653	3032	3791	4549▪	5307♦	6065•
	10	2.718	408	815	1223	1631	2039	2446	2854	3262	4077	4892▪	5708♦	6523•
	20	3.104	466	931	1397	1862	2328	2794	3259	3725	4656	5587▪	6518♦	7450•
	25	3.307	496	992	1488	1984	2480	2976	3472	3968	4961	5953▪	6945♦	7937•
	30	3.510	527	1053	1580	2106	2633	3159	3686	4212	5265	6318▪	7371♦	8424•
66	0	2.855	428	857	1285	1713	2141	2570	2998	3426	4283	5139▪	5996♦	6852•
	5	3.080	462	924	1386	1848	2310	2772	3234	3696	4620	5544▪	6468♦	7392•
	10	3.314	497	994	1491	1988	2486	2983	3480	3977	4971	5965▪	6959♦	7954•
	20	3.783	567	1135	1702	2270	2837	3405	3972	4540	5675	6809▪	7944♦	9079•
	25	4.030	605	1209	1814	2418	3023	3627	4232	4836	6045	7254▪	8463♦	9672•
	30	4.276	641	1283	1924	2566	3207	3848	4490	5131	6414	7697▪	8980♦	10262•
72	0	3.420	513	1026	1539	2052	2565	3078	3591	4104	5130	6156▪	7182♦	8208•
	5	3.689	553	1107	1660	2213	2767	3320	3873	4427	5534	6640▪	7747♦	8854•
	10	3.967	595	1190	1785	2380	2975	3570	4165	4760	5951	7141▪	8331♦	9521•
	20	4.528	679	1358	2038	2717	3396	4075	4754	5434	6792	8150▪	9509♦	10867•
	25	4.873	731	1462	2193	2924	3655	4386	5117	5848	7310	8771▪	10233♦	11695•
	30	5.118	768	1535	2303	3071	3839	4606	5374	6142	7677	9212▪	10748♦	12283•

Note: A Minimum Speed of at least 300 FPM is recommended for proper discharge.
▲ Maximum Suggested Belt Speeds
  Grain or other Free Flowing, Non Abrasive Materials•••
  Coal, Damp Clay, Soft Ores, Overburden and Earth, Fine Crushed Stone♦♦♦
  Heavy, Hard, Sharp Edged Ore, Coarse Crushed Stone▪▪▪

▲ Suggested Belt Speeds for Other Conditions
  Fine, Dry, Dusty or Fluffy Material 100-200 FPM Maximum
  Fragile Materials where degradation is harmful 150-250 FPM Maximum
  Wet Materials or materials which tend to cling to belt 300 FPM Min.

TABLE 8-13.   Recommended average spacing of idler rollers, in feet.

| Belt Width, Inches | CARRYING IDLERS | | | | | | RETURN IDLERS |
| | Weight of Material Conveyed Pounds Per Cubic Foot | | | | | | |
	30	50	75	100	150	200	
14	5½	5	5	5	4½	4½	10
16	5½	5	5	5	4½	4½	10
18	5½	5	5	5	4½	4½	10
20	5½	5	4½	4½	4	4	10
24	5	4½	4½	4	4	4	10
30	5	4½	4½	4	4	4	10
36	5	4½	4	4	3½	3½	10
42	4½	4½	4	3½	3	3	10
48	4½	4	4	3½	3	3	10
54	4½	4	3½	3½	3	3	10
60	4	4	3½	3	3	3	10
66	4	4	3½	3	3	2½	8
72	4	3½	3½	3	2½	2½	8

Note: In the shaded area, for more severe applications particulary for 35° and 45° idlers, the maximum allowable idler loading may be surpassed. In questionable cases consult REX CHAINBELT.

This table shows average values for constant steady loads; spacings of one-half the values shown should be used at the loading point to handle impact forces. When fine material is being loaded, idlers should be placed as close as possible.

Return idlers, which carry only the weight of the belt, should be spaced as shown in the last column of Table 8–13.

Roadways and Parking Layout

CHAPTER 9

PAVEMENTS

Concrete Pavement[1]

The following procedure is recommended for paving jobs that are not large enough to use the full series of pre-tests, including varied trial mixes, casting and curing beams, and strength measurements in the laboratory.

Table 9–1 gives quantities for a goal of 1- to 2-inch slump (see information on slump in Chapter 2), based on aggregate in a saturated, surface-dry condition with a specific gravity of 2.65. To change the slump to 2 to 3 inches, increase water by 1 or 2 gallons per cubic yard; slumps beyond 3 inches (emergency conditions) should be made by:

1. increasing sand content by 100 pounds;
2. decreasing coarse aggregate by 100 pounds; *and*
3. adding about 1 gallon of water per cubic yard.

Formulas and instructions for using this table are integrated in the following example.

Example

A paving job is to use aggregates with the following characteristics:

Coarse maximum size = 1 1/2 inches
        specific gravity = 2.71
        free moisture   = 2 percent
        appearance — angular
Fine   specific gravity = 2.69
        free moisture   = 4 percent

• Unadjusted quantities from Table 9–1 are:

---

[1]Portland Cement Association, "Design of Concrete Paving Mixtures," Skokie, Illinois. © Portland Cement Association, 1961.

TABLE 9-1. Trial mixes of air-entrained concrete for small paving jobs (1- to 2-inch slump).*

| | | Quantities per cubic yard of concrete | | | | | |
Max. size aggregate, inches	Air content, percent	Water, gallons	Water, pounds	Cement, sacks	Cement, pounds	Fine Aggregate, pounds	Coarse Aggregate, pounds
3/4 angular	6	33	275	7.0	658	1,333	1,581
3/4 round	6	30	250	7.0	658	938	2,041
1 angular	6	31	258	6.6	620	1,290	1,702
1 round	6	28	233	6.6	620	875	2,183
1 1/2 angular	5	29	242	6.1	573	1,245	1,872
1 1/2 round	5	26	217	6.1	573	802	2,381
2 angular	5	27	225	5.7	536	1,248	1,945
2 round	5	24	200	5.7	536	794	2,466
2 1/2 angular	5	26	217	5.5	517	1,189	2,042
2 1/2 round	5	23	192	5.5	517	747	2,552

*If more slumps become desirable an increase of 1-inch slump can be obtained by the addition of 1 to 2 gallons of water per cubic yard. In emergency conditions, if it becomes necessary to use a slump greater than 3 inches, it should be obtained by:

1. increasing the sand content by 100 pounds;
2. decreasing the coarse aggregate by 100 pounds; and
3. adding about 1 gallon of water per cubic yard.

$$\text{Air} \qquad\qquad = 5 \text{ percent}$$
$$\text{Water} \qquad\quad\;\, = 29 \text{ gallons}$$
$$\text{Cement} \qquad\quad = 6.1 \text{ sacks}$$
$$\text{Fine aggregate} \;\, = 1245 \text{ pounds}$$
$$\text{Coarse aggregate} = 1872 \text{ pounds}$$

• Adjust coarse aggregate requirement for specific gravity by writing ratios:

$$\frac{\text{actual requirement}}{\text{actual specific gravity}} = \frac{\text{table requirement}}{2.65}$$

$$\text{actual requirement} = \frac{\text{table requirement (actual specific gravity)}}{2.65}$$

$$= \frac{1872(2.71)}{2.65}$$

$$= 1914 \text{ pounds}$$

• Adjust fine aggregate requirement for specific gravity by same ratio as used for coarse aggregate:

$$\text{actual requirement} = \frac{1245(2.69)}{2.65}$$

$$= 1264 \text{ pounds}$$

• Determine weight of free moisture in aggregate:

$$1914 \,(2\%) = 38 \text{ pounds in coarse}$$
$$1264 \,(2\%) = 51 \text{ pounds in fine}$$

• Divide free moisture weight by 8.34 to convert to gallons:

$$\frac{38 + 51}{8.34} = 11 \text{ gallons total in aggregates}$$

• Determine net water requirement:

$$\text{net water} = \text{table requirement} - \text{free moisture}$$
$$= 29 - 11$$
$$= 18 \text{ gallons}$$

• Desired amount of aggregate is obtained by including free moisture in the weight:

$$\text{coarse aggregate} = 1914 + 38$$
$$= 1952 \text{ pounds}$$
$$\text{fine aggregate} \quad = 1264 + 51$$
$$= 1315 \text{ pounds}$$

Summary—First trial mix will contain:

$$\text{Water} \qquad\qquad\;\; = 18 \text{ gallons}$$
$$\text{Cement} \qquad\qquad = 6.1 \text{ sacks (573 pounds)}$$
$$\text{Fine aggregate} \quad\; = 1315 \text{ pounds}$$
$$\text{Coarse aggregate} = 1952 \text{ pounds}$$
$$\text{Air} \qquad\qquad\qquad = 5 \text{ percent, obtained by using air-entraining}$$
$$\text{cement or an air-entraining agent}$$

TABLE 9-2. Concrete pavement thickness and loading conditions.

Concrete pavement thickness, inches	Single axle			Tandem axle		
	Good for unlimited number of axle loads up to	Good for 50,000 axle loads up to	Good for 5,000 axle loads up to	Good for unlimited number of axle loads up to	Good for 50,000 axle loads up to	Good for 5,000 axle loads up to
5	10,000	12,500	15,000	16,500	21,000	26,000
6	14,500	17,500	20,500	24,500	30,000	35,000
7	19,000	22,500	26,500	31,500	37,500	43,000
8	23,500	28,000	33,000	38,500	45,500	52,500
9	28,500	34,500	41,500	45,500	54,000	63,500
10	34,500	42,000	51,000	53,000	64,000	76,000

TABLE 9-3. Thickness of full depth asphalt.*

Parking and Driveway Description	Subgrade Soil Type†	Minimum Depth Asphalt Concrete
Residential driveways; Parking Lots, up to 85 passenger cars	Good to Excellent	4 inches
	Medium	4
	Poor	4
Parking Lots, 85 to 500** passenger cars	Good to Excellent	4
	Medium	4 1/2
	Poor	6
Parking Lots, up to 20 heavy trucks†† per day; Service Stations; Passenger car parking lot Entrance and Traffic Lanes used by heavy trucks	Good to Excellent	5 1/2
	Medium	7
	Poor	9
Parking Lots (including Truck Stops), 20 to 400 heavy trucks per day; Passenger car parking lot Entrances and Traffic Lanes used by heavy trucks; Loading and Unloading areas	Good to Excellent	7 1/2
	Medium	9 1/2
	Poor	12

Notes:

*As the thickness design procedure calls for the use of asphalt paving mixtures similar to Asphalt Institute Type IV mixes, the same mix may be used for the base and surface.

†*Excellent* subgrade soils include clean and sharp sands and gravels, particularly those that are well graded; *good* subgrade soils include clean sands and sand-gravels and soils free of detrimental amounts of plastic materials; *medium* subgrade soils include loams, silty sands, and sand-gravels containing moderate amounts of clay and fine silt; *poor* subgrade soils include those having appreciable amounts of clay and fine silt.

**The Asphalt Institute can assist with parking lots for more than 500 stalls.

††Heavy trucks are heavy commercial vehicles, normally 2-axle 6-tire vehicles or larger; pickup and light panel trucks are not considered heavy trucks.

Depth of Concrete[2]

Table 9–2 gives acceptable loading conditions for concrete pavement of various thicknesses. Figures for 5000 and 50,000 pound axle loads indicate conditions that will use up 100 percent of the fatigue resistance of the pavement thickness listed.

Asphalt Pavement

Full-depth asphalt concrete[3]:

Table 9–3 gives recommended thickness, where full-depth means that asphalt concrete interfaces directly with subgrade.

Bases other than asphalt concrete[4]:

If a portion of the pavement is to be converted to a different base, the third column of Table 9–4 shows the thickness that should remain asphalt-concrete. The difference (full-depth thickness minus third column of Table 9–4) is then multiplied by the factor in the last column of Table 9–4 to determine the base thickness between subgrade and asphalt-concrete pavement.

TABLE 9-4. Conversion to bases other than asphalt concrete.

Base	Expected Traffic	Minimum Pavement	Conversion Factor
Hot-mix sand asphalt	Light	2 inches	1.3
	Medium	3	1.3
	Heavy	4	1.3
Liquid and asphalt	Light	2	1.4
	Medium	3	1.4
	Heavy	4	1.4
Low quality untreated granular		See Figure 9–1	2.7
High quality untreated granular		See Figure 9–1	2.0

PARKING STALL DESIGN[5]

Symbols used in this section are explained in Table 9–5, along with representative values that will be used in the examples.

[2]Portland Cement Association, "Concrete Industrial Driveways," Skokie, Illinois.© Portland Cement Association, 1969.
[3]The Asphalt Institute, "Full-Depth Asphalt Pavements for Parking Lots, Service Stations and Driveways" (IS-91), College Park, Maryland, 1970.
[4]The Asphalt Institute, Thickness Design—Full-Depth Asphalt Pavement Structures for Highways and Streets (MS-I), College Park, Maryland, 1969, pp. 35–42.
[5]Ricker, Edmund R., "Traffic Design of Parking Garages," The Eno Foundation for Highway Traffic Control, Inc., Saugatuck, Conn. Copyright, 1957, by the Eno Foundation for Highway Traffic Control, Inc.

FIGURE 9-1

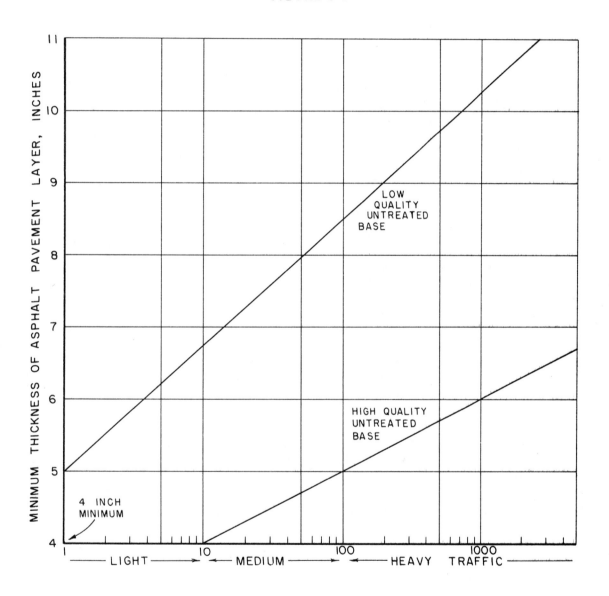

TABLE 9-5. Parking stall symbols.

Symbol	Meaning	Representative Value (inches)
L	Overall Length	216
W	Overall Width	78
O_f	Front Overhang (front axle to bumper)	36
O_r	Rear Overhang (rear axle to bumper)	54
O_s	Side Overhang (center of rear tire to fender)	9
t_r	Rear Tread (center to center of tires)	60
t_f	Front Tread (center to center of tires)	60
r	Minimum Turning Radius—inside rear wheel	164
r'	—inside front wheel	207
R	—outside point, front bumper	279
R'	—outside point, rear bumper	237
A	Aisle Width, inches	
E_f	Extension of front of car beyond curb, measured perpendicular to aisle, inches	
E_r	Extension of rear of car beyond curb, measured perpendicular to aisle, inches	
D	Distance along ramp, feet	
H	Floor-to-floor height, feet	
h	Height of curb	6
B	Angle of parking, measured from a line parallel to aisle	
c	Clearance between cars as one moves into or out of stall, inches	6
i	Inter-car distance, inches ($= S - W$)	40
S	Stall width, measured perpendicular to side of stall, inches	108
T	Slope of ramp, percent	
w	Width of stall, measured along aisle, inches	
l	Length of stall, measured perpendicular to aisle, inches	
X_h	Area wasted at end of herringbone parking line, square feet	
X_i	Area wasted at end of interlocked parking line, square feet	
X_s	Area wasted at end of single parking line, square feet	

Width of Stall: Number of stalls per given length of aisle

This calculation provides the plant engineer with a quick look at the interpendence of number of stalls, length of aisle, angle of parking, width of stall, and size of stall opening on aisle. A nomogram, Figure 9–2, allows rapid assessment of the effect of changing any of the variables. It is expected that some of the formulas appearing later will modify the choices initially made from this nomogram, but the design should start with this calculation.

Formula

$$w = \frac{S}{\sin B}$$

FIGURE 9-2

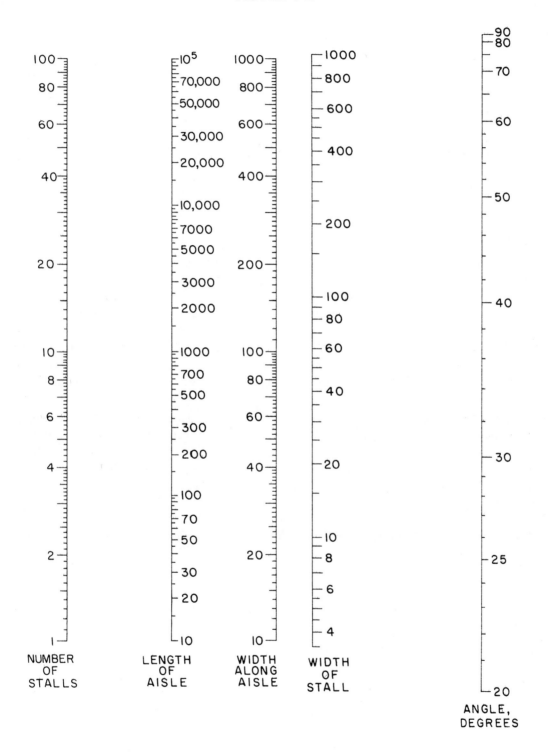

Example

How many stalls of representative dimensions can be placed along a 200-foot aisle if the stall angle is 45 degrees?

Solution

$$w = \frac{108}{\sin 45°}$$
$$= 153 \text{ inches}$$
$$= 12'9''$$

Dividing this line-to-line spacing into the aisle length gives number of stalls

$$n = \frac{200}{12.75}$$
$$= 16 \text{ stalls}$$

Using the nomogram

Except for the ANGLE scale, which is given in degrees, all scales in Figure 9–2 do not have specific units of measurement; the user can assume any units (inches, feet, tens of feet, meters, etc.) as long as the same units are used on all scales. For the preceding example, work the nomogram from right to left and assume the scales are in inches.

Draw a straight line through 45° on the ANGLE scale and 108 on the WIDTH OF STALL scale; where that line crosses the WIDTH ALONG AISLE scale, read a width of 153 inches. From that crossing draw a straight line through 2400 (200 feet) on the LENGTH OF AISLE scale and that line crosses the NUMBER OF STALLS scale between 15 and 16.

The nomogram can be worked in either direction, depending on which variables are dependent and which are independent. Another convenient mode of operation is to pivot a straightedge about one given value to see the various combinations of other variables that are compatible with that value, as when the length of aisle is fixed and the straightedge will show combinations of stall width and number of stalls that will give that aisle length.

Area Per Car (including allocation of half of aisle width)

Formula

$$\text{Area} = \frac{S}{\sin B}\left(L \sin B + S \cos B + \frac{A}{2}\right)$$

Example

For the stall dimensions just calculated, and an aisle width of 20 feet (240 inches), how much area must be allocated per car?

$$\text{Area} = \frac{108}{\sin 45°}\left(216 \sin 45° + 108 \cos 45° + \frac{240}{2}\right)$$
$$= 4443 \text{ square inches}$$
$$= 370 \text{ square feet}$$

Critical Angle: Angle at which minimum aisle width for clearing car on left equals aisle width for clearing car on right

Formula

$$B' = \text{arc cot } \frac{\sqrt{R^2 - (r + t_r + O_s + i - c)^2} + \sqrt{(r - O_s - i + c)^2}}{2S}$$

Example

What is the critical angle for a vehicle with representative dimensions as given in Table 9–5?

Solution

$$B' = \text{arc cot } \frac{\sqrt{279^2 - (164 + 60 + 9 + 40 - 6)^2} + \sqrt{(164 - 9)^2 - (164 - 9 - 40 + 6)^2}}{2(108)}$$

$$= 50.5 \text{ degrees}$$

Minimum Aisle Width (for drive-in stall angle greater than critical angle—movement limited by car parked on left)

Formula

$$A = R' + c + \sin B \sqrt{R^2 - (r + t_r + O_s + i - c)^2} - \cos B(r + t_r + O_s + S)$$

Example

What is the minimum aisle width for a vehicle of representative dimensions if stalls are at a 60-degree angle?

Solution

$$A = 237 + 6 + \sin 60° \sqrt{279^2 - (164 + 60 + 9 + 40 - 6)^2}$$
$$- \cos 60°(164 + 60 + 9 + 108)$$
$$= 163.6 \text{ inches}$$
$$= 13'6''$$

Minimum Aisle Width (for drive-in stall angle less than critical angle—movement limited by car parked on right)

Formula

$$A = R' + c - \sin B \sqrt{(r - O_s)^2 - (r - O_s - i + c)^2} - \cos B(r + t_r + O_s - S)$$

Example

What is the minimum aisle width for a vehicle of representative dimensions if stalls are at a 30-degree angle?

Solution

$$A = 237 + 6 - \sin 30° \sqrt{(164 - 9)^2 - (164 - 9 - 40 + 6)^2}$$
$$- \cos 30°(164 + 60 + 9 - 108)$$

$$= 86.3 \text{ inches}$$
$$= 7'2''$$

Minimum Aisle Width (for back-in stall angle less than critical angle—movement limited by car parked on right)

Formula

$$A = R + c - \sin B \sqrt{(r - O_s)^2 - (r - O_s - i + c)^2} - \cos B(r + t_r + O_s - S)$$

Example

What is the minimum aisle width for a vehicle of representative dimensions if stalls are at a 30-degree angle?

Solution

$$A = 279 + 6 - \sin 30° \sqrt{(164 - 9)^2 - (164 - 9 - 40 + 6)^2}$$
$$- \cos 30° \ (164 + 60 + 9 - 108)$$
$$= 128.3 \text{ inches}$$
$$= 10'7''$$

Length of Stall

Formula

$$1 = L \sin B + S \cos B$$

Example

What is the length of a stall, at an angle of 45 degrees, for a vehicle of representative dimensions?

Solution

$$1 = 216 \sin 45° + 108 \cos 45°$$
$$= 229 \text{ inches}$$

Overhang (wheels against curb)

Formula

$$E_f = \frac{S - T_f}{2} \cos B + \sin B \left[O_f - \sqrt{\frac{d^2}{4} - \frac{d}{2} - h^2} \right]$$

$$E_r = \frac{S - t_r}{2} \cos B + \sin B \left[O_r - \sqrt{\frac{d^2}{4} - \frac{d}{2} - h^2} \right]$$

Example

How far should a curb be placed from a wall to stop a representative vehicle in a

45° stall? Measurement is to the part of the curb where the rear wheel nearest the wall is expected to strike.

Solution

$$E_r = \frac{108 - 60}{2} \cos 45° + \sin 45° \left[54 - \sqrt{\frac{29^2}{4} - \frac{29}{2} - 6^2} \right]$$

$$= 63.82 \text{ inches}$$

Intermeshed Stalls: Figure 9-3

Formula

$$U = \frac{S}{2} \cos B$$

where:

$U =$ reduction in unit parking depth due to intermeshing

Example

How much saving in unit parking depth would result from intermeshing 108-inch wide stalls at 45 degrees?

Solution

$$U = \frac{108}{2} \cos 45°$$

$$= 38.18 \text{ inches}$$

Wasted Area at Each End of Parking Line

Formula—single parking line:

$$X_s = \frac{l^2}{288 \tan B}$$

$$= \frac{(L \sin B + S \cos B)^2}{288 \tan B}$$

Formula—interlocked parking line:

$$X_i = \frac{(L \sin B + \dfrac{S}{2} \cos B)^2}{72 \tan B} - \frac{SL}{144} - \frac{S^2}{288 \tan B}$$

Formula—herringbone parking line:

$$X_h = \frac{L^2}{288} + (L \sqrt{2} + 2L \sin B + S \cos B) \frac{0.354S}{144}$$

FIGURE 9-3

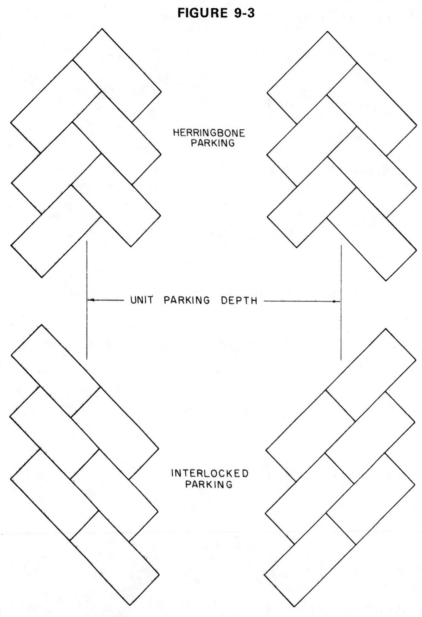

HERRINGBONE
PARKING

←——————— UNIT PARKING DEPTH ———————→

INTERLOCKED
PARKING

Example

How much area is lost at the end of a line of 45-degree interlocked stalls of representative dimensions?

Solution

$$X_t = \frac{\left(216 \sin 45° + \dfrac{108}{2} \cos 45°\right)^2}{72 \tan 45°} - \frac{108(216)}{144} - \frac{216^2}{288 \tan 45°}$$

$$= 182.25 \text{ square feet}$$

Slope and Rise of Ramp: Multistory parking

Formula

$$H = D(T/100)$$

Example

If floors are 1 foot thick how much floor-to-ceiling clearance will result from a 14 percent ramp 70 feet long?

Solution

$$H = 70(14/100)$$
$$= 9.8 \text{ feet}$$

Subtracting 1-foot floor thickness leaves 8.8 feet floor-to-ceiling clearance.

Temporary Holding

When arrival rate and parking rate are about the same there will be a build-up of cars waiting to be parked. Table 9–6 shows the number of holding spaces that will prevent overflow 99 percent of the time.

Table 9-6.   Holding requirements for peak inflow.

$$\frac{\text{Service per hour}}{\text{Arrival per hour}}$$

Arrivals per hour	0.85	0.90	0.95	1.00	1.05	1.10
0	0	0	0	0	0	0
20	15	14	13	12	11	10
40	22	20	18	16	14	12
60	29	26	23	20	16	13
80	35	31	27	23	18	14
100	40	35	30	25	20	15
120	45	39	33	27	21	15
140	51	43	36	29	22	15
160		47	38	31	22	15
180		50	41	32	23	15
200			43	34	23	15
220			46	36	24	15
240			48	37	24	15
260			51	38	25	15
280				40	25	15
300				41	25	15

Outdoor Signs—Design and Illumination

CHAPTER 10

This chapter presents some guidelines for planning of large and small signs, including mechanical requirements, size and readability, color, and illumination.

WIND FORCES

Wind Pressure

Formula—flat surface:

$$P_f = .0042 \ (V_m)^2$$
$$P_f = .0032 \ (V_n)^2$$
$$P_k = .0022 \ (V_k)^2$$

Formula—cylindrical surface:

$$P_f = .0025 \ (V_m)^2$$
$$P_f = .0019 \ (V_n)^2$$
$$P_k = .0013 \ (V_k)^2$$

where: P_f = Pressure in pounds per square foot
P_k = Pressure in kilograms per square meter
V_m = Velocity in miles per hour
V_n = Velocity in knots
V_k = Velocity in kilometers per hour

Example

A sign is composed of a framework of 1-inch aluminum tubing, which supports a 1-foot by 2-foot flat plate of plastic. What will be the wind pressure at 60 miles per hour if the tubing projects to a total of 1 square foot?

Solution

Substituting 60 miles per hour in the first equation for flat surfaces gives

$$P_f = .0042 \ (60)^2$$
$$= 10.12 \text{ pounds per square foot}$$

and since the flat surface has an area of 2 square feet the pressure due to this surface is $2(10.12) = 20.24$ pounds.

Substituting 60 miles per hour in the first equation for cylindrical surfaces gives

$$P_f = .0025 \ (60)^2$$
$$= 9.00 \text{ pounds per square foot}$$

This rate of pressure is applied to 1 square foot and therefore the pressure due to cylindrical surfaces is 9 pounds. Total wind pressure is the sum of that on flat surfaces and that on cylindrical surfaces, or 29.24 pounds.

Plexiglas Thickness[1]

For an unbraced sign face that is cut from a single piece of Plexiglas, Table 10–1 shows recommended maximum short dimension (usually height) as a function of wind pressure, aspect ratio, and thickness. Aspect ratio is defined as the longer dimension divided by the shorter: if the flat surface is not rectangular, aspect ratio is long side over short side of the smallest rectangular that will enclose the flat surface.

TABLE 10-1. Maximum Unbraced Short Dimension

Plexiglas Thickness	Aspect Ratio					Maximum Span
	1.0	1.5	2.0	2.5	3.0	
20 Pounds per square foot wind load						
0.125	6.2	4.9	4.0	3.5	3.0	30
0.187	9.5	6.3	4.8	4.0	3.5	36
0.250	—	8.7	5.2	4.4	4.0	42
30 Pounds per square foot wind load						
0.125	5.7	4.3	3.5	3.0	2.6	24
0.187	8.3	5.1	4.1	3.4	3.0	29
0.250	—	5.8	4.6	4.0	3.4	34
40 Pounds per square foot wind load						
0.125	5.0	3.9	3.2	2.9	2.6	21
0.187	7.0	4.8	3.8	3.1	2.9	26
0.250	9.7	5.6	4.3	3.7	3.3	30

To use Table 10–1, locate the section that is applicable for the design wind load

---

[1] Rohm and Haas Company, "Plexiglas Sign Manual," Philadelphia, Pennsylvania. Copyright © 1969 By Rohm and Haas Company. Based on "Plexiglas Handbook for Sign Shops," Copyright © 1961 By Rohm and Haas Company. "These suggestions and data are based on information we believe to be reliable. They are offered in good faith, but without guarantee, as conditions and methods of use of our products are beyond our control."

and follow down the column that is nearest to the actual aspect ratio until a figure is found that exceeds the sign's short dimension, in inches. At the left hand of that row will be found the required Plexiglas thickness. For all aspect ratios larger than 3, simply use the last column, which shows the recommended maximum free span between supports in inches.

This table is based on a permissible center deflection of the unbraced Plexiglas sign face of 3 inches or 5 per cent of the shorter dimension, whichever is greater. This deflection will not develop working stresses in excess of the established value of 3000 pounds per square inch.

Weights of Plexiglas are:

    0.125 inch thick—3/4 pound/square foot
    0.187   1 1/8
    0.250   1 1/2

Corrugating of the Plexiglas adds considerable strength in the direction of corrugations, as shown by Table 10–2, which gives maximum recommended length of short dimension for various standard forms of Plexiglas. This table is based on corrugations running parallel to the short dimension, using the same deflection and working stress criteria as for uncorrugated material.

TABLE 10-2. Maximum short dimension for corrugated Plexiglas.

Pattern	Frequency	Amplitude	Thickness	Maximum Wind Load (Pounds per Square Foot) 20	30	40
C	2 1/2 in.	1 in.	0.125	57	51	45
C	2 1/2 in.	1 in.	0.187	63	57	53
C	1 in.	3/8 in.	0.125	35	32	30
V	3 in.	1 in.	0.125	57	51	45
V	3 in.	1 in.	0.187	63	57	53
D	5 5/8 in.	1 in.	0.125	67	60	56
D	5 5/8 in.	1 1/4 in.	0.187	83	73	67

In the pattern symbol column, C represents standard corrugations, V represents standard waves which are somewhat flattened at the peaks, and D represents decking (fairly sharp transition between two flat faces). Amplitude is the outside-to-outside dimension between opposing peaks, and frequency is the distance from one peak to the next peak in the same direction.

A simple method of achieving the same effect as corrugating, if the sign is not to be made by painting the inside of clear Plexiglas, is to cement reinforcing ribs to the back of the sign face. One typical arrangement is to cement 3-inch by 1/4-inch ribs parallel to the short dimension. As shown in Table 10–3, this method gives results comparable to or superior to corrugated material.

TABLE 10-3. Maximum short dimension in inches for indicated spacing of reinforcing ribs.

Spacing Between Ribs (inches)	Design Wind Load, Pounds per Square Foot								
	20			30			40		
	Face Thickness			Face Thickness			Face Thickness		
	.125	.187	.250	.125	.187	.250	.125	.187	.250
20	78	82	87	60	64	68	50	53	56
30	60	64	67	46	49	52	38	41	44
40	50	53	56	39	41	53	32	34	36

TABLE 10-4. Edge engagement for unbraced Plexiglas sign faces.

Short Dimension	Expansion Clearance	Edge Engagement
Up to 42 inches	1/8 inch	1 1/4 inches
42 to 72 inches	1/4 inch	1 1/4 inches
72 to 96 inches	1/4 inch	1 1/2 inches
Over 96 inches	0.3% of short dimension	1.6% of short dimension

TABLE 10-5. Minimum gauge of sheet metal retaining channels.

Plexiglas Thickness (inch)	Aluminum (AWG)	Steel (US Standard)
0.125	18	20
0.187	14	18
0.250	11	16

Edge Engagement

Allowances have been provided for the following effects when preparing recommendations for edge engagement dimensions:

- Thermal and humidity expansion and contraction
- Foreshortening of the Plexiglas when deflected by wind
- Panel shifting flush with one end of sign cabinet
- Fabricating tolerances

Table 10–4 presents recommendations for attaching Plexiglas to the sign cabinet. Edge engagement is the depth of the channel that holds the Plexiglas, and values in the table are for light-colored sign backgrounds such as white, light blue, and light yellow. For darker colors, dimensions should be increased 1/32 inch per foot.

Since the Plexiglas will rest in the bottom channel, expansion clearance is the distance between the Plexiglas and the top of the top channel. Dimensions in the table assume the sign face is trimmed to fit the cabinet accurately with proper allowance for expansion clearance.

To ensure that the channel has sufficient strength to hold the Plexiglas under both positive and negative wind loading, the metal sizes given in Table 13–5 should be considered as the minimum size to be considered.

Size of Sign

A general rule is that 10 minutes of visual arc is the threshold of understandability, and 1 minute of arc is the absolute minimum for merely distinguishing an object.

Formula

$$A = \frac{L}{2.1 \times 10^{-4} \times D}$$

where: A = visual angle in minutes of arc
L = length of object being viewed
D = distance from eye to object

This formula is usable for angles up to several degrees, which includes all situations generally encountered in the design of signs. Lengths L and D can be in any units as long as the same unit is used for both lengths.

Example

Will 5-inch-wide letters be satisfactory for viewing at 100 feet (1200 inches)?

$$A = \frac{5}{2.1 \times 10^{-4} \times 1200}$$
$$= 11 \text{ minutes of arc}$$

This letter size would be satisfactory if all other conditions are normal.

Another way of approximating the rule expressed by this equation is to figure that a clear block letter should be one foot high for each 500 feet of viewing distance.

Composition of Letters[2]

It is generally considered that an optimum letter is one whose width is 0.6 times its height, and whose thickness of stroke is 0.15 times the height. For experimenting with letter style, figure that the effect of stroke thickness is linear; if it is either 0.26 or 0.04 times the letter height, legibility is reduced by 20 percent.

Effect of Color

It is difficult to form quantitative rules for selection of color, but the following list is in order of the distance that they appear from the viewer, e.g., red gives the appearance of being closer than blue.

Red
Orange
Yellow
Green
Blue
Violet
White

In another dimension, it is generally accepted that darker shades appear closer than lighter shades. This rule also applies to black-and-white signs.

If there is sufficient contrast between the letter color and the background color, they will stand out to a person of normal vision. However, if the contrasting colors are both of the same shade, the camouflage effect will destroy the contrast for a person who is color blind to at least those two colors. Therefore, if the sign carries a warning or some equally important message, contrast in hue should be supplemented by contrast in shade.

Some tests on lettering of only primary and secondary colors, of full hue and value, established readability of various combinations. Table 10–6 lists 18 combinations in order of readability, with the most readable first.[3]

TABLE 10-6. Comparative readability of full value combinations.

	Letter Color	Background Color
Most readable	Black	Yellow
	Black	White
	Yellow	Black
	White	Black
	Blue	White
	White	Blue
	Blue	Yellow

[2]General Electric, "Sign Lighting," Publication TP-124, Cleveland, Ohio, 1966.
[3]Institute of Outdoor Advertising, "Type Lettering Color for Outdoor Advertising," New York, New York, 1966.

Yellow	Blue
Green	White
White	Green
Brown	White
White	Brown
Brown	Yellow
Yellow	Brown
Red	White
White	Red
Red	Yellow
Yellow	Red

Internal Illumination

Internally lighted signs and luminous elements are most meaningfully specified in units of footlamberts, where Table 10–7[4] outlines the meaning of some general levels. A few general application guides are given in Table 10–8[5].

TABLE 10-7. Brightness categories.

Brightness Category	Type of District	Sign Brightness, Footlamberts
High	Urban center locations and shopping centers where high prevailing illumination exists; areas of high sign density	200–350
Medium	Suburban areas where sign competition and illumination are moderate	100–200
Low	Rural areas	25–100

TABLE 10-8. Brightness applications.

Surface Brightness, Footlamberts	Visual Appearance	Typical Application
20–100	Subtle	Fascia signs
75–150	Lustrous	Belt signs above storefronts
125–200	Vivid	Business signs in shopping centers
200–300	Radiant	Gasoline service stations and motel signs
300–400	Brilliant	Large or high-rise signs for distant viewing
400–500	Dazzling	Large or high-rise signs for viewing at long distances

[4]Rohm and Haas Company, Plexiglas Sign Manual, op. cit.
[5]Ibid.

TABLE 10-10.   Characteristics of colored Plexiglas.

Color Name	Reflected Light Hue	Transmitted Light Hue	Diffusion Qualities	Light Transmission %	Formed Flat Face Letters	Formed Curved Face Letters	Minimum Distance Ratio	Best Neon Color
Red	Primary Red	Vivid Red	High	2	OK	OK	1/3	Rose
Red	Primary Red	Red/Tangerine	Good	3	Optional	Optional	1/2	Clear Red
Red	Primary Red	Red/Tangerine	Good	2	Not Recom'd	OK	1/2	Clear Red
Red	Tomato Red	Red/Orange	High	2	OK	OK	1/2	Clear Red
Red	Light Red	Red/Orange	Low	12	Not Recom'd	OK	1/1 1/2	Clear Red
Red	Darker Red	Red/Orange	Low	11	Optional	OK	1/1 1/2	Clear Red
Orange	Brilliant Orange	Orange	High	7	OK	OK	1/2	Clear Red
Orange	Bright Orange	Bright Orange	Good	14	Optional	OK	2/3	Clear Red
Yellow	Chrome Yellow	Chrome Yellow	High	20	OK	OK	1/2	Clear Red
Yellow	Light Yellow	Light Yellow	Low	29	Optional	OK	1/2	Fluorescent Green
Pale Yellow	Pastel Yellow	Pales Slightly	Low	34	Optional	OK	2/3	Fluorescent Green
Green	Bright Green	Pastel Green	Good	5	Optional	Optional	2/3	Fluorescent Green
Green	Forest Green	Pastel Green	Medium	9	Not Recom'd	Not Recom'd	1/1	Not Recom'd

Green	Bluish Green	Pastel Blue/Green	Low	36	Not Recom'd	Not Recom'd	2/1	Fluorescent Green
Green	Primary Dk. Green	Primary Dk. Green	High	2	Optional	Optional	1/2	Fluorescent Green
Olive Green	Olive	Chartreuse	High	6	OK	OK	2/3	Fluorescent Green
Aqua	Green/Turquoise	Green/Turquoise	Good	16	OK	OK	2/3	Fluorescent Green
Blue	Dk. Blue	Vivid Primary Blue	Good	1	OK	OK	1/2	Not Recom'd
Blue	Medium Dk. Blue	Pastel Light Blue	Low	19	Optional	Optional	1/i	Fluorescent Green
Blue	Dk. Blue	Vivid Blue	Good	2	Optional	OK	2/3	Fluorescent Blue
Turquoise	Turquoise	Turquoise/Aqua	High	6	OK	OK	1/2	Fluorescent Green
Blue	Primary Blue	Richer Blue	High	5	Optional	OK	1/2	Fluorescent Green
Light Blue	Pastel Blue	Pastel Blue	High	13	OK	OK	2/3	Fluorescent Green
Ivory	Milk White	Ivory/Yellow	Medium	35	Optional	OK	2/3	Fluorescent Green
Violet	Dk. Purple	Deep Violet	Medium	6	Not Recom'd	Optional	1/1	Green/Red
Red	Pastel Red	Pastel Red	Good	6	Optional	OK	1/2	Clear Red
Rust	Brownish Red	Tan	Good	4	OK	OK	1/2	Clear Red

Lamp Spacing[6]

Formula

$$S = \frac{8.65(T)\dfrac{L}{\text{ft}}}{(B)R^{0.465}}$$

where: S = center-to-center spacing of lamps in sign

T = light transmittance of Plexiglas, in decimals (Tables 10–9 and 10–10)

L/ft = lumens per foot output of lamp (Table 10–11)

B = desired brightness of sign surface

R = ratio of lamp-to-Plexiglas-distance divided by center-to-center-lamp-spacing

In calculating lumens per foot, adjustment has been made in Table 10–11 for the fall-off of light output near the ends.

TABLE 10-9.   Light transmittance of standard white translucent Plexiglas.

Plexiglas Color Number	Thickness		
	0.125	0.187	0.250
W-7138	42%	32%	26%
W-7328	32%	22%	18%
W-7420	22%	15%	11%

TABLE 10-11.   Lumens per foot output of fluorescent lamps.

Nominal Tube Length	Published Lumen Output	Lumens per Foot
48 inches	3500	933
72 inches	5550	965
72 inches	6050	1052
96 inches	7600	981

Example

A sign is to use aqua Plexiglas and 48-inch lamps with a spacing ratio of 2:3. What spacing between lamps will give a surface brightness of 150 footlamberts?

Solution

Table 10–10 shows that this Plexiglas has a transmittance, in decimals, of 0.16, and Table 10–11 shows that the lamps have an output of 933 lumens per foot. Substituting these numbers into the equation gives

[6]Ibid. Information developed and presented by Rohm & Haas has been rearranged and combined in this equation.

$$S = \frac{8.65(0.16)933}{150(0.667)^{0.465}}$$
$$= 10.3 \text{ inches}$$

Exposed-Incandescent-Lamp Signs[7]

Spot size is important in figuring lamp spacing. It is actually an effective spot size, as the figures given take into consideration lamp candlepower, irradiation, number of lamps in sign, and competing brightness of the surrounding area. Table 10–12 gives the expected range of effective spot sizes for various commercial lamps, and it can be seen that the range is not too large to permit a reasonable first design using average values. At distances of 500 feet and less, spot size is of less importance in sign layout because physical dimensions limit lamp spacing to a minimum of about 2 or 2 1/2 inches.

TABLE 10-12. Effective spot size.

Viewing Distance (feet)	Effective Spot Size (inches)	
	Minimum	Maximum
1000	13	18
1500	15	21
2000	18	24
2500	23	27
3000	26	32
3500	31	36
4000	35	42
4500	42	48
5000	48	56

Each lamp is usually located on the perimeter of the next lamp's effective spot size; lamp spacing is one-half the spot size. This rule will give a line of light that is continuous, but if it is desired that the line of light appear smooth, closer spacing will be required.

Stroke Width (more than one row of lamps, spaced at one-half the spot size)

Formula

$$S = \frac{(n + 1)Z}{2}$$

where: S = stroke width
n = number of rows of lamps forming the stroke
Z = spot size

Example

How wide will the stroke appear if a letter is formed of 3 rows of lamps and the spot size is 20 inches?

---

[7]General Electric, "Sign Lighting." Op. Cit.

Solution

$$S = \frac{(3 + 1)20}{2}$$

$$= 40 \text{ inches}$$

Letter Height (based on a letter *E*)

Formula

$$H = 3S + 2(0.0035D)$$

$$= \frac{3(n + 1)Z}{2} + 2(0.0035D)$$

A legible letter with pleasing proportions results when the width of a letter is 60 percent of its height.

Example

A letter *E,* with two rows of lamps in all its legs, is to be legible at 2000 feet.

Solution

From Table 10–12, assume a spot size which is the mean value of the two values given, or 21 inches.

$$H = 3 \frac{(2 + 1)21}{2} + 2(0.0035)(2000)$$

$$= 109 \text{ inches}$$

The width should be 109 (0.60) = 65.4 inches.

Silhouette Signs[8]

The general rule is that 1200 lumens per square foot are required in a district of high brightness, 800 in medium brightness, and 400 in low brightness.

Figure 10–1 gives minimum height, width, and stroke for dark letters silhouetted against a bright background, as when letters are suspended in front of a surface flooded with light. If the procedure is reversed and lighted letters are suspended in front of a dark background, the stroke should be reduced by 20 percent to compensate for apparent thickening due to irradiation. Experience has shown that a good workable spacing between letters and floodlighted background is 1/4 the height of the background if it is a polished, concentrating reflector, or 1/2 the height if it is a diffuse reflector.

Since Figure 10–1 is based on linear relationships, its range can be extended by multiplying all values by a constant. For example, both scales can be doubled to show that 42-inch letters should be used at 2400-feet viewing distance. These values are minimum for understandability; they should be increased by at least 50 to 100 percent to gain attention and encourage reading.

Usable light available is so dependent on reflectivity, absorption, focusing, and other

---

[8]Ibid.

FIGURE 10-1

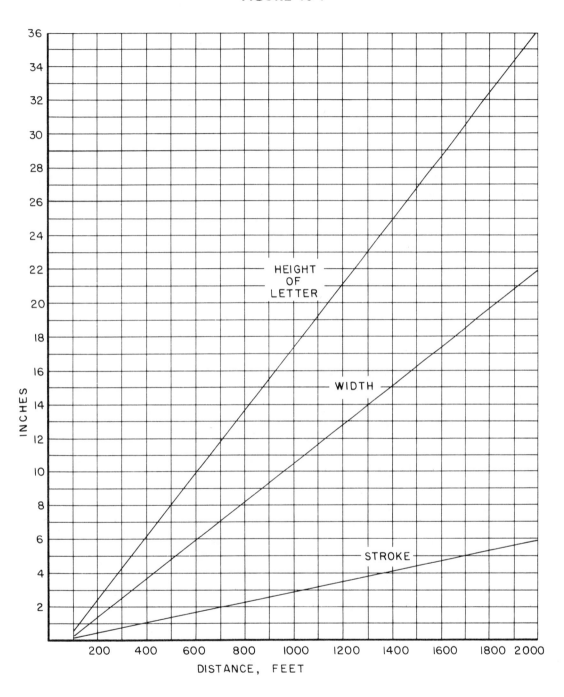

characteristics of the lampholder, that tables for general application become extremely complex. However, some *relative* color information is presented in Table 10–13; light outputs relative to Cool White are given.

TABLE 10-13.   Approximate relative light output of colored fluorescent lamps.

Cool White	1.00
Blue	0.39
Green	1.43
Gold	0.73
Pink	0.38
Red	0.06
Deep Blue	0.14

Torque and Power Transmission

CHAPTER 11

ROTATING SHAFT

Horsepower

Formula

$$HP = \frac{(T)R}{k}$$

where: T = torque

R = rotation speed in RPM

k = 63,025 if torque is in lbs. in.

= 5,252 if torque is in lbs. ft.

Example

What is the horsepower equivalent of 12 lbs. ft. torque rotating at 800 RPM?

Solution

$$HP = \frac{(12)800}{5252}$$
$$= 1.828 \text{ horsepower}$$

Torsional Stress

Formula

$$S = 5.093 \frac{DT}{D^4 - d^4}$$

where: S = shear stress due to torsion, psi

T = applied torque in inch-pounds

D = shaft outside diameter, inches

d = shaft inside diameter, inches

Example

How much torsional stress is a shaft of 4″ o.d. and 3.4″ i.d. subjected to if a torque of 3 inch-pounds is applied?

Solution

$$S = 5.093 \frac{4(3)}{4^4 - 3.4^4}$$

$$= 0.499 \text{ psi}$$

GEARS

The following symbols are used in this section:

D_σ = outside diameter
D_p = pitch diameter
L = center-to-center distance
L_w = worm lead
N = number of teeth
N_t = number of threads in worm
P_c = circular pitch
P_d = diametral pitch
P_{dwg} = worm gear diametral pitch

Outside Diameter

Formulas

$$D_\sigma = (N + 2)/P_d$$
$$D_\sigma = D_p + 2/P_d$$
$$D_\sigma = P_c \, (N + 2)/\pi$$
$$D_\sigma = D_p + 0.637 \, P_c$$

Example

What is the outside diameter of a gear that has 15 teeth and a diametral pitch of 6 inches?

Solution

Given values can be substituted directly into the first formula

$$D_\sigma = \frac{15 + 2}{6}$$

$$= 2.83 \text{ inches}$$

Diametral Pitch: Number of teeth per inch of pitch diameter

Formulas

$$P_d = \pi/P_c$$
$$P_d = N/D_p$$
$$P_d = (N + 2)/D_\sigma$$

Example

What is the diametral pitch of a gear that has 15 teeth and a pitch diameter of 2.5 inches?

Solution

Given values can be substituted directly into the second formula

$$P_d = \frac{15}{2.5}$$
$$= 6 \text{ inches}$$

Circular Pitch: Distance from tooth centers along pitch line

Formulas

$$P_c = \pi D_p / N$$
$$P_c = D_o / \left(2 + \frac{N}{\pi}\right)$$
$$P_c = \pi / P_d$$

Example

What is the circular pitch of a worm gear that has 15 teeth and a pitch diameter of 2.5 inches?

Solution

Given values can be substituted directly into the first formula

$$P_c = \pi 2.5 / 15$$
$$= 0.524 \text{ inch}$$

Pitch Diameter

Formulas

$$D_p = N / P_d$$
$$D_p = D_o N / (N + 2)$$
$$D_p = D_o - 2 / P_d$$
$$D_p = N P_c / \pi$$
$$D_p = D_o - 2 P_c / \pi$$

Example

What is the pitch diameter of a gear with outside diameter of 2.83 inches and diametral pitch of 6 inches?

Solution

Given values can be substituted directly into the third formula

$$D_p = 2.83 - \frac{2}{6}$$
$$= 2.5 \text{ inches}$$

Number of Teeth

Formulas

$$N = D_p P_d$$
$$N = D_o P_d - 2$$
$$N = \pi D_p / P_c$$

Example

How many teeth does a worm gear have if its pitch diameter is 2.5 inches and its circular pitch is 0.524?

Solution

Given values can be substituted directly into the last formula

$$N = \frac{2.5\pi}{0.524}$$
$$= 15$$

Center-to-Center Distance

Formula

$$L = \frac{\text{driven } D_p + \text{driver } D_p}{2}$$
$$L = \frac{\text{worm } D_p + \text{worm gear } D_p}{2}$$

Example

What distance will exist between spur gear centers if the pitch diameters are 2.5 for the driver and 3.67 for the driven?

Solution

Given values can be substituted directly into the first formula

$$L = \frac{3.67 + 2.5}{2}$$
$$= 3.09 \text{ inches}$$

Worm Lead

Formula

$$L_w = \frac{\pi}{P_{dwg}} N_t$$

Example

What is the lead of a worm which has double thread and a diametral pitch of 10?

Solution

$$L_w = \frac{\pi}{10}\,2$$
$$= 0.628$$

BELT OR CHAIN FORMULAS

Chain Speed

Formula

$$C = \frac{P(N)R}{12}$$

where: C = chain speed in feet per minute
P = pitch in per inch
N = number of teeth on sprocket
R = rotational speed of sprocket in RPM

Example

What is the linear speed of a chain whose pitch is 3 per inch if it is driven by a 12-tooth sprocket turning at 500 RPM?

Solution

$$C = \frac{3(12)500}{12}$$
$$= 1500 \text{ feet per minute}$$

Force on Chain or Belt (working load)

Formula

$$F = \frac{HP(33,000)}{S}$$

where: F = force in pounds
HP = horsepower
S = speed in feet per minute

Example

How much working load will there be on a chain that is driving a 5-horsepower load while moving at 250 feet per minute?

Solution

$$F = \frac{5(33,000)}{250}$$
$$= 660$$

Centrifugal Tension (caused by velocity and weight of chain or belt)

Formula

$$CT = \frac{W(S)^2}{115900}$$

where: CT = tension due to velocity and weight, in pounds

S = speed in feet per minute

Example

How much tension in a chain is caused by its weight and velocity if it weighs 4.5 pounds per foot and is traveling 600 feet per minute?

Solution

$$CT = \frac{4.5(600)^2}{115900}$$
$$= 13.98$$

Total Tension

Formula

$$TT = F + CT$$

where: TT = total tension

F = force due to working load

CT = tension due to velocity and weight

Example

What is the total tension in the chain in the two preceding examples?

Solution

$$TT = 660 + 13.98$$
$$= 673.98$$

Chain Length: Approximate length in pitches

Formula

$$L = \frac{S_t}{2} + 2D_c + \frac{.0253(D_t)^2}{D_c}$$

where: S_t = sum of teeth on both sprockets

D_c = distance between sprocket centers, in pitches

D_t = difference in number of teeth on sprockets

Example

How much chain will be required if sprockets of 12 and 36 teeth are separated by 100 pitches?

Solution

$$L = \frac{48}{2} + 2(100) + \frac{.0253(36 - 12)^2}{100}$$
$$= 224.15$$

Torque Required to Accelerate a Mass

Formula

$$T = \frac{k|R_f - R_i|W(R_e)^2}{t}$$

where: k = .0391 gives torque in in. lbs.
  = .0033 gives torque in ft. lbs.
  R_i = initial rotational velocity of mass in RPM
  R_f = final rotational velocity of mass in RPM
  W = weight of mass in pounds
  R_e = effective radius of mass in feet
  t = time to complete speed change in seconds

Example

How much torque is required to accelerate a 6.3–pound flywheel from 770 to 1250 RPM in 40 seconds? Flywheel construction is continuous from the center to its outside radius of 1 1/2 feet; effective radius is 3/4 foot.

Solution

$$T = \frac{.0391(1250 - 770)6.3(0.75)^2}{40}$$
$$= 26.48 \text{ in. lbs.}$$

Belt Length (uncrossed belt)

Formula

$$L = 2C + 1.57(D + d) + \frac{(D - d)^2}{4C}$$

where: $L =$ inside circumference
  $C =$ distance between pulley centers
  $D =$ diameter of large pulley
  $d =$ diameter of small pulley

Example

What length belt will be required if pulleys of 2 and 3 inches are mounted 14 inches apart?

Solution

$$L = 2(14) + 1.57(3 + 2) + \frac{(3 - 2)^2}{4(14)}$$
$$= 36 \text{ inches}$$

Belt Length (crossed belt)

Formula

$$L = 2C + 1.57(D + d) + \frac{(D + d)^2}{2}$$

where all symbols have the same meaning as for uncrossed belt

Example

What length belt will be required if pulleys of 4 and 5 inches are mounted 8 feet (96 inches) apart and the belt is crossed?

Solution

$$L = 2(96) + 1.57(4 + 5) + \frac{(4 + 5)^2}{2}$$

$$= 247 \text{ inches}$$

Angle of Contact on Small Pulley

Formula

$$A = 180 - 2 \text{ arc sin } \frac{D - d}{2C}$$

where: A = angle of contact, in degrees
       D = diameter of large pulley
       d = diameter of small pulley
       C = distance between pulley centers

Any unit of measure can be used on D, d, and C as long as the same unit is used on all three.

Example

What will be the angle of contact on a 4-inch pulley whose center is 60 inches from a 40-inch pulley?

Solution

$$A = 180 - 2 \text{ arc sin } \frac{40 - 4}{2(60)}$$

$$= 145 \text{ degrees}$$

Horsepower Capacities of Belts

Tables 11–1 through 11–9 give horsepower capacities for various types of belts, assuming 180 degrees of contact on the small pulley. Correction factors for other angles of contact are given in Table 11–10, and correction factors for variations to the belts in Tables 11–1 and 11–2 are given in Table 11–11.

TABLE 11-1. Horsepower capacities of 4-ply nylon stitched belts.

Speed, fpm	Light 4-ply				Pulley diameter, in. Medium 4-ply				Heavy 4-ply			
	1	2	3	6	1	2	3	6	1	2	3	6
1,000	0.45	0.64	0.76	0.83	0.60	0.90	1.03	1.25	0.90	1.40	1.70	2.21
2,000	0.94	1.27	1.38	1.56	1.15	1.67	1.95	2.33	1.66	2.06	3.21	4.19
3,000	1.28	1.81	2.07	2.35	1.59	2.44	2.85	3.50	2.35	3.82	4.75	6.15
5,000	1.89	2.73	3.18	3.75	1.80	3.09	3.80	4.85	3.03	5.51	7.00	9.49
6,000	1.92	2.91	3.35	4.05	1.86	3.30	4.17	5.31	2.99	6.17	8.21	11.30
7,000	1.93	2.94	3.57	4.51	1.82	3.35	4.25	5.54		6.10	8.39	12.20
8,000	1.87	2.98	3.63	4.72		3.33	4.27	5.67			8.31	12.48
9,000		2.92	3.68	4.79			4.21	5.71				12.25
10,000			3.64	4.85				5.62				
12,000				4.81								

TABLE 11-2. Horsepower capacities of medium 4-ply woven endless cotton belts.

Speed, fpm	Pulley diameter, in.			
	1-1½″	3″	4″	6″
500	0.25	0.35	0.4	0.5
1000	0.50	0.70	0.8	1.0
1500	0.80	1.0	1.3	1.5
2000	1.0	1.4	1.6	2.0
2500	1.3	1.8	2.0	2.3
3000	1.5	2.0	2.3	2.6
3500	1.8	2.4	2.5	3.0
4000	2.0	2.8	2.8	3.5
4500	2.1	3.2	3.2	4.1
5000	2.2	3.3	3.3	4.5

TABLE 11-3. Horsepower capacities per inch of width of regular single-ply Dacron belts.

Speed, fpm	Pulley diameter, in.						
	½	1	1½	2	3	4	6
1,000	0.5	1.0	1.0	1.2	1.4	1.5	1.6
2,000	1.5	2.0	2.1	2.2	2.5	2.7	2.9
3,000	1.9	2.4	3.0	3.3	3.9	4.1	4.4
4,000	2.3	2.9	3.7	4.2	4.8	5.2	5.7
5,000	2.5	3.2	4.2	4.7	5.5	6.0	6.7
6,000	2.6	3.5	4.6	5.1	6.0	6.7	7.5
7,000	2.6	3.6	4.8	5.4	6.5	7.4	8.4
8,000	2.5	3.7	5.0	5.6	6.8	7.8	8.9
9,000	2.3	3.8	5.1	5.7	6.9	8.0	9.2
10,000	2.0	3.8	5.2	5.8	7.0	8.2	9.4
12,000		3.6	5.2	5.8	7.0	8.2	9.5
15,000		3.3	5.0	5.7	6.9	8.2	9.5
18,000		3.0	4.8	5.6	6.9	8.1	9.5

TABLE 11-4. Horsepower capacities per inch of width of medium single-ply Dacron belts.

Speed, fpm	½	1	1½	2	3	4	6
				Pulley diameter, in.			
1,000	0.33	0.528	0.66	0.79	0.924	0.99	1.056
2,000	0.99	1.32	1.38	1.45	1.65	1.78	1.914
3,000	1.25	1.58	1.98	2.17	2.594	2.70	2.90
4,000	1.51	1.91	2.44	2.77	3.168	3.43	3.762
5,000	1.65	2.11	2.77	3.10	3.63	3.96	4.42
6,000	1.71	2.31	3.03	3.36	3.96	4.42	4.95
7,000	1.71	2.37	3.16	3.56	4.29	4.884	5.54
8,000	1.65	2.44	3.30	3.69	4.488	5.148	5.874
9,000	1.51	2.50	3.36	3.76	4.554	5.28	6.072
10,000	1.32	2.50	3.43	3.82	4.62	5.412	6.138
12,000		2.37	3.43	3.82	4.62	5.412	6.20
15,000		2.17	3.30	3.76	4.554	5.412	6.20
18,000		1.98	3.16	3.69	4.554	5.346	6.27

TABLE 11-5. Horsepower capacities per inch of width of light single-ply Dacron belts.

Speed, fpm	½	1	1½	2	3	4	6
				Pulley diameter, in.			
1,000	0.20	0.32	0.40	0.48	0.560	0.600	0.640
2,000	0.60	0.80	0.84	0.88	1.00	1.08	1.16
3,000	0.76	0.96	1.20	1.32	1.56	1.64	1.76
4,000	0.92	1.16	1.48	1.68	1.92	2.08	2.28
5,000	1.00	1.28	1.68	1.88	2.20	2.40	2.68
6,000	1.04	1.40	1.84	2.04	2.40	2.68	3.00
7,000	1.04	1.44	1.92	2.16	2.60	2.96	3.36
8,000	1.00	1.48	2.00	2.24	2.72	3.12	3.56
9,000	0.92	1.52	2.04	2.28	2.76	3.20	3.68
10,000	0.80	1.52	2.08	2.32	2.80	3.28	3.72
12,000		1.44	2.08	2.32	2.80	3.28	3.76
15,000		1.32	2.00	2.28	2.76	3.28	3.76
18,000		1.20	1.92	2.24	2.76	3.24	3.80

TABLE 11-6. Horsepower capacities per 1/4″ diameter braided endless round belts.

Belt speed, fpm	1½	2	3	4	5
		Pulley diameter, U-grooves, in.			
400	0.17	0.22	0.23	0.32	0.35
800	0.21	0.36	0.37	0.65	0.69
1200	0.33	0.45	0.45	0.79	0.83
1600	0.41	0.54	0.55	0.83	0.86
2000	0.44	0.58	0.59	0.98	1.04
2400	0.52	0.69	0.63	1.12	1.16
2800	0.54	0.72	0.68	1.24	1.28
3200	0.58	0.77	0.72	1.44	1.49
3600	0.63	0.84	0.74	1.59	1.60
4000	0.67	0.90	0.68	1.59	1.68
4800	0.69	0.92	0.59	1.57	1.70
5200	0.58	0.90	0.45	1.57	1.71
5600	0.63	0.85	0.28	1.56	1.70
6000	0.60	0.80	0.28	1.47	1.70

TABLE 11-7. Horsepower capacities of 3/8" diameter braided endless round belts.

Belt speed, fpm	Pulley diameter, U-grooves, in.			
	2	3	4	5
500	0.45	0.50	0.70	0.78
750	0.72	0.80	1.44	1.61
1000	0.90	1.00	1.75	1.83
1250	1.08	1.20	1.85	1.90
1500	1.20	1.30	2.20	2.30
2000	1.25	1.40	2.50	2.58
2500	1.35	1.52	2.75	2.85
3000	1.45	1.61	3.20	3.30
3500	1.47	1.65	3.54	3.65
4000	1.37	1.52	3.54	3.72
4500	1.18	1.30	3.50	3.75
5000	0.91	1.00	3.50	3.77
5500	0.54	0.60	3.40	3.80
6000	0.27	0.30	3.30	3.75

TABLE 11-8. Horsepower capacities of 9/16" diameter wound endless round belts.

Belt speed, fpm	Pitch diameter of pulley, In.					
	5.0	5.4	5.8	6.2	6.6	7.0
400	0.94	1.00	1.10	1.20	1.22	1.25
800	1.60	1.80	1.92	2.10	2.17	2.25
1200	2.20	2.45	2.70	2.90	3.00	3.20
1600	2.70	3.00	3.30	3.70	3.80	4.00
2000	3.10	3.50	3.90	4.40	4.50	4.70
2400	3.50	4.00	4.40	4.95	5.10	5.40
2800	3.75	4.30	4.80	5.50	5.70	6.00
3200	3.95	4.61	5.20	5.90	6.10	6.50
3600	4.10	4.80	5.40	6.00	6.50	6.90
4000	4.10	4.90	5.60	6.20	6.80	7.20
4400	3.96	4.45	5.70	6.34	6.90	7.50
4800	3.75	4.30	5.60	6.40	7.00	7.60
5200	3.40	4.00	5.40	6.20	6.90	7.60
5600	2.96	3.60	5.10	6.00	6.70	7.40
6000	2.40	3.00	4.70	5.60	6.40	7.10

TABLE 11-9. Horsepower capacities of 3/8" diameter wound endless round belts.

Belt speed, fpm	Pitch diameter of pulley, in.					
	3	3.4	3.8	4.2	4.6	5.0
400	0.46	0.54	0.61	0.66	0.70	0.74
800	0.76	1.10	1.27	1.40	1.51	1.61
1200	1.02	1.27	1.46	1.62	1.76	1.87
1600	1.22	1.56	1.82	2.03	2.21	2.36
2000	1.30	1.80	2.13	2.40	2.62	2.80
2400	1.51	2.01	2.41	2.70	3.00	3.20
2800	1.59	2.20	2.61	3.00	3.30	3.55
3200	1.61	2.30	2.80	3.23	3.60	3.87
3600	1.60	2.34	3.00	3.54	3.98	4.13
4000	1.50	2.34	3.00	3.54	3.98	4.35
4800	1.16	2.16	2.95	3.60	4.03	4.57
5200	0.90	2.00	2.80	3.50	4.10	4.60
5600	0.54	1.71	2.64	3.38	4.00	4.50
6000	0.12	1.40	2.40	3.20	3.80	4.40

TABLE 11-10. **Correction factors for small pulley angles of contact less than 180 degrees.**

Small Pulley Angle of Contact, Degrees

	45	90	110	120	130	140	150	160	170
Nylon Stitched and Woven Endless Cotton Belts			0.70	0.74	0.78	0.83	0.87	0.91	0.96
Regular, Medium, and Light Single Ply Dacron Belts	0.30	0.60	0.70	0.74	0.78	0.83	0.87	0.91	0.96
Endless Round Belts		0.69	0.79	0.82	0.86	0.89	0.92	0.95	0.97

TABLE 11-11. **Correction factors for variations of belts in in Tables 11-1 and 11-2.**

Type of Belt

	Light 4-ply	Heavy 4-ply	Light 6-ply	Medium 6-ply	Heavy 6-ply	Medium 8-ply	Heavy 8-ply
Nylon Stitched Belts			1.12	1.17		1.28	1.40
Woven Endless Cotton Belts	0.33	1.50	0.50	1.50			

Inventory Policies

CHAPTER 12

The following symbols and definitions are used in this chapter.

n_{max} = number in inventory after order is received
n_r = number in inventory when order is placed
r_i = daily production rate for inventory
r_u = daily usage rate
c_t = total cost of inventory policy
c_{to} = total cost of optimal policy
n = number in lot
n_o = number in optimal lot
u = requirements in units per year
c_i = costs of holding one unit in inventory for one year
c_w = costs of writing purchase or other order
c_s = costs of being short one unit for one year
t_d = time between placement and receipt of order, in fraction of year
t_o = time between orders or manufacturing runs for optimal solution

Total Inventory Costs (no shortages)

Formula

$$c_t = \frac{n\,c_i}{2} + \frac{u\,c_w}{L}$$

Example

A radio assembly plant uses 2400 of a certain resistor in a year and orders 200 at a time. It costs $8.00 to process an order and each resistor in inventory costs at the rate of $0.15 per year. What is the cost of this ordering policy?

Solution

$$c_t = \frac{0.15(200)}{2} + \frac{8(2400)}{200}$$
$$= \$111$$

233

Optimum Lot Size (no shortages)

Formula

$$n_o = \sqrt{\frac{2\ uc_w}{c_i}}$$

Example

In the preceding example, how many resistors should be ordered each time to minimize costs?

Solution

$$n_o = \sqrt{\frac{2(8)2400}{0.15}}$$
$$= 506$$

Cost of Optimum Order Size (no shortages)

Formula

$$c_{to} = \sqrt{2c_w c_i u}$$

Example

What is the cost of optimum inventory policy as found in the preceding example?

Solution

$$c_{to} = \sqrt{2(8)(0.15)2400}$$
$$= \$78.89$$

Reorder Point (no shortages)

Formula

$$n_r = t_d\, u$$

Example

At what inventory level should a purchase order be placed if it will take two weeks before the resistors are received in inventory?

Solution

$$n_r = \frac{2}{52}\, 2400$$
$$= 92$$

Optimum Order Quantity (considering cost of outages)

Formula

$$n_o = \sqrt{\frac{2\ c_w\ u}{c_i}}\ \sqrt{\frac{c_i + c_s}{c_s}}$$

Example

The preceding examples are modified by considering that allowing inventory to deplete while the assembly line still requires resistors will cost $0.30 per resistor per year. For minimum incremental costs, what quantity should be ordered each time a purchase order is written?

Solution

$$n_o = \sqrt{\frac{2(8)2400}{0.15}}\sqrt{\frac{0.15 + 0.30}{0.30}}$$
$$= 620$$

Cost of Optimum Order Size (considering cost of outages)

Formula

$$c_{to} = \sqrt{2c_w c_i u}\sqrt{\frac{c_s}{c_i + c_s}}$$

Example

What will the optimum policy of the preceding example cost?

Solution

$$c_{to} = \sqrt{2(8)0.15(2400)}\sqrt{\frac{0.30}{0.15 + 0.30}}$$
$$= \$61.97$$

Manufacturing for Inventory

Formula

$$c_t = \frac{c_w u}{n} + \frac{c_i n\left(1 - \frac{r_i}{r_u}\right)}{2}$$

Example

An assembly line draws subassemblies from inventory at the rate of 12 per day. When inventory is down to a given level the subassembly line, with setup costs of $20, begins manufacturing 300 subassemblies, adding to inventory at a rate of 30 per day. Other factors have the same values as in preceding examples. What is the incremental cost of the policy?

Solution

$$c_t = \frac{20(2400)}{300} + \frac{0.15(300)\left(1 - \frac{12}{30}\right)}{2}$$
$$= \$173.50$$

Optimum Lot Size (manufacturing for inventory)

Formula

$$n_o = \sqrt{\frac{2c_w u}{c_i \left(1 - \dfrac{r_i}{r_u}\right)}}$$

Example

To minimize incremental costs, how many units should be manufactured each time the subassembly line is started up? Other conditions are as described in the preceding example.

Solution

$$n_o = \sqrt{\frac{2(20)2400}{0.15\left(1 - \dfrac{12}{30}\right)}}$$

$$= 1033$$

Cost of Optimum Lot Size (manufacturing for inventory)

Formula

$$c_{to} = \sqrt{2c_w c_i u \left(1 - \frac{r_i}{r_u}\right)}$$

Example

What will the optimum policy of the preceding example cost?

Solution

$$c_{to} = \sqrt{2(20)0.15(2400)\left(1 = \frac{12}{30}\right)}$$

$$= \$92.95$$

APPENDIX

Engineering
Specification Tables

APPENDIX

COEFFICIENTS FOR FOUNDATION BEARING FORMULAS

The Standard Penetration Test is one of the tests a soil consultant conducts to obtain accurate figures on the soil's characteristics. In the test, a tube of 2-inch outside diameter and 1 1/2-inch inside diameter is driven by a 140-pound drop hammer falling 30 inches; tests are conducted at various locations and depths. The number of blows required to drive the tube 12 inches is the factor N, which can then be substituted into formulas in the foundations section of Chapter 1.

For preliminary estimates an approximation of N can be found by forming a general description of the soil's density and selecting a working value of N from this table. When there is a water table near ground level and it is above fine sand, an adjusted value of N, N_{adj}, must be used.

Other coefficients in the table are a summary of complex interrelationships among cohesion, angle of internal friction, and several other factors.

TABLE A-1.   Coefficients for foundation bearing formulas.

Description of Soil	N	N_{adj}	J	K	L
Very Loose	4	4	15	30	18
Loose	5–9	5–9	17	32	19
Low medium	10–15	10–15	23	41	26
Medium	16–23	16–19	31	49	32
Medium dense	24–36	20–25	47	62	46
Dense	37–43	26–29	80	82	68
High dense	44–55	30–35	150	115	100
Very dense	56–70	36–42	210	130	130
Extremely dense	70+	43+	320	170	170

TABLE A-2. Pile Array Factor.

Spacing/Diameter = 3

NUMBER PER ROW

ROWS	1	2	3	4	5	6	7	8	9	10	11	12	13	14	15
1		.90	.86	.85	.84	.83	.82	.82	.82	.82	.81	.81	.81	.81	.81
2	.90	.80	.76	.74	.73	.73	.72	.72	.72	.71	.71	.71	.71	.71	.71
3	.86	.76	.73	.71	.70	.69	.69	.68	.68	.68	.68	.68	.67	.67	.67
4	.85	.74	.71	.69	.68	.68	.67	.67	.66	.66	.66	.66	.66	.66	.66
5	.84	.73	.70	.68	.67	.67	.66	.66	.65	.65	.65	.65	.65	.65	.64
6	.83	.73	.69	.68	.67	.66	.65	.65	.65	.64	.64	.64	.64	.64	.64
7	.82	.72	.69	.67	.66	.65	.65	.65	.64	.64	.64	.64	.64	.63	.63
8	.82	.72	.68	.67	.66	.65	.65	.64	.64	.64	.63	.63	.63	.63	.63

Spacing/Diameter = 4

NUMBER PER ROW

ROWS	1	2	3	4	5	6	7	8	9	10	11	12	13	14	15
1		.92	.90	.88	.88	.87	.87	.86	.86	.86	.86	.86	.86	.86	.85
2	.92	.84	.82	.80	.80	.79	.79	.79	.78	.78	.78	.78	.78	.78	.78
3	.90	.82	.79	.78	.77	.77	.76	.76	.76	.76	.75	.75	.75	.75	.75
4	.88	.80	.78	.77	.76	.75	.75	.75	.74	.74	.74	.74	.74	.74	.74
5	.88	.80	.77	.76	.75	.75	.74	.74	.74	.73	.73	.73	.73	.73	.73
6	.87	.79	.77	.75	.75	.74	.74	.73	.73	.73	.73	.73	.73	.73	.72
7	.87	.79	.76	.75	.74	.74	.73	.73	.73	.73	.72	.72	.72	.72	.72
8	.86	.79	.76	.75	.74	.73	.73	.73	.72	.72	.72	.72	.72	.72	.72

Spacing/Diameter = 5

NUMBER PER ROW

ROWS	1	2	3	4	5	6	7	8	9	10	11	12	13	14	15
1		.94	.92	.91	.90	.90	.89	.89	.89	.89	.89	.88	.88	.88	.88
2	.94	.87	.85	.84	.84	.83	.83	.83	.83	.82	.82	.82	.82	.82	.82
3	.92	.85	.83	.82	.82	.81	.81	.81	.80	.80	.80	.80	.80	.80	.80
4	.91	.84	.82	.81	.81	.80	.80	.80	.79	.79	.79	.79	.79	.79	.79
5	.90	.84	.82	.81	.80	.79	.79	.79	.79	.79	.79	.78	.78	.78	.78
6	.90	.83	.81	.80	.79	.79	.79	.79	.78	.78	.78	.78	.78	.78	.78
7	.89	.83	.81	.80	.79	.79	.78	.78	.78	.78	.78	.78	.78	.78	.77
8	.89	.83	.81	.80	.79	.79	.78	.78	.78	.78	.78	.77	.77	.77	.77

Spacing/Diameter = 6

NUMBER PER ROW

ROWS	1	2	3	4	5	6	7	8	9	10	11	12	13	14	15
1		.95	.93	.92	.92	.91	.91	.91	.91	.91	.90	.90	.90	.90	.90
2	.95	.89	.88	.87	.86	.86	.86	.86	.85	.85	.85	.85	.85	.85	.85
3	.93	.88	.86	.85	.85	.84	.84	.84	.84	.84	.83	.83	.83	.83	.83
4	.92	.87	.85	.84	.84	.83	.83	.83	.83	.83	.83	.82	.82	.82	.82
5	.92	.86	.85	.84	.83	.83	.83	.82	.82	.82	.82	.82	.82	.82	.82
6	.91	.86	.84	.83	.83	.82	.82	.82	.82	.82	.82	.82	.82	.81	.81
7	.91	.86	.84	.83	.83	.82	.82	.82	.82	.82	.81	.81	.81	.81	.81
8	.91	.86	.84	.83	.82	.82	.82	.82	.81	.81	.81	.81	.81	.81	.81

Spacing/Diameter = 7

NUMBER PER ROW

ROWS	1	2	3	4	5	6	7	8	9	10	11	12	13	14	15
1		.95	.94	.93	.93	.92	.92	.92	.92	.92	.92	.92	.92	.92	.92
2	.95	.91	.89	.89	.88	.88	.88	.88	.87	.87	.87	.87	.87	.87	.87
3	.94	.89	.88	.87	.87	.86	.86	.86	.86	.86	.86	.86	.86	.86	.86
4	.93	.89	.87	.86	.86	.86	.85	.85	.85	.85	.85	.85	.85	.85	.85
5	.93	.88	.87	.86	.86	.85	.85	.85	.85	.85	.85	.84	.84	.84	.84
6	.92	.88	.86	.86	.85	.85	.85	.85	.84	.84	.84	.84	.84	.84	.84
7	.92	.88	.86	.85	.85	.85	.85	.84	.84	.84	.84	.84	.84	.84	.84
8	.92	.88	.86	.85	.85	.85	.84	.84	.84	.84	.84	.84	.84	.84	.84

Spacing/Diameter = 8

NUMBER PER ROW

ROWS	1	2	3	4	5	6	7	8	9	10	11	12	13	14	15
1		.96	.95	.94	.94	.93	.93	.93	.93	.93	.93	.93	.93	.93	.93
2	.96	.92	.91	.90	.90	.89	.89	.89	.89	.89	.89	.89	.89	.89	.89
3	.95	.91	.89	.89	.88	.88	.88	.88	.88	.88	.88	.87	.87	.87	.87
4	.94	.90	.89	.88	.88	.87	.87	.87	.87	.87	.87	.87	.87	.87	.87
5	.94	.90	.88	.88	.87	.87	.87	.87	.87	.87	.86	.86	.86	.86	.86
6	.93	.89	.88	.87	.87	.87	.87	.86	.86	.86	.86	.86	.86	.86	.86
7	.93	.89	.88	.87	.87	.87	.86	.86	.86	.86	.86	.86	.86	.86	.86
8	.93	.89	.88	.87	.87	.86	.86	.86	.86	.86	.86	.86	.86	.86	.86

Spacing/Diameter = 9

NUMBER PER ROW

ROWS	1	2	3	4	5	6	7	8	9	10	11	12	13	14	15
1		.96	.95	.95	.94	.94	.94	.94	.94	.94	.94	.94	.93	.93	.93
2	.96	.93	.92	.91	.91	.91	.90	.90	.90	.90	.90	.90	.90	.90	.90
3	.95	.92	.91	.90	.90	.89	.89	.89	.89	.89	.89	.89	.89	.89	.89
4	.95	.91	.90	.89	.89	.89	.89	.89	.88	.88	.88	.88	.88	.88	.88
5	.94	.91	.90	.89	.89	.88	.88	.88	.88	.88	.88	.88	.88	.88	.88
6	.94	.91	.89	.89	.88	.88	.88	.88	.88	.88	.88	.88	.88	.88	.88
7	.94	.90	.89	.89	.88	.88	.88	.88	.88	.88	.88	.87	.87	.87	.87
8	.94	.90	.89	.89	.88	.88	.88	.88	.88	.87	.87	.87	.87	.87	.87

Spacing/Diameter = 10

NUMBER PER ROW

ROWS	1	2	3	4	5	6	7	8	9	10	11	12	13	14	15
1		.97	.96	.95	.95	.95	.95	.94	.94	.94	.94	.94	.94	.94	.94
2	.97	.94	.93	.92	.92	.92	.91	.91	.91	.91	.91	.91	.91	.91	.91
3	.96	.93	.92	.91	.91	.90	.90	.90	.90	.90	.90	.90	.90	.90	.90
4	.95	.92	.91	.90	.90	.90	.90	.90	.90	.90	.89	.89	.89	.89	.89
5	.95	.92	.91	.90	.90	.90	.89	.89	.89	.89	.89	.89	.89	.89	.89
6	.95	.92	.90	.90	.90	.89	.89	.89	.89	.89	.89	.89	.89	.89	.89
7	.95	.91	.90	.90	.89	.89	.89	.89	.89	.89	.89	.89	.89	.89	.89
8	.94	.91	.90	.90	.89	.89	.89	.89	.89	.89	.89	.89	.89	.89	.89

Spacing/Diameter = 11

NUMBER PER ROW

ROWS	1	2	3	4	5	6	7	8	9	10	11	12	13	14	15
1		.97	.96	.96	.95	.95	.95	.95	.95	.95	.95	.95	.95	.95	.95
2	.97	.94	.93	.93	.92	.92	.92	.92	.92	.92	.92	.92	.92	.92	.92
3	.96	.93	.92	.92	.92	.91	.91	.91	.91	.91	.91	.91	.91	.91	.91
4	.96	.93	.92	.91	.91	.91	.91	.91	.91	.90	.90	.90	.90	.90	.90
5	.95	.92	.92	.91	.91	.91	.90	.90	.90	.90	.90	.90	.90	.90	.90
6	.95	.92	.91	.91	.91	.90	.90	.90	.90	.90	.90	.90	.90	.90	.90
7	.95	.92	.91	.91	.90	.90	.90	.90	.90	.90	.90	.90	.90	.90	.90
8	.95	.92	.91	.91	.90	.90	.90	.90	.90	.90	.90	.90	.90	.90	.90

CHARACTERISTICS OF GEOMETRIC SHAPES[1]

Whether the shapes are large and composed of structural metals or small and composed of electronic potting compound, the characteristics in this section are valid. As long as consistent units are used, the same equations apply in English, metric, or any other measurement system.

Depending on the problem at hand, an evaluation of any characteristic could give the final answer or it could give a partial answer for a series of calculations. For example, evaluation of cross-sectional area could be the final answer to a problem or it could be one of the steps toward calculating volume.

Example

Evaluate the characteristics of the structural aluminum I-beam shown in Figure A–1.

This shape is found as the first Configuration of Table A–3. Area of cross-section:

$$A = b(d - d_1) + d_1 t$$
$$= 4(6 - 5.3) + 5.3 \, (0.21)$$
$$= 2.8 + 1.1$$
$$= 3.9 \text{ square inches}$$

Distance from neutral axis to extreme fibre:

$$x = \frac{d}{2}$$
$$= 3 \text{ inches}$$

Moment of Inertia:

$$I = \frac{bd^3 - d_1^3(b - t)}{12}$$
$$= \frac{4(6)^3 - 5.3^3(4 - 0.21)}{12}$$
$$= 25.1$$

---

[1]Most of the shapes in Table A–3 are from: The Aluminum Association, "Engineering Data for Aluminum Structures," New York, 1969.

Section Modulus:

$$S = \frac{bd^3 - d_1{}^3(b - t)}{6d}$$

$$S = \frac{4(6)^3 - 5.3^3(4 - 0.21)}{6(6)}$$

$$= 8.36$$

Radius of gyration:

$$r = \sqrt{\frac{bd^3 - d_1{}^3(b - t)}{12\,[bd - d_1(b - t)]}}$$

$$= \sqrt{\frac{4(6)^3 - 5.3^3(4 - .21)}{12\,[4(6) - 5.3(4 - .21)]}}$$

$$= 2.53$$

FIGURE A-1

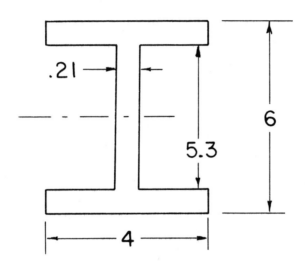

TABLE A-3. Geometric shapes.

I-BEAM

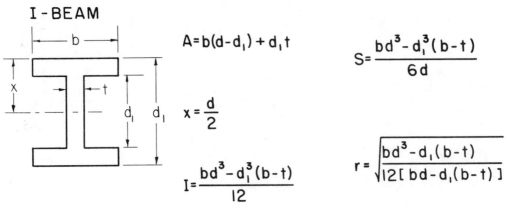

$$A = b(d-d_1) + d_1 t$$

$$x = \frac{d}{2}$$

$$I = \frac{bd^3 - d_1^3(b-t)}{12}$$

$$S = \frac{bd^3 - d_1^3(b-t)}{6d}$$

$$r = \sqrt{\frac{bd^3 - d_1(b-t)}{12[bd - d_1(b-t)]}}$$

H-BEAM

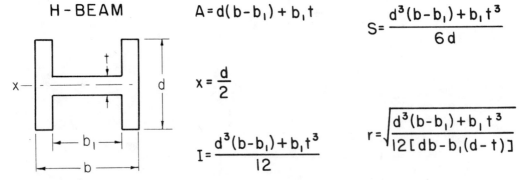

$$A = d(b-b_1) + b_1 t$$

$$x = \frac{d}{2}$$

$$I = \frac{d^3(b-b_1) + b_1 t^3}{12}$$

$$S = \frac{d^3(b-b_1) + b_1 t^3}{6d}$$

$$r = \sqrt{\frac{d^3(b-b_1) + b_1 t^3}{12[db - b_1(d-t)]}}$$

CHANNEL

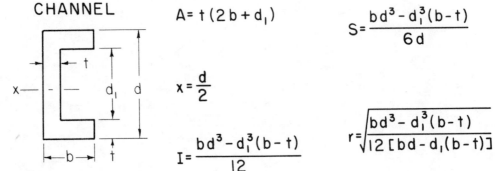

$$A = t(2b + d_1)$$

$$x = \frac{d}{2}$$

$$I = \frac{bd^3 - d_1^3(b-t)}{12}$$

$$S = \frac{bd^3 - d_1^3(b-t)}{6d}$$

$$r = \sqrt{\frac{bd^3 - d_1^3(b-t)}{12[bd - d_1(b-t)]}}$$

TABLE A-3. cont.

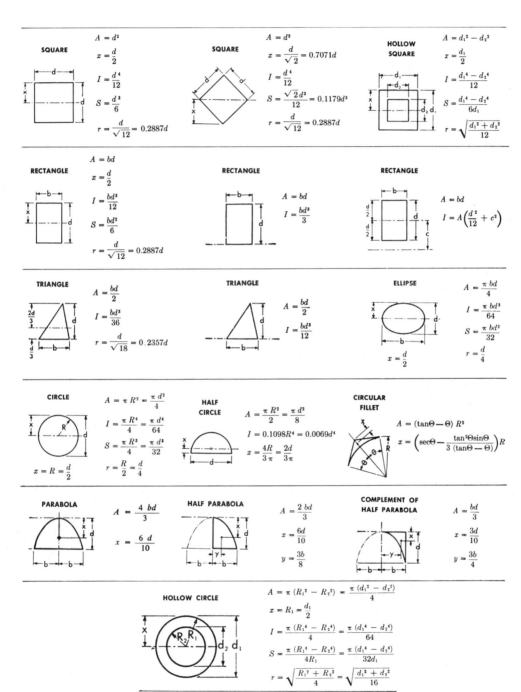

SQUARE

$$A = d^2$$
$$x = \frac{d}{2}$$
$$I = \frac{d^4}{12}$$
$$S = \frac{d^3}{6}$$
$$r = \frac{d}{\sqrt{12}} = 0.2887d$$

SQUARE

$$A = d^2$$
$$x = \frac{d}{\sqrt{2}} = 0.7071d$$
$$I = \frac{d^4}{12}$$
$$S = \frac{\sqrt{2}\,d^3}{12} = 0.1179d^3$$
$$r = \frac{d}{\sqrt{12}} = 0.2887d$$

HOLLOW SQUARE

$$A = d_1^2 - d_2^2$$
$$x = \frac{d_1}{2}$$
$$I = \frac{d_1^4 - d_2^4}{12}$$
$$S = \frac{d_1^4 - d_2^4}{6d_1}$$
$$r = \sqrt{\frac{d_1^2 + d_2^2}{12}}$$

RECTANGLE

$$A = bd$$
$$x = \frac{d}{2}$$
$$I = \frac{bd^3}{12}$$
$$S = \frac{bd^2}{6}$$
$$r = \frac{d}{\sqrt{12}} = 0.2887d$$

RECTANGLE

$$A = bd$$
$$I = \frac{bd^3}{3}$$

RECTANGLE

$$A = bd$$
$$I = A\left(\frac{d^2}{12} + c^2\right)$$

TRIANGLE

$$A = \frac{bd}{2}$$
$$I = \frac{bd^3}{36}$$
$$r = \frac{d}{\sqrt{18}} = 0.2357d$$

TRIANGLE

$$A = \frac{bd}{2}$$
$$I = \frac{bd^3}{12}$$

ELLIPSE

$$A = \frac{\pi\, bd}{4}$$
$$I = \frac{\pi\, bd^3}{64}$$
$$S = \frac{\pi\, bd^2}{32}$$
$$x = \frac{d}{2}$$
$$r = \frac{d}{4}$$

CIRCLE

$$A = \pi R^2 = \frac{\pi d^2}{4}$$
$$I = \frac{\pi R^4}{4} = \frac{\pi d^4}{64}$$
$$S = \frac{\pi R^3}{4} = \frac{\pi d^3}{32}$$
$$x = R = \frac{d}{2}$$
$$r = \frac{R}{2} = \frac{d}{4}$$

HALF CIRCLE

$$A = \frac{\pi R^2}{2} = \frac{\pi d^2}{8}$$
$$I = 0.1098R^4 = 0.0069d^4$$
$$x = \frac{4R}{3\pi} = \frac{2d}{3\pi}$$

CIRCULAR FILLET

$$A = (\tan\Theta - \Theta)R^2$$
$$x = \left(\sec\Theta - \frac{\tan^2\Theta\sin\Theta}{3(\tan\Theta - \Theta)}\right)R$$

PARABOLA

$$A = \frac{4\, bd}{3}$$
$$x = \frac{6\, d}{10}$$

HALF PARABOLA

$$A = \frac{2\, bd}{3}$$
$$x = \frac{6d}{10}$$
$$y = \frac{3b}{8}$$

COMPLEMENT OF HALF PARABOLA

$$A = \frac{bd}{3}$$
$$x = \frac{3d}{10}$$
$$y = \frac{3b}{4}$$

HOLLOW CIRCLE

$$A = \pi(R_1^2 - R_2^2) = \frac{\pi(d_1^2 - d_2^2)}{4}$$
$$x = R_1 = \frac{d_1}{2}$$
$$I = \frac{\pi(R_1^4 - R_2^4)}{4} = \frac{\pi(d_1^4 - d_2^4)}{64}$$
$$S = \frac{\pi(R_1^4 - R_2^4)}{4R_1} = \frac{\pi(d_1^4 - d_2^4)}{32d_1}$$
$$r = \sqrt{\frac{R_1^2 + R_2^2}{4}} = \sqrt{\frac{d_1^2 + d_2^2}{16}}$$

TABLE A-3. cont.

REGULAR POLYGON

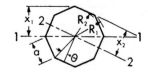

n = Number of Sides

$a = 2 \sqrt{R_1^2 - R_2^2}$, $\Theta = \dfrac{180°}{n}$

$$A = \frac{na^2 \cot \Theta}{4} = \frac{nR_1^2 \sin 2\,\Theta}{2} = nR_2^2 \tan \Theta$$

$$x_1 = R_1 = \frac{a}{2 \sin \Theta}, \qquad x_2 = R = \frac{a}{2 \tan \Theta}$$

$$I_{1-1} = I_{2-2} = \frac{A\,(6R_1^2 - a^2)}{24} = \frac{A\,(12R_2^2 + a^2)}{48}$$

$$S_{1-1} = \frac{A\,(6R_1^2 - a^2)}{24R_1}, \qquad S_{2-2} = \frac{A\,(12R_2^2 + a^2)}{48R_2}$$

$$r_{1-1} = \sqrt{\frac{6R_1^2 - a^2}{24}}, \qquad r_{2-2} = \sqrt{\frac{12R_2^2 + a^2}{48}}$$

ANGLE

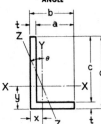

$$\mathbf{K} = \pm \frac{abcdt}{4\,(b + c)}$$

Product of Inertia about axes X-X and Y-Y.

$$\tan 2\Theta = \frac{2\,K}{I_v - I_x}$$

K is negative when heel of angle, with respect to center of gravity, is in 1st or 3d quadrant, positive when in 2d or 4th quadrant.

$$A = t\,(b + c) \qquad x = \frac{b^2 + ct}{2(b + c)} \qquad y = \frac{d^2 + at}{2(b + c)}$$

$$I_x = \frac{1}{3}\,[t(d - y)^3 + by^3 - a(y - t)^3]$$

$$I_v = \frac{1}{3}\,[t(b - x)^3 + dx^3 - c(x - t)^3]$$

$$I_z = I_x \sin^2\Theta + I_v \cos^2\Theta + K \sin 2\Theta$$

Z-Z is axis of minimum I

Axes of moments of inertia pass through the centroid.

CIRCULAR SECTOR

Area of sector $= \tfrac{1}{2}$ (length of arc $\times r$)

$= $ Area of circle $\times \dfrac{\Theta}{360}$

$= 0.0087266 \times r^2 \times \Theta$

r = radius of circle

Θ = sector angle in degrees

CIRCULAR SEGMENT

Area of top segment =

Area of top sector — Area of triangle $aa'c$

$$\frac{(\text{Length of top arc} \times r) - x\,(r - b)}{2}$$

r = radius of circle

x = chord b = rise

Area of bottom segment = Area of circle — Area of top segment

---

PROPERTIES OF THE CIRCLE

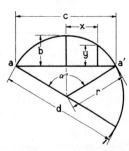

Circumference $= 6.28318r = 3.14159d$
Diameter $= 0.31831$ circumference
Area $= 3.14159\,r^2$

Arc $a\,a' = \dfrac{\pi r\,\alpha°}{180°} = 0.017453\,r\,\alpha°$

Angle $\alpha° = \dfrac{180°}{\pi r}\,aa' = 57.29578\,\dfrac{aa'}{r}$

Radius $r = \dfrac{4\,b^2 + c^2}{8\,b}$

Chord $c = 2\sqrt{2\,br - b^2} = 2\,r \sin \dfrac{\alpha}{2}$

Rise $b = r - \tfrac{1}{2}\sqrt{4\,r^2 - c^2} = \dfrac{c}{2} \tan \dfrac{\alpha}{4}$

$= 2\,r \sin^2 \dfrac{\alpha}{4} = r + y - \sqrt{r^2 - x^2}$

$y = b - r + \sqrt{r^2 - x^2}$

$x = \sqrt{r^2 - (r + y - b)^2}$

Diameter of circle of equal periphery as square $= 1.27324$ side of square
Side of square of equal periphery as circle $= 0.78540$ diameter of circle
Diameter of circle circumscribed about square $= 1.41421$ side of square
Side of square inscribed in circle $= 0.70711$ diameter of circle

FUNCTIONS OF π

$\pi = 3.14159265359$, log $= 0.4971499$

$\pi^2 = 9.8696044$, log $= 0.9942997$

$\pi^3 = 31.0062767$, log $= 1.4914496$

$\sqrt{\pi} = 1.7724539$, log $= 0.2485749$

$\dfrac{1}{\pi} = 0.3183099$, log $= \bar{1}.5028501$

$\dfrac{1}{\pi^2} = 0.1013212$, log $= \bar{1}.0057003$

$\dfrac{1}{\pi^3} = 0.0322515$, log $= \bar{2}.5085500$

$\sqrt{\dfrac{1}{\pi}} = 0.5641896$, log $= \bar{1}.7514251$

$\dfrac{\pi}{180} = 0.0174533$, log $= \bar{2}.2418774$

$\dfrac{180}{\pi} = 57.2957795$, log $= 1.7581226$

TABLE A-4. Beam formulas.[2]

Concentrated load P at center

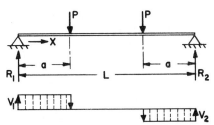

Reactions: $R_1 = R_2 = \dfrac{P}{2}$

Maximum shear forces:
$$V_1 = +P/2; \quad V_2 = -P/2$$

Maximum bending moment:
$$M_{\max} = \frac{PL}{4} \text{ at center}$$

Maximum deflection $= \dfrac{PL^3}{48EI}$ at center

$$\text{def.} = \frac{Px}{48EI}(3L^2 - 4x^2), \quad o \le x \le \frac{L}{2}$$

Two equal concentrated loads P equi-distant from the center

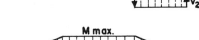

Reactions: $R_1 = R_2 = P$

Maximum shear forces:
$$V_1 = +P \; ; \; V_2 = -P$$

Maximum bending moment:
$$M_{\max} = Pa, \text{ between loads}$$

Maximum deflection $= \dfrac{Pa}{24EI}(3L^2 - 4a^2)$

$$\text{def.} = \frac{Px}{6EI}(3La - 3a^2 - x^2), \quad o \le x \le a$$

$$= \frac{Pa}{6EI}(3Lx - 3x^2 - a^2), \quad a \le x \le (L - a)$$

Concentrated load P at any point

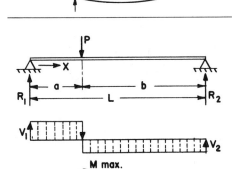

Reactions: $R_1 = \dfrac{Pb}{L}; \; R_2 = \dfrac{Pa}{L}$

Shear forces: $V_1 = +R_1; \; V_2 = -R_2$

Maximum bending moment:
$$M_{\max} = \frac{Pab}{L}, \text{ at } x = a$$

$$M = \frac{Pbx}{L}, o \le x \le a; M = \frac{Pa}{L}(L - x), a \le x \le L$$

Maximum deflection $= \dfrac{Pab\,(L + b)\,\sqrt{3a\,(L + b)}}{27\,EIL}$

at $x = \sqrt{a\,(L + b)/3}$

deflection under load $= \dfrac{Pa^2 b^2}{3\,EIL}, \quad x = a$

$$\text{def.} = \frac{Pbx}{6\,EIL}(L^2 - b^2 - x^2), \quad o \le x \le a$$

---

[2] The Aluminum Association, Engineering Data for Aluminum Structures, New York, 1969.

TABLE A-4. cont.

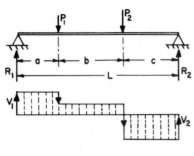

Two *unequal* concentrated loads unsymmetrically located

Reactions: $R_1 = \dfrac{P_1(L-a) + P_2 c}{L}$

$\qquad\qquad R_2 = \dfrac{P_2(L-c) + P_1 a}{L}$

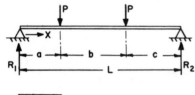

Shear forces: $V_1 = +R_1$

$\qquad\qquad V_2 = -R_2$

Bending moments:

$\qquad M_1 = R_1 a$, maximum if $R_1 < P_1$

$\qquad M_2 = R_2 c$, maximum if $R_2 < P_2$

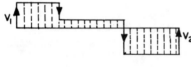

Two *equal* concentrated loads unsymmetrically located

Reactions: $R_1 = \dfrac{P(L-a+c)}{L}$

$\qquad\qquad R_2 = \dfrac{P(L-c+a)}{L}$

Shear forces: $V_1 = +R_1$
$\qquad\qquad V_2 = -R_2$

Bending moments:

$\qquad M_1 = R_1 a$, maximum if $a > c$
$\qquad M_2 = R_2 c$, maximum if $a < c$

$M = R_1 x - P(x-a), \quad a \le x \le (a+b)$

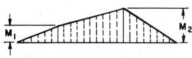

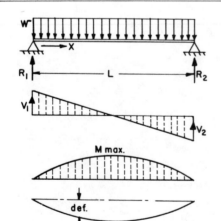

Uniformly distributed loading of w lb/in total load $W = wL$

Reactions: $R_1 = R_2 = \dfrac{wL}{2} = \dfrac{W}{2}$

Shear $= w\left(\dfrac{L}{2} - x\right), \; o \le x \le L$

Maximum bending moment $= \dfrac{wL^2}{8} = \dfrac{WL}{8}$, at center

$M = \dfrac{wx}{2}(L-x) = \dfrac{Wx}{2L}(L-x), \;\; o \le x \le L$

Maximum deflection $= \dfrac{5\,wL^4}{384\,EI} = \dfrac{5\,WL^3}{384\,EI}$, at center

$\qquad$ def. $= \dfrac{wx}{24\,EI}(L^3 - 2Lx^2 + x^3), \, o \le x \le L$

TABLE A-4. cont.

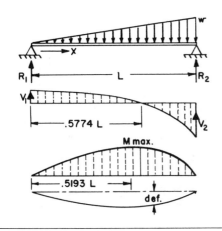

Distributed load increasing uniformly to one end

Total load $W = \dfrac{wL}{2}$, max. loading = w lb/in

Reactions: $R_1 = \dfrac{W}{3} = \dfrac{wL}{6}$

$R_2 = \dfrac{2W}{3} = \dfrac{wL}{3}$

Shear forces: $V_1 = +R_1; V_2 = -R_2$

$V = \dfrac{W}{3} - \dfrac{Wx^2}{L^2}, o \le x \le L$

Maximum bending moment $= 0.1283WL, x = 0.5774L$

$M = \dfrac{Wx}{3L^2}(L^2 - x^2), o \le x \le L$

Maximum deflection $= 0.01304\dfrac{WL^3}{EI}, x = 0.5193L$

def. $= \dfrac{Wx}{180\,EIL^2}(3x^4 - 10L^2x^2 + 7L^4), \quad o \le x \le L$

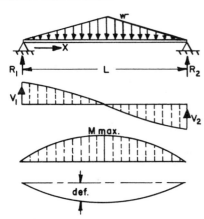

Distributed load increasing toward center

Total load $W = \dfrac{wL}{2}$, max. loading = w lb/in

Reactions: $R_1 = R_2 = \dfrac{W}{2} = \dfrac{wL}{4}$

Shear forces: $V_1 = +R_1 ; V_2 = -R_2$

$V = \dfrac{W}{2L^2}(L^2 - 4x^2), o \le x \le \dfrac{L}{2}$

Maximum bending moment $= \dfrac{WL}{6} = \dfrac{wL^2}{12}$

$M = \dfrac{Wx}{2}\left(1 - \dfrac{4x^2}{3L^2}\right), \quad o \le x \le \dfrac{L}{2}$

Maximum deflection $= \dfrac{WL^3}{60\,EI} = \dfrac{wL^4}{120\,EI}, x = \dfrac{L}{2}$

def. $= \dfrac{Wx}{480\,EIL^2}(5L^2 - 4x^2)^2, \quad o \le x \le \dfrac{L}{2}$

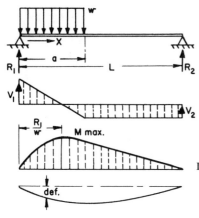

Load towards right end of beam—uniformly distributed

Total load $= wa$

Reactions: $R_1 = \dfrac{wa}{2L}(2L - a); R_2 = \dfrac{wa^2}{2L}$

Shear forces: $V_1 = +R_1; V_2 = -R_2$
$V = R_1 - wx, o \le x \le a$

Maximum bending moment:

$= \dfrac{wa^2}{8L^2}(2L - a)^2, x = \dfrac{R_1}{w}$

$M = R_1x - \dfrac{wx^2}{2}, o \le x \le a$

Def. $= \dfrac{wx}{24\,EIL}[a^2(2L - a)^2 - 2ax^2(2L - a) + Lx^3],$

$o \le x \le a$

$= \dfrac{wa^2(L - x)}{24\,EIL}(4Lx - 2x^2 - a^2), a \le x \le L$

TABLE A-4.   cont.

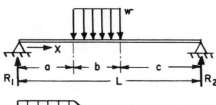

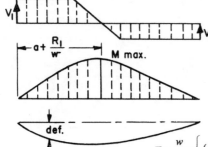

Partially distributed uniform load
Total load $= wb$

Reactions: $R_1 = \dfrac{wb}{2L}(2c + b)$

$R_2 = \dfrac{wb}{2L}(2a + b)$

Shear forces: $V_1 = +R_1 ; V_2 = -R_2$
$V = R_1 - w(x - a), a \leq x \leq a + b$

Maximum bending moment

$= \dfrac{wb}{8L^2}(2c + b)[4aL + b(2c + b)], x = a + \dfrac{R_1}{w}$

Deflection:

$$= \frac{w}{24\,EI}\left[\frac{b(b + 2c)x}{L}\right]\left[-2x^2 + 2a(2L - a) + b(b + 2c)\right]$$
$$\text{for } o \leq x \leq a$$

$$= \frac{w}{24\,EI}\left\{(x - a)^4 + \left[\frac{b(b + 2c)x}{L}\right]\left[-2x^2 + 2a(2L - a) + b(b + 2c)\right]\right\}$$
$$\text{for } a \leq x \leq a + b$$

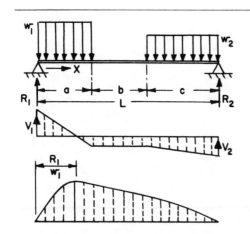

Partially distributed uniform load at each end
Total load $= w_1a + w_2c$

Reactions: $R_1 = \dfrac{w_1a(2L - a) + w_2c^2}{2L}$

$R_2 = \dfrac{w_2c(2L - c) + w_1a^2}{2L}$

Shear forces: $V_1 = +R_1 ; V_2 = -R_2$
Maximum bending moment

$= \dfrac{R_1^2}{2w_1}$, when $R_1 < w_1a$

$M = R_1x - \dfrac{w_1x^2}{2}, o \leq x \leq a$

$M = R_1x - \dfrac{w_1a}{2}(2x - a), a \leq x \leq a + b$

$M = R_2(L - x) - \dfrac{w_2(L - x)^2}{2}, a + b \leq x \leq L$

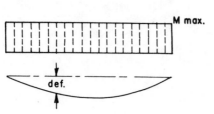

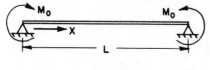

Two equal and opposite moments, M_0, at ends

Reactions: both zero

Shear forces: zero at all points

Maximum bending moment $= M_0$
$M = M_0$ at all points

Maximum deflection $= \dfrac{M_0L^2}{8\,EI}, x = \dfrac{L}{2}$

def. $= \dfrac{M_0x}{2\,EI}(L - x), o \leq x \leq L$

TABLE A-4. cont.

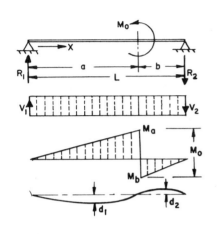

Moment, M_0, applied at $x = a$

Reactions: $R_1 = +\dfrac{M_0}{L}$; $R_2 = -\dfrac{M_0}{L}$

Shear force $V = +\dfrac{M_0}{L}$, $o \le x \le L$

Bending moment: $M_a = \dfrac{M_0 a}{L}$, $M_b = -\dfrac{M_0 b}{L}$

$$M_a - M_b = M_0$$

Deflection:

$$d_1 = \frac{M_0}{6\,EI}\left[\left(6a - \frac{3a^2}{L} - 2L\right)x - \frac{x^3}{L}\right], o \le x \le a$$

$$d_2 = \frac{M_0}{6\,EI}\left[3a^2 + 3x^2 - \frac{x^3}{L} - \left(2L + \frac{3a^2}{L}\right)x\right], a \le x \le L$$

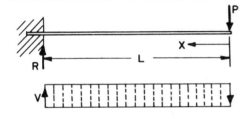

Concentrated load, P, at free end of cantilever beam

Reaction: $R = P$, at fixed end

Shear force $V = -P$, $o \le x \le L$

Maximum bending moment $= -PL$, $x = L$

Bending moment: $M = -Px$, $o \le x \le L$

Maximum deflection $= \dfrac{PL^3}{3\,EI}$, at free end, $x = o$

$$\text{def.} = \frac{P}{6\,EI}(2L^3 - 3L^2 x + x^3), o \le x \le L$$

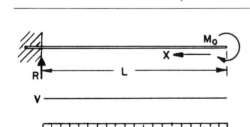

Moment, $-M_0$, at free end of cantilever beam

Reaction: $R = o$

Shear force: $V = o$, $o \le x \le L$

Maximum bending moment $= -M_0$

Bending moment $= -M_0$, $o \le x \le L$

Maximum deflection $= \dfrac{M_0 L^2}{2\,EI}$, at free end

$$\text{def.} = \frac{M_0 (L - x)^2}{2\,EI}, o \le x \le L$$

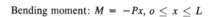

TABLE A-4. cont.

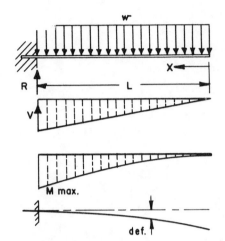

Uniformly distributed loading of w lb/in
    Total load $W = wL$

Reaction: $R = W = wL$

Maximum shear force $= -W = -wL$, at $x = L$
Shear force $= -wx$, $o \leq x \leq L$

Maximum bending moment $= -\dfrac{WL}{2} = -\dfrac{wL^2}{2}$, at fixed end

Bending moment: $M = -\dfrac{Wx^2}{2L} = -\dfrac{wx^2}{2}$, $o \leq x \leq L$

Maximum deflection $= \dfrac{WL^3}{8\ EI} = \dfrac{wL^4}{8\ EI}$, at free end

    $\mathrm{def} = \dfrac{w}{24\ EI}(x^4 - 4L^3 x + 3L^4)$, $o \leq x \leq L$

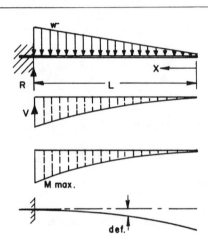

Distributed loading, increasing uniformly to fixed end

    Total load $= W = \dfrac{wL}{2}$

Reaction: $R = W = \dfrac{wL}{2}$

Maximum shear force $= -W = -\dfrac{wL}{2}$, at $x = L$

Shear force $= -\dfrac{Wx^2}{L^2}$, $o \leq x \leq L$.

Maximum bending moment $= -\dfrac{WL}{3}$, at fixed end

Bending moment $= -\dfrac{Wx^3}{3L^2}$, $o \leq x \leq L$

Maximum deflection $= \dfrac{WL^3}{15\ EI}$, at free end

    $\mathrm{def.} = \dfrac{W}{60\ EIL^2}(x^5 - 5L^4x + 4L^5)$, $o \leq x \leq L$

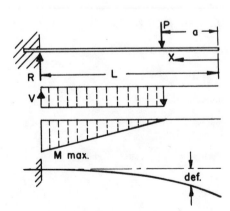

Concentrated load, P, inboard of free end

Reaction: $R = P$

Shear force: $V = 0$, $o \leq x < a$
               $V = -P$, $a < x \leq L$

Maximum bending moment $= -P\ (L - a)$, at fixed end

Maximum deflection $= \dfrac{P\ (L - a)^2}{6\ EI}(2L + a)$

TABLE A-4. cont.

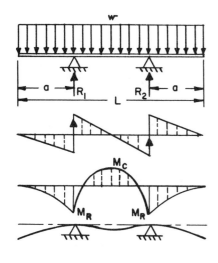

Uniformly distributed loading of w lb/in
Total load, $W = wL$

Reactions: $R_1 = R_2 = \dfrac{W}{2}$

Shear forces:

$V = wa$, just outboard of supports

$V = \dfrac{w}{2}(L - 2a)$, just inboard of supports

Bending moments:

$M_R = -\dfrac{wa^2}{2} = -\dfrac{Wa^2}{2L}$, at supports

$M_c = \dfrac{W}{8}(L - 4a)$, at center

def. $= \dfrac{W\,(L-2a)^3}{384\,EI}\left[\dfrac{5}{L}(L-2a) - \dfrac{24}{L}\left(\dfrac{a^2}{L-2a}\right)\right]$, at center

def. $= \dfrac{W\,(L-2a)^3 a}{24\,EIL}\left[-1 + 6\left(\dfrac{a}{L-2a}\right)^2 + 3\left(\dfrac{a}{L-2a}\right)^3\right]$, at ends

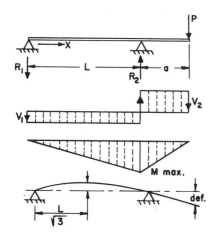

Concentrated load, P, at end of overhang

Reactions: $R_1 = -\dfrac{Pa}{L}$

$R_2 = \dfrac{P}{L}(L + a)$

Shear forces: $V_1 = -\dfrac{Pa}{L}$

$V_2 = P$

Maximum bending moment:

$M_{max} = -Pa$, at right support

Deflections:

Maximum downward def. $= \dfrac{Pa^2}{3\,EI}(L + a)$, at load

Maximum upward deflection; at $x = \dfrac{L}{\sqrt{3}}$

$= \dfrac{PaL^2}{9\sqrt{3}\,EI} = 0.06415\,\dfrac{PaL^2}{EI}$

Concentrated load, P, between supports

Reactions: $R_1 = \dfrac{Pb}{L}$; $R_2 = \dfrac{P\,(L-b)}{L}$

Maximum bending moment $= \dfrac{Pb\,(L-b)}{L}$, at load

Maximum downward deflection

$= \dfrac{Pb\,(L^2 - b^2)\,\sqrt{3\,(L^2 - b^2)}}{27\,EIL}$, at $x = \dfrac{\sqrt{3\,(L^2 - b^2)}}{3}$

Maximum upward deflection

$= -\dfrac{Pab}{6\,EI}\left(2L + \dfrac{b^2}{L} - 3b\right)$, at end of overhang

TABLE A-4. cont.

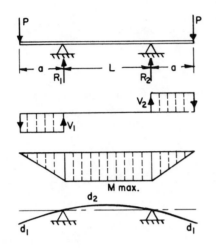

Two equal loads, P, at ends of overhang

Reactions: $R_1 = R_2 = P$

Shear forces: $V_1 = -P$; $V_2 = +P$

Maximum bending moment $= -Pa$, between supports

Deflections:

$$d_1 = \frac{Pa^2}{3\,EI}\left(a + \frac{3}{2}\,L\right), \text{ at point of load}$$

$$d_2 = -\frac{PL^2a}{8\,EI}, \text{ at center point}$$

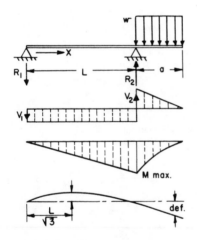

Uniformly distributed loading, w lb/in on overhang
   Total load $= wa$

Reactions: $R_1 = -\dfrac{wa^2}{2L}$

$\qquad\qquad R_2 = \dfrac{wa}{2L}(2L + a)$

Shear forces: $V_1 = R_1$
$\qquad\qquad\quad V_2 = wa$

Maximum bending moment:

$\qquad M_{\max} = -\dfrac{wa^2}{2}, \text{ at right support}$

Deflection at end of overhang:

$\qquad d_1 = \dfrac{wa^3}{24\,EIL}\,(4L + 3a)$

Maximum deflection between supports:

$$d_2 = -\frac{wa^2L^2}{18\sqrt{3}\,EI} = -0.03208\,\frac{wa^2L^2}{EI}$$

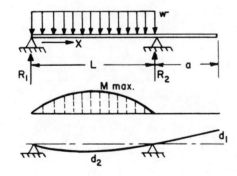

Uniformly distributed loading, w lb/in between supports
   Total load $= wL$

Reactions: $R_1 = R_2 = \dfrac{wL}{2}$

Maximum bending moment $= \dfrac{wL^2}{8}$, $x = \dfrac{L}{2}$

Deflection at end of overhang:

$\qquad d_1 = -\dfrac{wL^3a}{24\,EI}$

Maximum deflection between supports:

$\qquad d_2 = \dfrac{5wL^4}{384\,EI}$

TABLE A-4. cont.

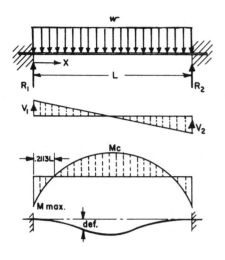

Uniformly distributed load, w lb/in
Total load $W = wL$

Reactions: $R_1 = R_2 = \dfrac{W}{2}$

Shear forces: $V_1 = +\dfrac{W}{2}$

$V_2 = -\dfrac{W}{2}$

Maximum (negative) bending moment
$$M_{max} = -\frac{wL^2}{12} = -\frac{WL}{12}, \text{ at end}$$

Maximum (positive) bending moment
$$M_c = \frac{wL^2}{24} = \frac{WL}{24}, \text{ at center}$$

Maximum deflection $= \dfrac{wL^4}{384\,EI} = \dfrac{WL^3}{384\,EI}$, at center

def. $= \dfrac{wx^2}{24\,EI}(L - x)^2,\ o \le x \le L$

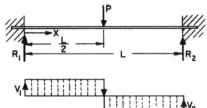

Concentrated load, P, at center

Reactions: $R_1 = R_2 = \dfrac{P}{2}$

Shear forces: $V_1 = +\dfrac{P}{2}$; $V_2 = -\dfrac{P}{2}$

Maximum bending moment
$$M_{max} = \frac{PL}{8}, \text{ at center}$$

$$M_{max} = -\frac{PL}{8}, \text{ at ends}$$

Maximum deflection $= \dfrac{PL^3}{192\,EI}$, at center

def. $= \dfrac{Px^2}{48\,EI}(3L - 4x),\ o \le x \le \dfrac{L}{2}$

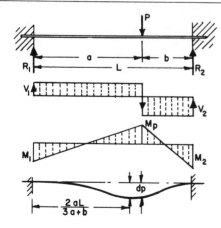

Concentrated load, P, at any point

Reactions: $R_1 = \dfrac{Pb^2}{L^3}(3a + b)$

$R_2 = \dfrac{Pa^2}{L^3}(3b + a)$

Shear forces: $V_1 = R_1$; $V_2 = -R_2$
Bending moments:

$M_1 = -\dfrac{Pab^2}{L^2}$, max. when $a < b$

$M_2 = -\dfrac{Pa^2b}{L^2}$, max. when $a > b$

$M_p = +\dfrac{2Pa^2b^2}{L^3}$, at point of load

Deflection $= \dfrac{Pa^3b^3}{3\,EIL^3}$, at point of load

Max. def. $= \dfrac{2Pa^3b^2}{3\,EI\,(3a + b)^2}$, at $x = \dfrac{2aL}{3a + b}$, for $a > b$

TABLE A-4. cont.

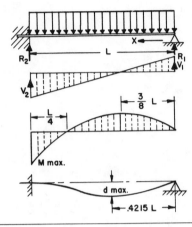

Uniformly distributed load, w lb/in

Total load $W \doteq wL$

Reactions: $R_1 = \dfrac{3wL}{8}$, $R_2 = \dfrac{5wL}{8}$

Shear forces: $V_1 = + R_1$; $V_2 = - R_2$

Bending moments:

    Max. negative moment $= -\dfrac{wL^2}{8}$, at left end

    Max. positive moment $= \dfrac{9}{128} wL^2$, $x = \dfrac{3}{8}L$

    $M = \dfrac{3wLx}{8} - \dfrac{wx^2}{2}$, $o \leq x \leq L$

Maximum deflection $= \dfrac{wL^4}{185EI}$, $x = 0.4215\,L$

    def. $= \dfrac{wx}{48EI}(L^3 - 3Lx^2 + 2x^3)$, $o \leq x \leq L$

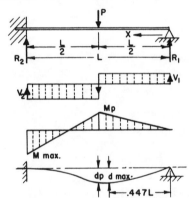

Concentrated load, P, at center

Reactions: $R_1 = \dfrac{5}{16}P$; $R_2 = \dfrac{11}{16}P$

Shear forces: $V_1 = R_1$; $V_2 = - R_2$

Bending moments:

    Max. negative moment $= -\dfrac{3\,PL}{16}$, at fixed end

    Max. positive moment $= \dfrac{5\,PL}{32}$, at center

Maximum deflection $= 0.009317\,\dfrac{PL^3}{EI}$, at $x = 0.447\,L$

Deflection at center under load $= \dfrac{7\,PL^3}{768\,EI}$

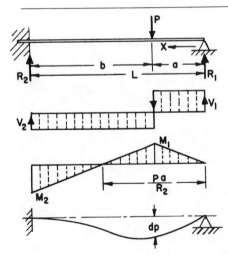

Concentrated load, P, at any point

Reactions: $R_1 = \dfrac{Pb^2}{2L^3}(a + 2L)$, $R_2 = \dfrac{Pa}{2L^3}(3L^2 - a^2)$

Shear forces: $V_1 = R_1$; $V_2 = - R_2$

Bending moments:

    Max. negative moment, $M_2 = -\dfrac{Pab}{2L^2}(a + L)$, at fixed end

    Max. positive moment, $M_1 = \dfrac{Pab^2}{2L^3}(a + 2L)$, at load

Deflections: $d_p = \dfrac{Pa^2b^3}{12\,EIL^3}(3L + a)$, at load

$d_{max} = \dfrac{Pa\,(L^2 - a^2)^3}{3\,EI\,(3L^2 - a^2)^2}$, at $x = \dfrac{L^2 + a^2}{3L^2 - a^2}L$, when $a < 0.414\,L$

$d_{max} = \dfrac{Pab^2}{6\,EI}\sqrt{\dfrac{a}{2L + a}}$, at $x = L\sqrt{\dfrac{a}{2L + a}}$, when $a > 0.414\,L$

TABLE A-4. cont.

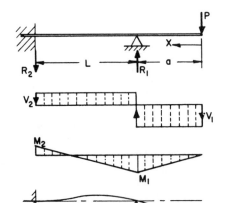

Concentrated load, P, at end of overhang

Reactions: $R_1 = P\left(1 + \dfrac{3a}{2L}\right)$

$R_2 = -\dfrac{3\,Pa}{2\,L}$

Shear forces: $V_1 = -P$

$V_2 = \dfrac{3\,Pa}{2\,L}$

Bending moments:

$M_1 = -Pa$, at R_1

$M_2 = \dfrac{Pa}{2}$, at fixed end

Deflection at end of overhang

def. $= \dfrac{PL^3}{EI}\left(\dfrac{a^2}{4\,L^2} + \dfrac{a^3}{3\,L^3}\right)$

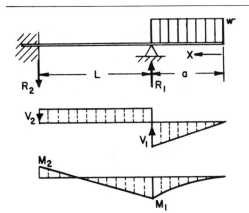

Distributed load, w lb/in. on overhang

Reactions: $R_1 = wa\left(1 + \dfrac{3a}{4L}\right)$

$R_2 = -\dfrac{3\,wa^2}{4\,L}$

Shear forces: $V_1 = -wa$

$V_2 = \dfrac{3\,wa^2}{4\,L}$

Bending moments:

$M_1 = -\dfrac{wa^2}{2}$, at R_1

$M_2 = \dfrac{wa^2}{4}$, at fixed end

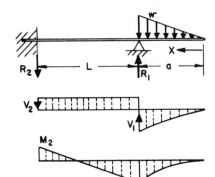

Distributed triangular loading of w lb/in. maximum intensity on overhang

Reactions: $R_1 = \dfrac{wa}{2}\left(1 + \dfrac{a}{2\,L}\right)$

$R_2 = -\dfrac{wa^2}{4\,L}$

Shear forces: $V_1 = -\dfrac{wa}{2}$

$V_2 = \dfrac{wa^2}{4\,L}$

Bending moments:

$M_1 = -\dfrac{wa^2}{6}$, at R_1

$M_2 = \dfrac{wa^2}{12}$, at fixed end

TABLE A-4. cont.

Continuous beam of two equal spans—equal concentrated loads, P, at center of each span

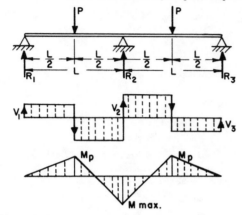

Reactions: $R_1 = R_3 = \dfrac{5}{16}\, P$

$$R_2 = 1.375\, P$$

Shear forces: $V_1 = -V_3 = \dfrac{5}{16}\, P$

$$V_2 = \pm\, \dfrac{11}{16}\, P$$

Bending moments:

$$M_{max} = -\dfrac{6}{32}\, PL,\ \text{at } R_2$$

$$M_p = \dfrac{5}{32}\, PL,\ \text{at point of load}$$

Continuous beam of two equal spans—concentrated loads, P, at third points of each span

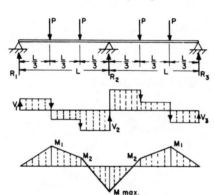

Reactions: $R_1 = R_3 = \dfrac{2}{3}\, P$

$$R_2 = \dfrac{8}{3}\, P$$

Shear forces: $V_1 = -V_3 = \dfrac{2}{3}\, P$

$$V_2 = \pm\, \dfrac{4}{3}\, P$$

Bending moments:

$$M_{max} = -\dfrac{1}{3}\, PL,\ \text{at } R_2$$

$$M_1 = \dfrac{2}{9}\, PL$$

$$M_2 = \dfrac{1}{9}\, PL$$

Continuous beam of two equal spans—uniformly distributed load of w lb/in.

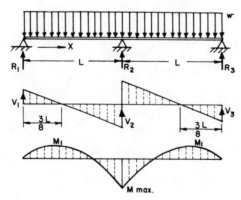

Reactions: $R_1 = R_3 = \dfrac{3}{8}\, wL$

$$R_2 = 1.25\, wL$$

Shear forces:

$$V_1 = -V_3 = \dfrac{3}{8}\, wL$$

$$V_2 = \pm\, \dfrac{5}{8}\, wL$$

Bending moments:

$$M_{max} = -\dfrac{1}{8}\, wL^2$$

$$M_1 = \dfrac{9}{128}\, wL^2$$

Maximum deflection $= 0.00541\, \dfrac{wL^4}{EI}$

at $x = 0.4215\, L$

Def. $= \dfrac{w}{48\,EI}(L^3 x - 3\,Lx^3 + 2x^4),\ o \leq x \leq L$

TABLE A-4.   cont.

Continuous beam of two equal spans—uniformly distributed load of w lb/in. on one span

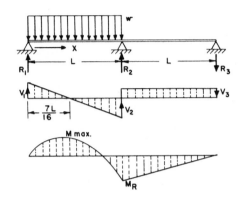

Reactions: $R_1 = \dfrac{7}{16}\, wL$, $R_2 = \dfrac{5}{8}\, wL$, $R_3 = -\dfrac{1}{16}\, wL$

Shear forces: $V_1 = \dfrac{7}{16}\, wL$, $V_2 = -\dfrac{9}{16}\, wL$, $V_3 = \dfrac{1}{16}\, wL$

Bending moments:

$$M_{max} = \frac{49}{512}\, wL^2,\ \text{at}\ x = \frac{7}{16}\, L$$

$$M_R = -\frac{1}{16}\, wL^2,\ \text{at}\ R_2$$

$$M = \frac{wx}{16}\, (7L - 8x),\ o \leq x \leq L$$

Continuous beam of two equal spans—concentrated load, P, at center of one span.

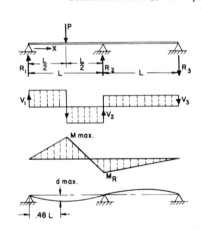

Reactions: $R_1 = \dfrac{13}{32}\, P$, $R_2 = \dfrac{11}{16}\, P$, $R_3 = -\dfrac{3}{32}\, P$

Shear forces: $V_1 = \dfrac{13}{32}\, P$, $V_2 = -\dfrac{19}{32}\, P$, $V_3 = \dfrac{3}{32}\, P$

Bending moments:

$$M_{max} = \frac{13}{64}\, PL,\ \text{at point of load}$$

$$M_R = -\frac{3}{32}\, PL,\ \text{at support}\ R_2$$

Maximum deflection:

$$d_{max} = \frac{0.96\, PL^3}{64\, EI},\ \text{at}\ x = 0.48L$$

Continuous beam of two equal spans—concentrated load, P, at any point on one span.

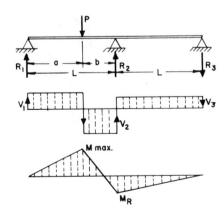

Reactions: $R_1 = \dfrac{Pb}{4L^3}\, [4L^2 - a\,(L + a)]$

$$R_2 = \frac{Pa}{2L^3}\, [2L^2 + b\,(L + a)]$$

$$R_3 = -\frac{Pab}{4L^3}\, (L + a)$$

Shear forces: $V_1 = \dfrac{Pb}{4L^3}\, [4L^2 - a\,(L + a)]$

$$V_2 = -\frac{Pa}{4L^3}\, [4L^2 + b\,(L + a)]$$

$$V_3 = \frac{Pab}{4L^3}\, (L + a)$$

Bending moments: $M_{max} = \dfrac{Pab}{4L^3}\, [4L^2 - a\,(L + a)]$

$$M_R = -\frac{Pab}{4L^2}\, (L + a)$$

TABLE A-4. cont.

Continuous beam of three equal spans—concentrated load, P, at center of each span

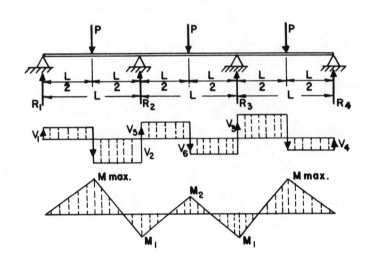

Reactions: $R_1 = R_4 = \dfrac{7}{20} P$

$\qquad\qquad R_2 = R_3 = \dfrac{23}{20} P$

Shear forces:

$$V_1 = -V_4 = \dfrac{7}{20} P$$

$$V_3 = -V_2 = \dfrac{13}{20} P$$

$$V_5 = -V_6 = \dfrac{P}{2}$$

Bending moments:

$$M_{max} = \dfrac{7}{40} PL$$

$$M_1 = -\dfrac{3}{20} PL$$

$$M_2 = \dfrac{1}{10} PL$$

Continuous beam of three equal spans—concentrated loads, P, at third points of each span

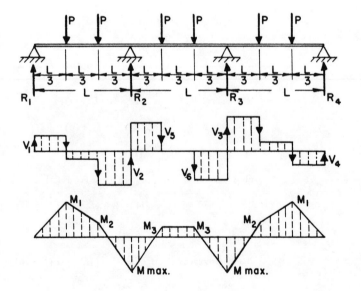

Reactions:

$$R_1 = R_4 = \dfrac{11}{15} P$$

$$R_2 = R_3 = \dfrac{34}{15} P$$

Shear forces:

$$V_1 = -V_4 = \dfrac{11}{15} P$$

$$V_3 = -V_2 = \dfrac{19}{15} P$$

$$V_5 = -V_6 = P$$

Bending moments:

$$M_{max} = -\dfrac{12}{45} PL$$

$$M_1 = \dfrac{11}{45} PL$$

$$M_2 = \dfrac{7}{45} PL$$

$$M_3 = \dfrac{3}{45} PL$$

TABLE A-4.   cont.

Continuous beam of three equal spans—uniformly distributed load

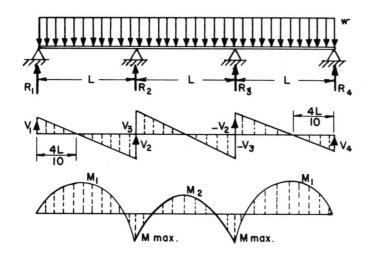

Loading: w lb/in
Reactions:

$$R_1 = R_4 = \frac{4wL}{10}$$

$$R_2 = R_3 = \frac{11wL}{10}$$

Shear forces:

$$V_1 = -V_4 = \frac{4wL}{10}$$

$$V_2 = -\frac{6wL}{10}$$

$$V_3 = \frac{5wL}{10}$$

Bending moments:

$$M_{max} = -\frac{wL^2}{10} \text{, at } R_2 \text{ and } R_3$$

$$M_1 = \frac{4wL^2}{50} \text{, at } 0.4L \text{ from } R_1 \text{ and } R_4$$

$$M_2 = \frac{wL^2}{40} \text{, at center}$$

Continuous beam of four equal spans—uniformly distributed load

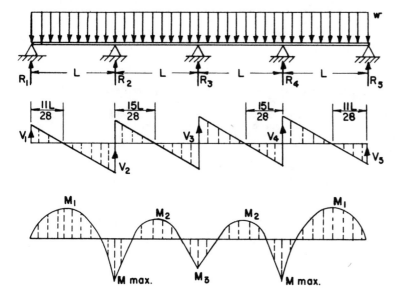

Loading: w lb/in

Reactions: $R_1 = R_5 = \dfrac{11wL}{28}$

$$R_2 = R_4 = \frac{32wL}{28}$$

$$R_3 = \frac{26wL}{28}$$

Shear forces:

$$V_1 = -V_5 = \frac{11wL}{28}$$

$$V_4 = -V_2 = \frac{17wL}{28}$$

$$V_3 = \frac{13wL}{28}$$

Bending moments:

$$M_{max} = -\frac{168wL^2}{1568} \text{, at } R_2 \text{ and } R_4$$

$$M_1 = \frac{121wL^2}{1568}$$

$$M_2 = \frac{57wL^2}{1568}$$

$$M_3 = -\frac{112wL^2}{1568}$$

TABLE A-4.   cont.

Values given in the formulas do not include any provision for impact

---

SIMPLE BEAM
One Concentrated Moving
Load

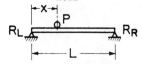

R_L max $= V_L$ max (at $x = 0$) $= P$

M max $\left(\text{at point of load, when } x = \dfrac{L}{2}\right) = \dfrac{PL}{4}$

SIMPLE BEAM
Two Equal Concentrated
Moving Loads

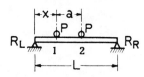

R_L max $= V_L$ max (at $x = 0$) $= P\left(2 - \dfrac{a}{L}\right)$

M max $\begin{cases} \left[\begin{array}{l} \text{when } a < (2 - \sqrt{2})\,L = 0.586L \\ \text{under load 1 at } x = \dfrac{1}{2}\left(L - \dfrac{a}{2}\right) \end{array}\right] = \dfrac{P}{2L}\left(L - \dfrac{a}{2}\right)^2 \\[20pt] \left[\begin{array}{l} \text{when } a > (2 - \sqrt{2})\,L = 0.586L \\ \text{with one load at center of span} \\ \text{(other load is then off span)} \end{array}\right] = \dfrac{PL}{4} \end{cases}$

SIMPLE BEAM
Two Unequal Concentrated
Moving Loads

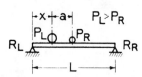

R_L max $= V_L$ max (at $x = 0$) $= P_L + P_R\dfrac{L - a}{L}$.

M max $\begin{cases} \left[\text{under } P_L, \text{ at } x = \dfrac{1}{2}\left(L - \dfrac{P_R a}{P_L + P_R}\right)\right] = (P_L + P_R)\dfrac{x^2}{L} \\[18pt] \left[\begin{array}{l} M \text{ max may occur with larger load at} \\ \text{center of span and other load off span} \end{array}\right] = \dfrac{P_L L}{4} \end{cases}$

GENERAL RULES FOR SIMPLE BEAMS CARRYING CONCENTRATED MOVING LOADS

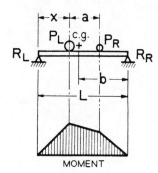

MOMENT

Maximum shear due to moving concentrated loads occurs at one support when one of the loads is at that support. With several moving loads, the point of maximum shear must be determined by trial.

Maximum bending moment produced by moving concentrated loads occurs under one of the loads when that load is as far from one support as the center of gravity of all the moving loads on the beam is from the other support.

In the diagram, maximum bending moment occurs under load P_L when $x = b$. It should also be noted that this condition occurs when the center line of the span is midway between the center of gravity of the loads and the nearest concentrated load.

Screw Thread Standards[3]

The following definitions, in conjunction with Figure A–3, explain the terms that are used in the tables on screws, bolts, and nuts.

A. Full Diameter Shank: Equal to major diameter of thread. Produced by cut thread or by roll thread on extruded blank. Characteristic of machine bolts and cap screws.

B. Undersized Shank: Equal approximately to pitch diameter of thread. Produced by roll threading a non-extruded blank. Characteristic of machine screws.

C. Pitch: The distance from a point on the screw thread to a corresponding point on the next thread measured parallel to the axis.

D. Pitch Diameter: The simple, effective diameter of screw thread. Approximately half way between the major and minor diameters.

E. Major Diameter: The largest diameter of a screw thread.

F. Minor Diameter: The smallest diameter of a screw thread.

Lead: The distance a screw thread advances axially in one turn.

Cut Thread: Threads are cut or chased; the unthreaded portion of shank will be equal to major diameter of thread.

Rolled Thread: Threads are cold formed by squeezing the blank between reciprocating serrated dies. This acts to increase the major diameter of the thread over and above the diameter of unthreaded shank (if any), unless an extruded blank is used.

Classes of thread are distinguished from each other by the amounts of tolerance and allowance specified. External threads or bolts are designated with the suffix "A"; internal or nut threads with "B."

Classes 1A and 1B: For work of rough commercial quality where loose fit for spin-on-assembly is desirable.

FIGURE A-2

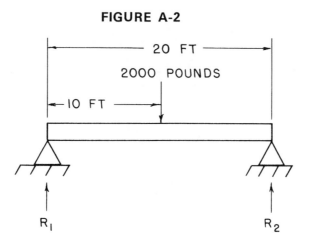

3H. M. Harper Company, "Thread Guide (Technical Bulletin Number 104)," Morton Grove, Illinois, 1968.

Classes 2A and 2B: The recognized standard for normal production of the great bulk of commercial bolts, nuts and screws.

Classes 3A and 3B: Used where a closed fit between mating parts for high quality work is required.

Class 4: A theoretical rather than practical class, now obsolete.

Class 5: For a wrench fit. Used principally for studs and their mating tapped holes. A force fit requiring the application of high torque for semi-permanent assembly.

FIGURE A-3

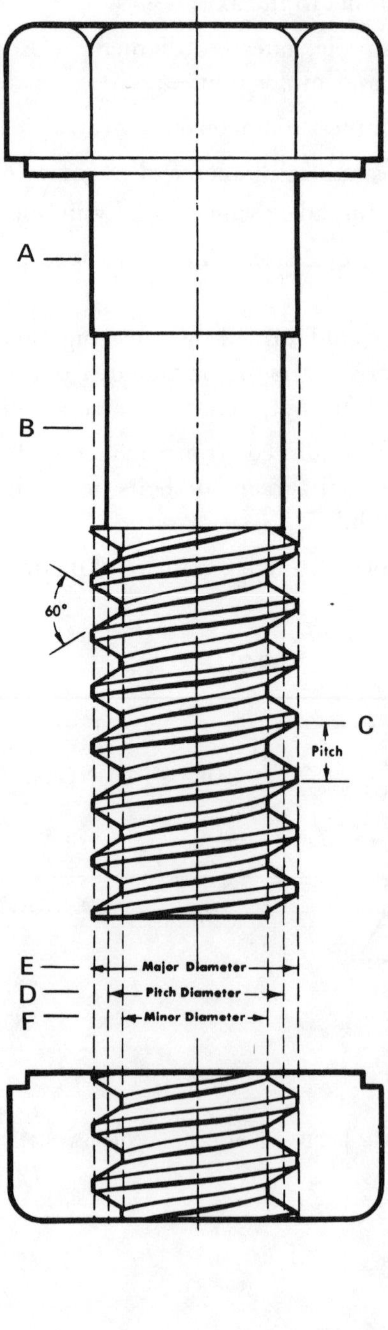

Thread details[4] for Classes 2 and 3 are given in inches in Table A–5 for screws and bolts, and in Table A–6 for nuts and tapped holes.

TABLE A-5. Inch standards for screws and bolts.

SIZE AND THREADS PER INCH	SERIES DESIGNATION	CLASS	ALLOWANCE	MAJOR DIAMETER			PITCH DIAMETER			NOMINAL MINOR DIAMETER
				LIMITS		TOLERANCE	LIMITS		TOLERANCE	
				MAXIMUM	MINIMUM		MAXIMUM	MINIMUM		
2–56	UNC	2A	0.0006	0.0854	0.0813	0.0041	0.0738	0.0717	0.0021	0.0635
		3A	0.0000	0.0860	0.0819	0.0041	0.0744	0.0728	0.0016	0.0641
2–64	UNF	2A	0.0006	0.0854	0.0816	0.0038	0.0753	0.0733	0.0020	0.0662
		3A	0.0000	0.0860	0.0822	0.0038	0.0759	0.0744	0.0015	0.0668
3–48	UNC	2A	0.0007	0.0983	0.0938	0.0045	0.0848	0.0825	0.0023	0.0727
		3A	0.0000	0.0990	0.0945	0.0045	0.0855	0.0838	0.0017	0.0734
3–56	UNF	2A	0.0007	0.0983	0.0942	0.0041	0.0867	0.0845	0.0022	0.0764
		3A	0.0000	0.0990	0.0949	0.0041	0.0874	0.0858	0.0016	0.0771
4–40	UNC	2A	0.0008	0.1112	0.1061	0.0051	0.0950	0.0925	0.0025	0.0805
		3A	0.0000	0.1120	0.1069	0.0051	0.0958	0.0939	0.0019	0.0813
4–48	UNF	2A	0.0007	0.1113	0.1068	0.0045	0.0978	0.0954	0.0024	0.0857
		3A	0.0000	0.1120	0.1075	0.0045	0.0985	0.0967	0.0018	0.0864
5–40	UNC	2A	0.0008	0.1242	0.1191	0.0051	0.1080	0.1054	0.0026	0.0935
		3A	0.0000	0.1250	0.1199	0.0051	0.1088	0.1069	0.0019	0.0943
5–44	UNF	2A	0.0007	0.1243	0.1195	0.0048	0.1095	0.1070	0.0025	0.0964
		3A	0.0000	0.1250	0.1202	0.0048	0.1102	0.1083	0.0019	0.0971
6–32	UNC	2A	0.0008	0.1372	0.1312	0.0060	0.1169	0.1141	0.0028	0.0989
		3A	0.0000	0.1380	0.1320	0.0060	0.1177	0.1156	0.0021	0.0997
6–40	UNF	2A	0.0008	0.1372	0.1321	0.0051	0.1210	0.1184	0.0026	0.1065
		3A	0.0000	0.1380	0.1329	0.0051	0.1218	0.1198	0.0020	0.1073
8–32	UNC	2A	0.0009	0.1631	0.1571	0.0060	0.1428	0.1399	0.0029	0.1248
		3A	0.0000	0.1640	0.1580	0.0060	0.1437	0.1415	0.0022	0.1257
8–36	UNF	2A	0.0008	0.1632	0.1577	0.0055	0.1452	0.1424	0.0028	0.1291
		3A	0.0000	0.1640	0.1585	0.0055	0.1460	0.1439	0.0021	0.1299
10–24	UNC	2A	0.0010	0.1890	0.1818	0.0072	0.1619	0.1586	0.0033	0.1379
		3A	0.0000	0.1900	0.1828	0.0072	0.1629	0.1604	0.0025	0.1389
10–32	UNF	2A	0.0009	0.1891	0.1831	0.0060	0.1688	0.1658	0.0030	0.1508
		3A	0.0000	0.1900	0.1840	0.0060	0.1697	0.1674	0.0023	0.1517
12–24	UNC	2A	0.0010	0.2150	0.2078	0.0072	0.1879	0.1845	0.0034	0.1639
		3A	0.0000	0.2160	0.2088	0.0072	0.1889	0.1863	0.0026	0.1649
12–28	UNF	2A	0.0010	0.2150	0.2085	0.0065	0.1918	0.1886	0.0032	0.1712
		3A	0.0000	0.2160	0.2095	0.0065	0.1928	0.1904	0.0024	0.1722
1/4–20	UNC	2A	0.0011	0.2489	0.2408	0.0081	0.2164	0.2127	0.0037	0.1876
		3A	0.0000	0.2500	0.2419	0.0081	0.2175	0.2147	0.0028	0.1887
1/4–28	UNF	2A	0.0010	0.2490	0.2425	0.0065	0.2258	0.2225	0.0033	0.2052
		3A	0.0000	0.2500	0.2435	0.0065	0.2268	0.2243	0.0025	0.2062
5/16–18	UNC	2A	0.0012	0.3113	0.3026	0.0087	0.2752	0.2712	0.0040	0.2431
		3A	0.0000	0.3125	0.3038	0.0087	0.2764	0.2734	0.0030	0.2443
5/16–24	UNF	2A	0.0011	0.3114	0.3042	0.0072	0.2843	0.2806	0.0037	0.2603
		3A	0.0000	0.3125	0.3053	0.0072	0.2854	0.2827	0.0027	0.2614
3/8–16	UNC	2A	0.0013	0.3737	0.3643	0.0094	0.3331	0.3287	0.0044	0.2970
		3A	0.0000	0.3750	0.3656	0.0094	0.3344	0.3311	0.0033	0.2983
3/8–24	UNF	2A	0.0011	0.3739	0.3667	0.0072	0.3468	0.3430	0.0038	0.3228
		3A	0.0000	0.3750	0.3678	0.0072	0.3479	0.3450	0.0029	0.3239
7/16–14	UNC	2A	0.0014	0.4361	0.4258	0.0103	0.3897	0.3850	0.0047	0.3485
		3A	0.0000	0.4375	0.4272	0.0103	0.3911	0.3876	0.0035	0.3499
7/16–20	UNF	2A	0.0013	0.4362	0.4281	0.0081	0.4037	0.3995	0.0042	0.3749
		3A	0.0000	0.4375	0.4294	0.0081	0.4050	0.4019	0.0031	0.3762
1/2–13	UNC	2A	0.0015	0.4985	0.4876	0.0109	0.4485	0.4435	0.0050	0.4041
		3A	0.0000	0.5000	0.4891	0.0109	0.4500	0.4463	0.0037	0.4056
1/2–20	UNF	2A	0.0013	0.4987	0.4906	0.0081	0.4662	0.4619	0.0043	0.4374
		3A	0.0000	0.5000	0.4919	0.0081	0.4675	0.4643	0.0032	0.4387
9/16–12	UNC	2A	0.0016	0.5609	0.5495	0.0114	0.5068	0.5016	0.0052	0.4587
		3A	0.0000	0.5625	0.5511	0.0114	0.5084	0.5045	0.0039	0.4603
9/16–18	UNF	2A	0.0014	0.5611	0.5524	0.0087	0.5250	0.5205	0.0045	0.4929
		3A	0.0000	0.5625	0.5538	0.0087	0.5264	0.5230	0.0034	0.4943

NOTE: SCREW THREAD FITS: Classes of thread are distinguished from each other by the amounts of tolerance and allowance specified. External threads or bolts are designated with the suffix "A," internal or nut threads with "B."

CLASSES 1A AND 1B: For work of rough commercial quality where a loose fit for spin-on assembly is desirable.

CLASSES 2A AND 2B: The recognized standard for normal production of the great bulk of commercial bolts, nuts, and screws.

---

[4]Ibid.

TABLE A-5. cont.

SIZE AND THREADS PER INCH	SERIES DESIGNATION	CLASS	ALLOWANCE	MAJOR DIAMETER			PITCH DIAMETER			NOMINAL MINOR DIAMETER
				LIMITS		TOLERANCE	LIMITS		TOLERANCE	
				MAXIMUM	MINIMUM		MAXIMUM	MINIMUM		
5/8–11	UNC	2A	0.0016	0.6234	0.6113	0.0121	0.5644	0.5589	0.0055	0.5119
		3A	0.0000	0.6250	0.6129	0.0121	0.5660	0.5619	0.0041	0.5135
5/8–18	UNF	2A	0.0014	0.6236	0.6149	0.0087	0.5875	0.5828	0.0047	0.5554
		3A	0.0000	0.6250	0.6163	0.0087	0.5889	0.5854	0.0035	0.5568
3/4–10	UNC	2A	0.0018	0.7482	0.7353	0.0129	0.6832	0.6773	0.0059	0.6255
		3A	0.0000	0.7500	0.7371	0.0129	0.6850	0.6806	0.0044	0.6255
3/4–16	UNF	2A	0.0015	0.7485	0.7391	0.0094	0.7079	0.7029	0.0050	0.6718
		3A	0.0000	0.7500	0.7406	0.0094	0.7094	0.7056	0.0038	0.6733
7/8–9	UNC	2A	0.0019	0.8731	0.8592	0.0139	0.8009	0.7946	0.0063	0.7368
		3A	0.0000	0.8750	0.8611	0.0139	0.8028	0.7981	0.0047	0.7387
7/8–14	UNF	2A	0.0016	0.8734	0.8631	0.0103	0.8270	0.8216	0.0054	0.7858
		3A	0.0000	0.8750	0.8647	0.0103	0.8286	0.8245	0.0041	0.7874
1–8	UNC	2A	0.0020	0.9980	0.9830	0.0150	0.9168	0.9100	0.0068	0.8446
		3A	0.0000	1.0000	0.9850	0.0150	0.9188	0.9137	0.0051	0.8466
1–12	UNF	2A	0.0018	0.9982	0.9868	0.0103	0.9441	0.9382	0.0059	0.8960
		3A	0.0000	1.0000	0.9886	0.0103	0.9459	0.9415	0.0044	0.8978
1-1/8–7	UNC	2A	0.0022	1.1228	1.1064	0.0164	1.0300	1.0228	0.0072	0.9475
		3A	0.0000	1.1250	1.1086	0.0164	1.0322	1.0268	0.0054	0.9497
1-1/8–8	UN	2A	0.0021	1.1229	1.1079	0.0150	1.0417	1.0348	0.0069	0.9695
		3A	0.0000	1.1250	1.1100	0.0150	1.0438	1.0386	0.0052	0.9716
1-1/8–12	UNF	2A	0.0018	1.1232	1.1118	0.0114	1.0691	1.0631	0.0060	1.0210
		3A	0.0000	1.1250	1.1136	0.0114	1.0709	1.0664	0.0045	1.0228
1-1/4–7	UNC	2A	0.0022	1.2478	1.2314	0.0164	1.1550	1.1476	0.0074	1.0725
		3A	0.0000	1.2500	1.2336	0.0164	1.1572	1.1517	0.0055	1.0747
1-1/4–8	UN	2A	0.0021	1.2479	1.2329	0.0150	1.1667	1.1597	0.0070	1.0945
		3A	0.0000	1.2500	1.2350	0.0150	1.1688	1.1635	0.0053	1.0966
1-1/4–12	UNF	2A	0.0018	1.2482	1.2368	0.0114	1.1941	1.1879	0.0062	1.1460
		3A	0.0000	1.2500	1.2386	1.0114	1.1959	1.1913	0.0046	1.1478
1-3/8–6	UNC	2A	0.0024	1.3726	1.3544	0.0182	1.2643	1.2563	0.0080	1.1681
		3A	0.0000	1.3750	1.3568	0.0182	1.2667	1.2607	0.0060	1.1705
1-3/8–8	UN	2A	0.0022	1.3728	1.3578	0.0150	1.2916	1.2844	0.0072	1.2194
		3A	0.0000	1.3750	1.3600	0.0150	1.2938	1.2884	0.0054	1.2216
1-3/8–12	UNF	2A	0.0019	1.3731	1.3617	0.0114	1.3190	1.3127	0.0063	1.2709
		3A	0.0000	1.3750	1.3636	0.0114	1.3209	1.3162	0.0047	1.2728
1-1/2–6	UNC	2A	0.0024	1.4976	1.4794	0.0182	1.3893	1.3812	0.0081	1.2931
		3A	0.0000	1.5000	1.4818	0.0182	1.3917	1.3856	0.0061	1.2955
1-1/2–8	UN	2A	0.0022	1.4978	1.4828	0.0150	1.4166	1.4093	0.0073	1.3444
		3A	0.0000	1.5000	1.4850	0.0150	1.4188	1.4133	0.0055	1.3466
1-1/2–12	UNF	2A	0.0019	1.4981	1.4867	0.0114	1.4440	1.4376	0.0064	1.3959
		3A	0.0000	1.5000	1.4886	0.0114	1.4459	1.4411	0.0048	1.3978
1-5/8–8	UN	2A	0.0022	1.6228	1.6078	0.0150	1.5416	1.5342	0.0074	1.4694
		3A	0.0000	1.6250	1.6100	0.0150	1.5438	1.5382	0.0056	1.4716
1-3/4–5	UNC	2A	0.0027	1.7473	1.7268	0.0205	1.6174	1.6085	0.0089	1.5019
		3A	0.0000	1.7500	1.7295	0.0205	1.6201	1.6134	0.0067	1.5046
1-3/4–8	UN	2A	0.0023	1.7477	1.7329	0.0150	1.6665	1.6590	0.0075	1.5943
		3A	0.0000	1.7500	1.7350	0.0150	1.6688	1.6632	0.0056	1.5966
1-7/8–8	UN	2A	0.0023	1.8727	1.8577	0.0150	1.7915	1.7838	0.0077	1.7193
		3A	0.0000	1.8750	1.8600	0.0150	1.7938	1.7881	0.0057	1.7216
2–4-1/2	UNC	2A	0.0029	1.9971	1.9751	0.0220	1.8528	1.8433	0.0095	1.7345
		3A	0.0000	2.0000	1.9780	0.0220	1.8557	1.8486	0.0071	1.7274
2–8	UN	2A	0.0023	1.9977	1.9827	0.0150	1.9165	1.9037	0.0078	1.8443
		3A	0.0000	2.0000	1.9850	0.0150	1.9188	1.9130	0.0058	1.8466

NOTE: SCREW THREAD FITS: Classes of thread are distinguished from each other by the amounts of tolerance and allowance specified. External threads or bolts are designated with the suffix "A," internal or nut threads with "B."

CLASSES 1A AND 1B: For work of rough commercial quality where a loose fit for spin-on assembly is desirable.

CLASSES 2A AND 2B: The recognized standard for normal production of the great bulk of commercial bolts, nuts, and screws.

TABLE A-6. Inch standards for nuts.

SIZE AND THREADS PER INCH	SERIES DESIGNATION	CLASS	MINOR DIAMETER			PITCH DIAMETER			MAJOR DIAMETER MINIMUM
			LIMITS		TOLERANCE	LIMITS		TOLERANCE	
			MINIMUM	MAXIMUM		MINIMUM	MAXIMUM		
2–56	UNC	2B	0.0667	0.0737	0.0070	0.0744	0.0772	0.0028	0.0860
		3B	0.0667	0.0737	0.0070	0.0744	0.0765	0.0021	0.0860
2–64	UNF	2B	0.0691	0.0753	0.0062	0.0759	0.0786	0.0027	0.0860
		3B	0.0691	0.0753	0.0062	0.0759	0.0779	0.0020	0.0860
3–48	UNC	2B	0.0764	0.0845	0.0081	0.0855	0.0885	0.0030	0.0990
		3B	0.0764	0.0845	0.0081	0.0855	0.0877	0.0022	0.0990
3–56	UNF	2B	0.0797	0.0865	0.0068	0.0874	0.0902	0.0028	0.0990
		3B	0.0797	0.0865	0.0068	0.0874	0.0895	0.0021	0.0990
4–40	UNC	2B	0.0849	0.0939	0.0090	0.0958	0.0991	0.0033	0.1120
		3B	0.0849	0.0939	0.0090	0.0958	0.0982	0.0024	0.1120
4–48	UNF	2B	0.0894	0.0968	0.0074	0.0985	0.1016	0.0031	0.1120
		3B	0.0894	0.0968	0.0074	0.0985	0.1008	0.0023	0.1120
5–40	UNC	2B	0.0979	0.1062	0.0083	0.1088	0.1121	0.0033	0.1250
		3B	0.0979	0.1062	0.0083	0.1088	0.1113	0.0025	0.1250
5–44	UNF	2B	0.1004	0.1079	0.0075	0.1102	0.1134	0.0032	0.1250
		3B	0.1004	0.1079	0.0075	0.1102	0.1126	0.0024	0.1250
6–32	UNC	2B	0.1040	0.1140	0.0100	0.1177	0.1214	0.0037	0.1380
		3B	0.1040	0.1140	0.0100	0.1177	0.1204	0.0027	0.1380
6–40	UNF	2B	0.1110	0.1190	0.0080	0.1218	0.1252	0.0034	0.1380
		3B	0.1110	0.1186	0.0076	0.1218	0.1243	0.0025	0.1380
8–32	UNC	2B	0.1300	0.1390	0.0090	0.1437	0.1475	0.0038	0.1640
		3B	0.1300	0.1389	0.0089	0.1437	0.1465	0.0028	0.1640
8–36	UNF	2B	0.1340	0.1420	0.0080	0.1460	0.1496	0.0036	0.1640
		3B	0.1340	0.1416	0.0076	0.1460	0.1487	0.0027	0.1640
10–24	UNC	2B	0.1450	0.1560	0.0110	0.1629	0.1672	0.0043	0.1900
		3B	0.1450	0.1555	0.0105	0.1629	0.1661	0.0032	0.1900
10–32	UNF	2B	0.1560	0.1640	0.0080	0.1697	0.1736	0.0039	0.1900
		3B	0.1560	0.1641	0.0081	0.1697	0.1726	0.0029	0.1900
12–24	UNC	2B	0.1710	0.1810	0.0100	0.1889	0.1933	0.0044	0.2160
		3B	0.1710	0.1807	0.0097	0.1889	0.1922	0.0033	0.2160
12–28	UNF	2B	0.1770	0.1860	0.0110	0.1928	0.1970	0.0042	0.2160
		3B	0.1770	0.1857	0.0087	0.1928	0.1959	0.0031	0.2160
1/4–20	UNC	2B	0.1960	0.2070	0.0090	0.2175	0.2223	0.0048	0.2500
		3B	0.1960	0.2067	0.0107	0.2175	0.2211	0.0036	0.2500
1/4–28	UNF	2B	0.2110	0.2200	0.0090	0.2268	0.2311	0.0043	0.2500
		3B	0.2110	0.2190	0.0080	0.2268	0.2300	0.0032	0.2500
5/16–18	UNC	2B	0.2520	0.2650	0.0130	0.2764	0.2817	0.0053	0.3125
		3B	0.2520	0.2630	0.0110	0.2764	0.2803	0.0039	0.3125
5/16–24	UNF	2B	0.2670	0.2770	0.0100	0.2854	0.2902	0.0048	0.3125
		3B	0.2670	0.2754	0.0084	0.2854	0.2890	0.0036	0.3125
3/8–16	UNC	2B	0.3070	0.3210	0.0140	0.3344	0.3401	0.0057	0.3750
		3B	0.3070	0.3182	0.0112	0.3344	0.3387	0.0043	0.3750
3/8–24	UNF	2B	0.3300	0.3400	0.0100	0.3479	0.3528	0.0049	0.3750
		3B	0.3300	0.3372	0.0072	0.3479	0.3516	0.0037	0.3750
7/16–14	UNC	2B	0.3600	0.3760	0.0160	0.3911	0.3972	0.0061	0.4375
		3B	0.3600	0.3717	0.0117	0.3911	0.3957	0.0046	0.4375
7/16–20	UNF	2B	0.3830	0.3950	0.0120	0.4050	0.4104	0.0054	0.4375
		3B	0.3830	0.3916	0.0086	0.4050	0.4091	0.0041	0.4375
1/2–13	UNC	2B	0.4170	0.4340	0.0170	0.4500	0.4565	0.0065	0.5000
		3B	0.4170	0.4284	0.0114	0.4500	0.4548	0.0048	0.5000
1/2–20	UNF	2B	0.4460	0.4570	0.0110	0.4675	0.4731	0.0056	0.5000
		3B	0.4460	0.4537	0.0077	0.4675	0.4717	0.0042	0.5000
9/16–12	UNC	2B	0.4720	0.4900	0.0180	0.5084	0.5152	0.0068	0.5625
		3B	0.4720	0.4843	0.0123	0.5084	0.5135	0.0051	0.5625
9/16–18	UNF	2B	0.5020	0.5150	0.0130	0.5264	0.5323	0.0059	0.5625
		3B	0.5020	0.5106	0.0086	0.5264	0.5308	0.0044	0.5625

CLASSES 3A AND 3B: Used where a closer fit between mating parts for high quality work is required.

CLASS 4: A theoretical rather than practical class, now obsolete.

CLASS 5: For a wrench fit. Used principally for studs and their mating tapped holes. A force fit requiring the application of high torque for semi-permanent assembly.

TABLE A-6.   cont.

SIZE AND THREADS PER INCH	SERIES DESIGNATION	CLASS	MINOR DIAMETER			PITCH DIAMETER			MAJOR DIAMETER MINIMUM
			LIMITS		TOLERANCE	LIMITS		TOLERANCE	
			MINIMUM	MAXIMUM		MINIMUM	MAXIMUM		
5/8–11	UNC	2B	0.5270	0.5460	0.0190	0.5660	0.5732	0.0072	0.6250
		3B	0.5270	0.5391	0.0121	0.5660	0.5714	0.0054	0.6250
5/8–18	UNF	2B	0.5650	0.5780	0.0130	0.5889	0.5949	0.0060	0.6250
		3B	0.5650	0.5730	0.0080	0.5889	0.5934	0.0045	0.6250
3/4–10	UNC	2B	0.6420	0.6630	0.0210	0.6850	0.6927	0.0077	0.7500
		3B	0.6420	0.6545	0.0125	0.6850	0.6907	0.0057	0.7500
3/4–16	UNF	2B	0.6820	0.6960	0.0140	0.7094	0.7159	0.0065	0.7500
		3B	0.6820	0.6908	0.0088	0.7094	0.7143	0.0049	0.7500
7/8–9	UNC	2B	0.7550	0.7780	0.0230	0.8028	0.8110	0.0082	0.8750
		3B	0.7550	0.7681	0.0131	0.8028	0.8089	0.0061	0.8750
7/8–14	UNF	2B	0.7980	0.8140	0.0160	0.8286	0.8356	0.0070	0.8750
		3B	0.7980	0.8068	0.0088	0.8286	0.8339	0.0053	0.8750
1–8	UNC	2B	0.8650	0.8900	0.0250	0.9188	0.9276	0.0088	1.0000
		3B	0.8650	0.8797	0.0147	0.9188	0.9254	0.0066	1.0000
1–12	UNF	2B	0.9100	0.9280	0.0150	0.9459	0.9535	0.0076	1.0000
		3B	0.9100	0.9198	0.0085	0.9459	0.9516	0.0057	1.0000
1-1/8–7	UNC	2B	0.9700	0.9980	0.0280	1.0322	1.0416	0.0094	1.1250
		3B	0.9700	0.9875	0.0175	1.0322	1.0393	0.0071	1.1250
1-1/8–8	UN	2B	0.9900	1.0150	0.0250	1.0438	1.0528	0.0090	1.1250
		3B	0.9900	1.0047	0.0147	1.0438	1.0505	0.0067	1.1250
1-1/8–12	UNF	2B	1.0350	1.0530	0.0180	1.0709	1.0787	0.0078	1.1250
		3B	1.0350	1.0448	0.0098	1.0709	1.0768	0.0059	1.1250
1-1/4–7	UNC	2B	1.0950	1.1230	0.0280	1.1572	1.1668	0.0096	1.2500
		3B	1.0950	1.1125	0.0175	1.1572	1.1644	0.0072	1.2500
1-1/4–8	UN	2B	1.1150	1.1400	0.0250	1.1688	1.1780	0.0092	1.2500
		3B	1.1150	1.1297	0.0147	1.1688	1.1757	0.0069	1.2500
1-1/4–12	UNF	2B	1.1600	1.1780	0.0180	1.1959	1.2039	0.0080	1.2500
		3B	1.1600	1.1698	0.0098	1.1959	1.2019	0.0060	1.2500
1-3/8–6	UNC	2B	1.1950	1.2250	0.0300	1.2667	1.2771	0.0104	1.3750
		3B	1.1950	1.2146	0.0196	1.2667	1.2745	0.0078	1.3750
1-3/8–8	UN	2B	1.2400	1.2650	0.0250	1.2938	1.3031	0.0093	1.3750
		3B	1.2400	1.2547	0.0147	1.2938	1.3008	0.0070	1.3750
1-3/8–12	UNF	2B	1.2850	1.3030	0.0180	1.3209	1.3291	0.0082	1.3750
		3B	1.2850	1.2948	0.0098	1.3209	1.3270	0.0061	1.3750
1-1/2–6	UNC	2B	1.3200	1.3500	0.0300	1.3917	1.4022	0.0105	1.5000
		3B	1.3200	1.3396	0.0196	1.3917	1.3996	0.0079	1.5000
1-1/2–8	UN	2B	1.3650	1.3900	0.0250	1.4188	1.4283	0.0095	1.5000
		3B	1.3650	1.3797	0.0147	1.4188	1.4259	0.0071	1.5000
1-1/2–12	UNF	2B	1.4100	1.4280	0.0180	1.4459	1.4542	0.0083	1.5000
		3B	1.4100	1.4198	0.0098	1.4459	1.4522	0.0063	1.5000
1-5/8–8	UN	2B	1.4900	1.5150	0.0250	1.5438	1.5535	0.0097	1.6250
		3B	1.4900	1.5047	0.0147	1.5438	1.5510	0.0072	1.6250
1-3/4–5	UNC	2B	1.5340	1.5680	0.0340	1.6201	1.6317	0.0116	1.7500
		3B	1.5340	1.5575	0.0235	1.6201	1.6288	0.0087	1.7500
1-3/4–8	UN	2B	1.6150	1.6400	0.0250	1.6688	1.6786	0.0098	1.7500
		3B	1.6150	1.6297	0.0147	1.6688	1.6762	0.0074	1.7500
1-7/8–8	UN	2B	1.7400	1.7650	0.0250	1.7938	1.8038	0.0100	1.8750
		3B	1.7400	1.7547	0.0147	1.7938	1.8013	0.0075	1.8750
2–4-1/2	UNC	2B	1.7590	1.7950	0.0360	1.8557	1.8681	0.0124	2.0000
		3B	1.7590	1.7861	0.0271	1.8557	1.8650	0.0093	2.0000
2–8	UN	2B	1.8650	1.8900	0.0250	1.9188	1.9289	0.0101	2.0000
		3B	1.8650	1.8797	0.0147	1.9188	1.9264	0.0076	2.0000

CLASSES 3A AND 3B: Used where a closer fit between mating parts for high quality work is required.

CLASS 4: A theoretical rather than practical class, now obsolete.

CLASS 5: For a wrench fit. Used principally for studs and their mating tapped holes. A force fit requiring the application of high torque for semi-permanent assembly.

Following the tables on thread details, Tables A–7 through A–11 present dimension details for a variety of screws[5], bolts[5], nuts[5], wood screws[4],[5], and lag screws[6].

[5]H. M. Harper Company, "Fastener Styles (Technical Bulletin Number 105–A)," Morton Grove, Illinois. Copyright 1969 H. M. Harper Co.

[6]Bethlehem Steel Corporation, "Bethlehem Standard Fasteners (Booklet 2669)," Bethlehem, Pa.

TABLE A-7.   Critical dimensions of various screws.

Square Head Set Screws

Nominal Size	F-Width Across Flats		G-Width Across Corners	H-Height of Head			X-Radius of Head
	Max.	Min.	Min.	Nom.	Max.	Min.	Nom.
#10	.190	.1875	.180	.247	9/64	.148	.134	15/32
#12	.216	.216	.208	.292	5/32	.163	.147	35/64
1/4	.250	.250	.241	.331	3/16	.196	.178	5/8
5/16	.3125	.3125	.302	.415	15/64	.245	.224	25/32
3/8	.3750	.375	.362	.497	9/32	.293	.270	15/16
7/16	.4375	.4375	.423	.581	21/64	.341	.315	1-3/32
1/2	.500	.500	.484	.665	3/8	.389	.361	1-1/4
9/16	.5625	.5625	.545	.748	27/64	.437	.407	1-13/32
5/8	.6250	.625	.606	.833	15/32	.485	.452	1-9/16
3/4	.750	.750	.729	1.001	9/16	.582	.544	1-7/8
7/8	.875	.875	.852	1.170	21/32	.678	.635	2-3/16
1	1.000	1.000	.974	1.337	3/4	.774	.726	2-1/2
1-1/8	1.125	1.125	1.096	1.505	27/32	.870	.817	2-13/16
1-1/4	1.250	1.250	1.219	1.674	15/16	.966	.908	3-1/8
1-3/8	1.375	1.375	1.342	1.843	1-1/32	1.063	1.000	3-7/16
1-1/2	1.500	1.500	1.464	2.010	1-1/8	1.159	1.091	3-3/4

Hexagonal Socket Type Set Screws

D-Nominal Diameter	C-Cup & Flat Point Diameter			R-Oval Point Radius	Y-Cone Point Angle		Full Dog Point & Half Dog Point				J-Socket Width Across Flats	
					118°±2° for these Lengths & Under	90°±2° for these Lengths & Over	P-Diameter					
	Mean	Max.	Min.				Max.	Min.	Q-Full	q-Half	Max.	Min.
5	1/16	0.067	0.057	3/32	1/8	3/16	0.083	0.078	0.06	0.03	0.0635	1/16
6	.069	0.074	0.064	7/64	1/8	3/16	0.092	0.087	0.07	0.035	0.0635	1/16
8	5/64	0.087	0.076	1/8	3/16	1/4	0.109	0.103	0.08	0.04	0.0791	5/64
10	3/32	0.102	0.088	9/64	3/16	1/4	0.127	0.120	0.09	0.045	0.0947	3/32
12	7/64	0.115	0.101	5/32	3/16	1/4	0.144	0.137	0.11	0.055	0.0947	3/32
1/4	1/8	0.132	0.118	3/16	1/4	5/16	5/32	0.149	1/8	1/16	0.1270	1/8
5/16	11/64	0.172	0.156	15/64	5/16	3/8	13/64	0.195	5/32	5/64	0.1582	5/32
3/8	13/64	0.212	0.194	9/32	3/8	7/16	1/4	0.241	3/16	3/32	0.1895	3/16
7/16	15/64	0.252	0.232	21/64	7/16	1/2	19/64	0.287	7/32	7/64	0.2207	7/32
1/2	9/32	0.291	0.270	3/8	1/2	9/16	11/32	0.334	1/4	1/8	0.2520	1/4
9/16	5/16	0.332	0.309	27/64	9/16	5/8	25/64	0.379	9/32	9/64	0.2520	1/4
5/8	23/64	0.371	0.347	15/32	5/8	3/4	15/32	0.456	5/16	5/32	0.3155	5/16
3/4	7/16	0.450	0.425	9/16	3/4	7/8	9/16	0.549	3/8	3/16	0.3780	3/8
7/8	33/64	0.530	0.502	21/32	7/8	1	21/32	0.642	7/16	7/32	0.5030	1/2
1	19/32	0.609	0.579	3/4	1	1-1/8	3/4	0.734	1/2	1/4	0.5655	9/16

Headless Slotted Set Screws

Nominal Size	D-Body Diameter of Screw	R-Radius of Oval Point Screw	I-Radius of Slotted Headless End	J-Width of Slot	T-Depth of Slot	C-Diameter of Cup & Flat Points		P-Diameter of Dog Point		Height of Dog	
						Max.	Min.	Max.	Min.	Q-Full	q-Half
5	0.125	0.094	0.125	0.023	0.031	·0.067	0.057	·0.083	0.078	0.060	0.030
6	0.138	0.109	0.138	0.025	0.035	0.074	0.064	0.092	0.087	0.070	0.035
8	0.164	0.125	0.164	0.029	0.041	0.087	0.076	0.109	0.103	0.080	0.040
10	0.190	0.141	0.190	0.032	0.048	0.102	0.088	0.127	0.120	0.090	0.045
12	0.216	0.156	0.216	0.036	0.054	0.115	0.101	0.144	0.137	0.110	0.055
1/4	0.250	0.188	0.250	0.045	0.063	0.132	0.118	0.156	0.149	0.125	0.063
5/16	0.312	0.234	0.313	0.051	0.078	0.172	0.156	0.203	0.195	0.156	0.078
3/8	0.375	0.281	0.375	0.064	0.094	0.212	0.194	0.250	0.241	0.188	0.094
7/16	0.438	0.328	0.438	0.072	0.109	0.252	0.232	0.297	0.287	0.219	0.109
1/2	0.500	0.375	0.500	0.081	0.125	0.291	0.270	0.344	0.334	0.250	0.125
9/16	0.562	0.422	0.563	0.091	0.141	0.332	0.309	0.391	0.379	0.281	0.140
5/8	0.625	0.469	0.625	0.102	0.156	0.371	0.347	0.469	0.456	0.313	0.156
3/4	0.750	0.563	0.750	0.129	0.188	0.450	0.425	0.563	0.549	0.375	0.188

Cup points are standard with stock sizes of all set screws. Other points are available on special order.

TABLE A-7. cont.

Flat Head

Machine Screws
Wood Screws
Tapping Screws

Nominal Size	Thread Diameter Maximum	A-Head Diameter			J-Width of Slot		T-Depth of Slot		D-Diameter of Recess		C-Depth of Recess
		Max.	Min.	Absol. Min.	Max.	Min.	Max.	Min.	Max.	Min.	Max.
2	.086	.172	.156	.147	.031	.023	.023	015	.102	.089	.063
3	.099	.199	.181	.171	.035	.027	.027	.017	.107	.094	.068
4	.112	.225	.207	.195	.039	.031	.030	.020	.128	.115	.089
5	.125	.252	.232	.220	.043	.035	.034	.022	.154	.141	.086
6	.138	.279	.257	.244	.048	.039	.038	.024	.174	.161	.106
7	.151	.305	.283	.268	.048	.039	.041	.027	.189	.176	.121
8	.164	.332	.308	.292	.054	.045	.045	.029	.189	.176	.121
8									**.204**	**.191**	**.113**
9	.177	.358	.334	.316	.054	.045	.049	.032	.214	.201	.123
10	.190	.385	.359	.340	.060	.050	.053	.034	.204	.191	.136
10									.258	.245	.146
12	.216	.438	.410	.389	.067	.056	.060	.039	.268	.255	.156
12									**.283**	**.270**	**.171**
14	.242	.491	.461	.437	.075	.064	.068	.044	.303	290	.191
1/4	.250	.507	.477	.452	.075	.064	.070	.046	.283	.270	.171
16	.268	.544	.512	.485	.075	.064	.075	.049	.327	.314	.216
18	.294	.597	.563	.534	.084	.072	.083	.054	.378	.365	.230
5/16	.312	.635	.600	.568	.084	.072	.088	.058	.365	.352	.216
3/8	.375	.762	.722	.685	.094	.081	.106	.070	.393	.380	.245
7/16	.436	.812	.771	.723	.094	.081	.103	.066	.409	.396	.261
1/2	.499	.875	.831	.775	.106	.091	.103	.065	.424	.411	.276

Additional tolerance for rounded edge.
Thread diameters for Tapping Screws are only approximate.
Phillips Recessed Head dimensions shown in bold type apply to Wood Screws.

Oval Head

Machine Screws
Wood Screws
Tapping Screws

Nominal Size	Thread Diameter Maximum	A-Head Diameter			J-Width of Slot		T-Depth of Slot		E-Total Height of Head		D-Diameter of Recess		C-Depth of Recess
		Max.	Min.	Absol. Min.	Max.	Min.	Max.	Min.	Max.	Min.	Max.	Min.	Max.
2	.086	.172	.156	.147	.031	.023	.045	.037	.080	.063	.112	.099	069
3	.099	.199	.181	.171	.035	.027	.052	.043	.092	.073	.124	.111	081
4	.112	.225	.207	.195	.039	.031	.059	.049	.104	.084	.136	.123	094
5	.125	.252	.232	.220	.043	.035	.067	.055	.116	.095	.158	.145	085
6	.138	.279	.257	.244	.048	.039	.074	.060	.128	.105	.178	.165	105
7	.151	.305	.283	.268	.048	.039	.081	.066	.140	.116	.189	.176	115
8	.164	.332	.308	.292	.054	.045	.088	.072	.152	.126	.192	.179	119
8											**.205**	**.292**	**.131**
9	.177	.358	.334	.316	.054	.045	.095	.078	.164	.137	.216	.203	144
10	.190	.385	.359	.340	.060	.050	103	.084	.176	.148	.209	.196	137
10											**.261**	**.248**	**.142**
12	.216	.438	.410	.389	.067	.056	.117	.096	.200	.169	.270	.257	152
12											**.283**	**.270**	**.165**
14	.242	.491	.461	.437	.075	064	.132	.108	.224	.190	.305	.292	188
1/4	.250	.507	.477	.452	.075	064	.136	.112	.232	.197	.290	.277	173
16	.268	.544	.512	.485	.075	.064	.146	.120	.248	.212	.332	.319	214
18	.294	.597	.563	.534	.084	.072	.171	.132	.272	.233	.381	.368	226
5/16	.312	.635	.600	.568	.084	.072	.160	.141	.290	.249	.390	.377	238
3/8	.375	.762	.722	.685	.094	.081	.206	.170	.347	.300	.410	.397	257
7/16	.436	.812	.771	.723	.094	.081	.210	.174	.345	.295	.422	.409	269
1/2	.499	.875	.831	.775	.106	.091	.216	.176	.354	.299	.437	.424	283

Thread diameters for tapping screws are only approximate.
Phillips Recessed Head dimensions shown in bold type apply to wood screws.

Binding Head

Machine Screws
Wood Screws
Tapping Screws

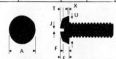

Nominal Size	Thread Diameter Maximum	A-Head Diameter		E-Height of Head		F-Height Of Oval		J-Width of Slot		T-Depth of Slot		U-*Diameter of Undercut		X-*Depth of Undercut	
		Max.	Min.	Max.	Min.	Max.	Min.	Max.	Min.	Max.	Min.	Max.	Min.	Max.	Min.
2	.086	181	.171	.050	.041	.018	.013	.031	.023	.030	.024	.141	.124	.010	.005
3	.099	208	.197	.059	.048	.022	.016	.035	.027	.036	.029	.162	.143	.011	.006
4	.112	235	.223	.068	.056	.025	.018	.039	.031	.042	.034	.184	.161	.012	.007
5	.125	263	.249	.078	.064	.029	.021	.043	.035	.048	.039	.205	.180	.014	.009
6	.138	290	.275	.087	.071	.032	.024	.048	.039	.053	.044	.226	.199	.015	.010
8	.164	344	.326	.105	.087	.039	.029	.054	.045	.065	.054	.269	.236	.017	.012
10	.190	399	.378	.123	.102	.045	.034	.060	.050	.077	.064	.312	.274	.020	.015
12	.216	454	.430	.141	.117	.052	.039	.067	.056	.089	.074	.354	.311	.023	.018
1/4	.250	513	.488	.165	.138	.061	.046	.075	.064	.105	.088	.410	.360	.026	.021
5/16	.312	641	.609	.209	.174	.077	.059	.084	.072	.134	.112	.513	.450	.032	.027
3/8	.375	769	.731	.253	.211	.094	.071	.094	.081	.163	.136	.615	.540	.039	034

*Undercut supplied only on special order

TABLE A-7. cont.

Round Head

Machine Screws
Wood Screws
Tapping Screws

Nominal Size	Thread Diameter Maximum	A-Head Diameter		E-Height of Head		J-Width of Slot		T-Depth of Slot		D-Diameter of Recess		C-Depth of Recess
		Max.	Min.	Max.	Min.	Max.	Min.	Max.	Min.	Max.	Min.	Max.
2	.086	.162	.146	.069	.059	.031	.023	.048	.037	.100	.087	.053
2										**.114**	**.101**	**.064**
3	.099	.187	.169	.078	.067	.035	.027	.053	.040	.109	.096	.062
3										**.122**	**.109**	**.073**
4	.112	.211	.193	.086	.075	.039	.031	.058	.044	.118	.105	.072
4										**.130**	**.117**	**.083**
5	.125	.236	.217	.095	.083	.043	.035	.063	.047	.154	.141	.074
6	.138	.260	.240	.103	.091	.048	.039	.068	.051	.162	.149	.084
7	.151	.285	.264	.111	.099	.048	.039	.072	.055	.170	.157	.092
8	.164	.309	.287	.120	.107	.054	.045	.077	.058	.178	.165	.101
9	.177	.334	.311	.128	.115	.054	.045	.082	.062	.186	.173	.110
10	.190	.359	.334	.137	.123	.060	.050	.087	.065	.195	.182	.119
12	.216	.408	.382	.153	.139	.067	.056	.096	.073	.249	.236	.125
14	.242	.457	.429	.170	.155	.075	.064	.106	.080	.265	.252	.142
1/4	.249	.472	.443	.175	.160	.075	.064	.109	.082	.268	.255	.147
16	.268	.506	.476	.187	.171	.075	.064	.115	.087	.281	.268	.159
18	.294	.555	.523	.204	.187	.084	.072	.125	.094	.339	.326	.176
5/16	.312	.590	.557	.216	.198	.084	.072	.132	.099	.308	.295	.187
3/8	.375	.708	.670	.256	.237	.094	.081	.155	.117	.387	.374	.228
7/16	.437	.750	.707	.328	.307	.094	.081	.196	.148	.402	.389	.241
1/2	.500	.813	.766	.355	.332	.106	.091	.211	.159	.416	.403	.256

Thread diameters for Tapping Screws are only approximate. Phillips Recessed Head dimensions shown in bold type apply to Wood Screws.

Pan Head

Machine Screws
Wood Screws
Tapping Screws

Nominal Size	Thread Diameter Maximum	A-Head Diameter		E-Height of Slotted Head		J-Width of Slot		T-Depth of Slot		R-Height of Recessed Head		D-Diameter of Recess		C-Depth of Recess
		Max.	Min.	Max.	Min.	Max.	Min.	Max.	Min.	Max.	Min.	Max.	Min.	Max.
2	.086	.167	.155	.053	.045	.031	.023	.031	.022	.062	.053	.104	.091	.059
3	.099	.193	.180	.060	.051	.035	.027	.036	.026	.071	.062	.112	.099	.068
4	.112	.219	.205	.068	.058	.039	.031	.040	.030	.080	.070	.122	.109	.078
5	.125	.245	.231	.075	.065	.043	.035	.045	.034	.089	.079	.158	.145	.083
6	.138	.270	.256	.082	.072	.048	.039	.050	.037	.097	.087	.166	.153	.091
8	.164	.322	.306	.096	.085	.054	.045	.058	.045	.115	.105	.182	.169	.108
10	.190	.373	.357	.110	.099	.060	.050	.068	.053	.133	.122	.199	.186	.124
12	.216	.425	.407	.125	.112	.067	.056	.077	.061	.151	.139	.259	.246	.141
1/4	.250	.492	.473	.144	.130	.075	.064	.087	.070	.175	.162	.281	.268	.161
5/16	.312	.615	.594	.178	.162	.084	.072	.106	.085	.218	.203	.350	.337	.193
3/8	.375	.740	.716	.212	.195	.094	.081	.124	.100	.261	.244	.393	.380	.233

Thread diameters for Tapping Screws are only approximate.

Fillister Head

Machine Screws
Wood Screws
Tapping Screws

Nominal Size	Thread Diameter Maximum	A-Head Diameter		H-Height of Head		J-Width of Slot		T-Depth of Slot		E-Total Height of Head		D-Diameter of Recess		C-Depth of Recess
		Max.	Min.	Max.	Min.	Max.	Min.	Max.	Min.	Max.	Min.	Max.	Min.	Max.
2	.086	.140	.124	.062	.053	.031	.023	.037	.025	.083	.066	.104	.091	.059
3	.099	.161	.145	.070	.061	.035	.027	.043	.030	.095	.077	.112	.099	.068
4	.112	.183	.166	.079	.069	.039	.031	.048	.035	.107	.088	.122	.109	.078
5	.125	.205	.187	.088	.078	.043	.035	.054	.040	.120	.100	.148	.135	.067
6	.138	.226	.208	.096	.086	.048	.039	.060	.045	.132	.111	.166	.153	.091
8	.164	.270	.250	.113	.102	.054	.045	.071	.054	.156	.133	.182	.169	.108
10	.190	.313	.292	.130	.118	.060	.050	.083	.064	.180	.156	.199	.186	.124
12	.216	.357	.334	.148	.134	.067	.056	.094	.074	.205	.178	.259	.246	.141
1/4	.250	.414	.389	.170	.155	.075	.064	.109	.087	.237	.207	.281	.268	.161
5/16	.312	.518	.490	.211	.194	.084	.072	.137	.110	.295	.262	.322	.309	.235
3/8	.375	.622	.590	.253	.233	.094	.081	.164	.133	.355	.315	.393	.380	.233
7/16	.436	.625	.589	.265	.242	.094	.081	.170	.135	.368	.321	.413	.400	.259
1/2	.499	.750	.710	.297	.273	.106	.091	.190	.151	.412	.362	.435	.422	.280

TABLE A-8. Dimensions of nuts.

A. S. Regular Hexagon Nuts

Nominal Size or Basic Major Diameter of Thread		F-Width Across Flats			G-Width Across Corners		H-Thickness (Full Nuts)			h-Thickness (Jam Nuts)		
		Max.	(Basic)	Min.	Max.	Min.	Nom.	Max.	Min.	Nom.	Max.	Min.
1/4	.2500	7/16	.4375	.425	.505	.485	13/64	.219	.187	9/64	.157	.125
5/16	.3125	9/16	.5625	.547	.650	.624	1/4	.267	.233	11/64	.189	.155
3/8	.3750	5/8	.6250	.606	.722	.691	5/16	.330	.294	13/64	.221	.185
7/16	.4375	3/4	.7500	.728	.866	.830	23/64	.378	.340	15/64	.253	.215
1/2	.5000	13/16	.8125	.788	.938	.898	27/64	.442	.402	19/64	.317	.277
9/16	.5625	7/8	.8750	.847	1.010	.966	31/64	.505	.463	21/64	.349	.307
5/8	.6250	1	1.0000	.969	1.155	1.104	17/32	.553	.509	23/64	.381	.337
*3/4	.7500	1-1/8	1.1250	1.088	1.299	1.240	41/64	.665	.617	27/64	.446	.398
*7/8	.8750	1-5/16	1.3125	1.269	1.516	1.447	3/4	.776	.724	31/64	.510	.458
*1	1.000	1-1/2	1.5000	1.450	1.732	1.653	55/64	.887	.831	35/64	.575	.519
*1-1/8	1.125	1-11/16	1.6875	1.631	1.949	1.859	31/32	.999	.939	39/64	.639	.579
*1-1/4	1.250	1-7/8	1.8750	1.812	2.165	2.066	1-1/16	1.094	1.030	23/32	.751	.687
*1-3/8	1.375	2-1/16	2.0625	1.994	2.382	2.273	1-11/64	1.206	1.138	25/32	.815	.747
*1-1/2	1.500	2-1/4	2.2500	2.175	2.598	2.480	1-9/32	1.317	1.245	27/32	.880	.808
*1-5/8	1.625	2-7/16	2.4375	2.356	2.815	2.686	1-25/64	1.429	1.353	29/32	.944	.868
*1-3/4	1.750	2-5/8	2.6250	2.538	3.031	2.893	1-1/2	1.540	1.460	31/32	1.009	.929
*1-7/8	1.875	2-13/16	2.8125	2.719	3.248	3.100	1-39/64	1.651	1.567	1-1/32	1.073	.989
*2	2.000	3	3.0000	2.900	3.464	3.306	1-23/32	1.763	1.675	1-3/32	1.138	1.050

*These sizes also conform to the new "Finished" Nut Standards.

Finished Hexagon Nuts

Nominal Size or Basic Major Diameter of Thread		F-Width Across Flats			G-Width Across Corners		H-Thickness (Full Nuts)			h-Thickness (Jam Nuts)		
		Max.	(Basic)	Min.	Max.	Min.	Nom.	Max.	Min.	Nom.	Max.	Min.
*1/4	.2500	7/16	.4375	.428	.505	.488	7/32	.226	.212	5/32	.163	.150
*5/16	.3125	1/2	.5000	.489	.577	.557	17/64	.273	.258	3/16	.195	.180
*3/8	.3750	9/16	.5625	.551	.650	.628	21/64	.337	.320	7/32	.227	.210
7/16	.4375	11/16	.6875	.675	.794	.768	3/8	.385	.365	1/4	.260	.240
*1/2	.5000	3/4	.7500	.736	.866	.840	7/16	.448	.427	5/16	.323	.302
*9/16	.5625	7/8	.8750	.861	1.010	.982	31/64	.496	.473	5/16	.324	.301
*5/8	.6250	15/16	.9375	.922	1.083	1.051	35/64	.559	.535	3/8	.387	.363
3/4	.7500	1-1/8	1.1250	1.088	1.299	1.240	41/64	.665	.617	27/64	.446	.398
7/8	.8750	1-5/16	1.3125	1.269	1.516	1.447	3/4	.776	.724	31/64	.510	.458
1	1.0000	1-1/2	1.5000	1.450	1.732	1.653	55/64	.887	.831	35/64	.575	.519
1-1/8	1.1250	1-11/16	1.6875	1.631	1.949	1.859	31/32	.999	.939	39/64	.639	.579
1-1/4	1.2500	1-7/8	1.8750	1.812	2.165	2.066	1-1/16	1.094	1.030	23/32	.751	.687
1-3/8	1.3750	2-1/16	2.0625	1.994	2.382	2.273	1-11/64	1.206	1.138	25/32	.815	.747
1-1/2	1.5000	2-1/4	2.2500	2.175	2.598	2.480	1-9/32	1.317	1.245	27/32	.880	.808

*These sizes also conform to old "A.S. Light" dimensions.

Finished Hexagon Castellated (Castle) Nuts

Nominal Size or Basic Major Diameter of Thread		F-Width Across Flats			G-Width Across Corners		H-Thickness			Nominal Height of Flats	Slot		Radius of Fillet (±010)	Dia. of Cylindrical Part
		Max.	(Basic)	Min.	Max.	Min.	Nom.	Max.	Min.		S-Width	T-Depth		
1/4	.2500	7/16	.4375	.428	.505	.488	9/32	.288	.274	3/16	.078	.094	3/32	.371
5/16	.3125	1/2	.5000	.489	.577	.557	21/64	.336	.320	15/64	.094	.094	3/32	.425
3/8	.3750	9/16	.5625	.551	.650	.628	13/32	.415	.398	9/32	.125	.125	3/32	.478
7/16	.4375	11/16	.6875	.675	.794	.768	29/64	.463	.444	19/64	.125	.156	3/32	.582
1/2	.5000	3/4	.7500	.736	.866	.840	9/16	.573	.552	13/32	.156	.156	1/8	.637
9/16	.5625	7/8	.8750	.861	1.010	.982	39/64	.621	.598	27/64	.156	.188	5/32	.744
5/8	.6250	15/16	.9375	.922	1.083	1.051	23/32	.731	.706	1/2	.188	.219	5/32	.797
3/4	.7500	1-1/8	1.1250	1.088	1.299	1.240	13/16	.827	.798	9/16	.188	.250	3/16	.941
7/8	.8750	1-5/16	1.3125	1.269	1.516	1.447	29/32	.922	.890	21/32	.188	.250	3/16	1.097
1	1.0000	1-1/2	1.5000	1.450	1.732	1.653	1	1.018	.982	23/32	.250	.281	3/16	1.254
1-1/8	1.1250	1-11/16	1.6875	1.631	1.949	1.859	1-5/32	1.176	1.136	13/16	.250	.344	1/4	1.411
1-1/4	1.2500	1-7/8	1.8750	1.812	2.165	2.066	1-1/4	1.272	1.228	7/8	.312	.375	1/4	1.570
1-3/8	1.3750	2-1/16	2.0625	1.994	2.382	2.273	1-3/8	1.399	1.351	1	.312	.375	1/4	1.726
1-1/2	1.5000	2-1/4	2.2500	2.175	2.598	2.480	1-1/2	1.526	1.474	1-1/16	.375	.438	1/4	1.881

TABLE A-8.   cont.

Hexagon and Square Machine Screw and Stove Bolts Nuts

Nominal Size or Basic Major Diameter of Thread		F-Width Across Flats			G-Width Across Corners				H-Thickness		
					Square		Hex.				
		Max.	(Basic)	Min.	Max.	Min.	Max.	Min.	Nom.	Max.	Min.
0	.0600	5/32	.1562	.150	.221	.206	.180	.171	3/64	.050	.043
1	.0730	5/32	.1562	.150	.221	.206	.180	.171	3/64	.050	.043
2	.0860	3/16	.1875	.180	.265	.247	.217	.205	1/16	.066	.057
3	.0990	3/16	.1875	.180	.265	.247	.217	.205	1/16	.066	.057
4	.1120	1/4	.2500	.241	.354	.331	.289	.275	3/32	.098	.087
5	.1250	5/16	.3125	.302	.442	.415	.361	.344	7/64	.114	.102
6	.1380	5/16	.3125	.302	.442	.415	.361	.344	7/64	.114	.102
8	.1640	11/32	.3438	.332	.486	.456	.397	.378	1/8	.130	.117
10	.1900	3/8	.3750	.362	.530	.497	.433	.413	1/8	.130	.117
12	.2160	7/16	.4375	.423	.619	.581	.505	.482	5/32	.161	.148
1/4	.2500	7/16	.4375	.423	.619	.581	.505	.482	3/16	.193	.178
5/16	.3125	9/16	.5625	.545	.795	.748	.650	.621	7/32	.225	.208
3/8	.3750	5/8	.6250	.607	.884	.833	.722	.692	1/4	.257	.239

Round (Button) Head Small Solid Rivets

D-Diameter of Body				A-Diameter of Head		H-Height of Head		R-Radius of Head	Length Tolerance	
Nominal		Max.	Min.	Max.	Min.	Max.	Min.	Approx.	Plus	Minus
3/32	.094	.096	.090	.182	.162	.077	.065	.084	.016	.016
1/8	.125	.127	.121	.235	.215	.100	.088	.111	.016	.016
5/32	.156	.158	.152	.290	.268	.124	.110	.138	.016	.016
3/16	.188	.191	.182	.348	.322	.147	.133	.166	.016	.016
7/32	.219	.222	.213	.405	.379	.172	.158	.195	.016	.016
1/4	.250	.253	.244	.460	.430	.196	.180	.221	.016	.016
9/32	.281	.285	.273	.518	.484	.220	.202	.249	.016	.016
5/16	.313	.317	.305	.572	.538	.243	.225	.276	.016	.016
11/32	.344	.348	.336	.630	.592	.267	.247	.304	.016	.016
3/8	.375	.380	.365	.684	.646	.291	.271	.332	.016	.016
7/16	.438	.443	.428	.798	.754	.339	.317	.387	.016	.016

Round (Button) Head Large Solid Rivets

D-Diameter of Body				A-Diameter of Head			H-Height of Head		G-Radius of Head
Nominal		Max.	Min.	Basic	Max.	Min.	Max.	Min. Basic	
1/2	0.500	0.520	0.478	0.875	0.938	0.844	0.406	0.375	0.443
5/8	0.625	0.655	0.600	1.094	1.157	1.063	0.500	0.469	0.553
3/4	0.750	0.780	0.725	1.312	1.390	1.281	0.593	0.562	0.664
7/8	0.875	0.905	0.850	1.531	1.609	1.500	0.687	0.656	0.775
1	1.000	1.030	0.975	1.750	1.828	1.719	0.781	0.750	0.885
1-1/8	1.125	1.160	1.098	1.969	1.063	1.938	0.891	0.844	0.996
1-1/4	1.250	1.285	1.223	2.188	2.282	2.157	0.985	0.938	1.107
1-3/8	1.375	1.415	1.345	2.406	2.500	2.375	1.078	1.031	1.217
1-1/2	1.500	1.540	1.470	2.625	2.719	2.594	1.188	1.125	1.328

90° Countersunk Head Small Solid Rivets

D-Diameter of Body				A-Diameter of Head		Length Tolerence	
Nominal		Max.	Min.	Max.	Min.	Plus	Minus
3/32	.094	.096	.090	.176	.171	.016	.016
1/8	.125	.127	.121	.235	.227	.016	.016
5/32	.156	.158	.152	.293	.284	.016	.016
3/16	.188	.191	.182	.351	.340	.016	.016
7/32	.219	.222	.213	.413	.400	.016	.016
1/4	.250	.253	.244	.469	.455	.016	.016
9/32	.281	.285	.273	.528	.511	.016	.016
5/16	.313	.317	.305	.588	.569	.016	.016
11/32	.344	.348	.336	.646	.626	.016	.016
3/8	.375	.380	.365	.704	.682	.016	.016
7/16	.438	.443	.428	.823	.797	.016	.016

TABLE A-8. cont.

78° Countersunk Head Large Solid Rivets

D-Diameter of Body				A-Diameter of Head			H-Height of Head	
Nominal		Max.	Min.	(Basic)	Max.	Min.	Max.	Min. (Basic)
1/2	0.500	0.520	0.478	0.905	0.936	0.874	0.281	0.250
5/8	0.625	0.655	0.600	1.131	1.194	1.068	0.343	0.312
3/4	0.750	0.780	0.725	1.358	1.421	1.295	0.406	0.375
7/8	0.875	0.905	0.850	1.584	1.647	1.521	0.469	0.438
1	1.000	1.030	0.975	1.810	1.873	1.747	0.531	0.500
1-1/8	1.125	1.160	1.098	2.036	2.114	1.973	0.609	0.562
1-1/4	1.250	1.285	1.223	2.262	2.340	2.199	0.672	0.625
1-3/8	1.375	1.415	1.345	2.489	2.567	2.246	0.751	0.688
1-1/2	1.500	1.540	1.470	2.715	2.793	2.652	0.813	0.750

Flat Head Small Solid Rivets

D-Diameter of Body			A-Diameter of Head		H-Height of Head		Length Tolerance	
Nominal		Max.	Min.	Max.	Min.	Max.	Min.	Plus	Minus
3/32	.094	.096	.090	.200	.180	.038	.026	.016	.016
1/8	.125	.127	.121	.260	.240	.048	.036	.016	.016
5/32	.156	.158	.152	.323	.301	.059	.045	.016	.016
3/16	.188	.191	.182	.387	.361	.069	.055	.016	.016
7/32	.219	.222	.213	.453	.427	.080	.067	.016	.016
1/4	.250	.253	.244	.515	.485	.091	.075	.016	.016
9/32	.281	.285	.273	.579	.545	.103	.085	.016	.016
5/16	.313	.317	.305	.641	.607	.113	.095	.016	.016
11/32	.344	.348	.336	.705	.667	.124	.104	.016	.016
3/8	.375	.380	.365	.769	.731	.135	.115	.016	.016
7/16	.438	.443	.428	.896	.852	.157	.135	.016	.016

Tinners Rivets

D-Diameter of Body			A-Diameter of Head		H-Height of Head		Length		
Nominal*	Max.	Min.	Max.	Min.	Max.	Min.	Nom.	Max.	Min.
6 oz.	.081	.075	.213	.193	.028	.016	1/8	.135	.115
8 oz.	.091	.085	.225	.205	.036	.024	5/32	.166	.146
10 oz.	.097	.091	.250	.230	.037	.025	11/64	.182	.162
12 oz.	.107	.101	.265	.245	.037	.025	3/16	.198	.178
14 oz.	.111	.105	.275	.255	.038	.026	3/16	.198	.178
1 lb.	.113	.107	.285	.265	.040	.028	13/64	.213	.193
1-1/4 lb.	.122	.116	.295	.275	.045	.033	7/32	.229	.209
1-1/2 lb.	.132	.126	.316	.294	.046	.034	15/64	.244	.224
1-3/4 lb.	.136	.130	.331	.309	.049	.035	1/4	.260	.240
2 lb.	.146	.140	.341	.319	.050	.036	17/64	.276	.256
2-1/2 lb.	.150	.144	.311	.289	.069	.055	9/32	.291	.271
3 lb.	.163	.154	.329	.303	.073	.059	5/16	.323	.303
3-1/2 lb.	.168	.159	.348	.322	.074	.060	21/64	.338	.318
4 lb.	.179	.170	.368	.342	.076	.062	11/32	.354	.334
5 lb.	.190	.181	.388	.362	.084	.070	3/8	.385	.365
6 lb.	.206	.197	.419	.393	.090	.076	25/64	.401	.381
7 lb.	.223	.214	.431	.405	.094	.080	13/32	.416	.396
8 lb.	.227	.218	.475	.445	.101	.085	7/16	.448	.428
9 lb.	.241	.232	.490	.460	.103	.087	29/64	.463	.443
10 lb.	.241	.232	.505	.475	.104	.088	15/32	.479	.459
12 lb.	.263	.251	.532	.498	.108	.090	1/2	.510	.490
14 lb.	.288	.276	.577	.543	.113	.095	33/64	.525	.505
16 lb.	.304	.292	.597	.563	.128	.110	17/32	.541	.521
18 lb.	.347	.335	.706	.668	.156	.136	19/32	.603	.583

*Size numbers refer to the approximate weight of 1,000 rivets.

TABLE A-9. Wood screw threads.

Size	Threads Per Inch	Major Dia. Max.	Major Dia. Min.	Root Dia. Max.	Root Dia. Min.
2	26	0.090	0.079	0.061	0.036
3	24	0.102	0.092	0.072	0.047
4	22	0.116	0.105	0.083	0.055
5	20	0.129	0.118	0.094	0.064
6	18	0.142	0.131	0.100	0.070
7	16	0.155	0.144	0.108	0.076
8	15	0.168	0.157	0.123	0.089
9	14	0.181	0.170	0.133	0.097
10	13	0.194	0.183	0.142	0.105
12	11	0.220	0.209	0.163	0.121
14	10	0.246	0.235	0.185	0.140
16	9	0.272	0.261	0.210	0.161
18	8	0.298	0.287	0.230	0.176
20	8	0.324	0.313	0.256	0.202
24	7	0.376	0.365	0.284	0.223

TABLE A-10. Wood screw pilot holes.

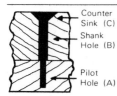

Counter Sink (C)
Shank Hole (B)
Pilot Hole (A)

Pilot Hole

Pilot holes for wood screws are recommended, especially for hard woods. They greatly lessen the possibility of damage to screws and to the wood. The hole in the first piece of wood should be bored large enough to accommodate freely the screw shank. In the second piece of wood the hole should be slightly smaller than the screw shank, as shown in the chart below. The hole depth should be about one-half the length of the screw in the second piece of wood. The length of screw chosen for the job will properly be at least an 1/8" shorter than the combined thickness of the wood.

Screw Size	Pilot Hole (A) Hard Woods Twist Bit (Nearest size in fractions of an inch)	Pilot Hole (A) Hard Woods Drill Gauge No. To be used for maximum holding power	Pilot Hole (A) Soft Woods Twist Bit (Nearest size in fractions of an inch)	Pilot Hole (A) Soft Woods Drill Gauge No. To be used for maximum holding power	Shank Clearance Holes (B) Twist Bit (Nearest size in fractions of an inch)	Shank Clearance Holes (B) Drill Gauge No. or Letter To be used for maximum holding power	Counter-Sink (C) Number of Auger Bit To counterbore for sinking head (by 16ths)
2	—	54	1/32	65	3/32	42	3
3	1/16	53	3/64	58	7/64	37	4
4	1/16	51	3/64	55	7/64	32	4
5	5/64	47	1/16	53	1/8	30	4
6	—	44	1/16	52	9/64	27	5
7	—	39	1/16	51	5/32	22	5
8	7/64	35	5/64	48	11/64	18	6
9	7/64	33	5/64	45	3/16	14	6
10	1/8	31	3/32	43	3/16	10	6
11	—	29	3/32	40	13/64	4	7
12	—	25	7/64	38	7/32	2	7
14	3/16	14	7/64	32	1/4	D	8
16	—	10	9/64	29	17/64	I	9
18	13/64	6	9/64	26	19/64	N	10
20	7/32	3	11/64	19	21/64	P	11
24	1/4	D	3/16	15	3/8	V	12

* Sizes for holes recommended for average application. Slightly larger or smaller holes may be required.

Holding Power of Lag Screws

Figure A–4 has been prepared to calculate a safe value that a lag screw can be expected to hold when used in the side grain of seasoned wood. It is assumed that the wood has been properly prepared to minimize splitting by drilling a pilot hole 40 to 70 percent of the bolt diameter for soft woods (roughly the top third of the nomogram's left-hand scale), 60 to 75 percent for medium woods, and 65 to 85 percent for hard woods. Pilot holes for very long bolts should be near the top of the range given here.

FIGURE A-4

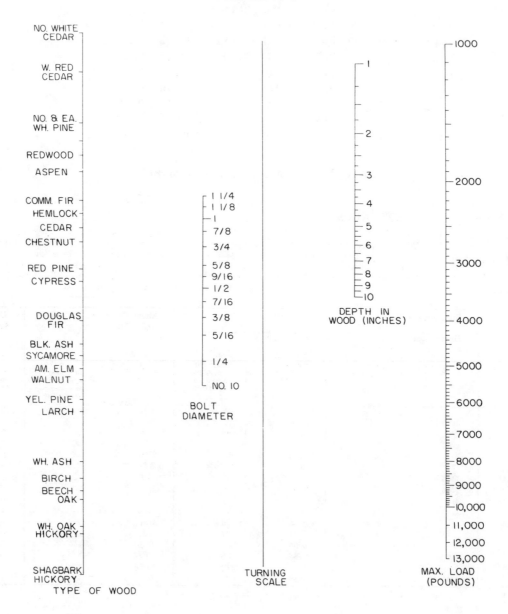

Example

A ledger board is to support 4800 pounds, evenly distributed, through four lag screws in 2 × 4's of douglas fir. What diameter screws should be used?

Since screw diameter is to be solved for, start on the right-hand scale. Locate 1200 (one-fourth of 4800) on the MAX. LOAD scale. Next, assume each bolt is to take full advantage of the amount of structural wood available in the 2 × 4's and therefore the DEPTH IN WOOD scale will be crossed at 3 1/2 inches. Draw a line through those two points and, from where that line crossed the TURNING SCALE, draw a line to DOUGLAS FIR on the TYPE OF WOOD scale. This second line will cross the BOLT DIAMETER scale between 3/8 and 7/16, showing that 7/16 inch diameter lag screws should be used.

TABLE A-11.   Lag screw details.

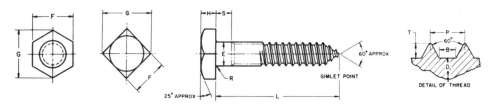

Hex Head for 6-in. lengths and shorter   **Square Head for lengths longer than 6 in.**

Note: When threads are roll formed (usual practice on smaller sizes) the un-threaded shank will be under size (see broken lines). A full size neck is furnished on screws of this type.

Square lag screw dimensions (in.)

Nominal Size or Basic Product Diam		Body or Shoulder Diam E		Width Across Flats F			Width Across Corners G		Height H			Shoulder Length S	Radius of Fillet R	Threads per Inch	Thread Dimensions			
		Max	Min	Basic	Max	Min	Max	Min	Basic	Max	Min	Min	Max		Pitch P	Flat at Root B	Depth of Thread T	Root Dia D₁
¼	0.2500	0.260	0.237	⅜	0.3750	0.362	0.530	0.498	¹¹⁄₆₄	0.188	0.156	0.094	0.031	10	0.100	0.043	0.039	0.173
⁵⁄₁₆	0.3125	0.324	0.298	½	0.5000	0.484	0.707	0.665	¹³⁄₆₄	0.220	0.186	0.125	0.031	9	0.111	0.048	0.043	0.227
⅜	0.3750	0.388	0.360	⁹⁄₁₆	0.5625	0.544	0.795	0.747	¼	0.268	0.232	0.125	0.031	7	0.143	0.062	0.055	0.265
⁷⁄₁₆	0.4375	0.452	0.421	⅝	0.6250	0.603	0.884	0.828	¹⁹⁄₆₄	0.316	0.278	0.156	0.031	7	0.143	0.062	0.055	0.328
½	0.5000	0.515	0.482	¾	0.7500	0.725	1.061	0.995	²¹⁄₆₄	0.348	0.308	0.156	0.031	6	0.167	0.072	0.064	0.371
⅝	0.6250	0.642	0.605	¹⁵⁄₁₆	0.9375	0.906	1.326	1.244	²⁷⁄₆₄	0.444	0.400	0.312	0.062	5	0.200	0.086	0.077	0.471
¾	0.7500	0.768	0.729	1⅛	1.1250	1.088	1.591	1.494	½	0.524	0.476	0.375	0.062	4½	0.222	0.096	0.085	0.579
⅞	0.8750	0.895	0.852	1⁵⁄₁₆	1.3125	1.269	1.856	1.742	¹⁹⁄₃₂	0.620	0.568	0.375	0.062	4	0.250	0.108	0.096	0.683
1	1.0000	1.022	0.976	1½	1.5000	1.450	2.121	1.991	²¹⁄₃₂	0.684	0.628	0.625	0.093	3½	0.286	0.123	0.110	0.780

Hex lag screw head dimensions (in.) (Note: Hex lag screws are identical in all respects to square lag screws except for head dimensions which are shown below.)

Nominal Size or Basic Product Diam		Width Across Flats F			Width Across Corners G		Height H		
		Basic	Max	Min	Max	Min	Basic	Max	Min
¼	0.2500	⁷⁄₁₆	0.4375	0.425	0.505	0.484	¹¹⁄₆₄	0.188	0.150
⁵⁄₁₆	0.3125	½	0.5000	0.484	0.577	0.552	⁷⁄₃₂	0.235	0.195
⅜	0.3750	⁹⁄₁₆	0.5625	0.544	0.650	0.620	¼	0.268	0.226
⁷⁄₁₆	0.4375	⅝	0.6250	0.603	0.722	0.687	¹⁹⁄₆₄	0.316	0.272
½	0.5000	¾	0.7500	0.725	0.866	0.826	¹¹⁄₃₂	0.364	0.302
⅝	0.6250	¹⁵⁄₁₆	0.9375	0.906	1.083	1.033	²⁷⁄₆₄	0.444	0.378

TABLE A-12. Construction bolts.

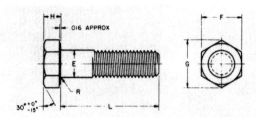

Dimensional data for all grades of hex cap screws are shown below.

Hex cap screw dimensions (in.)

Nominal Size or Basic Product Diam		Body Diam E		Width Across Flats F			Width Across Corners G		Height H			Radius of Fillet R	
		Max	Min	Basic	Max	Min	Max	Min	Basic	Max	Min	Max	Min
¼	0.2500	0.2500	0.2450	⁷⁄₁₆	0.4375	0.428	0.505	0.488	⁵⁄₃₂	0.163	0.150	0.025	0.015
⁵⁄₁₆	0.3125	0.3125	0.3065	½	0.5000	0.489	0.577	0.557	¹³⁄₆₄	0.211	0.195	0.025	0.015
⅜	0.3750	0.3750	0.3690	⁹⁄₁₆	0.5625	0.551	0.650	0.628	¹⁵⁄₆₄	0.243	0.226	0.025	0.015
⁷⁄₁₆	0.4375	0.4375	0.4305	⅝	0.6250	0.612	0.722	0.698	⁹⁄₃₂	0.291	0.272	0.025	0.015
½	0.5000	0.5000	0.4930	¾	0.7500	0.736	0.866	0.840	⁵⁄₁₆	0.323	0.302	0.025	0.015
⁹⁄₁₆	0.5625	0.5625	0.5545	¹³⁄₁₆	0.8125	0.798	0.938	0.910	²³⁄₆₄	0.371	0.348	0.045	0.020
⅝	0.6250	0.6250	0.6170	¹⁵⁄₁₆	0.9375	0.922	1.083	1.051	²⁵⁄₆₄	0.403	0.378	0.045	0.020
¾	0.7500	0.7500	0.7410	1⅛	1.1250	1.100	1.299	1.254	¹⁵⁄₃₂	0.483	0.455	0.045	0.020
⅞	0.8750	0.8750	0.8660	1⁵⁄₁₆	1.3125	1.285	1.516	1.465	³⁵⁄₆₄	0.563	0.531	0.065	0.040
1	1.0000	1.0000	0.9900	1½	1.5000	1.469	1.732	1.675	³⁹⁄₆₄	0.627	0.591	0.095	0.060
1⅛	1.1250	1.1250	1.1140	1¹¹⁄₁₆	1.6875	1.631	1.949	1.859	¹¹⁄₁₆	0.718	0.658	0.095	0.060
1¼	1.2500	1.2500	1.2390	1⅞	1.8750	1.812	2.165	2.066	²⁵⁄₃₂	0.813	0.749	0.095	0.060
1⅜	1.3750	1.3750	1.3630	2¹⁄₁₆	2.0625	1.994	2.382	2.273	²⁷⁄₃₂	0.878	0.810	0.095	0.060
1½	1.5000	1.5000	1.4880	2¼	2.2500	2.175	2.598	2.480	¹⁵⁄₁₆	0.974	0.902	0.095	0.060

Suggested assembly torques for hex cap screws

Cap Screw Diam	Grade 2				Grade 5				Grade 8		
	Minimum Yield Strength	Torque (ft-lb)			Minimum Yield Strength	Torque (ft-lb)			Minimum Yield Strength	Torque (ft-lb)	
		UNRC	UNRF			UNRC	UNRF			UNRC	UNRF
¼	57,000	6	7		92,000	10	11		130,000	14	15
⁵⁄₁₆	57,000	12	14		92,000	20	22		130,000	28	31
⅜	57,000	22	25		92,000	36	40		130,000	50	60
⁷⁄₁₆	57,000	35	39		92,000	57	64		130,000	80	90
½	57,000	54	61		92,000	90	100		130,000	125	140
⁹⁄₁₆	57,000	77	87		92,000	125	140		130,000	180	200
⅝	57,000	107	122		92,000	175	200		130,000	240	280
¾	57,000	190	212		92,000	310	340		130,000	430	480
⅞	36,000	193	216		92,000	500	550		130,000	700	770
1	36,000	290	320		92,000	740	810		130,000	1050	1150
1⅛	36,000	410	470		81,000	930	1040		—	—	—
1¼	36,000	580	645		81,000	1300	1440		—	—	—
1⅜	36,000	760	870		81,000	1700	1900		—	—	—
1½	36,000	1010	1115		81,000	2270	2550		—	—	—

TABLE A-12. cont.

Hex bolt dimensions (in.)

Nominal Size or Basic Product Diam		Body Diam E	Width Across Flats F			Width Across Corners G		Height H			Radius of Fillet R
		Max	Basic	Max	Min	Max	Min	Basic	Max	Min	Max
¼	0.2500	0.260	7/16	0.4375	0.425	0.505	0.484	11/64	0.188	0.150	0.031
5/16	0.3125	0.324	½	0.5000	0.484	0.577	0.552	7/32	0.235	0.195	0.031
⅜	0.3750	0.388	9/16	0.5625	0.544	0.650	0.620	¼	0.268	0.226	0.031
7/16	0.4375	0.452	⅝	0.6250	0.603	0.722	0.687	19/64	0.316	0.272	0.031
½	0.5000	0.515	¾	0.7500	0.725	0.866	0.826	11/32	0.364	0.302	0.031
⅝	0.6250	0.642	15/16	0.9375	0.906	1.083	1.033	27/64	0.444	0.378	0.062
¾	0.7500	0.768	1⅛	1.1250	1.088	1.299	1.240	½	0.524	0.455	0.062
⅞	0.8750	0.895	1 5/16	1.3125	1.269	1.516	1.447	37/64	0.604	0.531	0.062
1	1.0000	1.022	1½	1.5000	1.450	1.732	1.653	43/64	0.700	0.591	0.093
1⅛	1.1250	1.149	1 11/16	1.6875	1.631	1.949	1.859	¾	0.780	0.658	0.093
1¼	1.2500	1.277	1⅞	1.8750	1.812	2.165	2.066	27/32	0.876	0.749	0.093
1⅜	1.3750	1.404	2 1/16	2.0625	1.994	2.382	2.273	29/32	0.940	0.810	0.093
1½	1.5000	1.531	2¼	2.2500	2.175	2.598	2.480	1	1.036	0.902	0.093
1¾	1.7500	1.785	2⅝	2.6250	2.538	3.031	2.893	1 5/32	1.196	1.054	0.125
2	2.0000	2.039	3	3.0000	2.900	3.464	3.306	1 11/32	1.388	1.175	0.125

Heavy hex bolt dimensions (in.)

Nominal Size or Basic Product Diam		Body Diam E	Width Across Flats F			Width Across Corners G		Height H			Radius of Fillet R
		Max	Basic	Max	Min	Max	Min	Basic	Max	Min	Max
½	0.5000	0.515	⅞	0.8750	0.850	1.010	0.969	11/32	0.364	0.302	0.031
⅝	0.6250	0.642	1 1/16	1.0625	1.031	1.227	1.175	27/64	0.444	0.378	0.062
¾	0.7500	0.768	1¼	1.2500	1.212	1.443	1.383	½	0.524	0.455	0.062
⅞	0.8750	0.895	1 7/16	1.4375	1.394	1.660	1.589	37/64	0.604	0.531	0.062
1	1.0000	1.022	1⅝	1.6250	1.575	1.876	1.796	43/64	0.700	0.591	0.093
1⅛	1.1250	1.149	1 13/16	1.8125	1.756	2.093	2.002	¾	0.780	0.658	0.093
1¼	1.2500	1.277	2	2.0000	1.938	2.309	2.209	27/32	0.876	0.749	0.093
1⅜	1.3750	1.404	2 3/16	2.1875	2.119	2.526	2.416	29/32	0.940	0.810	0.093
1½	1.5000	1.531	2⅜	2.3750	2.300	2.742	2.622	1	1.036	0.902	0.093

TABLE A-12. cont.

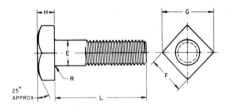

Square Bolt

Nominal Size or Basic Product Diam		Body Diam E	Width Across Flats F			Width Across Corners G		Height H			Radius of Fillet R
		Max	Basic	Max	Min	Max	Min	Basic	Max	Min	Max
¼	0.2500	0.260	⅜	0.3750	0.362	0.530	0.498	11/64	0.188	0.156	0.031
5/16	0.3125	0.324	½	0.5000	0.484	0.707	0.665	13/64	0.220	0.186	0.031
⅜	0.3750	0.388	9/16	0.5625	0.544	0.795	0.747	¼	0.268	0.232	0.031
7/16	0.4375	0.452	⅝	0.6250	0.603	0.884	0.828	19/64	0.316	0.278	0.031
½	0.5000	0.515	¾	0.7500	0.725	1.061	0.995	21/64	0.348	0.308	0.031
⅝	0.6250	0.642	15/16	0.9375	0.906	1.326	1.244	27/64	0.444	0.400	0.062
¾	0.7500	0.768	1⅛	1.1250	1.088	1.591	1.494	½	0.524	0.476	0.062
⅞	0.8750	0.895	1 5/16	1.3125	1.269	1.856	1.742	19/32	0.620	0.568	0.062
1	1.0000	1.022	1½	1.5000	1.450	2.121	1.991	21/32	0.684	0.628	0.093
1⅛	1.1250	1.149	1 11/16	1.6875	1.631	2.386	2.239	¾	0.780	0.720	0.093
1¼	1.2500	1.277	1⅞	1.8750	1.812	2.652	2.489	27/32	0.876	0.812	0.093
1⅜	1.3750	1.404	2 1/16	2.0625	1.994	2.917	2.738	29/32	0.940	0.872	0.093
1½	1.5000	1.531	2¼	2.2500	2.175	3.182	2.986	1	1.036	0.964	0.093
1¾	1.7500	1.785	2⅝	2.6250	2.538	3.712	3.485	1 5/32	1.196	1.116	0.125
2	2.0000	2.039	3	3.0000	2.900	4.243	3.982	1 11/32	1.388	1.300	0.125

TABLE A-13. Structural rib bolts.

THICKNESS OF THE WORK (GRIP), in.	3/8 (hole 7/16) Bolt Length L, in.	Wt, lb	1/2 (hole 9/16) Bolt Length L, in.	Wt, lb	5/8 (hole 11/16) Bolt Length L, in.	Wt, lb	3/4 (hole 13/16) Bolt Length L, in.	Wt, lb	7/8 (hole 15/16) Bolt Length L, in.	Wt, lb	1 (hole 1 1/16) Bolt Length L, in.	Wt, lb
5/16 to 3/8	15/16	8.0	1 3/16	17.0	1 5/16	31	1 1/2	50	1 5/8	78	1 7/8	114
7/16 to 1/2	1 1/16	8.5	1 5/16	17.5	1 7/16	32	1 5/8	52	1 3/4	80	2	120
9/16 to 5/8	1 3/16	9.0	1 7/16	18.5	1 9/16	33	1 3/4	53	1 7/8	82	2 1/4	122
11/16 to 3/4	1 5/16	9.5	1 9/16	19.5	1 11/16	34	1 7/8	55	2	84	2 3/8	123
13/16 to 7/8	1 7/16	10.0	1 11/16	20.0	1 13/16	35	2	57	2 1/8	86	2 1/2	125
15/16 to 1	1 9/16	10.5	1 13/16	21.0	1 15/16	38	2 1/8	58	2 1/4	88	2 5/8	128
1 1/16 to 1 1/8	1 11/16	11.0	1 15/16	21.5	2 1/16	39	2 1/4	60	2 3/8	90	2 3/4	130
1 3/16 to 1 1/4	1 13/16	11.5	2 1/16	22.5	2 3/16	41	2 3/8	61	2 1/2	92	2 7/8	133
1 5/16 to 1 3/8			2 3/16	23.0	2 5/16	42	2 1/2	63	2 5/8	94	3	135
1 7/16 to 1 1/2			2 5/16	24.0	2 7/16	43	2 5/8	65	2 3/4	96	3 1/8	138
1 9/16 to 1 5/8					2 9/16	44	2 3/4	67	2 7/8	98	3 1/4	142
1 11/16 to 1 3/4					2 11/16	45	2 7/8	69	3	100	3 3/8	144
1 13/16 to 1 7/8					2 13/16	46	3	71	3 1/8	103	3 1/2	147
1 15/16 to 2					2 15/16	47	3 1/8	73	3 1/4	105	3 5/8	150
2 1/16 to 2 1/8					3 1/16	48	3 1/4	74	3 3/8	107	3 7/8	153
2 3/16 to 2 1/4					3 3/16	49	3 3/8	76	3 1/2	109	4	155
2 5/16 to 2 3/8					3 5/16	51	3 1/2	78	3 5/8	111	4 1/8	158
2 7/16 to 2 1/2					3 7/16	53	3 5/8	79	3 3/4	114	4 1/4	161
2 9/16 to 2 5/8					3 9/16	54	3 3/4	81	3 7/8	116	4 3/8	165
2 11/16 to 2 3/4					3 13/16	55	3 7/8	83	4	118	4 1/2	168
2 13/16 to 2 7/8							4	84	4 1/8	120	4 5/8	171
2 15/16 to 3							4 1/8	85	4 1/4	122	4 7/8	174
3 1/16 to 3 1/8							4 1/4	86	4 3/8	125	5	177
3 3/16 to 3 1/4							4 3/8	88	4 1/2	127	5 1/8	179
3 5/16 to 3 3/8							4 1/2	90	4 5/8	129	5 1/4	181
3 7/16 to 3 1/2							4 5/8	92	4 3/4	131	5 3/8	184
3 9/16 to 3 5/8							4 3/4	94	4 7/8	133	5 1/2	187
3 11/16 to 3 3/4							4 7/8	96	5	135	5 5/8	191
3 13/16 to 3 7/8							5	98	5 1/8	138	5 3/4	194
3 15/16 to 4							5 1/8	101	5 1/4	140		

	3/8	1/2	5/8	3/4	7/8	1
HEAD DIAMETER—A, in.	21/32	29/32	1 9/64	1 3/8	1 19/32	1 53/64
HEAD HEIGHT—H, in.	9/32	3/8	15/32	9/16	21/32	3/4
DIAM ACROSS RIBS—C, in.	29/64	37/64	45/64	53/64	61/64	1 5/64
THREAD LENGTH—T, in.	15/32	23/32	27/32	1 1/32	1 5/32	1 9/32
NUT THICKNESS—N, in.	3/8	1/2	5/8	3/4	7/8	1
NUT WIDTH ACROSS FLATS—A.F., in.	11/16	7/8	1 1/16	1 1/4	1 7/16	1 5/8

Note: Length of rib (R) is approximately 1/32 in. shorter than maximum thickness of work.

TABLE A-14. Interference-body interrupted-rib bolts.

THICKNESS OF THE WORK (GRIP), in.	5/8 (hole 11/16) Bolt Length L, in.	Weight, lb	3/4 (hole 13/16) Bolt Length L, in.	Weight, lb	7/8 (hole 15/16) Bolt Length L, in.	Weight, lb	1 (hole 1 1/16) Bolt Length L, in.	Weight, lb
5/16 to 3/8	1 1/16	28	1 1/4	49	1 3/8	74	1 3/4	107
7/16 to 1/2	1 3/16	30	1 3/8	50	1 3/4	77	1 7/8	110
9/16 to 5/8	1 5/16	31	1 1/2	52	1 7/8	80	2	113
11/16 to 3/4	1 7/16	32	1 5/8	54	2	83	2 1/4	116
13/16 to 7/8	1 9/16	33	1 3/4	55	2 1/8	85	2 3/8	119
15/16 to 1	1 11/16	34	1 7/8	56	2 1/4	87	2 1/2	122
1 1/16 to 1 1/8	1 13/16	36	2	58	2 3/8	89	2 5/8	126
1 3/16 to 1 1/4	2	37	2 1/8	59	2 1/2	92	2 3/4	130
1 5/16 to 1 3/8	2 1/8	38	2 1/4	61	2 5/8	94	2 7/8	133
1 7/16 to 1 1/2	2 1/4	39	2 3/8	63	2 3/4	96	3	135
1 9/16 to 1 5/8	2 3/8	40	2 1/2	65	2 7/8	98	3 1/8	138
1 11/16 to 1 3/4	2 1/2	41	2 5/8	66	3	100	3 1/4	142
1 13/16 to 1 7/8	2 5/8	42	2 3/4	68	3 1/8	103	3 3/8	144
1 15/16 to 2	2 3/4	43	2 7/8	69	3 1/4	105	3 1/2	147
2 1/16 to 2 1/8			3	70	3 3/8	107	3 5/8	150
2 3/16 to 2 1/4			3 1/8	72	3 1/2	109	3 3/4	153
2 5/16 to 2 3/8			3 1/4	74	3 5/8	111	3 7/8	155
2 7/16 to 2 1/2			3 3/8	75	3 3/4	114	4	158
2 9/16 to 2 5/8			3 1/2	77	3 7/8	116	4 1/8	161
2 11/16 to 2 3/4			3 5/8	79	4	118	4 1/4	165
2 13/16 to 2 7/8			3 3/4	82	4 1/8	120	4 3/8	168
2 15/16 to 3			3 7/8	83	4 1/4	122	4 1/2	171
3 1/16 to 3 1/8			4	84	4 3/8	125	4 5/8	174
3 3/16 to 3 1/4			4 1/8	86	4 1/2	127	4 3/4	177
3 5/16 to 3 3/8			4 1/4	88	4 5/8	129	4 7/8	179
3 7/16 to 3 1/2					4 3/4	131	5	181
3 9/16 to 3 5/8					4 7/8	133	5 1/8	184
3 11/16 to 3 3/4					5	135	5 1/4	187
3 13/16 to 3 7/8					5 1/8	138	5 3/8	191
3 15/16 to 4					5 1/4	140	5 1/2	194
4 1/16 to 4 1/8					5 3/8	143	5 5/8	197
4 3/16 to 4 1/4							5 3/4	200
4 5/16 to 4 3/8							5 7/8	203
4 7/16 to 4 1/2							6	206
4 9/16 to 4 5/8							6 1/8	209
4 11/16 to 4 3/4							6 1/4	212
4 13/16 to 4 7/8							6 3/8	215
4 15/16 to 5							6 5/8	218
5 1/16 to 5 5/16								

	5/8	3/4	7/8	1
HEAD DIAMETER—A, in.	1 1/64	1 3/16	1 13/32	1 35/64
HEAD HEIGHT—H, in.	25/64	15/32	35/64	39/64
DIAMETER ACROSS RIBS—C, in.	45/64	53/64	61/64	1 5/64
THREAD LENGTH—T, in.	27/32	1 1/32	1 5/32	1 9/32
NUT THICKNESS—N, in.	5/8	3/4	7/8	1
NUT, ACROSS FLATS—A.F., in.	1 1/16	1 1/4	1 7/16	1 5/8
WASHER O.D., in.	1 1/2	1 3/4	2	2 1/4
WASHER I.D., in.	11/16	13/16	15/16	1 1/16
WASHER THICKNESS (nom.)—W, in.	0.134	0.148	0.165	0.165

Note: Length of rib (R) is approximately 1/32 in. shorter than maximum thickness of work.

TABLE A-15. Construction nuts.

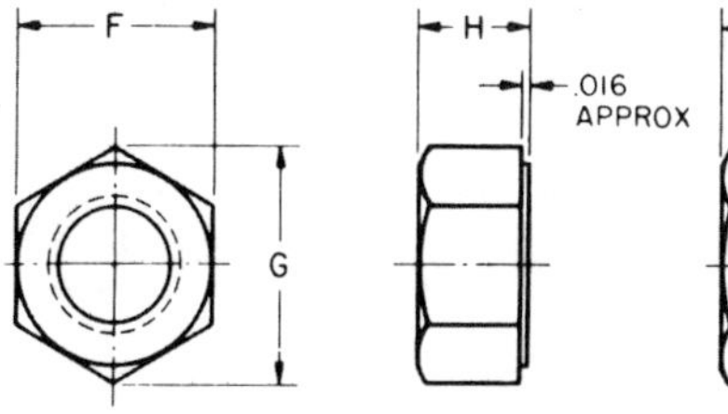

Hex Nuts, washer-faced and double-chamfered

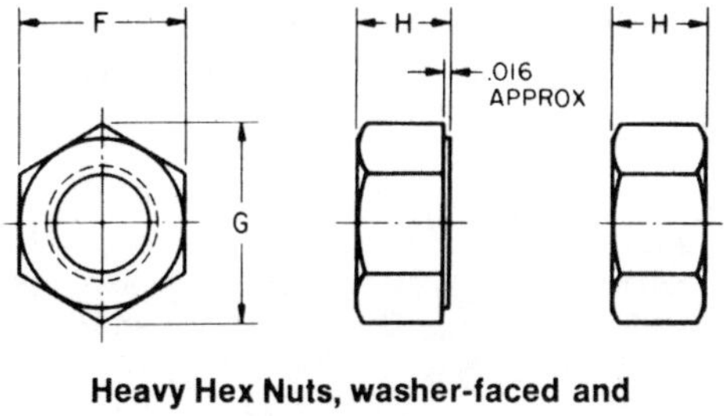

Heavy Hex Nuts, washer-faced and double-chamfered

Hex nut dimensions (in.)

Nominal Size or Basic Major Diam of Thread	Width Across Flats F			Width Across Corners G		Thickness Hex Nuts H		
	Basic	Max	Min	Max	Min	Basic	Max	Min
1/4 0.2500	7/16	0.4375	0.428	0.505	0.488	7/32	0.226	0.212
5/16 0.3125	1/2	0.5000	0.489	0.577	0.557	17/64	0.273	0.258
3/8 0.3750	9/16	0.5625	0.551	0.650	0.628	21/64	0.337	0.320
7/16 0.4375	11/16	0.6875	0.675	0.794	0.768	3/8	0.385	0.365
1/2 0.5000	3/4	0.7500	0.736	0.866	0.840	7/16	0.448	0.427
9/16 0.5625	7/8	0.8750	0.861	1.010	0.982	31/64	0.496	0.473
5/8 0.6250	15/16	0.9375	0.922	1.083	1.051	35/64	0.559	0.535
3/4 0.7500	1 1/8	1.1250	1.088	1.299	1.240	41/64	0.665	0.617
7/8 0.8750	1 5/16	1.3125	1.269	1.516	1.447	3/4	0.776	0.724
1 1.0000	1 1/2	1.5000	1.450	1.732	1.653	55/64	0.887	0.831
1 1/8 1.1250	1 11/16	1.6875	1.631	1.949	1.859	31/32	0.999	0.939
1 1/4 1.2500	1 7/8	1.8750	1.812	2.165	2.066	1 1/16	1.094	1.030
1 3/8 1.3750	2 1/16	2.0625	1.994	2.382	2.273	1 11/64	1.206	1.138
1 1/2 1.5000	2 1/4	2.2500	2.175	2.598	2.480	1 9/32	1.317	1.245
1 3/4 1.7500	2 5/8	2.6250	2.538	3.031	2.893	1 1/2	1.540	1.460
2 2.0000	3	3.0000	2.900	3.464	3.306	1 23/32	1.763	1.675

Heavy hex nut dimensions (in.)

Nominal Size or Basic Major Diam of Thread	Width Across Flats F			Width Across Corners G		Thickness Heavy Hex Nuts H		
	Basic	Max	Min	Max	Min	Basic	Max	Min
1/4 0.2500	1/2	0.5000	0.488	0.577	0.556	15/64	0.250	0.218
5/16 0.3125	9/16	0.5625	0.546	0.650	0.622	19/64	0.314	0.280
3/8 0.3750	11/16	0.6875	0.669	0.794	0.763	23/64	0.377	0.341
7/16 0.4375	3/4	0.7500	0.728	0.866	0.830	27/64	0.441	0.403
1/2 0.5000	7/8	0.8750	0.850	1.010	0.969	31/64	0.504	0.464
9/16 0.5625	15/16	0.9375	0.909	1.083	1.037	35/64	0.568	0.526
5/8 0.6250	1 1/16	1.0625	1.031	1.227	1.175	39/64	0.631	0.587
3/4 0.7500	1 1/4	1.2500	1.212	1.443	1.382	47/64	0.758	0.710
7/8 0.8750	1 7/16	1.4375	1.394	1.660	1.589	55/64	0.885	0.833
1 1.0000	1 5/8	1.6250	1.575	1.876	1.796	63/64	1.012	0.956
1 1/8 1.1250	1 13/16	1.8125	1.756	2.093	2.002	1 7/64	1.139	1.079
1 1/4 1.2500	2	2.0000	1.938	2.309	2.209	1 7/32	1.251	1.187
1 3/8 1.3750	2 3/16	2.1875	2.119	2.526	2.416	1 11/32	1.378	1.310
1 1/2 1.5000	2 3/8	2.3750	2.300	2.742	2.622	1 15/32	1.505	1.433
1 5/8 1.6250	2 9/16	2.5625	2.481	2.959	2.828	1 19/32	1.632	1.556
1 3/4 1.7500	2 3/4	2.7500	2.662	3.175	3.035	1 23/32	1.759	1.679
1 7/8 1.8750	2 15/16	2.9375	2.844	3.392	3.242	1 27/32	1.886	1.802
2 2.0000	3 1/8	3.1250	3.025	3.608	3.449	1 31/32	2.013	1.925
2 1/4 2.2500	3 1/2	3.5000	3.388	4.041	3.862	2 13/64	2.251	2.155
2 1/2 2.5000	3 7/8	3.8750	3.750	4.474	4.275	2 29/64	2.505	2.401
2 3/4 2.7500	4 1/4	4.2500	4.112	4.907	4.688	2 45/64	2.759	2.647
3 3.0000	4 5/8	4.6250	4.475	5.340	5.102	2 61/64	3.013	2.893
3 1/4 3.2500	5	5.0000	4.838	5.774	5.515	3 3/16	3.252	3.124
3 1/2 3.5000	5 3/8	5.3750	5.200	6.207	5.928	3 7/16	3.506	3.370
3 3/4 3.7500	5 3/4	5.7500	5.562	6.640	6.341	3 11/16	3.760	3.616
4 4.0000	6 1/8	6.1250	5.925	7.073	6.755	3 15/16	4.014	3.862

Heavier bolts and nuts, which are generally considered construction fasteners, are detailed in Tables A–12[7], A–13[8], A–14[8], and A–15[7]. Structural rib bolts shown in Table A–13 have, between the head and the threads, a section of longitudinal, triangular–shaped ribs which deform when the bolt is driven into a punched or drilled hole in structural steel. Nut dimensions in Table A–13 are for ANCO self-locking type with which the structural rib bolt is designed to mate.

---

[7]Ibid.

[8]Bethlehem Steel Corporation, "Bethlehem Construction Fasteners (Booklet 2373)," Bethlehem, Pennsylvania.

TABLE A-15. cont.

Square nut dimensions (in.)

Nominal Size or Basic Major Diam of Thread		Width Across Flats F			Width Across Corners G		Thickness H		
		Basic	Max	Min	Max	Min	Basic	Max	Min
¼	0.2500	⁷⁄₁₆	0.4375	0.425	0.619	0.584	⁷⁄₃₂	0.235	0.203
⁵⁄₁₆	0.3125	⁹⁄₁₆	0.5625	0.547	0.795	0.751	¹⁷⁄₆₄	0.283	0.249
⅜	0.3750	⅝	0.6250	0.606	0.884	0.832	²¹⁄₆₄	0.346	0.310
⁷⁄₁₆	0.4375	¾	0.7500	0.728	1.061	1.000	⅜	0.394	0.356
½	0.5000	¹³⁄₁₆	0.8125	0.788	1.149	1.082	⁷⁄₁₆	0.458	0.418
⅝	0.6250	1	1.0000	0.969	1.414	1.330	³⁵⁄₆₄	0.569	0.525
¾	0.7500	1⅛	1.1250	1.088	1.591	1.494	²¹⁄₃₂	0.680	0.632
⅞	0.8750	1⁵⁄₁₆	1.3125	1.269	1.856	1.742	⁴⁹⁄₆₄	0.792	0.740
1	1.0000	1½	1.5000	1.450	2.121	1.991	⅞	0.903	0.847
1⅛	1.1250	1¹¹⁄₁₆	1.6875	1.631	2.386	2.239	1	1.030	0.970
1¼	1.2500	1⅞	1.8750	1.812	2.652	2.489	1³⁄₃₂	1.126	1.062
1⅜	1.3750	2¹⁄₁₆	2.0625	1.994	2.917	2.738	1¹³⁄₆₄	1.237	1.169
1½	1.5000	2¼	2.2500	2.175	3.182	2.986	1⁵⁄₁₆	1.348	1.276
1¾	1.7500	2⅝	2.6250	2.538	3.712	3.485	1¹⁷⁄₃₂	1.571	1.491

Heavy square nut dimensions (in.)

Nominal Size or Basic Major Diam of Thread		Width Across Flats F			Width Across Corners G		Thickness H		
		Basic	Max	Min	Max	Min	Basic	Max	Min
¼	0.2500	½	0.5000	0.488	0.707	0.670	¼	0.266	0.218
⁵⁄₁₆	0.3125	⁹⁄₁₆	0.5625	0.546	0.795	0.750	⁵⁄₁₆	0.330	0.280
⅜	0.3750	¹¹⁄₁₆	0.6875	0.669	0.973	0.919	⅜	0.393	0.341
⁷⁄₁₆	0.4375	¾	0.7500	0.728	1.060	1.000	⁷⁄₁₆	0.456	0.403
½	0.5000	⅞	0.8750	0.850	1.237	1.167	½	0.520	0.464
⅝	0.6250	1¹⁄₁₆	1.0625	1.031	1.503	1.416	⅝	0.647	0.587
¾	0.7500	1¼	1.2500	1.212	1.768	1.665	¾	0.774	0.710
⅞	0.8750	1⁷⁄₁₆	1.4375	1.394	2.033	1.914	⅞	0.901	0.833
1	1.0000	1⅝	1.6250	1.575	2.298	2.162	1	1.028	0.956
1⅛	1.1250	1¹³⁄₁₆	1.8125	1.756	2.563	2.411	1⅛	1.155	1.079
1¼	1.2500	2	2.0000	1.938	2.828	2.661	1¼	1.282	1.187
1⅜	1.3750	2³⁄₁₆	2.1875	2.119	3.094	2.909	1⅜	1.409	1.310
1½	1.5000	2⅜	2.3750	2.300	3.359	3.158	1½	1.536	1.433
1¾	1.7500	2¾	2.7500	2.662	3.889	3.656	1¾	1.790	1.710
2	2.0000	3⅛	3.1250	3.025	4.419	4.153	2	2.044	1.956

Interference-body interrupted-rib bolts shown in Table A–14 have the ribbed section broken into segments each of which tapers for easier driving into a punched or drilled hole.

Weights[9] for some representative fastening devices are given in Table A–16. Multipliers are included on the first page of this table so that corrections can be made for the type of material used.

[9]H. M. Harper Company, "Fastener Styles." Op. Cit.

TABLE A-16.   Weights of various fastening devices.

MATERIAL	MULTIPLIER				
18-8 Stainless Steel	1.00	Carpenter No. 20	1.01	Monel	1.12
T-309 Stainless Steel	1.01	Hastelloy "C"	1.13	Nickel	1.13
T-316 Stainless Steel	1.01	Brass	1.08	Aluminum	.35
T-410 Stainless Steel	.98	Naval Bronze	1.06	Titanium	.68
T-416 Stainless Steel	.98	Silicon Bronze	1.11	Nylon	.14
T-430 Stainless Steel	.97	Copper	1.14		

Screws, Bolts, Nuts and Washers

Headless Slotted Set Screws

LENGTH	DIAMETER					
Inches	6-32	8-32	10-24	1/4-20	5/16-18	3/8-16
3/16	.06	.08	.11	.11		
1/4	.07	.11	.15	.26		
5/16	.09	.14	.18	.33	.51	
3/8	.11	.17	.21	.39	.63	.92
1/2	.15	.22	.29	.52	.84	1.23
3/4				.77	1.26	1.84
1				1.01	1.68	2.46

Square Head Set Screws

LENGTH	DIAMETER					
Inches	1/4-20	5/16-18	3/8-16	1/2-13	5/8-11	3/4-10
1/4	.59					
5/16	.65					
3/8	.72	1.27				
1/2	.85	1.47	2.32			
5/8	.97	1.68	2.60			
3/4	1.10	1.89	2.88	5.94		
1	1.36	2.31	3.54	7.06	12.15	
1-1/4	1.62	2.72	4.16	8.17	13.91	
1-1/2			4.77	9.29	15.69	24.36
1-3/4			5.38	10.40	17.45	26.92
2			6.00	11.52	19.22	29.55
2-1/2					22.77	34.74
3					26.20	39.91

Round Head Machine Screws

LENGTH	DIAMETER										
Inches	2-56	3-48	4-40	6-32	8-32	10-24	12-24	1/4-20	5/16-18	3/8-16	1/2-13
1/8	.04	.06	.07	.13							
3/16	.05	.07	.09	.15	.24						
1/4	.06	.07	.10	.17	.27	.39	.55	.81			
5/16	.06	.08	.11	.18	.29	.41	.58	.84			
3/8	.07	.09	.12	.20	.32	.44	.62	.90	1.64		
7/16	.07	.10	.14	.21	.34	.47	.67	.97	1.74		
1/2	.08	.11	.15	.23	.37	.51	.72	1.03	1.84	2.95	
5/8	.09	.13	.18	.27	.43	.59	.82	1.16	2.06	3.26	
3/4	.11	.15	.20	.31	.48	.66	.92	1.29	2.26	3.56	
7/8			.22	.34	.54	.73	1.01	1.42	2.47	3.87	
1			.26	.38	.60	.80	1.10	1.55	2.69	4.18	7.59
1-1/8			.29	.44	.67	.89	1.19	1.67			
1-1/4			.31	.46	.70	.93	1.28	1.79	3.05	4.72	8.57
1-1/2				.53	.81	1.07	1.48	2.04	3.47	5.34	9.68
1-3/4				.60	.92	1.22	1.68	2.30	3.89	5.95	10.8
2				.68	1.03	1.37	1.87	2.56	4.32	6.57	11.9
2-1/4					1.13	1.49	2.06	2.78	4.71	7.15	13.0
2-1/2					1.25	1.64	2.25	3.04	5.10	7.72	14.1
3					1.47	1.93	2.62	3.56	5.94	8.96	15.2
3-1/2						2.22		4.08	6.75	10.1	
4						2.51		4.59	7.59	11.4	
4-1/2						2.80		5.12	8.43	12.6	
5						3.09		5.63	9.26	13.8	
6						3.66		6.66	10.9	16.3	

TABLE A-16. cont.

Socket Type Set Screws

LENGTH DIAMETER

Inches	6-32	8-32	10-24	1/4-20	5/16-18	3/8-16	1/2-13	5/8-11	3/4-10
1/8	.03	.05							
3/16	.05	.07	.08	.15					
1/4	.06	.08	.12	.20	.32				
5/16	.07	.11	.14	.25	.40	.60			
3/8	.09	.14	.17	.30	.47	.69	1.33		
1/2	.13	.20	.23	.41	.64	.92	1.68		
5/8	.17	.26	.30	.53	.85	1.21	2.13	3.39	
3/4	.21	.32	.38	.66	1.04	1.51	2.67	4.25	6.04
1					1.45	2.11	3.75	5.96	8.55
1-1/4						2.79	4.83	7.67	11.1
1-1/2							5.91	9.39	13.6

Washers

Size	Outside Diameter	Inside Diameter	Thickness	Weight
#6	3/8	.147	.031	.08
#8	3/8	11/64	.031	.08
#10	7/16	.200	.037	.12
#12	1/2	15/64	.040	.18
1/4	11/16	17/64	.050	.44
5/16	7/8	11/32	.062	.88
3/8	1	25/64	.062	1.15
7/16	1-1/8	1/2	.062	1.41
1/2	1-1/4	9/16	.078	2.12
5/8	1-1/2	11/16	.078	3.00
3/4	1-7/8	13/16	.109	6.76
7/8	2-1/4	15/16	.109	9.90
1	2-1/2	1-1/16	.125	15.58
1-1/4	2-3/4	1-5/16	.125	24.86

Nuts

DIAMETER

	Heavy Hex Full	Heavy Hex Jam	Regular Hex Full	Regular Hex Jam	Finished Hex Full	Finished Hex Jam	Castle	Cap	Wing	Hex Machine Screw	Square
0										.03	
1										.03	
2										.04	
3										.04	
4								.27		.12	
5										.22	
6								.47	.35	.22	.26
8								.42	.33	.30	.33
10								.73	.78	.34	.39
12								.68	.80	.60	.68
1/4	1.09	.78	.67	.44	.76	.54	.77	.98	1.73	.67	.74
5/16	1.67	1.12	1.39	.92	1.12	.78	1.13	1.81	2.20	1.28	1.77
3/8	3.06	1.93	2.05	1.28	1.66	1.09	1.66	2.44	4.14	1.73	2.59
7/16	4.11	2.52	3.47	2.19	2.94	1.93	2.64		10.9		
1/2	6.54	3.91	4.61	3.18	3.89	2.75	4.19	3.57	10.4		5.78
9/16	8.19		5.95		6.08	3.62					
5/8	11.51	6.61	8.36	5.54	7.60	5.15	6.93	7.62	15.8		10.81
3/4	18.76	10.52	*	*	12.31	7.94	13.44		20.9		15.55
7/8	28.63	15.74	*	*	19.61	12.41	21.05				
1	41.44	22.50	*	*	29.32	18.31	29.69				
1-1/8	57.70	30.96	*	*	40.30	24.86					
1-1/4	76.13	44.06	*	*	53.94	35.97					
1-3/8	104.5	59.59			76.00						
1-1/2	133.4	75.55			98.11						
1-5/8	163.3										
1-3/4	208.1				157.0						
2	305.6				234.5						

* Regular Hex Nuts (Full and Jam) 3/4'' and larger are the same as Finished Hex Nuts (Full and Jam). Weights are for coarse thread nuts. Fine thread nuts weigh slightly less.

TABLE A-16. cont.

Studs, Rods, Wood Screws

Continuous Threaded Studs (Type "C")

LENGTH Inches	DIAMETER 6-32	8-32	10-24	1/4-20	5/16-18	3/8-16	1/2-13	5/8-11	3/4-10	7/8-9	1-8
3/4	.21	.33	.42								
7/8	.25	.39	.48								
1	.29	.45	.56	1.00	1.62	2.38					
1-1/8	.32	.51	.63	1.13	1.83	2.68					
1-1/4	.36	.57	.71	1.26	2.04	2.99					
1-1/2	.44	.68	.85	1.52	2.46	3.61	6.98				
1-3/4	.51	.80	.99	2.78	2.87	4.22	8.09				
2	.59	.91	1.13	2.04	3.29	4.84	9.21	14.60			
2-1/4				2.30	3.71	5.45	10.32	16.37			
2-1/2				2.55	4.13	6.06	11.44	18.14	26.60	36.56	
3				3.07	4.97	7.29	13.67	21.68	31.79	43.69	57.31
3-1/2						8.52	15.90	25.21	36.98	50.82	66.66
4						9.75	18.14	28.76	42.17	57.96	76.02
4-1/2							20.37	32.29	47.36	65.09	85.37
5							22.60	35.83	52.55	72.22	94.73
5-1/2							24.83	39.37	57.73	79.36	104.1
6							27.06	42.91	62.92	86.49	113.4

Tap End Studs (Type "A")

LENGTH Inches	DIAMETER 3/8-16	1/2-13	5/8-11	3/4-10	7/8-9	1-8
1	2.46					
1-1/4	3.07	5.58				
1-1/2	3.68	6.70				
1-3/4	4.30	7.81	12.39			
2	4.91	8.93	14.15	20.76		
2-1/4	5.52	10.04	15.92	23.35		
2-1/2	6.14	11.16	17.70	25.95		
2-3/4	6.75	12.28	19.46	28.54		
3	7.37	13.39	21.23	31.14	42.80	56.13
3-1/4		14.51	23.00	33.73	46.36	60.81
3-1/2		15.62	24.78	36.33	49.93	65.49
4			28.31	41.52	57.06	74.85
5				51.90	71.32	93.56
6					85.58	112.3

Threaded Rod

	WEIGHT PER 100 FT.
2-56	1.51
4-40	2.48
6-32	3.68
8-32	5.52
10-24	7.05
10-32	7.69
12-24	9.62
1/4-20	12.39
1/4-28	13.73
5/16-18	20.09
5/16-24	21.76
3/8-16	29.46
3/8-24	32.26
7/16-14	41.21
1/2-13	53.57
1/2-20	57.92
5/8-11	84.93
3/4-10	124.4
7/8-9	171.2
1/8	224.5
1-1/8-7	283.5
1-1/4-7	356.7

Flat Head Wood Screws

LENGTH Inches	DIAMETER #6	#8	#10	#12	#14	#16	#18	#20	#24	#30
3/8	.13									
1/2	.17	.24	.37							
5/8	.20	.29	.43							
3/4	.24	.34	.49	.67						
7/8	.28	.40	.56							
1	.31	.45	.63	.84	1.08					
1-1/4	.38	.55	.77	1.02	1.30					
1-1/2	.46	.66	.91	1.21	1.53	1.92	2.33			
1-3/4			.77	1.05	1.39	1.77	2.21	2.68		
2			.87	1.20	1.57	2.00	2.49	3.03	3.68	
2-1/2				1.48	1.93	2.47	3.07	3.73	4.53	
3				2.31	2.94	3.65	4.43	5.38	7.21	11.3
3-1/2						4.22	5.12	6.23	8.32	13.0
4						4.90	5.82	7.07	9.44	14.8
6									13.9	21.8

The next series of tables gives dimensions and installation data for concrete fastener anchors[10]. Proof tests consisted of axial tension applied to anchors in good grade concrete of 3000 psi compressive strength. Criteria were that the anchor was not removable and the concrete did not show any evidence of failure due to the anchor device. Most standards recommend one-fourth of the proof test as a safe working load.

Table A–17 is for lag screw expansion shields. This type of anchor is a two part unit that has tapered internal threads for a portion of its length, and circumferential ribs over a portion of the outside. Lag screw length should equal the expansion shell length, plus thickness of material to be fastened, plus one-quarter inch.

TABLE A-17. Lag screw expansion shields.

Diam of Lag Screw with Which Shield is Used	Length of Shield	Outside Diameter and Drill Required	Proof Test Loads (Pounds)
LONG STANDARD SIZES			
1/4″	1 1/2″	1/2″	200
5/16″	1 3/4″	1/2″	480
3/8″	2 1/2″	5/8″	960
1/2″	3″	3/4″	1600
5/8″	3 1/2″	7/8″	1725
3/4″	3 1/2″	1″	1850
SHORT STANDARD SIZES			
1/4″	1″	1/2″	160
5/16″	1 1/4″	1/2″	380
3/8″	1 3/4″	5/8″	640
1/2″	2″	3/4″	1300
5/8″	2″	7/8″	1400
3/4″	2″	1″	1500

A stud bolt anchor consists of a carbon steel rod and a cylindrically tapered expander plug. The rod is threaded at one end and the other end has a series of broaching rings and a slot through its diameter. The expander plug is preassembled in a longitudinal hole at the broaching ring end. Stud bolt anchors are expanded in place by use of a setting tool and a hammer. Table A–18 gives information on this type of anchor.

Sleeve-type stud bolt anchors are for medium to heavy duty fastening into solid masonry. These anchors are expanded by tightening the nut with a wrench and therefore

[10]Star Expansion Industries Corporation, "Anchor and Fastener Handbook," Mountainville, N.Y. Copyright 1969, Star Expansion Industries Corporation.

TABLE A-18. Stud bolt anchors.

Masonry Drill & Stud Size	Over-all Length	Stud Length	Minimum Drilled Depth	Proof Test Load (Pounds)
1/4"	1-3/4"	11/16"	1-5/16"	900
1/4"	2-1/4"	1-1/8"	1-5/16"	900
1/4"	3-1/4"	2-1/8"	1-5/16"	900
3/8"	2-1/4"	1"	1-5/8"	1500
3/8"	3-1/4"	1-15/16"	1-5/8"	1500
3/8"	3-3/4"	2-7/16"	1-5/8"	1500
1/2"	2-3/4"	1-1/4"	1-3/4"	2400
1/2"	4-1/4"	2-11/16"	1-3/4"	2400
1/2"	5-1/4"	3-11/16"	1-3/4"	2400
5/8"	3-3/8"	1-5/16"	2-3/8"	3200
5/8"	5"	2-15/16"	2-3/8"	3200
5/8"	7"	4-15/16"	2-3/8"	3200
3/4"	4-1/4"	1-11/16"	2-7/8"	4700
3/4"	6-1/4"	3-11/16"	2-7/8"	4700
3/4"	8-1/2"	5-15/16"	2-7/8"	4700

TABLE A-19. Sleeve-type stud bolt anchors.

Size	Head Style	Minimum Hole Depth	Maximum Thickness of Material To Be Fastened	Thread Size of Bolt	Proof Test Load	Min. Anchor Depth In Concrete
1/4 x 5/8	Acorn Nut	3/8"	1/4"			
1/4 x 1 3/8	Acorn Nut	1"	3/8"			
1/4 x 2 1/4	Acorn Nut	1"	1 1/4"			
1/4 x 1 3/8	Stud Bolt	1 3/8"	1"			
1/4 x 1 1/8	Flat Head	3/4"	3/8"			
1/4 x 2	Flat Head	1"	1"	10-24	900 lbs.	1 inch
1/4 x 2	Flat Threshold	1"	1"			
1/4 x 3	Flat Head	1"	2"			
1/4 x 4	Flat Head	1"	3"			
1/4 x 5 1/4	Flat Head	1"	4 1/4"			
5/16 x 1 1/2	Hex Nut	1"	1/2"			
5/16 x 2 1/2	Hex Nut	1"	1 1/2"			
5/16 x 1 1/2	Stud Bolt	1 1/2"	1"	1/4-20	1200 lbs.	1 inch
5/16 x 2 1/2	Flat Head	1"	1 1/2"			
5/16 x 3 1/2	Flat Head	1"	2 1/2"			
3/8 x 1 7/8	Hex Nut	1 1/4"	5/8"			
3/8 x 3	Hex Nut	1 1/4"	1 3/4"			
3/8 x 1 7/8	Stud Bolt	1 7/8"	1"	5/16-18	1600 lbs.	1 1/4 inches
3/8 x 2 3/4	Flat Head	1 1/4"	1 1/2"			
3/8 x 4	Flat Head	1 1/4"	2 3/4"			
1/2 x 2 1/4	Hex Nut	1 1/2"	3/4"			
1/2 x 3	Hex Nut	1 1/2"	1 1/2"	3/8-16	2800 lbs.	1 1/2 inches
1/2 x 2 1/4	Stud Bolt	2 1/4"	1"			
5/8 x 2 1/4	Hex Nut	2"	1/4"			
5/8 x 4	Hex Nut	2"	2"			
5/8 x 6	Hex Nut	2"	4"	1/2-13	4200 lbs.	2 inches
5/8 x 2	Stud Bolt	2"	2"			
3/4 x 2 1/2	Hex Nut	2"	1/2"			
3/4 x 4	Hex Nut	2"	2"	5/8-11	5600 lbs.	2 inches
3/4 x 5 3/4	Hex Nut	2"	3 3/4"			

do not have to bottom in their holes. The assembly consists of a threaded stud with an outwardly flared cone-shaped end over which is assembled a tubular expander sleeve. Table A–19 gives dimensions and other information on sleeve type-stud bolt anchors.

Imbedded nut screw anchors are medium duty anchors for use with standard machine screws or bolts. The anchor consists of a sleeve and an internally threaded cone with a series of integral ribs or lugs to prevent the cone-shaped nut from turning. All bolt size anchors except the 3/4-inch bolt size are preassembled into a single unit; the 3/4-inch bolt size is furnished as three separate parts: a cone shaped nut and two sleeves. An imbedded nut screw anchor is set in a drilled hole by using a special tamping tool and a hammer. Table A–20 gives details for this type of anchor.

TABLE A-20. Imbedded nut screw anchors.

Size of Bolt or Screw with Which Shield is Used	Dimensions of Minimum Holes Required		Proof Test Load (Pounds)†
	Diam. (Drill Size)	†Depth (Length of Anchor)	
6-32	5/16"	1/2"	150
8-32	5/16"	1/2"	250
10-24	3/8"	5/8"	300
12-24	1/2"	7/8"	400
1/4"-20	1/2"	7/8"	500
5/16"-18	5/8"	1"	850
3/8"-16	3/4"	1-1/4"	1250
7/16"-14	7/8"	1-1/2"	1650
1/2"-13	7/8"	1-1/2"	2300
5/8"-11	1-1/8"	1-3/4"	3200
3/4"-10	1-1/4"	2-1/4"	4000

†A deeper hole should be used in making attachments to poor masonry.

Power driven[11] tools for driving directly into concrete or steel without first drilling a hole use explosive charges such as standard .22 caliber, .38 caliber, or special power pellets. Fasteners available are in the form of drive pins, eyepins, threaded studs, and numerous other standard and special shapes.

Because holding power is a function of compression of the masonry or steel on the imbedded fastener shank, the holding power tables to follow are based on the assumption of no edge cracking and no interfastener effects within the material. Table A–21 gives minimum allowable fastener spacings that will fulfill these requirements.

When a power-driven fastener penetrates concrete, a ball-shaped area of compressed concrete is formed at the point of the fastener. This ball is a result of mechanical and chemical changes in the structure and it creates the majority of the holding power. To achieve maximum holding power, a power-driven fastener should penetrate the concrete

---

[11]Olin Mathieson Chemical Corp., Ramset Fastening Systems, "Fastening Handbook for Architects & Engineers," New Haven, Conn. Copyright 1958 and 1968 Olin Mathieson Chemical Corp., Ramset Fastening Systems.

TABLE A-21. Minimum fastener spacing in inches.

Shank	Diameter	Minimum fastener spacing		Minimum edge to fastener distance	
		steel	concrete	steel	concrete
1/8	.125	1.0	2.5	.500	3.0
9/64	.143	1.0	3.0	.500	3.0
5/32	.156	1.0	3.75	.500	3.0
11/64	.172	1.125	4.25	.625	3.0
3/16	.187	1.125	4.5	.625	3.0
7/32	.218	1.250	4.75	.750	3.0
1/4	.250	1.50	5.00	1.0	3.0

for a distance approximately equal to 6 to 8 times the fastener shank diameter. Table A–22 gives holding power in concrete.

Power fasteners driven into steel displace rather than remove material. This cold working and the elastic properties of steel provide holding power at a maximum if the fastener point penetrates completely through the steel. Table A–23 gives holding power in steel.

Information on types of nails most likely to be of interest to plant engineers is given in Table A–24[12]. All sizes shown are standard except those indicated by an asterisk. Nail diameters are given in terms of the gage wire from which the nail is made; Table A–25 gives sizes for Bethlehem Steel Wire Gage (formerly Washburn and Moen).

TABLE A-22. Predicted fastener holding power in concrete.

PREDICTED HOLDING POWER VALUES IN 2500 P.S.I. CONCRETE — LOW VELOCITY DRIVEN FASTENERS[1,2]
(PREDICTED MINIMUM AT 99.5% RELIABILITY)

SHANK DIAMETER (in Inches)		SHANK SURFACE	LOAD	PENETRATION INTO CONCRETE (in inches)								
				1/2	3/4	1	1 1/4	1 1/2	1 3/4	2	2 1/4	2 1/2
1/8	.125	Smooth	Tension	125	275	350	670	—				
			Shear	210	380	640	900	—				
9/64	.143	Smooth	Tension	150	320	380	700	—				
			Shear	250	400	760	1010	—				
5/32	.152	Smooth	Tension	160	340	410	710	810				
			Shear	275	450	850	1130	1510				

PREDICTED HOLDING POWER VALUES IN 3500 P.S.I. CONCRETE — LOW VELOCITY DRIVEN FASTENERS[1,2]
(PREDICTED MINIMUM AT 99.5% RELIABILITY)

SHANK DIAMETER (in Inches)		SHANK SURFACE	LOAD	PENETRATION INTO CONCRETE (in inches)								
				1/2	3/4	1	1 1/4	1 1/2	1 3/4	2	2 1/4	2 1/2
1/8	.125	Smooth	Tension	130	305	360	725	—				
			Shear	220	395	680	920	—				
9/64	.143	Smooth	Tension	145	315	390	775	—				
			Shear	270	415	785	1070	—				
5/32	.152	Smooth	Tension	150	325	415	810	890				
			Shear	275	470	880	1200	1600				

[1]The fasteners shall not be driven until the concrete has reached the designated ultimate compressive strength.
[2]The tension and shear values shown are for the fastener only. Wood or steel members connected must be investigated in accordance with accepted design criteria.

[12]Bethlehem Steel Corporation, "Bethlehem Nails and Other Wire Products," Bethlehem, Pennsylvania.

TABLE A-22. cont.

PREDICTED HOLDING POWER VALUES IN 5000 P.S.I. CONCRETE — LOW VELOCITY DRIVEN FASTENERS [1,2]
(PREDICTED MINIMUM AT 99.5% RELIABILITY)

SHANK DIAMETER (in Inches)		SHANK SURFACE	LOAD	PENETRATION INTO CONCRETE (in inches)								
				1/2	3/4	1	1 1/4	1 1/2	1 3/4	2	2 1/4	2 1/2
1/8	.125	Smooth	Tension	210	410	660	810	—				
			Shear	295	500	790	1110	—				
9/64	.143	Smooth	Tension	250	460	680	860	—				
			Shear	335	565	850	1425	—				
5/32	.152	Smooth	Tension	260	510	860	900	1200				
			Shear	345	590	985	1590	1935				

PREDICTED HOLDING POWER IN 2500 P.S.I. CONCRETE — STANDARD VELOCITY DRIVEN FASTENERS [1,2]
(PREDICTED MINIMUM AT 99.5% RELIABILITY)

SHANK DIAMETER (in Inches)		SHANK SURFACE	LOAD	PENETRATION INTO CONCRETE (in inches)								
				1/2	3/4	1	1 1/4	1 1/2	1 3/4	2	2 1/4	2 1/2
1/8	.125	Smooth	Tension		350	620	950					
			Shear		340	700	1220					
9/64	.143	Smooth	Tension		360	620	970					
			Shear		355	750	1280					
5/32	.156	Smooth	Tension			625	975	1400				
			Shear			755	1310	2010				
11/64	.172	Smooth	Tension			625	985	1415				
			Shear			765	1360	2115				
3/16	.187	Smooth	Tension				985	1425	1920			
			Shear				1365	2150	2715			
7/32	.218	Smooth	Tension					1430	1935	2100	3135	
			Shear					2210	2770	3480	4410	
1/4	.250	Smooth	Tension					1450	1940	2175	3180	3910
			Shear					2285	2845	3560	4500	5340

PREDICTED HOLDING POWER VALUES IN 3500 P.S.I. CONCRETE — STANDARD VELOCITY DRIVEN FASTENERS [1,2]
(PREDICTED MINIMUM AT 99.5% RELIABILITY)

SHANK DIAMETER (in Inches)		SHANK SURFACE	LOAD	PENETRATION INTO CONCRETE (in inches)								
				1/2	3/4	1	1 1/4	1 1/2	1 3/4	2	2 1/4	2 1/2
1/8	.125	Smooth	Tension		390	625	1140					
			Shear		335	710	1580					
9/64	.143	Smooth	Tension		395	615	1150					
			Shear		360	760	1615					
5/32	.156	Smooth	Tension			630	1145	1710				
			Shear			765	1620	2315				
11/64	.172	Smooth	Tension			620	1130	1715				
			Shear			730	1685	2320				
3/16	.187	Smooth	Tension				1140	1720	2495			
			Shear				1680	2365	2710			
7/32	.218	Smooth	Tension					1700	2515	3560	4290	
			Shear					2530	2865	4175	5290	
1/4	.250	Smooth	Tension					1725	2510	3575	4315	5280
			Shear					2780	3345	4360	5310	6415

PREDICTED HOLDING POWER VALUES IN 5000 P.S.I. CONCRETE — STANDARD VELOCITY DRIVEN FASTENERS [1,2]
(PREDICTED MINIMUM AT 99.5% RELIABILITY)

SHANK DIAMETER (in Inches)		SHANK SURFACE	LOAD	PENETRATION INTO CONCRETE (in inches)								
				1/2	3/4	1	1 1/4	1 1/2	1 3/4	2	2 1/4	2 1/2
1/8	.125	Smooth	Tension		610	1010	1625					
			Shear		830	1245	1940					
9/64	.143	Smooth	Tension		620	1015	1650					
			Shear		855	1260	1945					
5/32	.156	Smooth	Tension			1025	1650	2300				
			Shear			1280	1950	2580				
11/64	.172	Smooth	Tension			1040	1655	2315				
			Shear			1310	1980	2610				
3/16	.187	Smooth	Tension				1670	2325	3320			
			Shear				2015	2640	3715			
7/32	.218	Smooth	Tension					2340	3330	4210	5115	
			Shear					2810	3925	4435	5730	
1/4	.250	Smooth	Tension					2350	3345	4220	5135	6190
			Shear					3015	4010	4740	6130	6540

[1] The fasteners shall not be driven until the concrete has reached the designated ultimate compressive strength.
[2] The tension and shear values shown are for the fastener only. Wood or steel members connected must be investigated in accordance with accepted design criteria.

TABLE A-23.   Predicted fastener holding power in steel.

PREDICTED HOLDING POWER VALUES IN STEEL — LOW VELOCITY DRIVEN FASTENERS [1, 2, 3]
(PREDICTED MINIMUM AT 99.5% RELIABILITY)

SHANK DIAMETER (in inches)		Shank Surface	Load	STEEL PLATE THICKNESS IN INCHES				
				1/8	3/16	1/4	5/16	3/8
1/8	.125	Smooth	Tension	350	860	1030	1370	1725
			Shear	1380	1625	1710	1750	1790
9/64	.143	Smooth	Tension	510	1200	1500	1810	1950
			Shear	1530	1915	2140	2560	2630
5/32	.152	Smooth	Tension	805	1430	1860	2180	2350
			Shear	1730	2000	2810	3110	3200

PREDICTED HOLDING POWER VALUES IN STEEL — STANDARD VELOCITY DRIVEN FASTENERS [1, 2, 3]
(PREDICTED MINIMUM AT 99.5% RELIABILITY)

SHANK DIAMETER (in inches)		Shank Surface	Load	PLATE THICKNESS IN INCHES			
				1/4	3/8	1/2	3/4
1/8	.125	Smooth	Tension	1010	—	—	—
			Shear	2580	—	—	—
9/64	.143	Smooth	Tension	1332	—	—	—
			Shear	3010	—	—	—
5/32	.156	Smooth	Tension	1476	1715	2275	—
			Shear	3210	3480	3560	—
11/64	.172	Smooth	Tension	1685	1938	2317	—
			Shear	3580	3640	3720	—
3/16	.187	Smooth	Tension	2000	2480	2561	—
			Shear	3718	3800	4273	—
7/32	.218	Smooth	Tension	2319	3065	4700	—
			Shear	4015	4345	5650	—
1/4	.250	Smooth	Tension	2400	3090	3310	4700
			Shear	4380	4960	6320	7435

[1] The fasteners shall have sufficient length so that the entire pointed portion of the shank pierces the steel plate.
[2] The tension and shear values shown are for the fastener only. Wood or steel members connected must be investigated in accordance with accepted design criteria.
[3] Tests conducted in ASTM A7 Steel.

TABLE A-24.   Nail dimensions and weights.

Size	Length	Gage Number	Diameter of Head	Approximate Number per Pound
COMMON NAILS—flat head, diamond point—length is from point to underside of head				
2d	1	15	11/64	847
3d	1 1/4	14	13/64	543
4d	1 1/2	12 1/2	1/4	294
5d	1 3/4	12 1/2	1/4	254
6d	2	11 1/2	17/64	167
7d	2 1/4	11 1/2	17/64	150
8d	2 1/2	10 1/4	9/32	101
9d	2 3/4	10 1/4	9/32	92
10d	3	9	5/16	66
12d	3 1/4	9	5/16	61
16d	3 1/2	8	11/32	47
20d	4	6	11/32	29
30d	4 1/2	5	7/16	22
40d	5	4	15/32	17
50d	5 1/2	3	1/2	13
60d	6	2	17/32	10

TABLE A-24   cont.

BOX NAILS—large flat head, diamond point—length is from point to underside of head

2d*	1	15 1/2	3/16	
3d	1 1/4	14 1/2	7/32	588
4d	1 1/2	14	7/32	453
5d	1 3/4	14	7/32	389
6d	2	12 1/2	17/64	225
7d	2 1/4	12 1/2	17/64	200
8d	2 1/2	11 1/2	19/64	136
9d	2 3/4	11 1/2	19/64	
10d	3	10 1/2	5/16	90
12d*	3 1/4	10 1/2	5/16	
16d	3 1/2	10	11/32	69
20d	4	9	3/8	50
30d*	4 1/2	9	3/8	
40d*	5	8	13/32	
60d*	6	6	7/16	

FINISHING NAILS—brad head, cupped, diamond point—length is overall—head diameter is gage number

2d*	1	16 1/2	13 1/2	
3d	1 1/4	15 1/2	12 1/2	880
4d	1 1/2	15	12	630
5d*	1 3/4	15	12	
6d	2	13	10	288
7d*	2 1/4	13	10	
8d	2 1/2	12 1/2	9 1/2	196
9d*	2 3/4	12 1/2	9 1/2	
10d	3	11 1/2	8 1/2	124
12d*	3 1/4	11 1/2	8 1/2	
16d	3 1/2	11	8	87
20d*	3 1/2	10	7	
30d*	4 1/2	9	6	
40d*	5	8	5	

PLASTER BOARD NAILS—large flat head, long diamond point, blued—length is from point to underside of head

*	1	13	19/64	
*	1	13	3/8	
	1 1/8	13	19/64	473
*	1 1/8	13	3/8	
*	1 1/4	13	3/8	
	1 1/4	13	19/64	425
	1 1/4	12	3/8	310
*	1 1/2	13	19/64	
*	1 1/2	13	3/8	
*	1 3/4	13	19/64	
*	1 3/4	13	3/8	

TABLE A-24 cont.

Size	Length	Gage Number	Diameter of head	Approximate Number per Pound

GYPSUM WALLBOARD NAILS—flat head, diamond point, cement coated—length is overall

Size	Length	Gage Number	Diameter of head	Approximate Number per Pound
4d	1 3/8	14	7/32	493
5d	1 5/8	13 1/2	15/64	366
6d	1 7/8	13	1/4	278

PERFECT ROOFING NAILS—large checkered flat head, diamond point, smooth or barbed shank—length is from point to underside of head

Size	Length	Gage Number	Diameter of head	Approximate Number per Pound
	7/8	11	1/2	259
	1	11	1/2	235
	1 1/4	11	1/2	197
	1 1/2	11	1/2	170
	1 3/4	11	1/2	150

REGULAR HEAD ROOFING NAILS—flat head, diamond point, barbed or smooth shank—length is from point to underside of head

Size	Length	Gage Number	Diameter of head	Approximate Number per Pound
	1	12	9/32.	416
	1 1/4	11	5/16	250

Holding Power of Nails

Nails that are too large for a given task can be as expensive as nails that are too small when consideration is given to the individual cost of larger nails and to the extra labor cost of driving them. In addition, they may split the wood, leading to re-work costs. Figure A–5 helps calculate holding power under the following assumptions:

- Nail is driven at right angles to the wood's fibers. (Over a period of time the holding power of a nail driven into end-grain is usually negligible.)
- Wood is either seasoned or will be kept wet. (If a nail is driven into unseasoned wood, the nomogram value will be correct for the present but will decrease to about 1/4 that value when the wood seasons.)

Example

Finishing nails driven 1 3/4 inches into redwood must withstand a pull of 35 pounds. What size nails should be used?

Draw a straight line from 35 on the MAXIMUM LOAD scale, through 1 3/4 on the DEPTH OF NAIL scale, to the TURNING SCALE. From that point on the TURNING SCALE draw a straight line to REDWOOD on the TYPE OF WOOD scale. That line will cross the SIZE OF NAIL scale between 6 and 8 pennies, indicating that 8 is he minimum size that should be used.

FIGURE A-5. Nomogram for calculating holding power of nails.

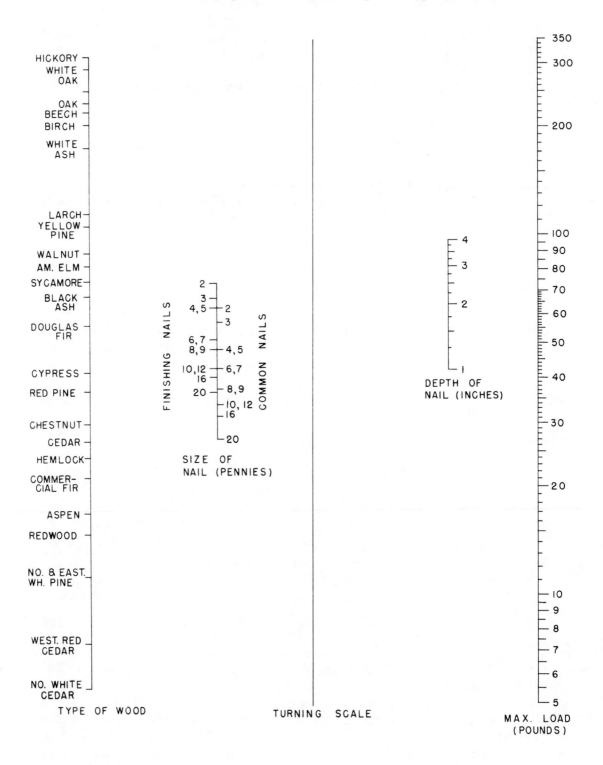

TABLE A-25.   Nail wire gage.

*Gage No.	in.	Decimal Size of Wire in.	Area sq in.	Lb per ft	Lb per mile	Ft per lb
	½	.5000	.1963	.6668	3521	1.500
7-0		.4900	.1886	.6404	3381	1.562
	15/32	.46875	.1726	.5861	3094	1.706
6-0		.4615	.1673	.5681	2999	1.76
	7/16	.4375	.1503	.5105	2696	1.959
5-0		.4305	.1456	.4943	2610	2.023
	13/32	.40625	.1296	.4402	2324	2.272
4-0		.3938	.1218	.4136	2184	2.418
	3/8	.3750	.1104	.3751	1980	2.666
3-0		.3625	.1032	.3505	1851	2.853
	11/32	.34375	.09281	.3152	1664	3.173
2-0		.3310	.08605	.2922	1543	3.422
	5/16	.3125	.07670	.2605	1375	3.839
1-0		.3065	.07378	.2506	1323	3.991
1		.2830	.06290	.2136	1128	4.681
	9/32	.28125	.06213	.2110	1114	4.74
2		.2625	.05412	.1838	970.4	5.441
	¼	.2500	.04909	.1667	880.2	5.999
3		.2437	.04664	.1584	836.4	6.313
4		.2253	.03987	.1354	714.8	7.386
	7/32	.21875	.03758	.1276	673.9	7.835
5		.2070	.03365	.1143	603.4	8.750
6		.1920	.02895	.09832	519.2	10.17
	3/16	.1875	.02761	.09377	495.1	10.66
7		.1770	.02461	.08356	441.2	11.97
8		.1620	.02062	.07000	369.6	14.29
	5/32	.15625	.01917	.06517	343.8	15.36
9		.1483	.01727	.05866	309.7	17.05
10		.1350	.01431	.04861	256.7	20.57
	1/8	.125	.01227	.04168	220.0	24.00
11		.1205	.01140	.03873	204.5	25.82
12		.1055	.008742	.02969	156.7	33.69
	3/32	.09375	.006903	.02344	123.8	42.66
13		.0915	.006576	.02233	117.9	44.78
14		.0800	.005027	.01707	90.13	58.58
15		.0720	.004072	.01383	73.01	72.32
16	1/16	.0625	.003068	.01042	55.01	95.98
17		.0540	.002290	.007778	41.07	128.60
18		.0475	.001772	.006018	31.77	166.20
19		.0410	.001320	.004484	23.67	223.00
20		.0348	.0009511	.003230	17.05	309.60

*Bethlehem Steel Wire Gage (formerly Washburn & Moen).

CONVERSION FACTORS[13]

Table A–26 lists conversion factors in alphabetical order of the given unit. Most of the entries are for conversion between metric and foot-pound units, but there are a few intra-system conversions such as horsepower to watts.

Entries are alphabetical in given unit and where any unit appears more than once the group is alphabetical in desired unit. To minimize questions on alphabetizing policy, most entries have been spelled out.

Conversion factors are in a form for direct use in computer programs and electronic data transmission systems; that is, each factor is written with one non-zero digit left of the decimal point and the appropriate power of ten is written following an E (for exponent). For example, the first conversion factor is

$$4.046856 \; E + 03$$

which is equal to

$$4.046856 \times 10^3$$

and therefore

$$\begin{matrix} \text{number} \\ \text{of acres} \end{matrix} \quad \text{times } 4046.856 = \begin{matrix} \text{number of} \\ \text{square meters} \end{matrix}$$

---

[13]Most conversion factors in Table A–27 are adapted from: U.S. Department of Commerce National Bureau of Standards, "ASTM Metric Practice Guide (Handbook 102)," Washington, D.C., 1967.

TABLE A-26. Conversion factors.

Given Unit	Times	Conversion Factor	Equals	Desired Unit
Acre		4.046856 E + 03		Meter squared
Atmosphere (Normal)		7.600023 E + 01		Centimeter of HG (0 C)
Atmosphere (Normal)		2.992135 E + 01		Inches of HG
Atmosphere (Normal)		1.013250*E + 05		Newton per square meter
British thermal unit (Mean)		1.05587 E + 03		Joule
Bushel (U.S.)		3.523907 E − 02		Meter cubed
Calorie (20 C)		4.18190 E + 00		Joule
Centimeter		3.280840 E − 02		Foot
Centimeter		3.937008 E − 01		Inch
Centimeter cubed		6.102339 E − 02		Inch cubed
Centimeter cubed		3.381402 E − 02		Ounce (Fluid)
Centimeter cubed		2.113376 E − 03		Pint
Centimeter of HG (0 C)		1.315785 E − 02		Atmosphere (Normal)
Centimeter of HG (0 C)		1.33322 E + 03		Newton per square meter
Centimeter of water (4 C)		9.80638 E + 01		Newton per square meter
Centimeter/second squared		3.280840 E − 02		Foot/second squared
Centimeter/second squared		3.937008 E − 01		Inch/second squared
Centimeter squared		1.973525 E + 05		Circular mil
Centimeter squared		1.550003 E − 01		Inch squared
Circular mil		5.067075 E − 06		Centimeter squared
Circular mil		5.067075 E − 10		Meter squared
Circular mil		5.067075 E − 04		Millimeter squared
Cup		2.365882 E − 04		Meter cubed
Degree (Angle)		1.745329 E − 02		Radian

TABLE A-26. Conversion factors (cont.)

Given Unit	Times	Conversion Factor	Equals	Desired Unit
Fathom		1.828800*E + 00		Meter
Foot		3.048000*E + 01		Centimeter
Foot		3.048000*E − 01		Meter
Foot candle		1.076391 E + 01		Lumen per square meter
Foot cubed		2.831685 E + 01		Liter
Foot cubed		2.831685 E − 02		Meter cubed
Foot-pound-force		1.355818 E + 00		Joule
Foot-pound force/minute		2.259697 E − 02		Watt
Foot-pound force per hour		3.766161 E − 04		Watt
Foot-pound force/second		1.355818 E + 00		Watt
Foot to fourth power		8.630975 E − 03		Meter to fourth power
Foot/second squared		3.048000*E + 01		Centimeter/second squared
Foot/second squared		3.048000*E − 01		Meter/second squared
Foot squared		9.290304*E − 02		Meter squared
Gallon		3.785412 E + 00		Liter
Gallon (U.S.)		3.785412 E − 03		Meter cubed
Grams per cubic centimeter		1.000000 E + 03		Kilogram per cubic meter
Horsepower (Electric)		7.460000*E + 02		Watt
Inch		2.540000*E + 00		Centimeter
Inch		2.540000*E − 02		Meter
Inch cubed		1.638706 E + 01		Centimeter cubed
Inch cubed		1.638706 E − 05		Meter cubed
Inch/second squared		2.540000*E + 00		Centimeter/second squared
Inch/second squared		2.540000*E − 02		Meter/second squared
Inch squared		6.451600 E + 00		Centimeter squared
Inch squared		6.451600 E − 04		Meter squared
Inches of HG		3.342095 E − 02		Atmosphere (Normal)
Inch to fourth power		4.162314 E − 07		Meter to fourth power

TABLE A-26. Conversion factors. (cont.)

Given Unit	Times	Conversion Factor	Equals	Desired Unit
Joule		9.47086 E − 04		British thermal unit (Mean)
Joule		2.39126 E − 01		Calorie (20 C)
Joule		7.37562 E − 01		Foot-pound-force
Joule		2.777778 E − 07		Kilowatt-hour
Joule		2.777778 E − 04		Watt-hour
Kilogram		3.527397 E + 01		Ounce mass (Avoir)
Kilogram		2.204622 E + 00		Pound mass
Kilogram		1.102311 E − 03		Ton (2000 pounds)
Kilogram force		9.806650 E + 00		Newton
Kilogram-meter squared		2.373035 E + 01		Pound mass-foot squared
Kilogram-meter squared		3.417171 E + 04		Pound mass-inch squared
Kilogram per cubic meter		1.000000 E − 03		Grams per cubic centimeter
Kilogram per cubic meter		3.612729 E − 05		Pound-mass per cubic inch
Kilogram per cubic meter		6.242797 E − 02		Pound-mass per cubic foot
Kilogram per square meter		2.048161 E − 01		Pound-mass per square foot
Kilogram per square meter		2.0482 E − 01		Pound-mass per square foot
Kilogram per square meter		1.422334 E − 03		Pound-mass per square inch
Kilogram/square centimeter		1.422334 E + 01		Pound-mass per square inch
Kilometer		6.213712 E − 01		Mile (U.S. statute)
Kilometer per hour		5.399568 E − 01		Knot (International)
Kilometer per hour		6.213712 E − 01		Mile per hour
Kilometer squared		3.861022 E − 01		Mile squared
Kilowatt-hour		3.600000*E + 06		Joule
Kip		4.448222 E + 03		Newton
Knot (International)		1.852000*E + 00		Kilometer per hour
Knot (International)		5.144444 E − 01		Meter per second
Knot (International)		8.689762 E − 01		Mile per hour

TABLE A-26. Conversion factors. (*cont.*)

Given Unit	Times	Conversion Factor	Equals	Desired Unit
Light year		9.46055 E + 15		Meter
Liter		3.531466 E − 02		Foot cubed
Liter		2.641720 E − 01		Gallon
Liter		1.056688 E + 00		Quart
Lumen per square meter		9.290304 E − 02		Foot candle
Meter		5.468066 E − 01		Fathom
Meter		3.280840 E + 00		Foot
Meter		3.937008 E + 01		Inch
Meter		1.05702 E − 16		Light year
Meter		6.213712 E − 04		Mile (U.S. statute)
Meter cubed		2.837959 E + 01		Bushel (U.S.)
Meter cubed		4.226753 E + 03		Cup
Meter cubed		3.531466 E + 01		Foot cubed
Meter cubed		2.641720 E + 02		Gallon (U.S.)
Meter cubed		6.102376 E + 04		Inch cubed
Meter cubed		3.360946 E + 04		Ounce (Fluid)
Meter cubed		2.113376 E + 03		Pint
Meter cubed		1.056688 E + 03		Quart
Meter cubed		6.762807 E + 04		Tablespoon
Meter cubed		2.028841 E + 05		Teaspoon
Meter per second		1.943845 E + 00		Knot (International)
Meter/second squared		3.280840 E + 00		Foot/second squared
Meter/second squared		3.937008 E + 01		Inch/second squared
Meter squared		1.973525 E + 09		Circular mil
Meter squared		1.076391 E + 01		Foot squared
Meter squared		1.550003 E + 03		Inch squared

TABLE A-26. Conversion factors. (cont.)

Given Unit	Times	Conversion Factor	Equals	Desired Unit
Meter squared		3.861022 E − 07		Mile squared
Meter to fourth power		1.158618 E + 02		Foot to fourth power
Meter to fourth power		2.402510 E + 06		Inch to fourth power
Mile per hour		1.609344*E + 00		Kilometer per hour
Mile per hour		1.150779 E + 00		Knot (International)
Meter squared		2.417054 E − 04		Acre
Mile squared		2.589988 E + 00		Kilometer squared
Mile squared		2.589988 E + 06		Meter squared
Mile (U.S. Statute)		1.609344 E + 00		Kilometer
Mile (U.S. Statute)		1.609344 E + 03		Meter
Millimeter squared		1.973525 E + 03		Circular mil
Minute (Angle)		2.908882 E − 04		Radian
Newton		1.019716 E − 01		Kilogram force
Newton		2.248222 E − 04		Kip
Newton		2.596942 E + 00		Ounce force (Avoir)
Newton		2.248089 E − 01		Pound force
Newton meter		1.416119 E + 02		Ounce force-inch
Newton meter		7.375621 E − 01		Pound force-foot
Newton meter		8.850748 E + 00		Pound force-inch
Newton per meter		6.852178 E − 02		Pound-force per foot
Newton per meter		5.710148 E − 03		Pound-force per inch
Newton per square meter		9.869233 E − 06		Atmosphere (Normal)
Newton per square meter		7.50064 E − 04		Centimeter of HG (0 C)
Newton per square meter		1.01974 E − 02		Centimeter of water (4 C)
Ounce (Fluid)		2.957353 E + 01		Centimeter cubed
Ounce (Fluid)		2.957353 E − 05		Meter cubed

TABLE A-26. Conversion factors. (*cont.*)

Given Unit	Times	Conversion Factor	Equals	Desired Unit
Ounce force (Avoir)		2.780139 E − 01		Newton
Ounce force-inch		7.061552 E − 03		Newton meter
Ounce mass (Avoir)		2.834952 E − 02		Kilogram
Pint		4.731765 E + 02		Centimeter cubed
Pint		4.731765 E − 04		Meter cubed
Pound force		4.448222 E + 00		Newton
Pound force-foot		1.355818 E + 00		Newton meter
Pound force-inch		1.129848 E − 01		Newton meter
Pound-force per foot		1.459390 E + 01		Newton per meter
Pound-force per inch		1.751268 E + 02		Newton per meter
Pound mass		4.535924 E − 01		Kilogram
Pound mass-foot squared		4.214012 E − 02		Kilogram-meter squared
Pound mass-inch squared		2.926397 E − 05		Kilogram-meter squared
Pound-mass per cubic foot		1.601846 E + 01		Kilogram per cubic meter
Pound-mass per cubic inch		2.767991 E + 04		Kilogram per cubic meter
Pound-mass per square foot		4.882428 E + 00		Kilogram per square meter
Pound-mass per square foot		4.88241 E + 00		Kilogram per square meter
Pound-mass per square inch		7.030696 E + 02		Kilogram per square meter
Pound-mass per square inch		7.030696 E − 02		Kilogram/square centimeter
Quart		9.463530 E − 01		Liter
Quart		9.463530 E − 04		Meter cubed
Radian		8.640000 E − 04		Degree (Angle)
Radian		3.437747 E + 03		Minute (Angle)
Radian		2.062648 E + 05		Second(Angle)
Second (Angle)		4.848137 E − 06		Radian

TABLE A-26. Conversion factors. (cont.)

Given Unit	Times	Conversion Factor	Equals	Desired Unit
Tablespoon		1.478676 E − 05		Meter cubed
Teaspoon		4.928922 E − 06		Meter cubed
Ton (2000 pounds)		9.071847 E + 02		Kilogram
Watt		4.425372 E + 01		Foot-pound force/minute
Watt		2.655224 E + 03		Foot-pound force per hour
Watt		7.375621 E − 01		Foot-pound force/second
Watt		1.340483 E − 03		Horsepower (Electric)
Watt-hour		3.600000*E + 03		Joule

*Conversion factor is exact; all subsequent digits are zero.

Index

A

B

E

F

G

T